Douglas Jerrold

Douglas Jerrold

1803-1857

Michael Slater

Duckworth

First published in 2002 by
Gerald Duckworth & Co. Ltd.
61 Frith Street, London W1D 3JL
Tel: 020 7434 4242
Fax: 020 7434 4420
Email: enquiries@duckworth-publishers.co.uk
www.ducknet.co.uk

A catalogue record for this book is available
from the British Library

ISBN 0 7156 2824 0

Typeset by Ray Davies
Printed in Great Britain by
Bookcraft (Bath) Ltd, Midsomer Norton, Avon

Contents

For my beloved sister

Barbara Parker

and my dear friend

Ann Watkins

Preface

Despite his centrality to the theatrical and journalistic life of the London of William IV and of the first twenty years of Victoria's reign, and his close involvement with both Dickens and Thackeray, there has been no attempt at a full-scale biographical study of Douglas Jerrold since his grandson Walter Jerrold's two-volume *Douglas Jerrold. Dramatist and Wit*, written in 1914 and published four years later. The present volume seeks to fill this gap.

Throughout the work I have made many references both to Walter Jerrold's biography and to the earlier *Life and Remains of Douglas Jerrold* published by Jerrold's eldest son, William Blanchard Jerrold, in 1859. To avoid too great a proliferation of footnotes I have not, generally, provided a precise reference for every quotation from, or detailed allusion to, these two books but trust that I have always made it clear to which of the two I am referring and believe that the reader who seeks to follow up these references should have little difficulty in locating them.

A big problem for anyone attempting a biography of Jerrold is that his surviving letters are nearly all undated except by day of the week and sometimes also month of the year, so that other evidence, if available, must often be relied upon to construct the basic chronological narrative of his life. A greater problem still is that his letters, even those to his son William, are, once he has established himself, mostly brief and business-like. (As he was only very rarely away from his wife it is the less surprising that only one or two letters to her are known.) Being someone who had, as he said, to feed his family out of his inkwell, he excused his epistolary brevity by pointing out that letter-writing was the only form of writing for which he was not paid. True, there is, among the many letters of his preserved in the Gordon N. Ray Collection in the Pierpont Morgan Library in New York, a long facetious one written to Mrs Charles Knight purporting to describe the Saturnalian behaviour of her eminently respectable husband, Jerrold's travelling-companion on a jaunt to Ireland, but this is an exceptional holiday indulgence. It was only to his much-loved friend Dickens, and sometimes also to Mark Lemon, his editor at *Punch*, that Jerrold would sometimes write intimately – for example, about his 'almost insane' dread of poverty in old age, or his distress over the disastrous improvidence of his son-in-law the journalist Henry Mayhew. Otherwise his surviving correspondence is generally about as unrewarding as Tennyson's for the biographical truffle-hound.

There is, on the other hand, a stack of evidence (of course, of varying degrees of reliability) about how Jerrold appeared to his contemporaries and a mass of comment on his public life contained in the reminiscences and private correspondence of those who came into contact with him. He was such a well-known figure, so celebrated for his caustic wit and for his democratic sympathies, that people wanted to meet him (unless, like the painter William Powell Frith, they felt too nervous of him) and to record their impressions for others. Naturally, too, Jerrold figures frequently in the flood of professional autobiographies, memoirs and biographies written by or about dramatists, actors, journalists, editors and publishers in the late 19th century.

The result of all this is that an authentic modern biography of Jerrold is bound to focus more upon the public than upon the private man. And it is appropriate that this should be the case. Jerrold was not a literary genius revealing in his work a complex inner life of the imagination but a remarkably talented and industrious satirical journalist, who was, and was seen at the time to be, very much a man of his age.

MICHAEL SLATER
London, July 2002

Acknowledgements

I wish to express my warmest thanks to Yvonne Jerrold for permission to quote from the unpublished correspondence and other papers of her great-great-great grandfather, as well as for all her kind encouragement and hospitality during my writing of this book.

I am deeply grateful to the late Nina Burgis, Dr Jean Elliott and John Grigg for much resourceful, meticulous, and quite invaluable, research assistance. I owe a great debt, too, to Amanda-Jane Doran, Curator of the Punch Collection 1988-1998, and to Miranda Taylor, former Punch Library Manager, for all their help and interest while I was researching in the *Punch* archives. I remember also with gratitude the unflagging interest taken in my Jerrold work by the late Professor Kathleen Tillotson, whose unrivalled knowledge of 19th-century literary history was a wonderful resource, and who kindly gave me a number of rare Jerrold items from her own library, notably one volume of *Douglas Jerrold's Weekly Newspaper*. Another generous book-donor and general encourager was Professor John Clubbe who presented me, at the outset of my work, with his own copy of Walter Jerrold's biography *Douglas Jerrold. Dramatist and Wit*.

It is a pleasure once again to record my appreciation of the support given to me in my scholarly work by Emma Robinson, Librarian of the University of London Library, and by her invariably helpful and courteous staff, especially Michael Mulcay. I am grateful also to the Leverhulme Foundation, and to the Society for Theatre Research, for grants which materially assisted the progress of the research for this book. And I would like here to thank also two good friends, Miriam Margolyes and Ann Green, each of whom provided me with a quiet retreat in which to work uninterruptedly at two crucial points in the gestation of this biography.

At the appropriate places in the Notes I have acknowledged expert help with particular points and thanked those who have provided me with pertinent information that I would otherwise never have come across. For more varied and extensive help and for general encouragement, often when this was sorely needed, I wish to thank the following friends and colleagues: Professor Richard D. Altick, Professor Rosemary Ashton, Dr Janet Birkett of the Theatre Museum, Professor Jacky Bratton, Barbara Cavanagh of Motley Books, Professor Philip Collins, Edward Costigan, Roy Davids, Liz Duval, Professor Angus Easson, Bob Flanagan, Paul Graham and Nicholas Reed of the Friends of West Norwood Cemetery, Professor Monica Fryckstedt, Dr Beryl Gray, Professor Barbara Hardy,

Acknowledgements

Michael Harris, Dr Adrian Harvey, Ron Heisler, Dr Peer Hultberg, Professor Anne Humpherys, Professor Louis James, John Kenworthy-Browne, William G. Knight, Valerie Browne Lester, Martin Nason, Professor Robert L. Patten, Cecilia Doidge Ripper, Martha Rosso of the Philadelphia Dickens Fellowship, the late George Rowell, Martin Rynja, Professor Andrew Sanders, Professor Toru Sasaki, Dr Paul Schlicke, Dr Angela Smith, Dr Klaus Stierstorfer, Professor John Sutherland, Ann Watkins, Janine Watrin, and Dr Tony Williams.

I am grateful to the following institutions that own Jerrold or Jerrold-related manuscript material for facilitating my access to it and for permission to quote from it: the Beinecke Rare Book and Manuscript Library, Yale University; the Berg Collection of English and American Literature, The New York Public Library (remembering especially the late Curator, Dr Lola Szladits, who once memorably said to me, 'You gonna write a *whole book* on Douglas Jerrold? This I have to read!' Sadly, I failed to finish it in time for her to do so); the Bodleian Library, University of Oxford; the British Library; the Brotherton Collection, University of Leeds Library, and Mr C.D.W Sheppard; the Trustees of the Chatsworth Settlement and Peter Day, Keeper of the Collection; the University of Chicago Library; the Churchill Archives Centre, Churchill College, Cambridge; the Fales Library, New York University; the Folger Shakespeare Library, Washington; the Harry Ransom Humanities Research Center, the University of Texas at Austin; the Houghton Library, Harvard University; the Harvard Theatre Collection, Harvard University; the Huntington Library, California; the Library of the University of Illinois at Urbana-Champaign; the University of Iowa Library; the John Rylands University Library of Manchester; Kent State University Library; the Pierpont Morgan Library, New York; the National Library of Scotland; Princeton University Library; Punch Ltd.; the National Portrait Gallery; the Templeman Library at the University of Kent and Steve Holland; the Master and Fellows of Trinity College, Cambridge.

Finally, I wish to record my grateful thanks to Jon Wilson and Christina Panagi of the Photographic Unit, Birkbeck College, for much help with preparing the illustrations for this book; to my friend Dr David Atkinson for meticulous proof-reading and for compiling the index with his usual exemplary skill; and to Lucy Nicholson and Eleanor Birne for being such very good editors.

M.S.

Illustrations

Plates (between pages 180 and 181)

Douglas Jerrold (? early 1830s). Watercolour (anonymous). *Reproduced by permission of the Fales Library & Special Collections, New York University.*
T.P. Cooke as William in *Black Eyed Susan*, 1829.
Samuel Laman Blanchard. From a miniature by Louisa Stuart Costello.
Title page of *More Frightened Than Hurt*, 1821.
J.P. Wilkinson as Popeseye in *More Frightened Than Hurt*. By Cruikshank.
Cover for first number of *Punch*, 1841. By Archibald S. Henning.
'Death and the Drawing Room' (*Illuminated Magazine*). By Kenny Meadows.
Henry Mayhew caricatured in *Punch* in 1841.
The Hermit of Bellyfulle (*Chronicles of Clovernook*). By Kenny Meadows.
Playbill advertisement for *Mrs Caudle's Curtain Lectures*, 1845.
Headed notepaper for *Douglas Jerrold's Weekly Newspaper. Reproduced by permission of the National Library of Scotland.*
The Amateur Players in *Every Man In His Humour*, 1845. By Kenny Meadows.
'Author's Miseries' (*Punch*, 1848). By Thackeray.
Douglas Jerrold in middle age (Wothlytype reproduction c. 1865 of earlier photograph).
Monthly cover for *A Man Made of Money*. By John Leech.
Advertisement for *Lloyd's Weekly Newspaper*, 1846/47.
William Blanchard Jerrold, 1873. Photograph by Elliott & Fry.
'The Manager's Pig', 1948. By Lewis C. Daniel. *Reproduced by courtesy of the Roedale Press*
Douglas Jerrold in May 1857. Photograph by Hugh Welch Diamond.

Illustrations in the text

Illustrations

Overture

The Passing of a Literary Hero

Monday 15 June 1857 was a beautiful day in London, 'the sky unclouded as in the sunniest Italian weather', according to *The Times*. Soon after mid-day a large crowd began gathering by the tall gates of West Norwood Cemetery waiting for the arrival of the funeral cortège of the writer Douglas Jerrold who had died suddenly at the age of fifty-four. Last respects were being paid to him both by the common people whose cause he had strenuously championed for so long, and by many leading figures from the world of mid-Victorian high culture. 'By this event', wrote the obituarist of the Liberal *Daily News* on 9 June, 'English literature has lost its most caustic and epigrammatic writer, London society its brightest wit, and cant, of every kind, its bitterest foe.'

Jerrold had died in harness as the (highly successful) editor of a mass-circulation Sunday paper, *Lloyd's Weekly Newspaper*. But it was as a 'leading champion of the people's rights and reformer of their wrongs'[1] on the radical *Punch* of the 1840s, as the author of two hugely and lastingly popular melodramas, *Black Eyed Susan* and *The Rent Day*, and as the creator of the sleepless Mrs Caudle and her nightly 'curtain lectures' to her hapless husband that he was chiefly cherished by the British public. Moreover, he was, in his own crooked little lion-maned person, a true hero of, and for, his times. James Hannay, a hard-hitting right-wing journalist, sometimes called 'the Douglas Jerrold of Conservatism', celebrated Jerrold in the lead article of the first number of the *Atlantic Monthly* (November 1857):

> ... he owed everything to nature and himself; no man of our age had so thoroughly fought his way; and no man of any age has had a much harder fight of it. To understand and appreciate him it was, and is, necessary to bear this fact in mind. It coloured him as the Syrian sun did the old crusading warrior. And hence, too, he was to a singular degree, a representative man of his age: his age having set him to wrestle with it, – having tried his force in every way and having left its mark on his entire surface. Jerrold and the century help to explain each other, and had found each other remarkably in earnest in all their dealings.

His image was familiar to many thousands through cartoons and photographs – in Mrs Gaskell's words, 'a very little almost deformed man with grey flowing hair, and very fine eyes' – and he was evidently an unforgettable physical presence for those like her who actually met him. 'How like

1

a little Nelson he stood, dashing back his hair, and quivering for the verbal combat!' remembered the critic David Masson, who had known him as a pivotal member of 'Our Club'. Others recalled his 'blue convex eye which seemed to pierce into the very heart of things' and his 'leonine head'

> which appeared to overweight the slender body by which it was supported ... the thin lips parted in a radiant smile, the long mane-like hair ... pushed back off the splendid forehead, the limbs and body ... restless with nervous excitement, and the genius of a giant [seeming] to animate the outlines of a dwarf.[2]

Now all that vitality and pugnacity had been abruptly extinguished by a death that, as his good friend George Henry Lewes wrote, 'created a great sensation all over England'. The voice of 'an ardent democrat, fierce against all injustice', of one who had made himself into 'a powerful people's advocate' was silenced for ever.[3] And now many thousands of those for whom he had spoken had come to Norwood to pay a final tribute to their hero.

*

The cemetery was in fact already overcrowded and the little Gothic chapel for Anglican burials was nearly full before the cortège arrived at the gates, in the shadow of St Luke's. This is one of London's so-called 'Waterloo Churches' commemorating that great battle, the horrific aftermath of which had so profoundly affected the twelve-year-old midshipman Jerrold as he helped to ferry dying and hideously wounded English soldiers back across the Channel. The hearse bearing the coffin, a plain oak one with no velvet covering, was followed by mourning coaches containing Jerrold's widow and immediate family (including his son-in-law, Henry Mayhew of *London Labour* fame). Reporters noted that none of the titled folk invited to the funeral, including the Duke of Devonshire and Lord John Russell, had troubled even to send what Dickens had recently characterised, in describing Mr Tulkinghorn's funeral in *Bleak House*, as an 'inconsolable carriage'. But a 'large concourse of gentlemen known to literature and art' was waiting at the cemetery gates to follow the funeral car up the hill to the chapel. Those who were to act as pall-bearers were: Dickens himself; Thackeray, Jerrold's old sparring partner on *Punch*, honouring the man he had once called 'a savage little Robespierre'; *Punch*'s editor, Mark Lemon; Sir Joseph Paxton, creator of the great building for the naming of which Jerrold was responsible, the 'Crystal Palace'; Hepworth Dixon, editor of the *Athenaeum*, the equivalent of today's *TLS*; the prominent Liberal MP and litérateur, Richard Monckton Milnes; Horace Mayhew, another member of the *Punch* fraternity; William Bradbury of Bradbury and Evans, the printers and proprietors of *Punch*; and another publisher friend of Jerrold's, Charles Knight, who had dedicated himself to helping

2

the spread of knowledge through his *Penny Cyclopedia* and other projects (he was perhaps now recalling the epitaph Jerrold had once proposed for him – 'Good Knight').

Among the other mourners who followed the coffin up the hill were Jerrold's old friend John Forster, whose domineering ways had once led Jerrold to nickname him 'the Beadle of the Universe', the dramatist Tom Taylor, and two leading 'Bohemians', or raffishly literary men about town, Albert Smith, the swaggering showman of Mont Blanc, and the journalist George Augustus Sala, one of 'Dickens's young men'. The veteran actor-managers J.B. Buckstone and Ben Webster were among those representing the theatrical profession and there was an impressive roll-call of artists – Cruikshank, Maclise, *Punch*'s John Leech, who illustrated two of Jerrold's satirical novels as well as the original Caudle Lectures, and, from the younger generation, John Tenniel, whom Jerrold had re-cruited for *Punch*, and William Powell Frith. Apologies for absence came from the literary idol of Jerrold's youth, the aged Leigh Hunt, who was troubled by a 'sorry cough', and from Thomas Carlyle. The latter was, he wrote to Monckton Milnes, prevented by a chance visitor from joining Milnes to perform 'that pious duty at Norwood today (not having heart for it by myself)'. 'It really was a kind of duty,' added Carlyle, 'a poor Brother Mortal and an *honest man* (I do believe) laying down his pen, and taking his departure from among us.' Evidently, he would have fully endorsed the verdict of the *Illustrated London News* on Jerrold: 'He did his work in the world like a brave and honest man.' (Jerrold had returned Carlyle's admiration but thought him too vague when it came to suggestions for 'the improvement of the age he rebuked. "Here", said he, "is a man who beats a big drum under my windows, and, when I come running downstairs has nowhere for me to go".')[4]

The Times of 15 June called the funeral arrangements 'unostentatious' but some thought otherwise, notably Dickens. According to Edmund Yates, another of his 'young men', Dickens 'spoke very sternly' at the Garrick Club that evening about the 'fuss and flourish' with which the ceremony had been conducted:

> The mourners, it seemed, wore bands of crape with the initials 'D.J.' round their arms, and there was a funeral-car of which Dickens declared he heard one old woman in the crowd say to another that it was 'just like the late Dook o' Wellinton's'.[5]

Dickens, we remember, had a lifelong abhorrence of pompous funeral customs and was soon to subject them to merciless ridicule in *Great Expectations*. On this occasion, even though it was the funeral of a much-loved friend, his sense of what he called 'the droll' was no doubt tickled by the contrast between the impressive effect that Jerrold's eldest son, William Blanchard, was clearly aiming at and the subversive behaviour of some elements in the crowd. 'The multitude', commented the *Morning*

Chronicle reporter on 16 June, 'was doubtless a striking tribute to the memory of one of the most eminent authors of his age' but

> ... the scene was anything but a decorous one. By far the larger number of the men had put on some sort of mourning, and at least half were there out of simple respect for the dead. But there was a large proportion of women, not one of them in mourning, with gaudy shawls on, some with children in their arms, evidently come to amuse themselves. They rushed about on all sides of the procession – pushing, hustling, and asking questions, making remarks, and utterly destroying not merely the solemnity but even the common decency of the scene. They were assisted in this, we are sorry to say, by a great many of the other sex. The rushing about the grounds by persons taking short cuts, the pressure over the very grave itself and the attempts of many actually to force their way into the chapel after it was declared to be full were most unseemly and indecorous.

One could almost imagine that by invading his funeral in this tumultuous manner the women were getting their revenge on Jerrold for Mrs Caudle, Miss Robinson Crusoe and a whole string of other comic female figures created by him for the amusement of *Punch*'s predominantly male readership.

All the pushing and hustling does not seem to have discomposed the Reverend Thomas Hugo, Vicar of St Botolph's and an old friend of Jerrold's. In the cemetery chapel he read the first part of the Church of England funeral service over the body of the man who, in his lifetime, had been such a scourge of bishops and other high-earning clerics, then the coffin was again placed on the hearse for another procession to the site of the grave. Masson, who like many other mourners had been unable to get into the chapel, followed the cortège as it passed the grandiose tomb of the theatre manager, George Bolwell Davidge, Jerrold's hard taskmaster in years gone by, and proceeded

> stepping slowly downwards along the path, which curved as it approached the grave. So, as I walked, I could see the coffin borne slowly onwards and downwards. Dickens was ... bareheaded, and his hair [was] slightly blown back by the breeze. And a little way behind him came Thackeray also bareheaded, tall among the rest, like Saul the son of Kish, – a head taller than any of his fellows.[6]

Hepworth Dixon had in his flowery way written in the *Athenaeum* on 13 June that Jerrold's friends and admirers 'would whisper over the grave the last farewells of the heart'. They might well have done so but nothing beyond the remainder of the funeral service was actually said at the graveside, perhaps because of the crowd's unruliness. Then the mourners left, reporters making a last note that Jerrold's grave was just across the path from the graceful monument that marked the final resting-place of the beloved friend of his youth, the poet Samuel Laman Blanchard.[7] The somewhat chaotic funeral had been, in the view of the *Morning Chronicle* reporter, only too true an emblem of 'many a literary career, restless and unquiet, sacrificing decency and delicacy for the object of the moment. The turmoil of his life attended the literary man even in his death.'

Meanwhile, the post-interment antics of Hepworth Dixon were greatly irritating a young journalist with the wonderful name of Eneas Sweetland Dallas, another of Jerrold's former companions at 'Our Club'. Dallas wrote to the publisher William Blackwood that Dixon was 'horridly coarse of nature':

> I could have knocked him down as I saw him at the funeral with his ostentation of sorrow. With a white pocket handkerchief in his hand, he walked solitary among the tombs, as you advanced to him he stretched out his hand to you, gave a look of unutterable grief, and suddenly turned on his heel without saying a word in speechless agony.[8]

Eventually even this Pecksniffian figure departed and so, to quote Masson again,

> Jerrold was left in his solitary place, where the rains were to fall, and the nights were to roll overhead, and, but now and then, on a summer's day, a chance stroller would linger in curiosity; and then back into the roar of London dispersed the funeral crowd.

Until a few years ago Masson's 'chance stroller' would have been able to see Jerrold's tomb and read the simple if over-optimistic inscription: 'An English writer whose works will keep his memory green better than any epitaph.'[9] The gravestone, however, fell victim to the local Council's 'nature park' conversion scheme for this magnificent Victorian cemetery, a scheme intended to enable visitors to 'relax in tranquil surroundings' unimpeded by the dead. Fortunately, there has been a change of policy in recent years and there are now plans to restore Jerrold's tomb as a number of others have been that were also removed. A comparable restoration of Jerrold to the fame that he enjoyed at the time of his death is hardly possible, but it is surely now time that we should try to recover from the obscurity of specialist academic studies and learned footnotes this dynamic little figure who was so much at the centre of popular culture and of journalistic and theatrical life in the London of William IV and the first two decades of Victoria's reign. Apart from the intrinsic cultural-historical interest of Jerrold's career in itself, such a work of recuperation should help us to understand something of the feelings of personal and national loss that were so widespread in England on that lovely June day in 1857.

Chapter One

Strolling Players and
'Theatres Rural'

1803-1813

The figure of the strolling player was a great stand-by for all writers of comic fiction during the early and mid 19th century, with Peregrine Proteus, the hero of Pierce Egan's *The Life of an Actor* (1825) standing as the great prototype. Swaggeringly ebullient, shabby-genteel in appearance, ever optimistic, fondly convinced of his own histrionic genius, and none too scrupulous when it came to economic survival, the strolling player features over and over again in comic stories and farcical dramas. Mr Jingle in Dickens's *Pickwick* and (gloriously) Vincent Crummles and his troupe in *Nicholas Nickleby* are the outstanding examples, but we might also remember Bingley's troupe (with the Fotheringay as its bright particular star) in Thackeray's *Pendennis* (1850) and Fuggleston's in Theodore Hook's *Gilbert Gurney* (1836).

Douglas Jerrold's view of strolling players was rather different, however. Instead of treating them with affectionate ridicule like Dickens or Thackeray, he presents them as quasi-heroic cultural missionaries 'of high social importance'. In a serial tale for the *New Monthly*, 'Bajazet Gag: the Manager in search of a Star', he puts into the manager's mouth a eulogy of the country actor:

> It is his noble privilege to awaken the sympathies of the humblest of his fellows, and it may be, often to startle them with a consciousness of the 'mystery of mysteries' which has slumbered within them. Look at the actor treading the threshing floor of a village barn. Behold the village clowns, rapt by his 'so potent art,' carried for a time beyond the 'ignorant present' by the genius of the poet and the passion of the player. Who shall say that these men are not, without knowing it, refined, exalted, by the 'cunning of the scene?'

Gag is being satirically presented by Jerrold as an unscrupulous showman but here the satire drops away as he expresses Jerrold's own sentiments. Gag pictures the player trudging from town to town humbly begging permission from 'beef-trained magistrates'

> to make some bumpkins happy – to busy them, for a time, with a picture of the human affections; in fact, to bestow upon them more real, more human-

ising good than many of the said justices ever even dreamt of in their long
dreams of official usefulness. Why, if the purpose of the stage were duly
acknowledged, were truly allowed, the magistrate himself, followed by his
constables, would, with floral wreaths and crown of laurel meet the strolling
players at the outskirts of every town and hamlet – yea, would lodge them in
the best inns, best houses, and banquet them as benefactors to the human
family. They would be received with pipe and tabor, and treated as befits the
humble, much-enduring missionaries for the diffusion of Shakesperianity![1]

Many other 19th-century writers, notably Hazlitt in his glowing 1820
essay on strollers, paid tribute to the way in which the players in 'village
barn, or travelling booth, or old-fashioned town-hall, or more genteel
assembly-room' had stirred and stimulated the imagination of childhood,
'introduced us, for the first time in our lives, to that strange anomaly in
existence, the fanciful reality, that gay waking dream, *a company of
strolling players!*'.[2] But none idealises the strolling player as cultural hero
and moral force (a somewhat unlikely role for Mr Jingle) in the way that
Jerrold does here. In doing so he was not only expressing some of his most
deeply-held beliefs about literature in general, and Shakespeare in particular, with regard to ethical and social concerns – but also showing filial
piety. For he himself had been born into the world of the strollers and been
very much a part of it for the first ten years of his life, 'appearing on the
paternal stage in several pieces when a child was needed'.[3] The most
notable of these appearances was in the arms of Edmund Kean when the
future superstar of Drury Lane was acting the eponymous Peruvian hero
in *Rolla* ('Monk' Lewis's translation of Kotzebue's *Die Spanier in Peru*).

Jerrold's father, Samuel, born in 1749, claimed to be the son of a
prosperous Hackney man, 'a large dealer in horses ... and the descendant
of yet richer forefathers'. Whether he was, like Dickens's Nicholas Nickleby, cast off by his family and turned player to keep alive or whether, like
many stage-struck young men of his day and later, he ran away of his own
free will to join a strolling company is not known. His frequent references
to having 'played in a barn upon the estate that was rightfully his own'
sounds like the former, but his glorying in the ownership of a pair of
Garrick's shoes, which he always wore on stage whatever his role, sounds
more like the latter. By the time he first appears in surviving theatrical
records he has just turned thirty and is married to an actress called
Elizabeth Simpson. They have at least two children, the elder, Robert,
being apparently illegitimate. The family formed part of a twenty-strong
company performing for a few months early in 1780 at the Crown Inn,
Islington. The Jerrolds took a 'benefit night' (i.e., when most of the night's
takings went to them) on April 19 playing opposite each other in a stock
comedy, *The Suspicious Husband*, with their three-year-old daughter
speaking the prologue. They then disappear from the record for nine years,
turning up again at Eastbourne in 1789 as part of another strolling
company with a 'circuit' based on Dover.[4]

The most desperately struggling kind of strolling company was like the one that so disillusioned the aspiring young actor Francis Wemyss in Falkirk in 1814 when he went to his first rehearsal. As described in his *Theatrical Biography*, his initial shock was that the theatre was a mere barn, his second the appearance of his fellow-actors:

> Falstaff's ragged regiment in apparel were princes to them – with the solitary exception of the manager, there was not a decently-dressed individual ... yet there was a shabby genteel appearance among them, which spoke of better days, and a certain strut by which the strolling player is readily detected by the eye of a professional brother.

The Dover Company seem to have been a cut above this but the actors were still 'sharers' rather than salaried. Thomas Dibdin, a natural son of the great Charles, made his début with the 'far-famed Dover company' as he calls it in his *Reminiscences*, where he also explains the system of 'sharing':

> a portion of all money taken at the doors went first to pay rent, servants, and tradesmen; and the remainder being divided into a certain number of aliquot parts, the manager took six of those portions for his trouble, and the use of his scenery and wardrobe; and every other member of the corps took one; the prompter had something additional: and if any actor had interest or address to procure the theatre a night's patronage for any family of rank, he claimed an additional share for what was a very important service.[5]

Samuel Jerrold (described by Dibdin as a 'melancholy comedian') may have got an extra share on account of his illustrious footwear. He would certainly have got one for being printer to the company (this, incidentally, strongly suggests that he had been a printer's apprentice who forsook his trade for acting, one of the most common routes to the stage for over a hundred years). Papering the town with playbills crammed with promise of rich and varied entertainment, was an essential part of any strolling company's campaign. 'Think what capital bills a man of your education could write for the shop-windows,' says Crummles to Nicholas Nickleby.

The early 1790s was, even for those without Samuel's advantages, a favourable time to turn stroller. In 1788 Parliament restored to local magistrates and mayors the power to license dramatic performances taken from them in 1737. In the interim actors outside London, legally classified as 'rogues and vagabonds' if they were not fortunate enough to be employed at one of the Royal Patent Theatres like Bath or York, had had to depend on the private patronage of country squires, or on the local authorities turning a blind eye to them as must have been the case in Islington when Samuel and his family played at the Crown. Now, however, began a boom in the building of provincial theatres for the accommodation of itinerant companies and by 1805 there were upwards of three hundred purpose-built theatres or recognised places of dramatic entertainment across the country.

After Dover Samuel seems to have 'strolled' northwards. He is found

9

acting at Gainsborough, Lincolnshire, in December 1792 and at South Shields in July 1795. A 'Mrs Jerrold' also appears on the South Shields playbill but this is not the Mrs Jerrold née Simpson. The latter had evidently died some time before April 1794, because in that month Samuel, now aged forty-five, married again at Wirksworth in Derbyshire. This time his bride was a twenty-two-year-old actress 'of great energy and ability' called Mary Reid. She had a mother with her as was fitting (we learn from Theodore Hook's *Gervase Skinner* that in order for travelling actresses to maintain their respectability 'it was generally understood that each un-married Miss was to carry her mamma with her ... or, if not, some discreet matron in the low-comedy line, as a chaperone') and this Mrs Reid, who was younger than her son-in-law, was to prove an important help to him and her daughter both professionally and domestically. Of Scottish origin, she had been a Miss Douglas and it was in compliment to her that Samuel and Mary Jerrold named their first son.

Mary Jerrold's name appears on a playbill for Wheatley's Riding School, Greenwich, on 17 May 1799 as part of a fourteen-strong company perform-ing *She Stoops To Conquer* (Goldsmith) and O'Keeffe's *The Agreeable Surprise*.[6] Samuel's name does not appear as a performer and it is possible that he was the troupe's manager. He had certainly gone in for manage-ment by 1802 when he had a company at Watford.[7] Hazlitt paints a glowing picture of a country manager's life:

> This fellow, who floats over the troubles of life as the froth above the idle wave, with all his little expedients and disappointments, with pawned paste-buckles, mortgaged scenery, empty exchequer, and rebellious orches-tra, is not of all men the most miserable – he is little less happy than a king, though not much better off than a beggar. He has little to think of, much to do, more to say; and is accompanied, in his incessant daily round of trifling occupations, with a never-failing sense of authority and self-importance, the one thing needful (above all others) to the heart of man.[8]

This description seems to fit Dickens's Mr Crummles or Thackeray's Mr Bingley very well but the truth was probably closer to the experience of that comedian beloved of Charles Lamb, Joe Munden (1758-1832), who briefly managed some strolling companies in the north-west. According to the profile of him published in the *Theatrical Inquisitor* in July 1813, Munden found himself 'beset with numerous vexations' such as 'the differ-ent tastes of audiences, the varied tempers of actors too ready to quarrel with the parts allotted to them, and the uncertain tenure of different theatres'.

The kind of 'vexation' a manager had constantly to deal with may be illustrated by a problem of Samuel's reported in the *Theatrical Inquisitor* for November 1812. 'Some respectable inhabitants' of Watford required him to put on Colman's new comedy *John Bull or, An Englishman's Fire-side*, which had just taken London by storm and was already in his company's repertoire. The play features a character called Dan, a broadly comic yokel inn-servant. This part was taken by Mrs Draper, Samuel's 'low-comedy woman', evidently an invaluable figure in any strolling company ('Young women, with pretty faces and good figures, are plenty enough in England,' says Hook's Manager Fuggleston, 'but a steady-going [sober], fat, low comedy woman with broad humour and strong lungs is, indeed, a treasure.'). But Samuel suddenly lost his 'treasure' and, in order to gratify the respectable Watfordians, had to cajole another of this troupe, young William Oxberry, into giving up the role of the mysterious Peregrine and clowning it as Dan, 'much against his inclination'.

Besides his family of actors, Samuel had by this time started a second family of his own, Mary having borne him a daughter, Elizabeth Sarah, and now she was again pregnant. As regards his first family, the elder son Robert had by this time struck out on his own, adopting the name Fitzgerald, and had joined the Norwich circuit where he specialised in playing Irishmen and sailors, 'his naturally hoarse voice and rolling walk' no doubt greatly helping in the latter case. Like his father, he turned manager and was running the famous York circuit (York, Hull, Leeds, Doncaster, Wakefield) when he died in 1818. Little seems to be known about Samuel's other son by his first marriage, Charles, beyond the facts that he went into the Navy, became a boatswain, and died in about 1846. And we know even less about the daughter, the three-year-old speaker of that prologue at the Crown, Islington, back in 1780.[9]

Samuel's company played at St Albans as well as Watford and perhaps in or near London during the winter of 1802/03 which might explain why Douglas was born there (in Greek Street, Soho, 'it has been said') on 3 January 1803. In his *Life of Douglas Jerrold* Blanchard Jerrold states that the baby was christened and then 'carried in swaddling clothes to Cranbrook [Kent] by his grandmother' and it may be that the Jerrolds had already established a family base there, in the village of Willsley near Cranbrook, though we have no definite evidence for this before 1806. However, Samuel was later described in *Oxberry's Dramatic Biography*[10] as having once been a 'proprietor of many Theatres *Rural*' so it may be that he had already acquired or leased the Cranbrook theatre whilst still active at Watford. Blanchard Jerrold is certainly wrong about the christening, for this did not take place until a full four years and nine months later, at St Anne's, Soho, as the parish records show (the Jerrolds evidently had some sort of London base in Soho). The detail about old Mrs Reid carrying the newly-born child down into Kent in its swaddling clothes (which sounds like family 'folk-memory' of a real occurrence) does suggest that the family needed to get to Cranbrook quickly so that there was no time to wait for the christening; but it was, in any case, not at all uncommon at this time for children to be baptised several years after they were born. Less common were men of Samuel's age begetting children and, if we are to believe the lengthy obituary of Jerrold, almost certainly written by his friend Hepworth Dixon, in the *Athenaeum* for 13 June 1857, he felt himself to have been marked for life (and death) by being born to an elderly father:

11

'he held a theory that the sons of old men are always nervous, facile, and short-lived.'

For the season of 1803/04 Samuel did not apparently play in Cranbrook but took his company to the dockyard town of Sheerness where, in a theatre 'fitted up with more than usual elegance', he presented a gala performance of *John Bull* on 14 November, in the presence of 'the Port Admiral and a very brilliant assemblage of elegance and fashion', with Oxberry giving 'a most humorous and correct performance' as Dan, and Samuel himself performing 'respectably' as the heavy-father figure, Sir Simon Rochdale.[11] On Easter Monday 1804 the company was strengthened by the recruitment of the seventeen-year-old Edmund Kean who already had a chaotic London career as 'the celebrated theatrical child' behind him. Thirty years later, when Jerrold's friend B.W. Procter ('Barry Cornwall') was writing his *Life of Edmund Kean*, he asked Jerrold for information about Kean's engagement with Samuel. Jerrold's notes printed in the *Life* give us a glimpse of the very varied fare that Samuel and his company had to provide to keep their audiences happy. Kean, 'then still in boy's costume',

> opened in *George Barnwell* [Lillo's ever-popular drama of 1731 about a London apprentice going spectacularly to the bad] and *Harlequin* in a Pantomime. His salary was fifteen shillings per week. ... he continued to play the whole round of tragedy, comedy, opera, farce, interlude, and panto-mime, until the close of the season. His comedy was very successful. In *Watty Cockney* and *Risk*, and in the song 'Unfortunate Miss Bailey' he made a great impression on the tasteful critics of Sheerness.

('A good song,' Dibdin remarks in his *Reminiscences*,[12] 'in a village, is thought more of by the audience than all the acting on the stage'; this was evidently true of Sheerness's nautical audiences also.) Jerrold, we note, makes no specific mention of Kean's having played the title role in *Rolla*, yet it must have been during this season that he himself figured as the kidnapped baby Kean rescues in that play (to be dramatically restored to its distracted parents by the dying, self-sacrificing Rolla just before the curtain falls). Probably, Jerrold was reluctant to reveal just how closely he had been, even in his earliest months, involved in his father's often hand-to-mouth enterprise – not that Samuel was all that low on the strolling scale. At least one of his productions seems to have become legendary in the profession: in his *Thirty Years Passed Among the Players* Joe Cowell records meeting in 1812 a strolling player called Howard at Plymouth who loftily informed him:

> yes, sir, I am an *actor* and have been ever since I was an infant in arms; played the child that cries in the third act of the comedy of 'The Chances' when it was got up with splendour by Old Gerald [*sic*] at Sheerness, when I was only nine weeks old; and I recollect, that is, my mother told me that I cried louder, and more naturally, than any child they'd ever had.

After the 1803/04 Sheerness season Samuel seems to have centred his managerial activities on Cranbrook, formerly the chief market town of the Weald of Kent, where, surrounded by 'rich pastures and leafy lanes', Douglas's earliest years were passed. He was later to say that his earliest memories were of the sound of sheep-bells and flower-gathering rambles with his grandmother, who seems to have divided her time between caring for him and taking the money at her son-in-saw's little thatched barn theatre. Two young actors who later made big names for themselves on the London stage and were important to Jerrold joined Samuel's Cranbrook company. One was James Pimbury Wilkinson (1787-1873) whose first attempt at a tragic part was, according to the *Mirror of the Stage* (21 January 1823), apparently so funny that Samuel 'prevailed upon him' to switch to comic roles whereupon he began building up that low-comedy repertoire of simpletons, eccentrics and boors which, ten years later, was to make his name. Samuel's anxiety to get Wilkinson into these roles probably had something to do with having lost Oxberry – as, indeed, he was for a while to lose Wilkinson – to a rival manager, Thomas Trotter of Worthing. The other notable recruit was John Pritt Harley (1786-1858), a lawyer's clerk who, according to *Oxberry's Dramatic Biography*,

> bade adieu to quill-driving, and ... padded off to Cranbrook where the late Mr Jerrold was astonishing the natives with a company particularly select but by no means numerous. Harley had but little knowledge of the technicalities of his new profession ... and, as most *managers* look on this as the criterion of merit, Mr Jerrold cast him but a few characters, and those of no considerable importance.[13]

Harley was soon to fare better with Samuel, who seems generally to have been much liked by his actors and actresses, one of whom, James Russell, described him to Blanchard Jerrold as 'the only really honest manager I ever knew'. He could hold his company together even when reduced to pawning his watch and 'pink satin suit' and playing 'in a carpenter's shop at Harrow'. But he had formidable rivals in the world of itinerant theatre-managers in Kent, none more so than the legendary Mrs Sarah Baker (1736-1816), who died worth a staggering sum of upwards of £16,000, having managed all her affairs herself despite her lack of education (she was the daughter of an acrobatic dancer called Ann Wakelin who toured the fairs). With her many purpose-built theatres at Canterbury, Rochester, Faversham, Maidstone, Tunbridge Wells and elsewhere, she became known as 'the Governess General and Sole Autocrat of Kentish Drama'. These theatres were all identical in plan and size so that the same scenery fitted in them all and Sarah could shift her company from one venue to another with minimal fuss and no need for rehearsals to adapt to the new place.[14]

More competition for Samuel was provided by another, much younger, manager, Thomas Trotter (1779-1851), whose company is first recorded in 1802 playing in a barn at Worthing. Although forced to yield to Mrs Baker in Faversham and Rochester, Trotter established a flourishing little theatre at newly-fashionable Southend in 1804 where he managed to attract the patronage of Lady Hamilton. Here Kean appeared after his season with Samuel Jerrold at Sheerness and took a benefit night in which he played Shylock, danced on the tight rope, sang all Apollo's music in Kane O'Hara's 'burletta' *Midas*, fought a pugilist and wound up the evening by playing Harlequin.[15] But he returned to Samuel in 1807 and all the other rising actors already mentioned – Oxberry, Wilkinson, Harley – seem also to have gone back and forth between Samuel's company and Trotter's.

By 1807 Trotter had leased barn theatres for seasons at Arundel, Marsham and Malling and had his own purpose-built theatres at Hythe and at his 'home base', Worthing. His opening production at the latter place on 7 July 1807 was *The Merchant of Venice*, starring no less a personage than Henry Siddons, son of the great Sarah, as Shylock. The Worthing Theatre, with its elegant little Doric portico and niche containing Shakespeare's bust, held between six and seven hundred people and next door to it stood a little cottage orné that Trotter had built for himself. The cost of building both theatre and cottage was £11,278 7s 6d, the kind of sum poor Samuel could only dream about.[16]

By 1806/07 Samuel would surely have been feeling himself pretty well encircled at Cranbrook by Baker and Trotter. The former had, for example, leased a theatre at Deal while continuing to operate all those she owned, and Trotter had added Gravesend to *his* circuit. Mindful perhaps of their successful Sheerness season three years before, Samuel and Mary decided to leave the pastoral beauty of central Kent for the seething, brawling atmosphere of a dockyard town on the Isle of Sheppey with closely-huddled little wooden houses, every other one of which was a tavern and every third one a brothel.[17] Here in a heady atmosphere compounded of navy and theatre, where 'a kind of seaport smell ... [took] hold of your nose with insulting tenacity',[18] the future author of *Black Eyed Susan* was to pass his childhood until just before his eleventh birthday.

The growth of Sheerness had been much accelerated by the war against the French that began in 1792. Initially, most of the dockyard labourers lived in the rotting hulks of old ships where 'there was no species of infamy unpracticed and they were unobserved'. In 1802 they were ejected, not without riotous opposition on their part, and replaced by convicts. The labourers either moved into barracks or crowded into the 'feverous alleys, noisome courts ... wooden huts called by a kind of poetic license, homes' that clustered round the dockyard walls. These huts, or 'cabins' were built of 'chips' or wood taken from the dockyard and painted with grey-blue dockyard paint, hence the area acquired the name of Blue Town. This was strictly a private enterprise development, and water delivered (by donkey) to houses cost a halfpenny a pail, a dockyard labourer's wages being at this time between ten and twelve shillings a week.

However unpleasant life may have been for the labouring population of Sheerness, it was at least not subject to the harsh brutality of military or naval discipline, to the ferocious floggings for comparatively trivial offences which Jerrold was to be forced to witness later on, and which he would never forget. These and other grievances led to mutinous outbreaks first at Spithead and then, more threateningly, at the Nore in 1797. The memory of the Nore mutineers marching triumphantly through Sheerness with Richard Parker, a common sailor, at their head waving the red flag of rebellion, would still have been vivid in local memory during the first decade of the 19th century, as would the eventual crushing of the mutiny and the hanging of Parker from the yard-arm of HMS *Sandwich*. Jerrold dramatised these events over thirty years later in his play *The Mutiny at the Nore* and – interestingly – took care to present Parker in a tragic-heroic light. Also noteworthy, to a lesser degree, is the fact that, apart from a joke or two about the Isle of Grain adjacent to Sheerness ('a precious island it is, very like a lark's turf afloat in a washing tub', says one character), his play is remarkably devoid of local colour.

The streets and alleys of Sheerness during the first decade of the 19th century would have provided rich materials for a budding Zola. The town was, Jerrold wrote later, 'famed for navigators, cyprian queens [prostitutes] and bowers of bliss [brothels]' and as a boy he would certainly have seen plenty of what one reviewer of his son's biography of him delicately termed 'the ruder realities of life'.[19] Sailors on the spree with their prize-money tumbled in and out of the beer-shops and brothels, often ending up with a filthy death in the ditches that were the town's only drainage system, fights were commonplace and there was, in general, 'so much trouble that the courts were always full of unsavoury cases, and magistrates complained that nowhere was as bad as Sheerness'.[20] Nothing of this – apart from the one phrase I have already quoted – gets into Jerrold's later writing, however.

Given an abundant and free-spending transient population eager for entertainment of all kinds, it is easy to see why leasing the Sheerness theatre was a good move for Samuel and Mary Jerrold in 1807. As long as the war with Napoleon lasted it remained a good investment. On 27 January Samuel agreed with the theatre's proprietor, a Londoner called Jacob Johnson, on a rental of £50 per annum but his company had already been performing there since at least 6 January. On that date an advertisement in the *Kentish Gazette* announced that the following night, a Wednesday, there would be presented at the Theatre, Sheerness, 'a favorite Comedy in two acts' called *The Jew and the Doctor* with Samuel as the Jew Abednego (a part requiring some versatility of the actor playing it), Harley in the light-comedy role of Changeable and Mary Jerrold as Mrs Changeable. This was to be followed by another piece written by Thomas Dibdin, 'a grand serious Romantic Melo Drama, performed upwards of 100 nights at the Theatre Royal, Covent Garden, called VALENTINE AND ORSON; or *The Wild Man of the Woods*' (this had been first produced at Covent Garden in 1804). 'Mr Jerrold', said this not every grammatical announcement, 'presents his respects to the Ladies and Gentlemen of

Sheerness, and its vicinity, that he has spared no expence to render the above piece worthy their notice'. In *Valentine and Orson*, the athletic Harley played Orson and also directed the pantomime while both Mrs Jerrold and 'Miss Jerrold', that is Elizabeth, played minor parts (Elizabeth was 'a Page' and 'The Genius Pacolet'). The piece, the spectacular nature of which presumably made it worth seeing more than once, was announced for repetition every night until the end of the week with varying farcical comedies as first pieces. Audiences would normally have expected to get in at half price after the first piece had been performed but Samuel's announcement states: 'On account of the great expence attending the getting up of this piece [*Valentine and Orson*], nothing under full price can be taken.' Full price was three shillings for a box, two for the pit, and one for the gallery.

For the next five years Samuel and his wife ran the theatre and, with the help of old Mrs Reid, raised their family. Two more children were born, Jane Matilda, to whom Douglas was always to be particularly attached (Walter Jerrold records a family tradition that Elizabeth was '"too like Douglas" in temperament and quickness of wits for them to be special chums') and Henry, who was to come to little good.[21] The attainment of a certain level of prosperity is indicated by the fact that Samuel and Mary were able to send Elizabeth to boarding-school in genteel Rochester, and judging by those programmes I have seen, they had the resources to offer a good mix of old favourites and new pieces with plenty of spectacle for the delectation of their audiences, which were 'almost wholly composed of "hearts of oak" with ivy (*vulgo*, sea-port nymphs) clinging around them'.[22] In his *Retrospections of the Stage* the actor John Bernard, recalling his time as a sharer in a joint-stock company at Plymouth in 1788, noted that sailors generally seemed to be 'very fond of playhouses' and had their own terms for the three sections of contemporary theatre auditoriums: 'The pit they called the hold; the gallery, up aloft or the maintop landing; the boxes, the cabin; and the stage, the quarter-deck.' And while, according to Bernard, they disliked representations of sea-fights since they would be sure to detect 'some blunder' (sea-fights would, in any case, have been beyond the resources of Samuel's little theatre), they loved to watch a land-fight

> particularly if Richard or Macbeth took a great deal of killing ... but they
> required the villain, whoever he was, to roll about a few minutes, like a
> jolly-boat in a tempest, in order to evince the pangs of his conscience and his
> wounds, when a *secundum artem* kick and shiver to conclude were the sure
> precursors of their thunder.

None of the programmes for Samuel's theatre I have seen feature any Shakespeare but the box-office favourites of the early 19th century – *Macbeth, Richard III, Hamlet, Merchant of Venice, Othello* – no doubt turned up as regularly at the Sheerness Theatre as the various non-Shakespearian stock pieces that do appear on these programmes. Samuel himself took whatever part needed filling – 'he was not particular what he played' said Jogrum Brown, his former doorkeeper, when interviewed by Blanchard Jerrold. Brown remembered Samuel as Richmond in *Richard III* and as the Ghost in *Hamlet* and, as we have seen, he also had in his repertoire Sir Simon Rochdale in *John Bull* and the comic but good-hearted Jew Abednego in *The Jew and the Doctor*.

By 1 December 1807 Wilkinson and Harley seem to have left the company as they do not appear in a playbill for that date.[23] Kean, however, had rejoined it and played the lead, Job Thornberry, in *John Bull* with Samuel, of course, as Rochdale. Thornberry is a very passionate tragi-comic role, the honest-tradesman father of a beautiful daughter seduced by a local nobleman, and would have provided useful practice for the Shylock with which Kean soon afterwards took Drury Lane by storm. His delivery of Job's fierce exclamation, 'Rot me if I won't make a baronet's son shake in his shoes for betraying a brazier's daughter!', no doubt drew 'thunders' from the Sheerness gallery if not from the boxes. The officers in the boxes, incidentally, could sometimes be as troublesome in their way as the sailors in the gallery in theirs. The somewhat undersized Kean opened in *Alexander the Great* and was annoyed by an officer constantly calling out in a jeering tone 'Alexander *the Little*!'. Jerrold recalled the incident later for Procter to use in his *Life of Kean*, having presumably himself heard it from Samuel and Mary:

> At length, making use of his (even then) impressive and peculiar powers, Mr. Kean folded his arms, and approached the intruder, who again sneeringly repeated 'Alexander the Little!' and, with a vehemence of manner and a glaring look that appalled the offender, retorted, 'Yes, with a GREAT SOUL!' In the farce of the *Young Hussar*, which followed, one of the actresses fainted, in consequence of the powerful acting of Mr Kean.

On 1 December 1807 Kean played the title role in another of Samuel's stock pieces, the 'musical entertainment' *Peeping Tom of Coventry*, played as an afterpiece to *John Bull*, and soon built up, 'even in such a place', as Jerrold puts it, a following for his histrionic powers, as well as for 'the elasticity and sprightliness of his quaint Harlequin'. But he incurred the enmity of someone in the town who set the dreaded press-gang on him. After acting for four more nights under a magistrate's protection, he had to make a nocturnal escape on the Chatham boat. Undoubtedly, he was a great loss to Samuel's enterprise, though by now there was another promising young actor, James Russell, in the company. Russell succeeded to Oxberry's part of Dan in *John Bull* and, according to a profile of him in *Roscius* (9 August 1825)

> was considered an acquisition to a theatre which has had many of our first actors on its boards, but which never boasted an audience capable of distinguishing humour from vulgarity – passion from bombast. The Sheerness

17

folks were not the most punctilious critics – a clog-hornpipe, and a comic song, were their most dainty delights.

However true this may have been, the Jerrolds evidently did not simply succumb to providing such 'delights' but strove to keep abreast of the theatrical times. The 1 December playbill already cited announces the last new Comedy called *Time's a Tell Tale* as shortly to be produced, which was certainly being up-to-the-minute as Henry Siddons's play had opened at Drury Lane only on 27 October. The staple fare, however, had to be the standard repertoire, comfortably familiar to both actors and public. Dickens, remembering in *The Uncommercial Traveller* the provincial theatre – Mrs Baker's Rochester – of his childhood in 'Dullborough Town', recalls *Macbeth* and *Richard III*, 'poor Jane Shore, dressed all in white, and with her brown hair hanging down, [going] starving through the streets', and George Barnwell killing the 'the worthiest uncle that ever man had' and afterwards being 'so sorry for it that he ought to have been let off'. And, sure enough, we find both of these two last 18th-century evergreens, *Jane Shore* and *George Barnwell*, featured in Samuel's bill of fare published in the *Kentish Gazette* for the week beginning 19 February 1810. By this time the theatre is designated as 'New Theatre, Sheerness' which suggests some rebuilding and renovation since 1807, hence good business. (On the other hand, the performances are no longer grandly described as being given 'by their Majesties Servants'.) Samuel seems to be following the same formula as in the previous year, with a different stock first piece every night, followed by a spectacular second piece, in this case Sheridan's 'grand Dramatic Romance', *The Forty Thieves*, 'with entire new Scenery, Machinery, Dresses, and Decorations'. The *Gazette* advertisement contains the announcement:

> Mr Jerrold, from the liberal encouragement his unremitting efforts to please have met with, induces him again [*sic*] to expend a considerable sum, in bringing forward this popular Dramatic Romance; and he most respectfully trusts his exertions will meet the public approbation.

Crummles himself could hardly have bettered such caressing of the public, though Nicholas Nickleby would have helped him improve the grammar.

As was customary, the Jerrolds made regular use of their young children on stage, even though they did not set up any 'Infant Phenomenon'. In the first piece on Monday night (19 February 1810) a comedy called *Heighho! for a Husband* first staged in London in 1793, Samuel, Mary and little Jane were all in the cast. In the 'Grand Dramatic romance' that followed, *The Forty Thieves*, Mary played Morgiana, little Jane 'Gossamer', 'Master Jerrold' [Douglas] Hassan and 'Master J.H. Jerrold' an anonymous fairy. Such a family *levée en masse* was probably a fairly regular occurrence, distracting the seven-year-old Douglas from things that, it seems, interested him more than the stage. 'He had,' his son recorded, 'no inclination towards the foot-lights; and never cared, in after-life, for the drama – seen from *behind* the scenes.' Later on it would require all the irresistible enthusiasm of Dickens, that passionate aficionado of the foot-lights, to get Jerrold behind them – apart, that is, from one very short-lived business venture in the actor-manager line.

The only source we have for any direct knowledge of Jerrold's Sheerness childhood is Blanchard Jerrold's somewhat hagiographic memoir in which we learn that he was mainly cared for by his loving grandmother, his mother (remembered locally as a 'more active manager' of the theatre than Samuel) being otherwise engaged. Blanchard tells us how old Mrs Reid would not let the little boy go out without his pattens on, even in dry weather, and, indeed, would not let him out much at all unless he was walking with her. He cites some old inhabitants of Sheerness who 'have yet a very vivid recollection of my father when a boy, and of his constant walks with his good grandmother'. When blind and bedridden, Mrs Reid would reminisce about locking up 'the dear child' in his own room with his books before she went to take money at the theatre – this, presumably, on nights when he was not needed on stage to be one of Mrs Haller's children in Kotzebue's ever-popular sentimental drama *The Stranger*, or Hassan in *The Forty Thieves*, or any other role. He was certainly not allowed out on the fifth of November when, as he wrote later, 'it was the custom of the authorities of an Isle of Sheppey dockyard to bestow upon their appren-tices a few waggon-loads of resinous timber, that a bonfire worthy of the cause it celebrated might be kindled from the public purse.' He describes himself lying in bed at midnight eagerly listening for the noise of the boys' procession and their chant about 'gunpowder treason and plot' and 'oh! how we wish to be with them!':

> We feel an unutterable pang, for loudest among the loud, we hear the shrill voice of Jack Tarleton. 'Ha!' we sigh, '*his* mother lets *him* out.' ... And now the procession moves on, and the voices die in the distance, and we feel we are left alone; and, in a few minutes, we hear new revellers ....[24]

In case he is making his father sound too mollycoddled as a child, Blanchard hastens to emphasise his pugnacity, quoting Jogrum Brown's decription of him as 'a stout, well-made, white-haired, and rosy-cheeked child ... somewhat unusually ready "to show fight"'. He may well have been one of the ringleaders, Blanchard believes, of 'the Blue Town juveniles' in their pitched battles with boys from Mile Town (Mile Town was another part of Sheerness, at a remove from the immediate vicinity of the dock-yard). Such a picture would have seemed quite appropriate to Blanchard's readers who had known Jerrold as the fearless and aggressive 'people's champion' of the 1840s and 1850s. So would his intense childhood patriot-ism and Nelson-worship, also much emphasised by Blanchard. Young Jerrold was serious beyond his years, 'graver than other children' – 'boys, and the games of boys, were not for him'. This may have been the result of physical ineptitude (Jerrold was physically clumsy all his life) rather than natural 'gravity' perhaps – he himself would say in later life that the only athletic sport he ever mastered was backgammon. 'Gravity' seems, anyway, somewhat hard to reconcile with the fights with the Mile Town boys, as does Jerrold's much-quoted remark later in life about the loneliness of his childhood ('The only other boy I knew was the buoy at the Nore'), or with Jerrold's own memories of longing to join in the Guy Fawkes fun. But Blanchard is evidently keen to depict his father as displaying as a child all that earnestness about life and physical courage which, along with a capacity for domestic affections and determined efforts at self-improvement, were among the qualities most looked for and expected in accounts of the childhood of Victorian heroes.

Regarding Jerrold's formal education, Blanchard tells us that Samuel paid Wilkinson to teach the little boy to read and write and then, after Wilkinson left the company, the child was sent to a local elementary school run by a Mr Herbert who, when questioned by Blanchard years later, unsurprisingly remembered his famous pupil as having been very well behaved and 'particularly studious'. Blanchard also cites old Mrs Reid's testimony that Jerrold had a 'remarkable love of reading'. Hepworth Dixon's *Athenaeum* obituary of 13 June 1857 paints rather a different picture, however, and one that sounds as though it derived directly from Jerrold himself:

> Jerrold's school-days were few and the results of his studies at Sheerness unimportant . He used to say, with a merry melancholy, that the only prize he carried home from school was a prize ringworm. In all ways, he was considered a dull boy; at nine years of age he could scarcely read. Breakers were the books which he liked to study ...

Smollett's novel *Roderick Random* with its classic honest-British-tar character Tom Bowling, the hero's uncle, was probably the nearest thing to studying the breakers so it is not surprising to find it mentioned by Blanchard as having been read 'passionately' by the young boy. However, as Smollett does not spare his readers any details of the brutality and squalor of life on board a man-of-war, memories of this book can hardly have been reassuring for the ten-year-old Jerrold when the time came for him to leave home for service in the Navy.

The only other book Blanchard mentions as having been favourite childhood reading of Jerrold's is the now forgotten *Death of Abel* by Saloman Gessner, the so-called 'Swiss Theocritus'. Mary Collier's florid 1761 translation of this became, and remained, hugely popular with 'that portion of the people who are below what is called the public, but form a far more numerous class': 'it has been repeatedly printed at country presses', commented the *Quarterly* in 1814 'with worn types and on coarse paper; and it is found at country fairs, and in little shops of remote towns almost as certainly as is the Pilgrim's Progress and Robinson Crusoe'.[25]

Gessner's rhythmic prose turns the story of the first murderer into a domestic drama variegated with some of the 'idyllic' nature-descriptions that first made him famous and also the insinuation of some pre-revolutionary doctrine (a comfort Byron was to deny the readers of his drama *Cain* in 1821). Gessner's Cain is immediately flooded with remorse after killing his brother ('Ah what tortures do I feel – how his head hangs! – how it bleeds ...') and becomes a figure of pre-Gothic terror. ('The furious winds shook his erect hair. Wild fear at length forced from his livid and quivering lips these horrid accents ... [etc.]'.) What with all this, and its being 'a dream from Hell' that dupes him into killing to save from 'misery and bondage' his children (twin boys who appear in Book 5 to charm the reader with their artless prattle), as well as his love for his devoted wife ('Thou art to me as a gracious angel!'), Gessner's first murderer becomes a highly sympathetic as well as a fearful figure. He surely remained somewhere in the recesses of Jerrold's imagination and contributed to the dramatist's conception of that series of agonised transgressors who appear in his plays beginning with Grayling in his first, and very successful, melodrama, *Ambrose Gwinnet* (1828).

More significant, however, than the remorseful murderer-hero, for Jerrold's later development, was Gessner's elaborately worked out image of labouring slaves and 'voluptuous idlers'. So much of Jerold's later writings revolve around one big, fierce simplification – that society as a whole is divided into the toiling and suffering masses, 'the people', on the one hand, and, on the other, those with wealth, privilege and power who exploit and abuse them – that it seems likely that this image of Gessner's had considerable impact on his childish imagination as he pored repeatedly over this favourite book. And, although the fable may proclaim the image to be 'a dream from Hell', the authenticity of Gessner's division of mankind would have seemed very much confirmed to any observant child looking at the life around him in Regency England.

His schooling at Mr Herbert's seems also to have encouraged a critical view of opulence: 'A wise man will desire no more than he may get justly, use soberly, distribute cheerfully and live upon contentedly' runs the copy-book sentence so neatly transcribed and signed by 'Ds. Wm. Jerrold' as part of a Christmas exercise in 1812.[26] Wealth might be the subject of cautionary maxims but that other English obsession, rank, was no doubt sacrosanct. And from his later schoolmaster, a Dickensian-sounding Southend tailor called Glasscock 'who had lost a leg through trimming standards with a bill-hook for a Guy Fawkes Festival', young Jerrold might have caught a faint aroma of royalty itself. Glasscock's mother owned several bathing-machines and boasted on her trade card that she had been dipper to both Princess Caroline of Wales and Princess Charlotte, moreover both his daughters had been in service with Princess Caroline during her residence in Southend.[27]

Royalty had forsaken Southend by the time the Jerrolds and their company were playing summer seasons there but fashionable visitors still came, although in dwindling numbers. The theatre that Thomas Trotter had built in 1804 was a very modest affair with one entrance for boxes, pit and gallery: a visitor stumbling on it in 1817 noted that if it had not been designated 'in large letters Theatre Royal' he would have taken it 'for a very small chapel or rather meeting-house'.[28] Samuel Jerrold and his family acted there for Trotter, the owner and licensee, in August and September 1810, Samuel taking a benefit night, supported by Harley, on 29 August. Young Douglas and little Jane were called to the colours to play Norman page-boys on 1 September in a production of 'Monk' Lewis's three-year-old Byzantine melodrama *Adelgitha; or the Fruits of a Single Error* (during which, despite the smallness of the theatre, the audience were thrillingly promised sight of 'Rocks, and a Water-Fall, *Grand Gothic Palace*, Subterraneous Cavern, and Grand Banquet'). For the next four years Samuel himself became licensee of the Southend Theatre with permission from the Court of Quarter Sessions to perform plays for sixty days from the end of each June but the only playbills that seem to have survived are a couple from August 1811, one featuring *The Surrender of Calais* and Millingen's *The Bee-Hive* ('Act 1st. The British Fleet at Anchor') and the other one *Macbeth* with Samuel as First Witch, Mary as one of the 'Singing Witches', customarily introduced into the play at this time, and little Douglas as Fleance.[29] During the 1812 season the theatre was 'but thinly attended', Samuel's 'spirited exertions' apparently not being 'seconded either by the visitors or the inhabitants', and there seems to be some evidence that 1813 was a year of financial retrenchment for the family. Elizabeth was still at her boarding-school in December 1812 but may have left it soon thereafter. She was to follow her parents into the profession and, like her sister after her, married into it.[30] In June Samuel sold the lease of the Sheerness house to his elder son by his first marriage, Robert Fitzgerald. He and Mary must have begun to be concerned about Douglas's future, given that, unlike his siblings, he showed no inclination for treading the boards. His passion for the sea and ardent Nelson-worship pointed rather towards some kind of nautical career and, fortunately, there was at hand a distinguished patron of the Southend Theatre who was able and willing to help the Jerrolds in this respect.

Chapter Two

In Nelson's Navy

1813-1815

Charles Austen, younger brother of Jane, was Captain of the *Namur*, which was stationed at the Nore, from November 1811 and would have been a patron of Samuel's Southend theatre during the summers of 1812 and 1813. The *Namur* was a seventy-four gun man-of-war that had seen service against the French on the 'Glorious First of June' but was now relegated to the status of 'guard-ship' – it was kept fully rigged and partly armed, stored and manned so that it could be made ready for active service in a few days. It was also used as a holding base for seamen (including pressed men) to be used to make up crews for outgoing ships, a fact later exploited by Jerrold in 'Jack Runnymede', one of the stories in his *Men of Character*. Captain Austen, a devoted family man who needed at this time to live as cheaply as possible, had his young wife and their two little girls sharing his quarters on board but seems also to have had summer lodgings in Southend. Austen, described by Jane on a visit to their oldest brother in October 1813 as 'all affectionate, placid, quiet, chearful good humour' was clearly a very approachable man and this no doubt emboldened Samuel to ask him if he might be willing to take young Douglas on board the *Namur* as a 'volunteer of the first class'.[1]

This category of boy-entrant into the navy came into being in 1794 when the Admiralty did away with the 'captain's servant' fiction whereby the sons of the nobility and gentry or, more frequently, of professional men (Nelson's father was a country parson) had previously entered the service in order to acquire the requisite three years 'sea-time' before they could be rated as midshipmen. This system had led to considerable abuse, hence the new regulation creating the new designation of 'Volunteer Class I' – 'to consist of young gentlemen intended for the sea service (whether the sons of sea officers or not) provided they are not under the age of eleven years; to be styled Volunteers, and allowed wages at the rate of six pounds per annum'.[2] Admission of these lads into a ship's company was still, however, wholly at the discretion of the captain, so Austen was quite free to oblige the Jerrolds.

Accordingly, the ten-year-old Douglas went aboard the *Namur* as potential officer material, a remarkable social opportunity for a strolling player's son, on 22 December 1813, just a couple of weeks before his eleventh birthday (it seems odd that he should join the ship just before Christmas and when he was just under age – there must presumably have been some special circumstances).[3] We know just when he went aboard but can only speculate about how he was feeling. Both his son and grandson present him as a brave-hearted little boy proud of his new uniform and eager for an heroic life of French-bashing on the ocean wave, but Jerrold's own comments in later life, as reported by a German journalist, Ludwig Kalisch, who interviewed him in 1855, strike a rather different note. Here is Kalisch's account:

> With tears in his eyes he told me several times during our talk he had never been young. While he was still a young boy he went through all of life's bitterness. The son of parents without fortune, he was put in the Navy by his father at a very early age. But Douglas the little cabin-boy (*Schiffsjunge*) who had a soft and good-natured heart witnessed at close quarters much coarseness and cruelty on board ship; he was so hurt and revolted that he suddenly renounced life at sea.[4]

As we have seen, a 'Volunteer of the First Class' had a status and prospects better than the term 'Schiffsjunge' suggests, and Blanchard is quite clear that Samuel was gratifying his son's ardent desire by placing him in the Navy. So why the tears in the Kalisch interview? Perhaps, speaking to a foreigner who would be reporting what he said where it was unlikely to be seen by many British readers, Jerrold felt able to indulge in a bout of retrospective self-pity (very minor compared with Dickens's in his 'autobiographical fragment', unpublished till after his death). Blanchard Jerrold writes, 'I have often heard my father dwell upon the great emotion with which he first ascended the gangway ... of one of his Majesty's ships.' This sounds, and is intended to sound, like uncomplicated glowing patriotism but I think that we may get more sense of what the little boy was really feeling on that winter's day in 1813 from an unpublished quasi-autobiographical piece, 'The Fate of Wilbert', that Jerrold wrote twelve years after the actual event.[5] This story, a hectic exercise in ultra-Byronism, relates how Wilbert, 'cursed ... with a mind sensitive and generous', had the further misfortune to be placed by Nature 'in a low and obscure calling' and was destined 'at an early period of boyhood ... to begin his varied part in this world of perplexities, as a sailor'. Piercing through the rhapsodical vapours of 'Wilbert's' prose is a sudden sharp image of 'a bleak and miserable day in the month of January' with an apprehensive child being carried towards a big ship 'frowning black and cheerless from out the wintry mist' and weeping as he looks back towards the shore across 'the brown universe of waters'. He disdains the offer to take him back home, however, and 'with a dry eye mounted the ship's side'.

Once aboard, Wilbert 'found but few to protect him. Left to the mad riot of older beings, he shared their pastime as he shared their duty'. In real life, however, young Jerrold was a good deal more fortunate. Captain Austen, Blanchard Jerrold tells us, received the child kindly, 'and petted him throughout the year and one hundred and twenty-three days which he passed under his command' though he did not, one presumes, pay too much attention to the anxious letter he received from old Mrs Reid asking him to ensure that her little grandson should always wear his pattens whenever he walked on the wet deck. Jerrold was allowed to keep pigeons and 'loved to see his flight of birds sweeping round the fleet'. He was even permitted to pore over the fascinating volumes of Buffon's *Natural History* in the Captain's cabin, storing his imagination with innumerable curious 'facts' on which to draw for illustrative and satirical purposes in his later writings.[6] Life on a guard-ship was comparatively relaxed and on the *Namur* there was even time for amateur theatricals among the young midshipmen and First-class Volunteers:

> In the cockpit, the Middy Jerrold would 'strut his hour upon the stage' and aspired to the important character of the 'Robber' in the *Iron Chest* [definitely an advance on playing Fleance in *Macbeth*!]. STANSFIELD was scene painter to the company, principal decorator, and master of ceremonies to the gentlemen and ladies who might be selected from such as at the period we describe, were in the habit of visiting a man-of-war.[7]

'STANSFIELD' was the future great marine artist and scene-painter Clarkson Stanfield. Twenty years old in 1813, he had been captured on Tower Hill by a press-gang (as a merchant seaman he was legitimate prey) and was serving as foremastman on the *Namur* under the assumed name of 'Roderick Bland'.[8] He and Jerrold were to meet again, on a rather more imposing stage, eleven years later when his scenic art was helping to 'realise' Jerrold's drama *The Rent Day* at Drury Lane.

Life on board was not all play for Captain Austen's young volunteers and midshipmen, however. Jane, writing to her sister Cassandra on 14 October 1813 reports:

> I have made Charles furnish me with something to say about Young Kendall. – He is going on very well. When he first joined the Namur, my Br. did not find him forward enough to be what they call put in the Office, & therefore placed him under the Schoolmaster, but he is very much improved, & goes into the Office now every afternoon – still attending School in the morning.[9]

Jerrold may also have been 'placed under the schoolmaster' but, Jane's report on young Kendall notwithstanding, this may have been of dubious educational advantage. Schoolmasters on board ship occupied a very inferior position at this time – captains were not obliged to have them and it was hardly a tempting situation. They were paid a pittance and were rated no higher than midshipmen but without the latter's officer privileges. Unsurprisingly, therefore, they tended to be scholastic rejects at best and at worst completely untrained. It is unlikely, however, that Captain Austen would have recruited any of his schoolmasters (two or three different ones figure in the *Namur*'s muster-rolls for 1813-14) quite in the way that Jerrold describes in 'Jack Runnymede'. Nankin the schoolmaster had arrived on board as a marine, a sailor informs Jack, and they drills him ... and mounts him on the gangway. One day, captain coming up the side sees Nankin's hands ... 'Dickson,' says the Captain [to the first Lieutenant], 'that marine's either a scholard or a pickpocket ... he's got such smooth hands.' Well, they wanted somebody to learn the ship's boys, and they tries Nankin, and finds he can read, and write, and sum; and so they promotes him to the gun-room [used as a school-room in men-of-war]; and bit by bit, he casts his red and pipe-clay [marine's uniform], and has the impudence to let his hair grow.

Nor does the school-room scene in 'Jack Runnymede' in which the first lieutenant orders a seven-year-old to be flogged by the bosun's mate for spinning his peg-top on the after-deck seem, on the face of it, likely to have been drawn from life on board the *Namur*; but we should remember that, although 'young gentlemen' such as Jerrold might be allowed by a kindly captain to keep pigeons or get up plays, such privileges would not have applied to other boys on board, boys of the second or third class, or the children of warrant officers and ordinary seamen. Indulged though he might be by Captain Austen, young Jerrold would certainly have found many aspects of life on the *Namur* pretty rough. He would have seen and heard much in the way of sometimes brutal horseplay (Hannay, who, like Jerrold, had been a Volunteer of the First Class, remembered youngsters having the tips of their noses slit and salt rubbed in the wound[10]), petty tyranny and foul language (in 'Wilbert' swaggering juvenile midshipmen are depicted as 'mouthing the big oath and screaming at human flesh'). But he was apparently taken under someone else's wing besides the Captain's. In a sketch, 'The Ship-Clergyman', published in the *Monthly Magazine* in November 1827, he recalls in vivid detail a certain 'Mr E. – ', presumably the chaplain of the *Namur*, who was

the patron of the poor child who had stepped from the nursery to the riot of the cock-pit: he would take the ten-years old midshipman with him in his shore rambles – would feed him with cakes and good counsel and, as much as possible, cleanse the mind of the infant from the moral mildew of a man-of-war![11]

In later years he would, his son tells us, say that, although he believed in boys being made to 'rough it' in order to develop their 'manliness', he saw 'in the life of a "middy" something too rough to be good – something that might make a very brutal man'.

In 'Jack Runnymede', where he is writing in a predominantly comic-satiric vein, he deals more light-heartedly with one aspect of the 'roughness', the legendary antagonism between young midshipmen (including trainee ones like Volunteers of the First-class) and the petty officers with whom they lived in such close juxtaposition.

Young midshipmen, like young dogs, very soon discover the antipathies of those it is their destiny to live with; but unlike the more useful animal, the young midshipman does not avoid the prejudices of the party, but takes every opportunity of revenging himself upon them. Such was the state of things between the juvenile midshipmen of the guard-ship – for, of course, we do not include the midshipmen of forty and fifty – and Mr Mac Acid, the gunner .... Thus it gave a particular edge to the pleasure of flirting with the carpenter's black-eyed daughter, that the time and place for such relaxation, was 'evening, the fore cock-pit,' close to Mac Acid's berth. ... On the present evening Mr Mac Acid, like a thrifty officer, sat conning his volume ... with his door ajar, and a heavy cane at his side, prepared at all points for the enemy. When his stick smote the neck of Runnymede, how, for a brief moment did the old man rejoice! To kill a spider, a rat, a pole-cat, a snake, great as may be the satisfaction to those who loathe such things, was nothing to the delight that Mac Acid would have felt at the destruction of a young midshipman. We verily believe the extacy of the sport would have carried the old man off.

'Is there no way, Mr Mac Acid,' asked the good-natured captain of the gunner, 'is there no way of reconciling you to the young gentlemen? Can't you, by any means, be brought to stomach a midshipman?'

'I think, sir,' replied the venerable Mr Mac Acid, shaking his white head – 'I think I could like one – in a pie.'

One would like to think that the exchange at the end of this passage recalled an actual exchange between Jane Austen's indisputably 'good-natured' brother and one of his petty officers but probably it is only a W.C. Fields joke brought into the world before its time.

In April 1814 Napoleon, with his capital city in enemy hands and his generals deserting him, abdicated and went into exile on Elba. The long wars seemed to be over at last but France, stinging from defeat, did not take kindly to the Allies' stripping her of her empire and the restoration of the Bourbon monarchy in the uninspiring form of gouty old Louis XVIII. Napoleon bided his time. On 26 February 1815 he escaped from Elba and made his triumphant return to French soil near Antibes on 1 March. When Jerrold was drafted on 24 April, with a company of 44 men, from the *Namur* to the gun-brig *Earnest*, he must have felt that he was going to see some action at last – not, however, that this was likely to be in battle, since French naval power had been broken by Nelson years before and British naval hostilities at this time mainly took the form of skirmishes with the Americans. Jerrold was the only 'Volunteer Class I' drafted on to the *Earnest* and it may indeed be that he had, as his son writes, 'touched his hat to the captain [no longer Captain Austen – he had resigned his post on the *Namur* in September 1814], and begged to be sent to glory'.[12] In fact, the *Earnest* was used to convoy military transports to Ostend in preparation for the great battle fought at Waterloo on 18 June which finally put an end to Napoleon's empire. Later, the brig helped to return some of the wounded British soldiers to Sheerness. Blanchard Jerrold underlines the powerful effect of this experience on the young volunteer. The soldiers'

raw stumps and festering wounds, went far to give my father that lively sense of the horror of war, which abided with him throughout his life. He often described the disgust with which he beheld the poor invalids binding their sores upon the deck – the groans and curses that fell upon his ear. Here was ... war behind the scenes!

The theatrical metaphor is well chosen because it was in one of his dramas, *The Mutiny at the Nore*, that Jerrold tried hardest to bring home to his audience this aspect of the reality of war. Although he himself escaped direct experience of battle he had no difficulty in creating a vivid picture of its consequences on board a man-of-war, building on his memories of scenes on board the *Earnest*:

> Well, the ship's cleared for action; now Dick is a fine, strong, healthy fellow; the first broadside's poured in – where's Dick? – sprawling a cripple for life upon the deck ... what's Dick's luck? Why, he's lying in the cockpit, with the surgeon and his mates, with their shirtsleeves tucked up, clattering their knives and saws, and there the poor fellow lies with a docked limb ... amid groans and sobs and prayers for water ...

This transporting of the Waterloo-wounded was one of Jerrold's most intense experiences during his six-months' service on the *Earnest*. Another was having to witness the punishment of an ordinary seaman called Michael Ryan that was recorded in the brig's log for 30 June (P.R.O.). Ryan was convicted of theft and condemned to eighteen lashes of the cat-o'-nine-tails (a particularly vicious instrument consisting of nine strips of leather bound to a handle with lead shot sewn to the ends of the thongs). This seems not to have been the only flogging at which the young Jerrold was compelled to be present. He later asserted that he had 'frequently' witnessed this 'cold-blooded and brutalising operation' and, according to his obituarist in the *Gentleman's Magazine* (July 1857) he had even seen it in its most extreme form: 'We have seen his eyes fill with tears, and his lips quiver, as he detailed his feelings at seeing a sailor flogged through the fleet.' The hideous brutality of naval discipline appears again and again in his writing, very much as a paradigm of man's inhumanity to man (especially as aggravated by distinction of rank), and of the moral cant that was in the 19th century so often associated with it. A debate in the House of Commons in July 1846 occasioned by a soldier's having been flogged to death provoked one of his most savage diatribes, quoted in his son's biography:

> The British oak which, on the authority of the song, supplies his heart to every British sailor, flourishes the more, like the British walnut, the more it is thrashed. This opinion is recommended to us by legislative wisdom – wisdom clubbed to by both sailors and landmen in the House of Commons; for a great part of Monday evening was devoted to the praises of the cat-o'-nine-tails. The eulogies were so glowing, so ingenious – the natural and social benefits of knotted cord administered by the boatswain's mate till the flesh blackens and blood gushes, so deep and manifold that, after the eloquence, the fancy, bestowed upon the scourge, we do not despair to hear sweet things said of the rack .....

In his *Mutiny at the Nore* Jerrold puts into the mouth of his hero, the mutineers' leader Richard Parker, some passionate speeches about the way in which such savage punishments tend to produce the very opposite effect to that which their defenders asserted. Parker has been wrongly convicted of the theft of a watch (according to the plot of the play, that is – Jerrold invents much in order to maximise sympathy for his mutineer-hero) and is telling his wife how he was punished. He speaks of himself in the third person as though to try and distance the horror:

PARKER: ... they did not hang the man, and thereby bury in his grave the remembrance of his shame; no they mercifully sent him through the fleet.

MARY: The fleet?

PARKER: Listen, then wonder that men with hearts of throbbing flesh look upon, much less inflict, such tortures. – They sent him to receive five hundred lashes, so many at the side of every vessel, whilst the thronging crew hung upon the yards and rigging, to hear the wretch's cries, and look upon his opening wounds. What was the result? Why, the wretch they tied up, a suffering, persecuted man, they loos'd a raging tiger!

His time on board the *Namur* and the *Earnest* left Jerrold with a fervent admiration of the ordinary British seaman. In his play *Black Eyed Susan* he placed, for the first time in dramatic history, this figure centre-stage as an heroic, potentially tragic, protagonist, and in *The Mutiny at the Nore* he touched on the horrors that threatened a sailor's life in war and in peace. Already in 'Wilbert' we see him clearly registering the double effect his naval experience had upon him:

The very young mind of Wilbert had been awakened into admiration by mortal daring, and sickened at mortal debasement. His breast had glowed to see the cool sailor hanging from the yard, whilst the tempest flapped its hundred wings around him. And the waters yawned unnumbered graves beneath: – and his heart was chilled to see the same being, who has with calm-set muscle outstared death in all its horrors, striped like a beast for some casual fault, taking, perhaps, much of its enormity from the whim of his master.

This hero-worship of the British ordinary seaman had, I believe, certain limiting consequences for the political aspect of Jerrold's later dramas and satirical fiction. The first was that his pre-eminent representative of the moral worth, and even nobility, of the common people was a figure fixed at the bottom of a rigid hierarchical structure. This structure defined him, gave him his meaning, and required his unquestioning support. A sailor's total loyalty and submission to the King, and to those holding his commission, must inevitably be an integral part of his virtue and worth. Parker in *The Mutiny at the Nore* is driven by rage against personally experienced injustice, not rage against the system, as at least one spectator of the play

29

thought he should be (see below, p. 79). William in *Black Eyed Susan* would no more question the basic distribution of wealth, power and privilege in society than would Dickens's Sam Weller.

The second consequence, closely related to the first, was that the villains in Jerrold tended always to be society's NCOs, as it were, or, at most, its junior officers rather than the 'high command'. It is the boatswains, the petty lawyers and lower-grade officials (beadles, for example) who persecute and oppress the people while the captains of society are essentially benevolent once their attention is drawn to the mischief being caused by their underlings. The higher ranks of society may produce morally inadequate people such as Old Grantley is revealed to have been in *The Rent Day*, or the Countess of Blushrose in *The Story of a Feather* (for good measure Jerrold makes her a bit of a kleptomaniac as well) but it is still Grantley *fils* and the good Lord Blushrose who put everything right at the end, showering benefits on the long-suffering hero of the play and heroine of the novel respectively. From the perspective of the lower decks, oppression must generally seem more a matter of malicious or tyrannical petty officers than the result of actions or the characters of the more remote figures above them, or of the system as a whole.

Jerrold's earliest social experiences had been in his father's theatre company. Here there would also have been a hierarchy but one based (theoretically at least) on individual merit, also quite fluid in nature with rising actors and actresses graduating to, or succeeding to, 'first business' in the company, or sometimes being eclipsed by wandering stars. Outside the theatre's walls, however, in the so-called 'real world', all the company were merely 'poor players' while, even inside the building, the 'real world' in the shape of the audience was clearly and literally structured into three distinct classes – upper- and upper-middle class boxes, middle- and lower-middle-class pit, and plebeian gallery – so Jerrold would have been well conditioned from his childhood to accept the naturalness of a similar social structuring when he began 'real' life in the Royal Navy.

By the late summer of 1815 outside reality was pressing hard on the Jerrolds. Samuel appears to have been depressed by the 'unjust dealings' of builders he had employed to restructure the Sheerness theatre and a further blow was the government's requisitioning of the land on which the theatre stood for expansion of the dockyard. He had not applied again for a summer lease of the Southend theatre, the 1814 season having presumably proved as disappointing as its predecessors, and now seems to have suffered a kind of *coup de vieillesse* and to have decided that his management career was at an end. He was sixty-six but far from sharing the vigour of another sexagenarian manager cited by Robert Dyer in his *Nine Years of an Actor's Life* who insisted on continuing to play juvenile tragedy heroes ('Why, I've played George Barnwell for forty years, and it's damned hard if I can't play him now'). The Sheerness theatre and its contents were sold by auction and it was left to Mrs Jerrold, still young and vigorous, to take steps to ensure the family's economic survival.

She decided to try for work in the London theatres. Leaving her husband and all her children in the care of her mother (except Henry, the youngest, whom she took with her), she left Sheerness for London and set about finding work and a place for the family to live. Meanwhile, Douglas had been paid off with the rest of the *Earnest*'s crew on 21 October, in effect ending his naval career almost before it had properly begun, for he had not yet qualified for rating as a midshipman. It may have been that he abandoned the navy in disgust, as he later told Kalisch, or he may have been summoned home by his mother to help the family in its hour of need. Whatever the reason for this abrupt termination of his naval career, ten years later when Jerrold was writing his autobiography in the Byronic-tragic terms of the story of 'Wilbert', he represents it as a fortunate thing that his hero's 'nautical existence was but of short duration': 'Had it continued till dawning manhood ... some omnipotent captain might have arraigned his spirit for rebellion, and the yard-arm or marine's musket had paid the traitor'.

Alternatively, Wilbert might have simply stuck for years, even decades, at the rank of midshipman as so many did who had no strings to pull, no relatives, friends or patrons who could use their interest at the Admiralty on their behalf. So, quite apart from his disillusionment with navy life, it was better for him to quit the service so young:

> At thirteen behold Wilbert thrown back upon the land, to begin the world anew; congratulating himself, that at so early a period he is free; for had his poor services been required some years longer, incapable of new pursuits on shore, what would have been the fate of the man-midshipman? Had his 'love of country' been ever so unbounded it would have been surely unreturned by the object of his affections.

Wilbert's domestic situation is, as we might expect, very cloudily expressed. Apart from 'one heart whose sisterly throb ... beat towards him' (Jerrold's tribute to his little sister Jane perhaps?), his family seem reprehensibly unappreciative of, and insensitive to, the suffering genius in their midst. To have him cared for by a doting grandmother would have detracted disastrously from his Byronic/Shelleyan hero status, so there is no equivalent of old Mrs Reid in the story. It was she, however, who seems to have been chiefly responsible for keeping the family fed, clothed and sheltered during the autumn of 1815 as they waited for Mary Jerrold's summons for them to come to London. This duly came in late December and 7 am on New Year's Day 1816 found the family disembarking from the Chatham boat (Jerrold's coat having been stolen on board[13]) at Westminster pier and making their way to modest lodgings in the shadow of that great Covent Garden Theatre of which the young boy would have heard so much talk among his father's acting troupe in earlier days.

Chapter Three

Beginning the World

1816-1827

When the Jerrolds moved to London they naturally gravitated towards
Broad Court. Linking Bow Street, in which Covent Garden Theatre
stands, with Drury Lane, Broad Court's proximity to the two great national theatres recommended it to the acting profession: 'I'm to be found in
Broad Court, Bow Street, when I'm in town' announces Mr Snevellici in
Nicholas Nickleby (1839); 'If I am not at home, let any one ask for me at
the stage door.' It was hardly a salubrious address, since it formed part of
what Disraeli called in *Sybil* (1845) 'those half-tawdry, half-squalid streets
that one finds in the vicinity of our theatres'. Jerrold's chief memories of
the place as it was in 1816 seem, according to his son, to have been of
dinginess and 'noisy, ragged boys' with whom he fought, but there was also
a notable site of festivity in the Court. The Wrekin Tavern had been 'time
out of mind the favorite resort of authors, actors, poets, painters and
penny-a-liners'.[1] Here celebrities like Theodore Hook, the Kembles, Charles Mathews (the great comic actor idolised by both Jerrold and, later, the
young Dickens), 'Monk' Lewis, the bestselling author of Gothic romance,
and many others, gathered for jolly meetings of their 'Catamarans Club'
(Sheridan, who died the year the Jerrolds came to London, had also been
a member). This would have been Jerrold's first glimpse of a social
phenomenon later to be so dear to him, the clubbing together, in some
suitably bibulous and smoky setting, of men connected with the world of
journalism and the arts, especially the theatre.

Life cannot have been particularly festive for young Jerrold in 1816,
however. The family's fortunes were at a low ebb, Samuel having apparently become a mere shell of a man. Every family member who could earn
any money had to set about doing so, quickly. Mary Jerrold and her elder
daughter, Elizabeth, got what stage work they could – probably in the
provinces as much as in London (the earliest records Walter Jerrold could
find of either mother or daughter acting in London dated from 1821 and
1822, respectively) and Jerrold himself became an apprentice, though
apparently not formally indentured, in Mr Sidney's printing-shop in
Northumberland Street, Strand. 'The labours of a printer's apprentice,'
Charles Knight remarks, writing on Jerrold in his *English Cyclopedia*, 'are
not ordinarily favourable to intellectual development ... the duties are so
purely mechanical, and yet demand constant attention, that the subject-
matter of his employ can rarely engage his thoughts.' But Pierce Egan

paints a different picture in his *Life of an Actor* (it has to be said, however, that his Mr Quarto's printing-house is a rather larger-scale establishment than Sidney's probably was). Egan's young hero, Peregrine Proteus, is apprenticed to Quarto who employs twenty 'typos' (the name printers use for each other, Egan tells us) setting up a whole variety of works – history, plays, biographies, poetry, etc.:

> From such invaluable sources the compositor has the opportunity of skimming the cream off all the good things before they meet the eyes of the public. Information is thus pouring in upon his mind continually without his seeking after it, and he has always the opinion of other men in his hands respecting anything new in the wide and extensive field of literature, including the daily occurrences of life. ... Such opportunities beget criticism amongst them, and very severe critics and first-rate scholars are to be found in printing offices. ...There is likewise a great fondness for satire among them....

Whether or not Sidney's printing-shop was like this, young Jerrold evidently became fired with a strong desire to become himself a contributor to literature and set about filling in gaps in his education and deepening his knowledge of great writers past and present. Blanchard Jerrold pictures his father at this time rising betimes to study Latin before going to work, eagerly reading his way through Shakespeare and scraping together enough money to borrow Scott's novels (some of the greatest of the Waverley Novels were appearing during Jerrold's first years in London) from a circulating library for reading aloud to his father. In later life Jerrold would dwell, 'with honest pride', on this time of his life and was fond of telling a particular story about using his first wages to buy the ingredients of a pie which he then made for his father and himself: ' "Yes, sir," he would say, emphatically, "I earned the pie, I made the pie, I took it to the bakehouse, I fetched it home; and my father said, 'Really the boy made the crust remarkably well'." '

Old Jerrold was not forgotten by former members of his company. James Russell took him off to see Kemble's Hamlet at Covent Garden, and encouraged young Douglas in his literary aspirations. Russell's being a friend of Scott's must have given him immense cachet in the boy's eyes as the actor patted him on the back, advised him on his reading and was kind about his earliest attempts at poetry. 'Russell,' Jerrold's son reported him as saying in later years, 'was the only man, when I was a poor boy, who gave me hope.' His former tutor of Sheerness days, J.P. Wilkinson, also turned up to make his London debut (15 June 1816) at the Lyceum Theatre, Strand, which had been completely rebuilt by its manager Samuel Arnold and was now called the English Opera House. Wilkinson wrote later to Blanchard Jerrold, 'I cannot forget how glad he [Jerrold] was to see me, and how sanguine he was of my success, saying ... "Oh, Mr Wilkinson! you are sure to succeed, and I'll write a piece for you."' Wilkinson did indeed make his mark as Sam Spatterdash in Samuel Beazley's

musical farce *Five Hours at Brighton* but it was another two years before
he scored a really major hit with his Geoffrey Muffincap, a clownish
charity-boy in another farce, Peake's *Amateurs and Actors*.

As for Samuel and Mary, there were to be no triumphant London débuts
for them even though Mary was still a working actress. But they did have
their past provincial acclaim, modest as it may have been, to look back on.
When, thirty years later, Jerrold was writing his *Story of a Feather* for
Punch he drew on memories of talk between his parents at Broad Court
when depicting the heroine's parents, a superannuated theatre couple, in
chapter 36. With empty cupboards, 'only a handful of sleepy fire in the
winter's grate', and 'pale-faced children about them', the Davises yet
contrive to enjoy themselves by praising each other as the 'greatest artists
in the world', disparaging the reigning London stars by comparison:

> 'Well, John,' Mrs Davis would begin, 'I saw *Hamlet* last night. People may
> call it a wife's prejudice, but it was nothing like your *Hamlet* at Cranbrook.
> I shall never forget that point of yours in the *Ghost's* speech, "I am thy
> father's spirit." As for Garrick, he quite missed it'. 'It's very odd, Mary,' said
> Davis, 'I was just then thinking of the new *Juliet* and your *Juliet* at Grave-
> send. That line of yours – ' 'What line, John?' Mrs Davis asked with the
> prettiest innocence. 'Oh, my dear, that line that struck the mayor so much –
> "As with a club strike out my desperate brains!" There, Mary, though you're
> my own wife, I will say it, you went quite through the heart. The poor girl of
> the other night scarcely touched one's waistcoat.'

Like the Davises' daughter, the young Jerrolds, now all well into their
teens, had to rely very much on their own exertions for their daily bread
(the beef-steak pie sounds to have been rather a special treat). Henry
Jerrold followed his brother into the printing trade and the two girls got
what stage work they could, like their mother.

Jerrold continued to work at the printer's in Northumberland Street
until he was sixteen, when his employer apparently went bankrupt
(though no official record of this seems traceable) and he transferred to
another printer called Bigg in Lombard Street. Bigg printed and edited a
paper called the *Sunday Monitor*, which was the oldest-established Sunday newspaper, having been founded as the *British Gazette and Sunday
Monitor* in 1804. Jerrold was to be connected with the *Monitor* in one form
or another, for some while.[2] He may also have worked about this time as
a reader on a daily paper, the *Globe*.

Jerrold found himself living, in post-war London, through a period of
intense social and political turmoil. The passing of the 1815 Corn Laws had
stirred up much discontent in the country. Although London itself largely
escaped what M. Dorothy George calls the 'torrent of pauperisation' that
'deluged the greater part of agricultural England', mass anti-Government
demonstrations took place at Spa Fields, Islington, in November and
December 1816. The second one was followed by a march on the Royal
Exchange and the Tower of London by a small number of demonstrators

waving the Republican tricolour and raiding gunsmiths' shops. They were easily dispersed but the Government, panicked by fears of 'Jacobinism' and the smashing of the windows of the Prince Regent's coach on his way to open Parliament (January 1817), suspended Habeas Corpus. In 1819, a year when, according to the *Annual Register,* 'Pecuniary distress' was 'nearly universal', came the 'Peterloo Massacre' in Manchester and the passing of fiercely repressive legislation. The arrest, early in 1820, of the so-called 'Cato Street Conspirators', bent on assassinating the entire Cabinet at a dinner-party, marked the end of the period of intense political agitation. The economy was recovering, the House of Lords trial for adultery of Queen Caroline, wife of the deeply unpopular George IV, provided a handy alternative focus for anti-Government feelings, and the succeeding decade was (apart from the financial crisis of 1825) compara- tively tranquil. The years of Jerrold's middle teens, however, were ones of great political and social tension, reflected in the ferocious cartoons of Gillray and equally ferocious polemics in the contemporary periodical press.

Journalism was not the only form of highly politicised writing at this time and Jerrold could hardly have been unaffected by this aspect of so much of the notable poetry that was appearing as he grew towards manhood. He was, like so many of his generation, a Byron-worshipper and would have eagerly devoured the stupendously subversive poetry emanat- ing from that exiled demi-god – Cantos III and IV of *Childe Harold,* *Manfred, Don Juan, A Vision of Judgment.* He would also have known Shelley's rousingly Radical *Queen Mab* (1813), which was circulating widely in pirated form:

> Whence, think'st thou, kings and parasites arose?
> Whence that unnatural line of drones, who heap
> Toil and unvanquishable penury
> On those who build their palaces, and bring
> Their daily bread? – From vice, black loathsome vice;
> From rapine, madness, treachery, and wrong ... .

Shelley and Keats were to be alluded to by Jerrold a few years later in his first major literary effort, as literary martyr-heros (see below p. 50). Given Jerrold's passion for Shakespeare, it seems certain that he would have read Hazlitt's *Characters of Shakespeare's Plays* (1817) and very likely that he would have attended the Surrey Institution to hear Hazlitt himself lecturing on 'The English Poets' in January 1818, 'The English Comic Writers' in the winter of 1818/19, and 'Dramatic Literature of the Age of Elizabeth' in 1820. If so, he would have heard the hisses from the more conservative elements in the audience provoked by Hazlitt's Radical re- marks.[3] (In April 1819 the leading Tory journal *Blackwood's* mocked Hazlitt as 'the Cockney Aristotle' and jeered that he could not 'look round him at the Surrey, without resting his smart eye on the idiot admiring grin of several dozens of aspiring apprentices and critical clerks'.) But for the young Jerrold the most important, inspiring and nourishing figure among the major Romantics was undoubtedly the poet, essayist, theatre critic and 'indefatigable journaliser' James Henry Leigh Hunt.

Having spent two years in prison (1813-15) for libelling the Prince Regent as a 'fat old Florizel of forty', Hunt was an established Radical hero but it was rather Hunt the inspiring guide to literature, art and the beauties of nature, the moral and aesthetic teacher, who was so important and so formative for Jerrold. He wrote to Hunt some twenty years later:

> I am ashamed to think how many years it is, since your writings first gave direction to my thoughts, – strengthening my belief in the good and the beautiful ... and sending me to books, as to undreamt of places in fairy-land.[4]

And in another letter, later still, he tells Hunt (of whom Dickens wrote on 12 June 1847 that he believed he had done more than anyone 'to instruct the young men of England and to lend a helping hand to those who educate themselves ...'):

> I look upon you as my literary parent: it was you who directed me to my earliest choice of books: it was from the *Examiner* that, as a boy, I began to ponder on the political and social duties that we owe towards one another.[5]

When he died Jerrold's library still contained the two volumes (1820-21; all published) of the *Indicator*, one of the best-loved of Hunt's many journals, that were almost certainly acquired by him at this time. Most of the essays in them were written by Hunt himself, promoting his philosophy of 'cheer', the sweetening of life by the enjoyment of books, art, nature and the simple pleasures of everyday life, and among the 'original verses' Hunt had promised his readers appeared Keats's 'La Belle Dame sans Merci'. Writing in the *North British Review* in November 1860 Alexander Kinnear described the *Indicator* as full of Hunt's 'own peculiar excellencies ... exuberant fancy ... the imagination which invests with poetry the most trivial common-places' and Charles Knight had earlier praised it for being 'full of fancies rich and rare, of glances deep into the heart of things ... of tenderness, of humour often most quaint and original'.[6]

Of the older writers Jerrold studied at this time, it was the great masters of sonorous and ornate 17th-century English, Thomas Fuller, Sir Thomas Browne, and Jeremy Taylor (an 1820 edition of Taylor's *Holy Living and Holy Dying* was also in his library) who had the greatest influence on him stylistically, and whom he set himself deliberately to imitate. Many years later, when giving stylistic advice to the young Sala, he said, 'Imitate as many old writers as you can, until you find somebody is imitating you' and added, 'By that time you will find that you have got a style of your own.'[7] It was probably about this time, too, that he first encountered the work of Rabelais who was throughout his career to be a major influence on him as a satirist.

Like all other young men in London who aspired to the professional theatre, whether as an actor or writer ('directors' in our modern sense did not exist, the role was subsumed in that of theatre manager), Jerrold gravitated towards the feverish little world of private theatres so scathingly portrayed by Dickens in *Sketches by Boz* some twenty years later. There were many such theatres in London in the early 19th century, run by speculators who traded on novices prepared to pay to perform such classic showy roles as Macbeth, Richard III, the young villain-hero George Barnwell or the 'heavy' Gothic villain Osmond in Lewis's *The Castle Spectre*; and if they could not afford to pay for leads they could pay proportionally less to enact secondary roles. Dickens's description of these places as being patronised by 'dirty boys, low copying-clerks in attorneys' offices ... shop-boys who now and then mistake their master's money for their own', chimed with much middle-class disapproval of them. They were 'the sink of almost every iniquity which ingenuity can contrive, or villainy execute', declared an indignant writer to *The Times* on 9 January 1808, places into which silly young apprentices and 'inferior clerks' were decoyed by prostitutes and drank more than was good for them. Dyer has some bitter comments about them in his *Nine Years of an Actor's Life*:

> A young man of limited means cannot be constantly honest in a private theatre. He has to pay his entrance fee ... for his books – his stage dresses: but there the evil does not end, for after the play it is usual to adjourn to some tavern, and there sup ale and flattery... .

The continuity with the activities of modern local Amateur Dramatic Societies might seem quite striking but such eminently respectable diversions of today's suburban middle-classes seldom lead to court proceedings. *The Times* for 17 July 1829 reports a case at the Mansion House magistrates' court in which a policeman described the 'romping ... and very indecent conduct' in which he had seen boys and girls indulging at the Catherine Street Theatre in the Strand (one of the most famous of these establishments, and specifically mentioned by Dickens): 'The mischiefs produced in society by places of this kind,' declared this officer, 'were incalculable.'

Yet private theatres did provide a valuable, if rough-and-ready, sort of drama school for those seriously set on an acting career and also, it seems, a venue for would-be dramatists to try out their work. A particularly fruitful source of recruits seems to have been the printing-shops of Regency London, which, to judge from the evidence of Victorian theatrical memoirs (to say nothing of Egan), would seem to have been positively awash with aspiring young actors and dramatists. Sometimes the master was quite as stage-struck as his apprentices – like Mr Seale of Tottenham Court Road, for example, who rehearsed Glenalvon (another 'heavy' villain) in one corner while his apprentice, William Oxberry, sat studying the role of the same play's hero, Douglas (alias 'Young Norval'), in another.[8]

At Mr Bigg's shop in Lombard Street Jerrold was within easy walking distance of several little private theatres to be found in Clerkenwell. Of these the principal one was located in Rawstorne Place, Rawstorne Street, not far from Sadler's Wells. Here, according to some reminiscences published in 1887, was first presented Jerrold's little farce *The Smoked Miser; or, The Benefit of Hanging* that was later to make a great hit at the Wells.[9] Here also, in 1821, he witnessed his fellow-apprentice Samuel Phelps (later the Wells's great Shakespeare impresario) playing Osmond in the inevitable *Castle Spectre*. Phelps had paid five guineas for the role which Jerrold felt was money wasted: 'Stick to your printing;' he told his irritated colleague, 'you'll never earn twenty-five shillings a week by spouting.' Phelps's Victorian biographer's statement that for the years 1821-26 Jerrold, Phelps, and another young man, William Love who became a famous 'polyphonist' (ventriloquist), were 'the principal members' of the Rawstorne Street amateur company, giving from one to three performances every week, is probably exaggerated. One or other of them, or all three, may well be lurking, however, behind the probably fictitious names printed on the only playbill for the theatre that seems to have survived.[10] Dated 9 August 1825, it announces a performance of *Richard III* followed by 'A Scotch Hornpipe by Miss Gonin', and then a favourite melodrama *The Miller and his Men*. At the foot of the bill appear the words 'N.B. – *No Admittance in Dishabille*' which suggests that Rawstorne Street at least aimed at greater decorum in its audiences than did Catherine Street. Confusing though the testimony is about Jerrold's early associations with Phelps, it seems clear that they were both involved, to a greater or lesser extent, with this little theatre and also that they were fellow-seekers after culture generally, studying French and Latin together under the auspices of 'an old Dutch gentleman' after Jerrold had, one day in the printing office, instigated a mutual scrutiny of their deficient education.[11]

Phelps had a long provincial apprenticeship to serve in the professional theatre before he started to come into his own under Macready at Covent Garden. As for Jerrold, by the time his first play was professionally produced in 1821 he had already had a prophetic taste of the trials and tribulations attendant on any career in the theatre. Wilkinson's great success as Muffincap at the English Opera House (29 August 1818) provided an opportunity for young Jerrold to submit to Arnold the manager the two-act farce he had written, as promised, for Wilkinson (complete with obligatory comic song for the star to sing). However, the script stayed at the theatre, probably never even read by Arnold, who, like all managers, was constantly inundated with unsolicited manuscripts. Two more years had to pass before Wilkinson was again in a position to bring Jerrold's play forward, and then it was only with some difficulty, apparently, that the precious manuscript was extracted from Arnold's stockpile.

The London theatre world into which Jerrold was trying to break in the 1820s was a complex one with many features requiring explanation for today's non-specialist readers. Here I can offer only a brief and much over-simplified general sketch of the situation.[12] It was dominated by the two great so-called 'Patent Theatres', Covent Garden and Drury Lane, both recently rebuilt on a vast scale, each having an audience capacity of over 3,000. These two houses claimed – on dubious legal grounds – exclusive rights, under patents granted by Charles II, to the staging in London of Shakespeare and what was called the 'legitimate' drama generally (what we should nowadays call 'straight plays'). A third theatre, the more intimate Haymarket, specialising in comedy, had a patent to present 'legitimate' drama during the summer when the other two theatres were closed. Then there were the so-called 'Minor Theatres' that mostly came into being in the early years of the 19th century, both in Westminster, where the Lord Chamberlain could license them, and in the suburbs where local magistrates could do so. Westminster theatres included Arnold's English Opera House (Lyceum), the Adelphi and the Olympic; and among the most notable suburban theatres were Sadler's Wells in Islington and the Coburg (later the Old Vic) and its rival the Surrey in Lambeth.

The 'Minors', debarred from presenting 'legitimate' drama, tended to develop special lines of their own, like the spectacular aquatic drama at Sadler's Wells, Madame Vestris's refined 'comediettas' at the Olympic, lurid melodramas at the Adelphi and the Coburg, and so on. But the line between 'legitimate' and 'illegitimate' became increasingly blurred during the first two decades of the 19th century. The much-disputed term 'burletta' came into use to describe the production of a play into which one or two songs, or other musical elements, had been introduced (such as the 'singing witches' in *Macbeth*) so it could be regarded as not trespassing into 'legitimate' territory and the manager could escape prosecution or being closed down by the Lord Chamberlain. This musical element tended to become ever more vestigial in many productions – one song, or even, as George Rowell says, 'an occasional chord on the piano' during the performance of any piece could still, arguably, allow it to qualify as a 'burletta'.[13] Meanwhile, successive managers of Covent Garden and Drury Lane found that in order to fill their huge auditoria they had to compete with the Minors in presenting melodramas, burlettas, pantomimes, pageants like Elliston's spectacular version of the coronation of George IV at Drury Lane, animal-dramas like *The Dog of Montargis* (Covent Garden, 1814), and so on, thereby outraging upholders of the national drama. There was constant friction between the Patent Theatres and the Minors, including a number of successful legal prosecutions of the latter by the former for infringement of their rights by 'straight' productions of Shakespeare's plays, for example. Individual actors, managers and actor-managers moved freely between the two spheres, the two latter categories of personnel altering their views according to the side of the fence on which they were currently operating.

Jerrold was to become very active in the campaign, not finally successful until 1843, to break the so-called 'monopoly' (more accurately to be described as a cartel, as Tracy Davis has shown[14]) exercised by the Patent

Theatres. The literati saw getting rid of this system as one the key factors in 'reviving the drama' – restoring to English theatre, that is, something of the literary glory of Shakespeare's time. Also relevant, as the dramatists vehemently argued, was ensuring that they got a fair financial reward for their work as well as some copyright protection for it. As things were in the 1820s, and as they essentially remained for the next three decades, payment for original dramas was very poor. It was much cheaper, in the absence of any form of international copyright, for managers simply to have plays pirated from the French. The inflated salaries paid to star performers and the costs of staging the kind of spectacular productions the general public wanted left the managers with very little money to spare for paying for new plays. As late as 1848 a satirical observer of the London theatre scene could still define a dramatic author as ' a humble personage, who, by the condescension of the manager and actors, is allowed to write the plays by which the latter get their living'.[15] In a piece on 'The Degeneracy of the Drama' a writer in the *Drama* lamented, in October 1824, that dramatists were wholly dependent on 'the taste, caprice, avarice or jealousy of the Managers of our London theatres' for getting their work staged and, even when a piece is accepted the hapless dramatist has to accommodate 'not only ... the pretensions, vanity, and abilities of the actors and actresses, but their age and corpulency; he must, in fact, take the measure of them, as well as the stage tailor does.' And if his work was printed, it was, as David Morris, manager of the Haymarket, said to the 1832 Parliamentary Commission on Dramatic Literature, 'generally considered' to be 'public property' so that it could be performed with impunity at any other theatre. Following the tremendous success of his nautical melodrama *Black Eyed Susan* at the Surrey in 1829, Jerrold was to be one of the greatest sufferers from this injustice, as well as from managerial meanness.

Such embittering experiences still lay in the future for him in 1821 when he at last saw his first play staged. Daniel Egerton, a well-established Covent Garden actor, took over the management of Sadler's Wells Theatre, Islington, in April. He remodelled it in 'a superior style of elegance and splendour',[16] but failed to retain the services of its star, the great clown Grimaldi. He did, however, manage to engage Wilkinson for a short season and this time the actor succeeded in bringing forward the little farce that his young friend had written for him. So at last Jerrold's first play, *More Frightened than Hurt*, billed as a 'New Comic Burletta', was produced on 30 April 1821. It starred Wilkinson as Popeseye, a naïve and cowardly young butcher ('popeseye' is the name of a particularly delicious mutton tit-bit) who has learned to swagger at his local drinking club. He and his friend Ajax Hector, a small-time *miles gloriosus*, are the intended sons-in-law of old Easy but the latter's daughters, aided by the two young men they really love, contrive to frighten off their unwanted suitors by means of a threatened duel. Jerrold manages to create some good farcical situations which must have worked well on stage, as when Popeseye and

41

Hector each think the other has been killed and is now a ghost. There is lively dialogue throughout and already some touches of what came to be thought of as characteristic Jerroldian wit, as when one of the lovers pretends to encourage Popeseye before the duel by telling him he is 'a lad of fine metal' to which he promptly replies, 'That's why I don't wish to be mixed with lead.' Jerrold also supplies Wilkinson with a spirited comic song to sing at the end of Act II, telling the story of Ned Nappy, a young hatter who elopes with his master's daughter, marries her at Shoreditch on Easter Monday, is promptly arrested and finally thrown in jail. It ends with a mildly risqué pun (to be 'in the straw' was a slang phrase for being pregnant):

> And yet, though you may think it strange, such wonders works the law
> That one hour after marriage poor Ned was in the *straw*!

Not surprisingly, Wilkinson scored a hit in his tailor-made role, performing it at least twenty times during his month's engagement at the Wells. The play's theatrical effectiveness (it 'still keeps the stage' noted the *Gentleman's Magazine* in its obituary of Jerrold) no doubt encouraged Egerton to commission more work from its eighteen-year-old author. This commission – if indeed it was a commission and not a proposal originating with the young dramatist himself – was for a work very different from the sprightly little farce, however. It was for something that would bring into play the unique resources of the Wells but use them for loftier ends than previous managements had done – in the service of Literature rather than merely for sensational effects. Egerton, after all, was a leading Covent Garden actor, and his wife Sarah had an established reputation as the 'Mrs Siddons of melodrama' (acting Scott's Meg Merrilies at Drury Lane in 1816 she had, wrote Hazlitt in his *View of the English Stage*, made his 'blood run cold'). They were aiming to raise the cultural level of the fare offered to the Wells's patrons, something with which the young Jerrold would have ardently sympathised.

The Wells in the first two decades of the 19th century was famous not only as the theatre of Grimaldi but also as the home of 'aqua-drama'. Patriotic pageants like *The Siege of Gibraltar* (1804) staged the triumphs of the British navy with mimic ships manoeuvring about in a huge water-tank. This tank, about five feet deep, thirty feet wide and ninety feet from front to back of the stage area, was installed under the stage by Charles Dibdin the younger who managed the theatre 1800-19. Like the later supplementary roof-tank which provided 'real waterfalls', it was fed from the adjacent New River Head. The enticement 'Last Scene on Real Water with a Cataract' appeared frequently on Wells playbills and, as patriotic fervour subsided following the end of the war, new scenarios were devised to exploit these aquatic facilities. Among the attractions of *Albert and Emira; or, the Dumb Boy and His Horse* (3 July 1820), for example, was a Grand Combat of Four, by Mrs J. Usher [she played Albert] who will defend herself against Three Assailants; and a Splendid last Scene displaying the Real Water, and the Conflagration of the Tyrant's Castle, during which Two Horses Plunge into the Waves and a Combat takes place between the Riders on Horseback in the Water.[17]

Egerton could hardly have ignored such a remarkable theatrical re-source as his water-tanks. On 30 July he announced as the concluding attraction of the evening 'A GRAND NEW AQUATIC SPECTACLE (in Two Acts) dramatized from the Poems of Ossian by Mr D.W. Jerrold, and which has been long in preparation called *The Chieftain's Oath; or, The Rival Clans'*. No script survives but Jerrold's words must have got rather lost amidst

the grandeur of the Scenery, the beauty and strong national character of the Music, the reflection of the rising Moon on the REAL WATER (to be wit-nessed only in this Theatre), the burning of the Camp, the plunging of Maclean and his adherents into the Lake, the novel and romantic effect of the last Scene ....[18]

We can be pretty sure, though, that he would have written some smart dialogue for the rising young comedian Robert Keeley (who would star in several of his later plays). Keeley played 'Rundy Ramble, a Trader in Trifles', according to the playbill – evidently some sort of Autolycus figure. But it was clearly the Moon, 'rising (as seen in nature) large and red, decreasing in size, and becoming paler as she ascends', which was, so to speak, the star of the show, though at least Jerrold does get to share billing with her. His name does not, however, appear on the bill for his next piece, *The Gipsy of Derncleugh,* a new three-act adaptation of Scott's novel *Guy Mannering* 'combining', according to Egerton's playbill of 27 August, 'most of the interesting events of that celebrated Work, with the powerful Dramatic effect of the French Melo Drama on the same subject, now performing in Paris'.[19] It is ironic, in view of Jerrold's later fierce campaign against the English stage's dependence on Paris for so much of its stock in trade, that his third professionally-produced play (which he was happy to have printed under his name) should be a piece of this sort. Doubtless, however, he was keen to oblige Mrs Egerton by providing her with an opportunity to chill some more blood with her performance as Meg Mer-rilies. His work was perhaps facilitated by a visit or two to the Lyceum where another adaptation of the French play, J.R. Planché's *The Witch of Derncleugh,* had been playing since the end of July with Wilkinson as Dominie Sampson and where Elizabeth Jerrold had a small part as a servant-girl (Mrs Jerrold was not in the cast but was probably already a member of Samuel Arnold's stock company; her name appears regularly in Lyceum playbills from September 1821 onwards).

Meanwhile a Holborn publisher called John Duncombe had decided to start a series called 'The New Acting Drama', publishing plays in shilling paperback editions. In 1821 he used Jerrold's *More Frightened than Hurt* to launch the series and later added *The Gipsy* to it. In each case the author's name, 'D.W. Jerrold', was prominent on the title-page in Gothic type. It seems, however, that Jerrold had no wish to put his name to his next piece for Egerton. This was produced at the Olympic Theatre, just off the Strand, on 9 January 1822 (Egerton had taken over the management of the Olympic in addition to the Wells, which was closed during the winter months). Advertised as 'a Burlesque, Tragico, Comico, Operatico, Extravaganza, called The Brisket Family; or, the Running of the Rat!!!', it parodied Arnold's immensely popular *The Maid and the Magpie* (based on Rossini's *La Gaza Ladra* and first performed 1815) and featured a mechanical rat, described in the cast-list as 'Gnaw'em … a Performer well acquainted with his Business'. This burlesque, renamed *Dolly and the Rat*, was revived by Egerton at both his theatres in 1823 and provided a good vehicle for a popular low comedian called Vale (he was, Jerrold wrote in the *Mirror of the Stage* on 28 August 1824, one of those actors who 'at their entrance, shake hands with the entire audience'). It was published by Duncombe but never acknowledged by Jerrold, doubtless because it was a mere pot-boiler with no claim to any dramatic (as opposed to theatrical) or literary merit, in spite of being stuffed with comically-used Shakespearian quotations. Of the remaining two pieces Jerrold supplied for Egerton, the first was *The Smoked Miser* which may have been privately premiered earlier at the Rawstorne Street theatre. Produced at the Wells on 23 June 1823, it was a great hit. Vale as the miser's servant Goliah Spiderlimb was particularly relished by the audience, especially his 'introduced' comic song, full of jokes about London landmarks, entitled 'The Good Old Days of Adam and Eve'. The *Miser* was also included in Duncombe's series and carried its author's name on the title-page. Jerrold's last piece for Egerton (premiered 28 July) was another unpublished aquatic spectacular, *The Island*, based on Byron's poem about the *Bounty* mutineers – 'hashed', said the *Mirror of the Stage* on 4 August 1823 'for the classic stomachs of Islington with a necessary libation of milk and water'. As with *The Chieftain's Oath*, the dramatist's art must have been somewhat eclipsed by the staging, the tank scenes and the 'admirable' presentation of the deck of the *Bounty* 'with all its appendages of rigging, sails, and guns'. One sailor in the gallery was apparently so taken with all this realism that he called out to one of the actors to 'go leeward of the capstan'.[20]

Exciting as it must have been to the young devotee of Shakespeare to see his first plays professionally staged, Jerrold would still have been sharply aware of the vexations of the contemporary dramatist's lot – the meagre financial rewards (his first four plays earned him the magnificent sum of twenty pounds between them) and the frustrations of having to subjugate his work to the needs and desires of the leading players and of the theatre manager (the Sadler's Wells tank and its 'real water' was but a grander variant of the 'real pump and two washing-tubs' that Mr

Crummles tells Nicholas Nickleby must feature prominently in the drama Nicholas has to write for his troupe).

It must have been some compensation for Jerrold that, thanks to that other string to his bow, journalism, he could hold both leading actors and theatre managers – those all-powerful rulers of the stage – up to public ridicule. By this time he and his family had probably moved, perhaps following the death of poor old Samuel in 1820 and the engagement of Mary Jerrold and her elder daughter at the Lyceum, from Broad Court to Little Queen Street, Holborn. (Swept away by the Kingsway development later in the century, this street used to link Holborn and Great Queen Street.) Here the Jerrolds were neighbours of Douglas's publisher John Duncombe who had his premises at number 19. While continuing to deal in Radical periodicals like the *Republican,* Duncombe and his brother Edward had developed a lucrative line what we would now call 'soft porn' – such publications as *The Frisky Songster, The Amatory Poems and Songs of the Earl of Rochester*, and highly scurrilous fake 'Memoirs' of celebrated actresses, or of Byron, 'comprising his voluptuous amours'.[21] He had also, as we have seen, begun theatrical publishing and in August 1822 he expanded this side of the business by starting the fortnightly paper which has already been cited called the *Mirror of the Stage.* Jerrold's initials first appear in its pages (24 February 1823) appended to a nine-verse (non-pornographic) poem on the delights of sharing a chair with one's beloved, but he may well have made earlier anonymous contributions, including a review of his own play *The Smoked Miser* on 14 July 1823 ('The dialogue is infinitely superior to the pieces usually brought out at this house; the situations are novel and well contrived ...'). In September 1823, however, he begins a regular series entitled 'The Minor-ies' (punning on the City of London street-name) signed with the Greek letter 'oe'. 'The Minor-ies' is a series of critical notices of star actors and actresses at the Minor Theatres, modelled, no doubt, on Leigh Hunt's *Critical Essays on the Performers at the London Theatres* (1807) and Hazlitt's *View of the English Stage* (1818). The dominant tone of the series is one of a kind of baroque exasperation with the falsities and follies of so many contemporary actors:

> Mr Sloman at the Coburg, has all the popularity of a harassed dog, who has lent his tail to the appendage of a tin-kettle, for the sport and pastime of hallooing urchins .... His *acting* is a continual exclamation, between the cry of a whipped schoolboy and the tenor-note of an ill-blown bag-pipe. It is the very feast of vacancy to attend his representations .... (17 November 1823)

Over the next seven months other actors came under Jerrold's lash. One is criticised for his 'transitions to violent rage' which are like 'a tap set in action by a baby': 'away he goes with his hands to his hair, and his feet like a culprit's at a tread-mill; – head shaking, spitting, starting, – a very tornado *in little*.' Another is adjured, 'Do not be so *active* in your operations – do not attempt to express love or loyalty by the movement of a windmill.'

The Coburg's 'stock cut-throat', Mr Bradley, is a ludicrous figure who 'meets all our infantile ideas of the wicked Ogre, who would make a roast meal of a father and mother, and hash them up with their babies for the next day's dinner'. The romantic lead Mr Stanley, with his voice 'like a high wind playing at whoop in a field of reeds', is a 'very pinmaker's apprentice come to maturity'. Mrs Stanley, too, is found wanting though she had 'promised to be a good actress': she has not the discernment to choose between portraying 'a momentary excitation of spirit and daring of heart' and 'a monotonous vociferation continual as unmeaning'.

Deeply believing in the actor as 'an artist who skilfully pourtrays the passions of human nature, who calls up feeling, and who meets it – and who, where reality ceases to exist, employs imagination', Jerrold deploys his budding satirical powers to castigate incompetents at the Coburg and elsewhere. He inveighs, too, against the timidity of managers who pander to the lowest elements in Minor Theatre audiences – by hiring a popular pugilist to appear, for example, or by putting on shows like dramatisations of Pierce Egan's sensational best-seller *Tom and Jerry, or Life in London* (Egerton did very well at Sadler's Wells and the Olympic from April 1822 through to January 1823 with a version by Egan himself, which climaxed with a spectacular six-pony race around a specially constructed course in the auditorium). Egan's book, claimed a correspondent of the *Mirror* (4 August 1823), 'has done more to demoralise the rising generation, and unhinge the sacred bonds of society, than any publication during the last fifty years' and it may have been Jerrold who described it as 'that filthy drug at which "the gorge rises"' (17 November 1823); it was certainly he who, in February 1824, called Egan 'that villanous corrupter of the English' and the next month referred to the Sadler's Wells production as a 'vile abortion'. Young Jerrold would have been more than human if he had felt no twinge of envy at the huge success of the *Tom and Jerry* dramatisations, but there can be no doubt that his reverence for the English language had much to do with his anger against Egan's classic of low-life and 'fast' slang, just as his passion for restoring the greatness of English drama had much to do with his criticism of Minor-Theatre managers content to truckle to the kind of audience found only in those places: 'if these caterers for public entertainment would vary their bill of fare, and present something less "ungracious to the taste", they would perceive their guests crowding to their board, after a temporary abstinence, notwithstanding that *rational* enjoyment, which they [managers] so much despise' (16 March 1824).

The gap between reality and stage conventions was one of Jerrold's constant themes in his writing for the *Mirror*, whether it was stage sailors made to 'talk of liberality, glory, honor, independence of Britain, when our every day observation assures us that many have been and are reduced to all possible misery by the retention of money earned by the loss of blood and limb', or comic heroes from the 'moral work-bag' of prolific hack dramatist, Edward Ball (soon to rename himself Fitzball), who are all 'well-behaved young gentlemen with pinafores, continually mouthing the lozenge of "benevolence", "patriotism", etc.' (23 August 1824).

Among the other contributors to Duncombe's journal was a young man who was the same age as Jerrold and just as passionately concerned with literature. This was Samuel Laman Blanchard, a glazier's son who had had a good schooling but had to give up a university place because his father could not afford to keep him there. He was a clerk in Doctors' Commons and in his free time scribbled lyrics, sonnets, blank-verse 'dramatic fragments' and so on. Like Jerrold, he revered Leigh Hunt and worshipped Shakespeare and Byron. He was good-looking and had great personal charm. In a memoir written after Blanchard's untimely death Bulwer Lytton recalled 'that simple cheerfulness ... that inborn and exquisite urbanity – that child-like readiness to be pleased with all – that acute and delicate sensibility' and, years later, the old publisher Vizetelly still remembered him as 'a general favourite ... genial in disposition, amiable in manner, and lively in conversation, with a perpetual smile playing over his dark, handsome Jewish features'.[22] Jerrold first met him in 1822, probably through Duncombe, and the two young men formed an intense romantic friendship. They were united not only by their literary passions and ambitions but also by their political ideals. Jerrold's son describes how one day in 1823 they excitedly determined to follow in Byron's glowing footsteps and go to fight for Greek independence but had second thoughts after getting 'heroically wet through' in a sudden cloudburst – 'the rain,' Jerrold commented later, 'washed all the Greece out of us'.

The surviving records of this friendship, undoubtedly the most important of Jerrold's life, show the gentle, sweet-natured Blanchard playing a comforting and consoling 'wifely' role, always trying to soften what he called the 'needless asperity' of many of his friend's opinions. Jerrold, on the other hand, appears to have exercised a 19th-century-husband-like influence over Blanchard: 'Such as my nature is,' Blanchard wrote to him in 1826 in a letter quoted by Blanchard Jerrold, 'it is not too much to say that it has been almost moulded by you; and certainly, of late years, nothing has been admitted into it that has not received your stamp and sanction.'[23] In 1824 he prophesied literary greatness for Jerrold in a sonnet which stands, in his *Lyric Offerings*, next to another paying tribute to the memory of Keats:

> The time shall be
> When men may find a music in thy name,
> To rouse deep fancies and opinions free;
> Affections fervid as the sun's bright flame,
> And sympathies unfathom'd as the sea.

Blanchard Jerrold includes in the second edition of his *Life of Douglas Jerrold* a very passionately – not to say melodramatically – written document addressed by his father to his friend. It is dated 'Friday night, 12 o'clock, Jan 2nd, 1824' and headed 'My Debt'. It begins:

> Yes, I am your debtor. I owe you not ingots of gold, whose borrowing damns the mind with sense of obligation: but I owe you some delirious throbs, a quick pulsation of the heart, a delicious wildering of the brain; a dew, which in my short pilgrimage thro' this world's desert, few have proffered to my parched spirit.

Jerrold has, it emerges from the barely-controlled swoopings and soarings of his prose ('I do not stay to turn a sentence … my heart is in every word'), only a few hours before been with Blanchard, and perhaps other friends, 'in the enjoyment of responsive hearts and congenial souls'. Since then he has been bitterly hurt, insulted or humiliated by 'a worldly reptile', one of 'those leeches of the heart, that from a hundred lacerated pores lick in their loathsome meal', and has experienced a nightmarish sense of alienation from the whole human race as he walked the streets:

> I felt as if each face came *forcibly dull* upon my sense; a ponderous look that beat back the peering outstretched form of hope; statues had gained animation; each form around me was mechanically precise, one wheeled eastward, another west. I stood upon the pavement, and methought as I gazed on the insensible crowd around me, at times *enlivened* by the skippings of frivolity, that I was isolated from humanity, – shut out from the world. Oh, how my soul sickened as I thought on my loneliness!

Even reaching his home and family has not lightened his mood. He has found affection but no understanding of his distress: 'If that I am sad, a worldly, surprised "Why?" makes me more wretched … I looked around the *inhabited* apartment, and found it empty.' But, going into another room, he begins to read one of Blanchard's poems and soon finds his heart leaping

> as though it had long been wandering … amid foreign mobs, and far from all it prized, was chilled by the freezing apathy around it, when, to awaken its torpor … a well-known, valued, long-beloved being darted from the crowd, and greeted it with blessed fellowship. *Such were my feelings*; BELIEVE THEM.

Eight months after this outpouring Jerrold added a new dimension to his domestic life which doubtless made a great difference in his attitude to home. On 15 August 1824 he married Mary Ann Swann in their parish church of St Giles in the Fields and brought her back to live with his mother, sisters and grandmother in Little Queen Street. Mary Ann was the daughter of a London postman Thomas Swann or Swan, originally from Wetherby in Yorkshire. She was born in 1806 or 1807, and her father died in 1812.[24] We know nothing else about her family circumstances or how she survived economically. Her son says that she was Jerrold's 'boyhood love' but gives no clue as to how they first met. The marriage certificate states that Mary Ann was also of St Giles's parish, so the relationship perhaps began as a boy-and-girl neighbourhood romance (in the 1851 Census she gives her place of birth as Middlesex). Possibly Jerrold met her through the theatre – she may have been an actress in a small way. We simply do not know. But it was certainly a bold move for a twenty-one-year-old who had not long since been describing himself as 'a hunted pauper', and who was eking out a living with hack journalism and playwriting. Perhaps he was influenced by Blanchard's marriage the previous year. Out of the latter's own great happiness came his epithalamium for Jerrold's wedding. After praising his friend's courage and tenacity in the face of unrelenting adversity ('Alas! in youth, that best of time, / What do we see but pain and crime?'), Blanchard depicts marriage, with a sort of sub-Keatsian eroticism, as a magical new country in which the young bridegroom will be soothed and restored to a happier state of mind:

> An isle that lifts its rainbow breast
> From out its bed of crystal sea,
> ...
> Methinks thy timid, trusting Mary
> Would well beseem this land of fairy.
> Such time would soon restore the tint
> Half lost in sorrow's withering print ... [25]

Poor Mary Ann had indeed high expectations to live up to if we are to judge from a rhapsody on the theme of 'Woman' into which Jerrold had launched in the course of one of his 'Minor-ies' articles in the *Mirror* (26 April 1824):

> There is a mysterious power attached to the name of 'woman' that awakens all our kindlier feelings, and busies imagination in its most beautiful delights; ... we live but under the heaven of beaming eyes, and are conscious of nothing but the presence of blooming lips and animated features ... 'Woman' is the spell-word, the universal charm, that calls up expectation of the very being of affection, sensibility and tenderness. We expect most largely, and, therefore, when disappointment comes, we feel its visitation more keenly ...

Jerrold seems to have been very fortunate in his choice of partner. Mary Ann proved a devoted wife and mother 'whose loving eyes', according to her eldest son, 'no worldly pleasures could ever turn for one moment from her children'. The journalist George Hodder, who was close to Jerrold in the 1840s and once stayed with the family in Boulogne, describes her as 'the most thoughtful and considerate of housewives' and retails a scrap of table-talk which suggests how greatly the physically clumsy and domestically helpless Jerrold appreciated Mary Ann's home-making skills and her ability to provide him with order and comfort, even with such limited and uncertain resources as she must have had to work with in the earlier years of their marriage. Jerrold told Hodder later that he 'would never advise a man to choose a wife on account of her intellect any more than for her money', adding, 'As to myself ...since I have been married I have never known what it is to turn down my own socks.'[26]

We shall inevitably recur to the subject of Jerrold's marital relationship when we come to discuss his creation of Mrs Caudle, that notable subverter of the Victorian wifely ideal. For the present, in the absence of any contemporary information about her at this time, we must let Mary Ann disappear into that household in Little Queen Street, already so full of women, where, a year later, she will give birth to her first child, Jane Matilda, and, after another fifteen months, to her first son, William Blanchard Jerrold, whose middle name commemorated the other great love of his young father's life.

By 1826, therefore, Jerrold had four mouths to feed and must have been eagerly anticipating the publication of his three-volume magnum opus *Facts and Fancies*. With its imposing title-page adorned with epigraphs from Shakespeare and Burton, its high-flown style, allegorical sequences and complicated structure, this work was clearly intended to establish its young author's literary reputation. The dedication – to Laman Blanchard naturally – is dated August 1826. After the sheets for the first volume had been printed, however, publication was aborted owing to the publishers' bankruptcy following the financial crisis of 1825.[27] Meanwhile Blanchard's fate was altogether more propitious. Through family connections, he obtained a three-year appointment as Assistant Secretary to the Zoological Society which, unlike his previous drudging clerkship, allowed him leisure for literary work; and at the end of the period he had ready for the press his first volume of poems, *Lyric Offerings*. Published in 1828 under the auspices of William Harrison Ainsworth, dedicated to Charles Lamb, and eagerly purchased by the young Robert Browning among others, it was to launch him smoothly on a successful literary career.

Before continuing the story of Jerrold's continuing struggle to scrape a living with his pen as best he could by writing whatever he could sell, at whatever price, for ephemeral periodicals and minor theatres, we might pause to consider what *Facts and Fancies* shows us about its author's psychological and emotional state at this time. One thing that seems clear from the surviving volume is that Blanchard's hopes that his friend's marriage to his 'timid, trustful Mary' might make him generally happier have not been fulfilled. The dominant emotions are those of rage, alienation and bitterness. The shame of wearing shabby clothes, and of being humiliated by the better off, is a motif that recurs again and again (and connects with some unpleasantly racist passages about Jews, the second-hand clothing market being pretty well a Jewish monopoly at this time). There is a remarkably violent little story called 'The Fiends' about the terrible fate of a young man full of romantic visions who is seduced by three fiends 'presenting to him pen, ink and paper'. The ink is 'mingled with the tear that lay in the hollow cheek of the corpse of Chatterton', the paper is 'skin ript from the left breast of the murdered John Keats'. These fatal gifts have sometimes 'raised him above mortality' but 'often have they dashed him beneath the car of the idol wealth'. The Juggernaut image may be rather confused – Jerrold does not mean, presumably, that the young writer sacrifices himself to wealth – but the bitterness is unmistakable.

The theme of frustrated or wasted literary endeavour is also strong in *Facts and Fancies* which paradoxically strains to make Byronic-type literary capital out of the wrecked hopes and tormented 'misunderstood-outcast' life it describes. But underlying all the purple prose is a very deep feeling of hurt and of anger directed towards the prosperous and powerful. This super-sensitive and burningly ambitious youth in his second-hand clothes, this 'little Shakespeare in a camlet cloak', must, one feels, have met with some really lacerating rudeness and contemptuous treatment on the part of the wealthy or the socially superior, permanently affecting his attitude towards them as a class and leading to so many charges of 'bitterness' and rancorous radicalism in later years.

In the most obviously autobiographical piece in the book, 'The Fate of Wilbert', from which I have already quoted in connection with his child-hood years in the Navy, Jerrold develops an idea of himself as a Byronic soul born into the wrong class who, after his brief naval experience, was 'at thirteen ... thrown back upon the land, to begin the world anew' and who was then

> prompted by independence of mind to submit to the drudgery of a trade, – to tie up his bursting heart in apron-strings; to laugh, to jest; to seem one of the things whose delights he pitied as he scorned; to be herded up with beings whose bodies were hired; where mind was not the bargain; where the image of the gross fancy was applauded by the vulgar throat ... .

It is easy to laugh at, or to be put off by, such youthful hyperbolic self-dramatising and self-pitying, and it was no doubt just as well that these particular 'early mutterings', as Jerrold called his juvenilia, re-mained unpublished. But they should help us to understand just how passionately Jerrold felt about Shakespeare and the great writers whose work he devoured, and the intensity with which he felt both the sense of his own literary vocation and the harshness of the economic circumstances in which he was struggling to work out his destiny (a telling image for the working day occurs at one point in *Facts and Fancies*: 'arming himself for the fight, he sallies out to the combat of the day'). The loving support of Mary Ann and delight in their infant family (Jerrold was a lover of children all his life) must have been a real mainstay to him at this time.

Another source of consolation and inspiration was the formation – perhaps by Jerrold himself – of the Mulberries Club, named after Shake-speare's famous mulberry tree. Jerrold, Blanchard and a loosely-knit group of other young or youngish journalists, actors, artists and scribblers for the minor theatres gathered for a weekly 'club-night' at a pub in

Vinegar-yard, Catherine Street, where, in the 'tobacco-impregnated, slightly alcoholic atmosphere' characteristic of such places, they could swap jokes, trade professional gossip, and read each other poems and essays exalting Shakespeare (so-called 'Mulberry leaves'). Jerrold was to become famous as the leading light of many similar clubs – he gets a whole chapter to himself in John Timbs's *Club Life of London* (1866) – but I doubt if any of them meant as much to him as the Mulberries did in the 1820s. Proclaiming through its very name allegiance to the most revered and inspiring figure in all English literature, the Club provided struggling young aspirants to literary, artistic or dramatic fame with what Jerrold, looking fondly back on it years later, described as a 'society of kindred thoughts and sympathising hopes'.[28] It must also have been important for what we now call 'networking'. Among its members was a young actor and playwright destined to become one of the great actor-managers of mid-Victorian theatre, John Baldwin Buckstone, who shared with Jerrold a boyhood naval background. According to Bulwer Lytton[29] Buckstone was much impressed by Jerrold and volunteered to transcribe 'three volumes of Moral Philosophy' the latter had written (presumably the ill-fated *Facts and Fancies*). It may well have been Buckstone who recommended Jerrold to the enterprising manager of the Coburg Theatre, George Davidge. Buckstone worked at the Coburg from 1824 and his first play, *The Bear Hunters; or, The Fatal Ravine,* had been produced there in April 1825. Four months later Davidge, seeking to cash in on the excitement caused by a grossly emaciated Frenchman called Seurat's putting himself on exhibition in Pall Mall as 'The Living Skeleton', had paid Jerrold to write a farcical *pièce de circonstance* with that title in which Davidge himself played Sparerib, '*a Student of Surgery, who ... having been brought* to Bones, *is determined* to live upon them', and Buckstone a comic waiter called Hobnail. Jerrold seems to have put his own stamp on the affair by including in the dialogue such remarks as 'the public would rather give half-a-crown apiece to see a man without flesh than sixpence apiece to put one in good condition' and it was well received by Davidge's patrons, being announced (as 'the very Laughable Burletta') for its thirteenth performance on 29 August.

Work for the Coburg must have helped to replace income lost following the folding of Duncombe's *Mirror* in October 1824, and over the next ten months Jerrold wrote at least three more pieces for Davidge – a skit on London tradesmen's advertisements, a workmanlike adaptation of a Haymarket hit, Poole's *Paul Pry,* and another skit, or 'burletta', called *Popular Felons,* among the 'felons' being Frankenstein and his 'Man-monster' (subjects of another West End hit), 'charged with a malicious attempt at perverting the Morals of the Land, and doubling the Price of Eau de Cologne, and Sal Volatile'.[30] Jerrold would have been wretchedly enough paid for writing these things, and of course it would always have been a question of a one-off payment. As noted above, successful theatre pieces benefited managers and actors at this time, not authors.

What must have have been particularly galling for young Jerrold was that, in order to escape from being a mere 'hired body' in Mr Bigg's printing-shop, he had had to use his literary talent in what would have seemed to him debased and debasing ways. He had written theatre notices for an ephemeral rag launched by a small-time publisher of unsavoury reputation and although, thanks to J.P. Wilkinson, he had eventually seen his first play staged (at a suburban minor house), this had led to very little in the way of playwriting opportunities – none at all in the 'legitimate' theatre. He had done adaptation work for Egerton and his wife at Sadler's Wells and the Olympic and after that, as we have seen, on a rather lower level for Davidge at the Coburg. Other young dramatists had been more fortunate. The one-time bookseller's apprentice, J.R. Planché, seven years Jerrold's senior, had had his first piece, *Amoroso, King of Little Britain,* a burlesque of a burlesque, produced at Drury Lane when he was 22, thanks to the interest of the rising comic actor John Pritt Harley (who, like Wilkinson, had once been a member of Samuel Jerrold's troupe). *Amoroso* ran for seventeen performances, and Planché's career never looked back thereafter. By the time Jerrold was writing *Facts and Fancies* Planché had seen over 40 of his dramatic works staged – burlettas, melodramas, 'interludes', operas – and was comfortably established as Charles Kemble's stock-author at Covent Garden, where he also supervised Kemble's groundbreaking 'archaeological' productions of Shakespeare which created a sensation by using 'historically accurate' dress. Planché's regular habit of pirating French plays for his own pieces would have added offence to envy as far as Jerrold was concerned. In the *Weekly Times* for 10 February 1828 he ridiculed the idea of calling Planché an author: 'A diver might as well call himself the maker of every pearl he brings from the bottom of the sea.'

The Sunday paper in which this scathing reference to Planché appears was one with which Jerrold had been closely involved from its inception two years earlier and by late 1828 was apparently editing (see quotation from the *Stage*, below, p. 62). In its first number of 3 June 1826 it proclaimed both its freedom from party and its patriotism: 'we feel a pride in the splendor of our public establishments, yet, we would not have that built upon the sufferings or privations of our fellow-subjects.' The first issue also contains, most probably from Jerrold's pen, a blistering attack on the 'utterly contemptible and insignificant condition' of the two great national theatres with their 'pasteboard shows' concocted by 'patchers': this situation results from the 'paltry payments' offered to dramatists and the great difficulty they have in getting their work even considered by theatre managers. The second issue has an initialled piece by Jerrold ('J') called 'Ned Sadgett' in a genre that he was to make very much his own – a moralistic sketch of a character with one strongly-marked peculiarity or *idée fixe* (in this case refusal ever to break a sworn oath). Its wordiness suggests that Jerrold was paid by the column-inch though he claims it is for ease – 'I might have consigned my anecdote to the meagre capacity of a chair-like paragraph, but I prefer lying loosely and at full length along the sofa column – it is so comfortable!' Another piece headed 'Kings and Little Girls' (23 July), unsigned but unmistakably Jerroldian, looks forward to the stinging satirist of *Punch*: stimulated by a report that George IV is yet again going to alter the army's uniform at enormous cost to the public purse, it compares him, after several other unflattering comparisons, to a little girl playing with dolls and ends with a grim joke:

> We believe the suits of the Guards trumpeters cost each seventy-two pounds: should their habiliments be newly-fashioned, we would humbly submit that a figure of a five-shillings per week cotton-spinner be worked in the back or on the lappets: it would speak most eloquently to the feelings of all men.

Most of Jerrold's acknowledged work for the *Weekly Times* took the form of theatre criticism. From 20 August 1826 onwards he had a regular column headed DRAMA signed first with the letter D reversed and then with it the correct way round. This gave him a platform to continue the scornful mockery of the two great Patent Theatres' degradation that he had already begun in the paper:

> Was not Drury-lane, a few months since, fitted up, like a Bartholomew fair booth, for the capers of Signor ANTONIO on the *corde volante*; and beneath whom were there not two or three ladies ... tossing up golden balls, with others stalking on stilts and ladders? (23 July 1826)

Nor did he omit to mention the scandal of the crowds of prostitutes to be found milling around inside the building at Covent Garden Theatre:

> No female can ... reach the boxes without having her ears assaulted by the most disgusting language, alike from mere children of fourteen to wrinkled harridans of three score. Vice is here encountered in all its brutal gradation. (29 October 1826)

He lavishes praise on the Adelphi ('this elegant and well-directed little establishment'), on the wonderful sailor-acting of T.P. Cooke (as in Buckstone's highly successful melodrama *Luke the Labourer*, which Jerrold also praises), and on the scene-painting of his former shipmate Stanfield whom he calls 'the stage Claude'. He eulogises Wilkinson whenever he gets a chance, and has reservations about Miss Mitford's 'energetically written' *Two Foscari* produced at Covent Garden on 12 November 1826: 'the torrent of feeling and action is too frequently weakened by spreading into mere rivulets.' At his best, as in his detailed analysis of Fanny Jarman's Covent Garden debut as Juliet on 11 February 1827, he is an acute and illuminating critic. And he writes with pleasing gusto about the blood-and-thunder repertoire of Davidge's Coburg:

> This may be called the magazine of dramatic gunpowder ... A death's head and cross-bones would form its most pertinent proscenium ornament; or a

pyramid of jaw-bones, and a little imp at the top, smoking a blue light, and dangling a newly-strangled babe, or tickling a living one with an assassin's dagger, might serve as well to characterise the productions of this theatre ... The very door-keepers ought to be dressed as demons ... smoke and flame should be the livery of the house. (6 August 1826)

In September 1826 Jerrold found another opening for his writing in the new series of the *Monthly Magazine* that had been running since January. Founded in 1796 as 'an enterprise on behalf of intellectual liberty against the panic forces of conservatism',[31] the *Monthly* had been primarily concerned with political, economic and social matters though it had also published some poetry (Coleridge had contributed under a pseudonym). In 1824 Richard Phillips, its founder, sold it and in January 1826 the new owners appointed George Croly as editor. Croly, an Irish clergyman pursuing a literary career in London, shifted the journal from a Radical to a Liberal stance and began publishing 'Original Papers' (humorous, historical, pathetic) and short fiction – Dickens's earliest stories were to appear in the *Monthly* seven years later. A series of 'Village Sketches' by the already-celebrated Mary Russell Mitford began appearing with Croly's first number which also featured Sydney Smith's humorous 'Advice to the Clergy' and a long piece 'On the Decline of the British Drama' lamenting the 'complete schism between the reading and the playgoing public' and deploring the 'melodrames' that have 'grown up on the ruins of the regular drama'. Jerrold would certainly have endorsed the views expressed and would also have found Croly's Liberalism congenial. The first number of the *Monthly* for which he wrote (September 1826) has a lead article, perhaps by Croly himself, which is an anti-Corn-Law piece arguing that 'the mass of misery and pauperism cannot go on increasing ... The poor must be relieved, and who but the rich can relieve them?' It ends with words that might serve as an epigraph for all Jerrold's subsequent social journalism: 'We will not preach contentment to the poor, for that is to lull the fears of the rich, and harden their hearts. Too long, too long have they had all their own way.'

Jerrold made his *Monthly* debut with a couple of sub-early-Keatsian poems, both about being a poet and both signed with his full initials. In the next number appeared the first of an intermittent series called 'Full Lengths', signed 'J'. These were sketches of types representing various trades and callings, a genre much favoured by the Romantic essayists, especially Leigh Hunt, and one with an ancient lineage going all the way back via La Bruyère and Sir Thomas Overbury to Theophrastus. Jerrold continued to practise this popular genre for many years, eventually collaborating with Hunt, Blanchard, Thackeray and others in the periodical work called *Heads of the People* (see p. 114 below). He begins the series in the *Monthly* with a type dear to his heart, the Greenwich Pensioner, painting an admiring and affectionate portrait of the superannuated old sailor with a wooden leg (made from a splinter of the mainmast of Nelson's

Victory) and other battle-wounds. With a characteristically elaborate conceit (into which he smuggles a compliment to the *Monthly*'s most distinguished contributor) Jerrold makes the point that the sailor's ravaged body is the visible record of the nation's debt to him:

> let us consider as we look at his wooden supporter, that if it had not been for his leg, the cannon-ball might have scattered us in our tea-parlour – the bullet which deprived him of his orb of vision, might have stricken *Our Village* from our hand, whilst ensconced in our study; the cutlass which cleaved his shoulder, might have demolished our china vase ... hemmed round by such walls of stout and honest flesh, we have lived securely ...

Even these brief quotations, together with the earlier ones from *Facts and Fancies*, show that when Jerrold wrote 'literature' as opposed to workaday dramatic criticism he took pains to notch up his style – with negative results for his readability today. Jonson's criticism of Spenser, that 'in affecting the ancients, he writ no language', might be applied to Jerrold's humbler case if for 'the ancients' we substitute Shakespeare and the great stylists of the 17th century so eagerly studied by the young Jerrold. 'Imitate as many old writers as you can' was, as we have seen, the advice Jerrold gave to the young Sala. But mere imitation needs to become active appropriation if a writer is to find his own voice. The would-be elegant periphrasis of such phrases as 'orb of vision' may have worked well in Augustan English but was available only for comic purposes by the 1820s: such obsolete language awaited the genius of Dickens to realise its full potential in that respect. Similarly, Lamb does not just copy the celebrated 'quaintness' of Fuller or Browne but repackages it for post-French-Revolution (Romantic) readers. Whenever Jerrold begins to appropriate the old writers' elaborate conceits, or their convoluted or recherché comparisons, for the purposes of satire rather than for sentiment or for moral reflection, his own writing becomes individual and therefore interesting.

Whatever their stylistic shortcomings, however, the 'Full Lengths' were at least based on observed life and retain the same *sort* of interest that Mayhew's characters do – though lacking the vividness given to those descriptions by all the *ipsissima verba* of Mayhew's subjects. Jerrold's self-conscious 'literary' style may jar occasionally but in his descriptions of various contemporary vocational types he is essentially writing as a journalist and not as a creative artist. His subject-matter remains of interest to the social historian if not to the literary critic, and there are some grotesque or satirical touches which can still entertain. But, as was to be the case throughout his career, whenever he abandoned the journalistic mode and tried any kind of fiction other than farcical or satirical anecdote, the work that he produced has not stood the test of time. His narrative shortcomings are all too evident in a meandering 'Oriental' tale, 'The Moth with the Golden Wings' (*Monthly,* November 1826), which reads like an *Arabian Nights* story retold by a verbose Sunday School teacher.

Sometime during 1827 Jerrold moved his growing family from his mother's home in Little Queen Street to Somers Town in the parish of St Pancras, taking a house in Seymour Street (now Eversholt Street). Originally projected towards the end of the 18th century as a fashionable suburb north of the New (now Euston) Road, Somers Town soon fell into the hands of speculative builders who went in for cheaper high-density housing. By the late 1820s it had become very much a working-class area with a large immigrant population of French and Spanish political refugees. Another struggling family that came briefly to rest in Somers Town just at this time was that of John and Elizabeth Dickens and, many years later, when their famous son was writing *Bleak House*, he located the down-at-heel Skimpole here. Seymour Street consisted of standard late-Georgian 'Third Class' terraced housing ('two bays wide with three storeys and a basement ... a single arched window on the ground floor and two tall windows on the *piano nobile*'[32]), and it seems most likely that the Jerrolds would have been able to rent only lodgings, not a whole house. By July 1828 the family numbered five, Mary Ann having given birth to a second boy, Douglas Edmund, always known as Edmund or Ned and destined in due course to become the family's problem child.

The young paterfamilias needed to generate more in the way of regular income than could be supplied by his work for the *Sunday Monitor* (and this particular paper may by this time have become more of a drain on his finances than a source of income – see below, p. 101), the *Weekly Times*, occasional pieces for the *Monthly*, and such odds and ends as *The Statue Lover*, a little 'vaudeville' written for performance in the Vauxhall pleasure gardens in June. He turned again to the desperate trade of creating dramatic fodder for the voracious audiences of the minor theatres, this time on a regular-wage basis. The obvious theatre to turn to was the Coburg, where he had already had work accepted, and so the late summer of 1828 saw him joining the prolific melodramatist H.M. Milner as one of Davidge's house dramatists at a salary of five pounds a week.

On 6 August 1826 Jerrold had characterised the Coburg in the *Weekly Times* as being the 'most favored resort of those whose imaginations revel in a broad-sword fight, a hornpipe in fetters and a conflagration'. During the 1827/28 season, however, Davidge had been raising the tone – and baiting the Patent Theatres – by putting on Shakespeare, albeit Shakespeare somewhat transformed as in 'A Favourite Melodramatic Burletta, founded on a play of Shakespeare's, *The Jew of Venice*'. Much as Jerrold would have hated such sacrilegious treatment of the Bard, he would certainly have supported Davidge's campaign to cock a snook at Covent Garden and Drury Lane and this perhaps made the idea of working for him seem more palatable. Most likely, however, it was sheer financial need that made him willing to become a hired hack for someone he found as uncongenial as he evidently found Davidge. In the event, the experience of being a Coburg house-dramatist was to prove quite as disagreeable as he could possibly have anticipated.

Chapter Four

'The Sorry Shakespeare'

1828-1830

We have already noted Jerrold's satirical tale about a Minor Theatre actor-manager entitled 'Bajazet Gag; the Manager in Search of a "Star"' which was serialised in the *New Monthly Magazine* between July 1841 and February 1842. Energetically written and full of obvious 'insider' knowledge, it provides the modern reader with a comprehensive and entertaining guide to the bizarre world in which Gag's original, Davidge, and his competitors operated, a world in which artistic creativity and vulgar trickery, high-flown fantasy and sordid reality were strangely intertwined.

Gag has a sycophantic sidekick, Slimely Duckweed, who does his dirty work for him ('in a theatre, as Mr Bazajet Gag would frequently lament, "it was often impossible to be a gentleman"') and functions also as his purveyor of dramatic fodder:

> Duckweed was an author. Yes; having in his possession a very excellent pair of scissors, he was a dramatic writer. It is said of the Hottentot that he makes to himself a fantastic wardrobe from the intestines of oxen and sheep; Slimely Duckweed clothed himself ... with the reeking bowels of half-published novelists.

(Jerrold may well have had in mind Dickens's recent onslaught in *Nicholas Nickleby* on adaptors like William Moncrieff who dramatised popular novels even before their monthly-part serialisation was complete.) The French drama provides another fertile source for Gag's repertoire. He seizes on a packet Duckweed has just received from France:

> '... let's see what they've been doing at the shops in Paris – something may offer itself. Come, let's rummage the brains of our lively neighbours.'
> Saying this, the manager cut the string of the packet; and there were some fifteen dramas, of every variety, from classic tragedy to pancake vaudeville – all wet, as imported, to be undone into English, at the choice of Duckweed; or rather at the choice of his wife, – Duckweed, like a good husband, fathering all the offspring, human and literary, of his indefatigable spouse.

Gag also has a tame 'red-fire' dramatist who supplies him with a succession of 'original' sensation pieces with titles like *The Blue-Bottle of Babylon* and *The Demon Vulture* and who attends rehearsals following at Gag's heels 'like a spaniel compelled to trudge after its tyrant owner'. This pathetic figure, 'Mr Gentle', evidently recalls Davidge's dramatist-of-all-work, Milner, who between 1821 and 1829 contributed, according to George Rowell, 'at least fifty-six new pieces' to the Coburg's repertoire, among them an adaptation of Mary Shelley's novel called *Frankenstein; or, The Demon of Switzerland*.[1]

Gag has in rehearsal Gentle's latest effort, *The Devil's Concubine*, and Jerrold's description of the Manager's fawning on his star performers and his overbearingly brutal behaviour towards the dramatist and the actors playing minor parts (he addresses the women as 'you tuppenny trollops') no doubt reflects what Jerrold himself suffered and witnessed often enough at the Coburg. The same applies to his vivid depiction of the audience's rowdy behaviour at the first night of the *Concubine*'s representation and of the manager's tricks for humouring and placating his disgruntled patrons when the curtain falls ('to an uproar', Jerrold notes with savage irony, that must be 'so grateful to the feelings of the man of taste and the moralist'). To keep his audiences coming and to keep them happy Gag must be always on the look-out for some new sensation, of whatever kind. His hopes are raised when he is offered a piece called *The Prince of Greenland* but his interest vanishes the moment he finds that it is not a question of a real live blubber-eating, whale-oil-drinking Greenlander, complete with canoe and paddles, to whom he could have given 'forty minutes between the pieces' but 'an historical tragedy in five acts' ('"And have I had my time taken up with a damned tragedy?" cried manager Gag'). He fails in an attempt to filch 'Marc Antony', a domino-playing dog, from his chief rival and finally arrives in the unsavoury neighbourhood of Houndsditch too late to secure a man called Southcote, whose name he had found in *The London Directory* and whom he was going to bring out as the veritable 'Shiloh', the miraculous son of the 18th-century religious fanatic Joanna Southcott.

Davidge had a reputation to maintain in regard to what the *Theatrical Examiner* called (19 May 1827) 'the promptitude he observes in the production of novelty'.[2] The stock fare of the Coburg, wrote Timbs in his 1829 *Companion to the Theatres*, consisted of 'burlettas, melo-dramatic spectacles, and broad farces' and he commended 'the extraordinary speed with which these pieces are produced', adding, 'the prolific invention of the manager, and those who write for his stage, is truly astonishing'. During his three months (September–November 1828) at the Coburg Jerrold wrote or adapted six pieces: a couple of two-act melodramas (*Descart, the French Buccaneer* and *The Tower of Lochlain*, both premièred 1 September 1828); a well-received satirical farce (*Wives by Advertisement; or, Courting in the Newspapers*, 8 September – the playbill for this piece includes the line 'N.B. Wedding Rings are on Sale in the Lobby and in the Saloon'); a one-act 'broad extravaganza' (*Two Eyes Between Two; or, Pay Me For My Eye*, 12 October); and two rather more ambitious efforts, both three-act melodramas, *Ambrose Gwinnett; or, A Sea-side Story* (6 October) and *Fifteen Years of a Drunkard's Life* (24 November). *Gwinnett* dramatised a macabre incident at Deal in 1779. The historical Gwinnett was convicted of murdering a man who had, in fact, been kidnapped by a press-gang; he was hung in chains on the sea-shore but secretly rescued by friends who had spotted that he was still alive and spirited away abroad, returning after many years to establish his innocence. The main interest in Jerrold's play focuses on his invented villain, Grayling, who knows the truth but conceals it because of his hatred for Gwinnett, his rival in love. In place of the usual thoroughly black-hearted villain familiar from Gothic melodrama, Jerrold tries to portray in Grayling a more complex character, a man of strong passions whose humanity has been perverted partly by his treatment by the community and partly by frustrated love. Hatred and vengeance struggle within him against more humane feelings and he dies with the heroine's compassionate tears falling on his face. It was a strong part for Davidge and he evidently made the most of it. He also, in his 'Manager Gag' capacity, knew how to exploit the property: his playbill for the week beginning 13 October (during which time every single item performed came from Jerrold's pen though his name appears nowhere on the bill) included a lengthy quotation, purportedly from the historical Gwinnett himself, describing his sensations during the time that he was being hanged and gibbetted.[3] The play was a great hit, hailed by Moncrieff as

> one of the very best dramas the minor stage has produced for some time, and has the merit, in these translating times, of being purely English 'from top to toe' ... pity and suspense are alternately excited, and unmixed satisfaction attends the denouement.[4]

It quickly became a stock piece for theatres all over Britain and America and was printed in both Cumberland's Minor Theatre and Richardson's New Minor Drama series. In August 1829 it was being advertised in Scarborough as 'the New interesting and highly popular Domestic Drama, as performed upwards of one Hundred Nights at most of the London Theatres'; 1830 saw productions in Boston, Philadelphia and New York; and it remained in the repertory of the acting drama for at least the next forty years. It was back – not, certainly, for the first time – at the Coburg, now called the Victoria, in 1860, three years after Jerrold's death, with a different subtitle, *The Gibbet on the Sands*, and billed as 'this extraordinary and unprecedented Drama, of which the celebrated Author ... was justly proud, considering it the best and most effective Drama he had ever written'.[5] Needless to say, Jerrold, who would have derived some bitter mirth from this elevation of his early hack-work above his later 'legitimate' high comedies, never earned a penny more from it than was included in his meagre weekly stipend from Davidge.

The second of his full-length (three-act) melodramas for the Coburg was *Fifteen Years of a Drunkard's Life,* intended by Davidge to follow up the success of Milner's *The Hut of the Red Mountains; or, Thirty Years of a Gambler's Life* (first produced on 3 September 1827) which Milner had 'adapted' – very much as Gentle 'adapts' *The Devil's Concubine* in 'Bajazet Gag' – from a popular success of the Paris theatre *Trente Ans ou la Vie d'un Joueur*. In his guise as Moral Reformer of the Nation (always a good line for theatre managers in the early 19th century), Davidge announced:

> The immense advantages that resulted from the thrilling Representation of a late Melo-Drama, in which were developed the frightful effects of the career of a Gambler have induced the Proprietor to attempt ... a fearful display of the innumerable Evils that wait upon the Habits of a Drunkard ... .[6]

As with *Gwinnett*, Jerrold shows distinct originality in carrying out his commission. In the first place he has *two* drunkards: Vernon, a member of the wealthy middle classes, and Copsewood, a young tenant farmer. Both follow a Hogarthian downward progress (Hogarth's 'Gin Lane' is specifically invoked on the playbill); no more than Hogarth is Jerrold prepared to present vice as a class issue. Secondly, he shows both men as true alcoholics, people who really cannot help themselves once the poison has entered their system, and whose every effort to reform is doomed. This, as Louis James has noted, tends to subvert the mode of melodrama, rendering the villain, Vernon's libertine friend Glanville, irrelevant to the main plot; he can achieve his wicked schemes *as a result* of the protagonists' drunkenness but he is not the cause of it.[7] Nor can there be a happy ending; instead the play's finale consists, in James's words, in 'the nightmare, inconsequential slaughter of Jacobean tragedy'. Vernon stabs his faithful wife by mistake, then is killed by a bullet intended for someone else by Glanville, who is killed by Copsewood, who is left to be hanged for murder. Vernon lingers long enough to realise he has murdered his beloved Alicia. The focus throughout is intensely domestic, as was to be the case later in Cruikshank's famous series of *The Bottle*. The emphasis on the ruin of families rather than just individuals would have been a strong contributing factor to the drama's success with its Coburg audience.

By this time Jerrold was beginning to attract attention as a rather remarkable young man. In its highly favourable review of *Fifteen Years*, the *Stage* wrote on 24 November 1828:

> The author must indeed be possessed of the pen of a ready writer – for he not only produces a new melodrama, or burletta, at this house, almost every other week, and has also, we understand, been engaged at Sadler's Wells on the same terms, [I have found no corroborative evidence of this however] but he is editor of a Sunday newspaper (*the Weekly Times*) besides. One would almost think the compilation of the latter, was fully sufficient to employ every moment of his time ... His indefatigability well deserves the reward it meets with – for his dramatic pieces are generally allowed to be the best of their kind – and his Sunday paper for amusement, entertainment, and sound observation, is not to be equalled by any one of the like class.

The word 'reward' must have galled Jerrold, given his situation at the Coburg. He later dramatised the degradation of such a position and the hypocritical meanness of Davidge in 'The Manager's Pig', a farcical little tale written in the same year as 'Gag' and later collected in *Cakes And Ale*. Davidge is here lampooned under the name of Aristides Tinfoil. Having become the owner of a pig, Tinfoil commands his house dramatist to write a play for the creature:

'For a pig, sir?' exclaimed the author.
'Measure him', said Tinfoil [to 'measure' an actor was to consider his peculiar talents before deciding on what parts he should be given] ...
'But, my dear sir, it is impossible that –'
'Sir! impossible is a word which I cannot allow in my establishment. By this time, sir, you ought to know that my will, sir, is sufficient for all things, sir, – that, in a word, sir, there is a great deal of Napoleon about me, sir.'

A 'perfect swinish drama' is duly forthcoming and Tinfoil boasts to a friend about his writer's ability: 'An extraordinary young man, sir! – I have brought him out, sir – a wonderful young man, sir ... Only wants working, sir – requires nothing but being kept at it, sir.' He also professes huge admiration for literary talent, saying that those who show it should be highly rewarded: 'sir, it is perfectly unknown, my liberality towards that young man.' Of course, the moment the pig ceases to draw the crowds, Tinfoil has it killed and his family enjoys a succulent feast of pork.

Jerrold had no intention of labouring on for Davidge until he too should, metaphorically speaking, be consumed. Quite apart from the gross inadequacy of his financial rewards, he seems to have found Davidge himself very antipathetic. It was immediately after Davidge's death in 1842 that he portrayed him both as Gag and as Tinfoil. (No doubt the fact that Davidge died a very prosperous man irritated him further.) He is reputed to have said after hearing that Davidge had died about 4 pm, 'Humph! I didn't think he'd die before the half-price had come in!'[8]

Back in 1828, the critical and popular success of *Fifteen Years*, following on the success of *Wives by Advertisement* and *Gwinnett*, would not have gone unnoticed by Davidge's majestic rival, the 'Great Lessee', Robert William Elliston, who, after bankrupting himself in his efforts to make Drury Lane pay, was now in what Charles Lamb called 'the last retreat, and recess, of his every-day waning grandeur'. Since June 1827 he had been managing the Surrey Theatre, which he had memorably managed once before (1809-12) when it was still called the Royal Circus. The Surrey (finally demolished in 1934) stood in Blackfriars Road, just a few blocks from the Coburg, and the two competed fiercely for audiences. (Elliston, however, had great pretensions to gentility and disdained to get into a price war with Davidge when the latter sought to boost his audience numbers with 'shilling orders' that admitted their purchasers to any part of the house: the *Stage* reviewer sitting in the pit on 8 September to witness Jerrold's *Wives by Advertisement* was horrified to find himself 'on one side ... supported by a Dustman, and on the other by a Coalheaver! – reader only figure to yourself our situation!'.) Elliston features in 'Bajazet

Gag' as Gag's arch-rival, Trombone, the name alluding to his supreme skill
in blowing his own and his theatre's trumpet, and he probably contributes
not a little to the portrait of Gag himself, especially as regards flowery
speeches and pompous self-importance. Davidge, according to Fitzball's
account in his *Thirty-five Years of a Dramatic Author's Life*, was 'a blunt
man'.

Elliston the manager may be largely forgotten today, apart from Christopher Murray's excellent book on him, but his fame as one of the greatest
comic actors ever to tread the English stage endures. Hazlitt, Leigh Hunt
and Lamb were only some of the most distinguished of his admirers.
Lamb's Elian essay 'Ellistoniana' wonderfully evokes the essential theat-
ricality of the man which Jerrold himself had also noted, in a less
charitable way, in the *Mirror of the Stage* (26 July 1824): 'Perhaps there is
no man in the world so completely *professional* as Mr ELLISTON: he was
born an ACTOR; ... nature formed him to look, speak, and move, as if *he
felt* – but not *to feel*.' Elliston was, wrote Wemyss in his *Theatrical
Biography*,

> the Napoleon of drama, of whom it has been justly said, if thrown overboard,
> in rags, from one side of a ship, he would appear, before his tormentors could
> turn round, upon the other side of the deck dressed as a gentleman, ready to
> begin the world again; ... the favourite of the public by whom he was spoiled;
> honoured by the smiles of royalty, until on one occasion at least, he actually
> imagined himself a king – in representing the character of George the
> Fourth, in the pageant of the coronation responding to the applause of his
> audience by the emphatic phrase of '*Bless you, my people*'.

By December 1828 Elliston had made the Surrey one of the most successful
of all the Minor Theatres, having regaled its audiences with a skilful mix
of varied entertainment including Shakespeare, with his own incompara-
ble Falstaff, novelties like the talented Irish child actor Master Burke,
opera, pantomime and elaborately-staged original melodramas like
Fitzball's *The Inchcape Bell*. Believing that young Jerrold was 'the most
rising Dramatist that we have', he managed to lure him from the Coburg
to further strengthen the Surrey's repertoire. Given Jerrold's detestation
of Davidge, this was presumably not too difficult a matter to arrange, and
the appearance of *Ambrose Gwinnett* as the main attraction on the Surrey's playbill for New Year's Day 1829 signalled its author's new allegiance. Alas, he was soon to discover that Elliston could be quite as mean
an employer as Davidge, if not more so, and that his habitual drunkenness
created additional problems. Once, when some self-important person complained that he could see a duke or a prime minister any time in the
morning but never Elliston, Jerrold replied, 'if Elliston is invisible in the
morning, he'll do the handsome thing any afternoon by seeing you twice,
for at that time of day he invariably sees double'.[9]

Jerrold's first task for Elliston was to revamp an old pantomime into a
melodrama. His major project was a full-scale melodrama based on an old

London legend, *John Overy, the Miser; or, the Southwark Ferry,* with which Elliston opened his summer season on 20 April 1829. Drawing his inspiration from memories of Kean's overwhelming portrayal of the monstrously avaricious Sir Giles Overreach in Massinger's *A New Way to Pay Old Debts,* Jerrold creates in Overy a gold-obsessed figure who rejects his starving orphaned grandson and connives at the kidnapping of his loving, virtuous daughter when she refuses to sell herself in marriage to a decadent aristocrat (later, Overy runs mad and tries to stab her). It is a startling departure from the loving father/daughter relationship that is one of melodrama's basic configurations and Moncrieff in his preface to the play as published in Richardson's New Minor Drama series interestingly suggests that Jerrold and Elliston might not have got away with it at Covent Garden or Drury Lane. 'Minor' dramatists could, it seems, take greater risks. With Overy, as with Grayling in *Ambrose Gwinnett,* Jerrold is depicting a man corrupted by evil passions rather than the black-hearted villain of conventional melodrama, but here it seems likely that a strongly personal element comes into the picture. Overy has a long, highly rhetorical, speech (melodrama's equivalent of the operatic aria) narrating how he became a miser. It reads very much as though Jerrold is fearfully imagining how he himself might become warped and dehumanised by his scorching sense of social and economic injustice:

> ... the world! there was a time when I looked upon it with a melting eye ... I painted it a garden of flowers – I found it a heap of ashes. What did I see? The weak smote down and goaded by the strong ... the knave's head plumed and glistening with diamonds – poor honesty shoeless and unbonneted; he whose tongue gave utterance to his heart, shunned like a pestilence, or hunted like a beast – he, who would lick the hands of fools or hum a lie within the ear of crime, clothed with the richest – fed with the best. I saw this and my heart grew hard, my eyes sullen ... .

When Overy asks himself what causes 'so much baseness, so much un-merited contempt' his answer is 'Gold!' There is a clear continuity here with the bitter broodings so prominent three years earlier in *Facts and Fancies.*

The play was felt by some to be something of a throwback, as for example by the *Monthly Magazine* which noted in May 1829:

> Elliston, the indefatigable Elliston, fights his battle at the Surrey with great intrepidity. 'John Overy ...' is the grand piece ... one of those old monstrosities that used to keep children out of their beds in wonder, and to send old fools to their beds in fear ... The scenery, story and songs were received with *high* applause, the galleries being infinitely delighted.

Jerrold followed up this popular success for Elliston with another in a different vein, a bustling two-act farce called *Law and Lions!* satirising 'the present rage for the "Education of the People" ' in which Vale played a clownish linkman (someone who carried a torch for pedestrians to light them through dark streets) with a ludicrously-presented passion for natural history. He is called Jemmy Mammoth and his favourite exclamation is 'Oh Buffon!'. It is his clumsy attempt to play the *savant* that Jerrold satirises rather than the Society for the Diffusion of Useful Knowledge (founded 1827) but, as with his successful Coburg farce, *Wives by Advertisement*, *Laws and Lions!* shows how adept he was in that necessary skill for the successful 19th century *farceur*, the ability to give his work a topical spin. It is also in his farce-writing rather than in his serious melodramas (when he tends to lapse into a sort of pastiche 17th-century English) that we find Jerrold's most original use of language, often in the form of some witty elaboration of some 'high-culture' reference, such as a remark of Mammoth's lodger, a starving young poet called Epic: 'My Muse has never been a graceful one, having been spurred on by hunger; and what Pegasus can mount freely with a knife and fork in his flanks?'

A fine opportunity for the exercise of Jerrold's peculiar linguistic ingenuity presented itself, as we shall see, with his next job for Elliston, a job that was to result in a quantum leap in his fame; though it made fortunes only for others. Elliston had engaged the services for a few weeks of the hugely popular T.P. Cooke, who at this period usually starred at the Adelphi, and he needed a new piece written to 'showcase' the actor and his unique abilities. Cooke, born in 1786, was a real-life naval hero with a fine muscular figure and a 'handsome expressive countenance'.[10] He became an actor in 1804 and by the 1820s was far and away the most celebrated exponent of the stage sailor: others who played the role were, wrote Dyer in his *Nine Years of an Actor's Life*, 'land-lubbers, he is a *son of the sea*, a very amphibious animal; his hands are used like fins, and he moves on the shore like a fish out of water'. One of his greatest successes in the genre was the coxswain Long Tom Coffin in Fitzball's 'Nautical Burletta', *The Pilot* (Adelphi, 30 October 1825), an adaptation, or rather reversal, of Fenimore Cooper's novel which made the Americans the villains and the British the good guys. In this part he gave, according to Leman Rede in his *Road to the Stage*, a 'characteristic touch' which was 'invariably recognised and applauded': 'previous to commencing his combat with the [American] Sergeant he pauses to take tobacco, and afterwards, when he has driven his adversary from him, claps his sword into his mouth whilst he hitches up his trousers'; this, says Rede; dramatically illustrates 'cool, habitual bravery'.

The brave, patriotic and carefree Jack Tar figure had a long history on the English stage before Cooke (Jack Bannister was his most notable predecessor), Dibdin's immensely popular sea-songs and Nelson's victories having contributed powerfully to his continued popularity.[11] Before Cooke, however, he had been very much a low-comedy figure, given to roystering drunkenness. Cooke, who belonged to the same school of Romantic acting as Kean (fiery Highland chiefs and spectacularly eerie figures like Frankenstein's monster and Vanderdecken the Flying Dutchman, were among his most celebrated non-nautical roles) brought a depth of feeling and a touch of nobility to his sailor roles. The *Stage*'s reviewer of *The Pilot* found his Long Tom Coffin 'highly picturesque and deeply impressive; giving to the sailor character a new feature of thoughtfulness and mystery, and a tinge of the romantic' (January 1829).

The play Jerrold wrote for Cooke was a three-act 'Nautical Drama' called *Black Eyed Susan; or, All in the Downs*, the title being derived from Gay's famous ballad. It was an ideal vehicle for the actor's special genius (over the next thirty years Cooke was to play Jerrold's Sweet William over eight hundred times, more than any other role) and it brilliantly fuses a whole number of elements of passionate concern to Jerrold himself and to contemporary theatre audiences. He pays tribute to the real-life sailors with whom he had served, and for whom he had such strong admiration, by making his ordinary seaman unequivocally the hero and central figure in the play, and even, in the later scenes, placing him in a situation that invests him with genuine tragic dignity and later helped to inspire Melville's *Billy Budd*.[12] But Jerrold also gives the play a domestic focus. In place of the swashbuckling British tar fighting any number of inferior foreigners (in *The Pilot* Tom Coffin defeats six Yankee soldiers armed only with his harpoon), he presents William as a devoted husband, returning eagerly to his Susan after three years' brave service in his nation's wars. In Jerrold's play there is no trace of the triumphal jingoism usually associated with the nautical drama; everything is focused on the husband/wife relationship. It was the poverty of the rural labourer's existence that had caused William to join the navy and thus Jerrold brings in a third element, sympathy for the plight of the poor. Legal and economic power in the little seaport town of Deal where the action takes place is in the hands of the secretly criminal but outwardly respectable Doggrass, Susan's rapacious landlord who is also her unfeeling uncle (a domesticated and bowdlerised – i.e. non-incestuous – version of the uncle-villain in 'Monk' Lewis's Gothic melodrama *The Castle Spectre*). William returns in time to save his Susan from eviction, and from the threat to her virtue posed by Hatchet, Doggrass's partner in a clandestine smuggling racket. This gives Jerrold an opportunity to show his sailor in the obligatory cutlass-fight, there being no battle-scenes in the play. Susan, the play's domestic icon, is again threatened, however, when drunkenly assaulted by William's captain, Crosstree, to whom he is devoted and whose life he once saved. Hearing her cries, William rushes in and strikes down her assailant before he knows who it is. This leads to his court-martial for striking a superior officer, inevitable condemnation, a harrowing farewell scene with Susan, and the elaborate preparations for carrying out the death sentence. Just as William is about to be hanged from the yard-arm the conscience-stricken Crosstree rushes in with a document (which had been intercepted and kept back by Doggrass) proving that William had already got his discharge from the navy when he struck the blow. He is immediately freed and reunited with Susan amid the cheers of the sailors in which, no doubt, the audience also joined.

The court-martial and execution scenes on board William's ship were staged with the utmost realism and attention to detail. Both Jerrold and Cooke, being ex-sailors, would have brought their expertise to bear on this and the scenes amply provided the spectacular element needed for successful melodrama, with the additional thrill for the audience of witnessing an authentic representation of two of the most highly dramatic rituals of a closed community. The stage-directions for the last scene show the degree of realism:

The Forecastle of the ship – Procession along the starboard gangway; minute bell tolls. MASTER-AT-ARMS *with drawn sword under his arm, point next to the prisoner;* WILLIAM *follows without his neckcloth and jacket, a* MARINE *on each side;* OFFICERS OF MARINES *next;* ADMIRAL, CAPTAIN, LIEUTENANT, *and* MIDSHIPMEN *following. ...* MARINE OFFICER *delivers up prisoner to the* MASTER-AT-ARMS *and* BOATSWAIN, *a* SAILOR *standing at one of the forecastle guns, with the lock-string in his hand; a platform extends from the cat-head to the fore-rigging. Yellow flag flying at the fore. Colours half-mast down – Music –* WILLIAM *embraces the union jack – shakes the* ADMIRAL's *hand.*

It is not hard to imagine the tremendous tension created in the theatre by this ritual, following as it does immediately on the intensely pathetic scene of William's parting with his weeping Susan, or the effect of the sudden release of that tension when Crosstree rushes on with the reprieving document. At the same time the grotesquely implausible way, explained by a minor character in a hasty aside, whereby this vital piece of paper has (literally) surfaced, attached to the corpse of the drowned Doggrass, may be seen as Jerrold the radical's way of subverting – for those that have ears to hear – his happy ending. It does this through its implicit mockery of the audience's wish to rest in the reassuring effect of melodrama in which plot mechanisms (coincidences, sudden revelations of unsuspected relationships, discovery of lost or hidden documents, etc.) ensure that threatened and beleaguered goodness and innocence will always be ultimately triumphant. Gay may have contributed more to Jerrold's play than the title. Writing his dénouement, Jerrold may well have had in mind the Beggar's words in the last scene of *The Beggar's Opera* when the Player protests that he cannot upset the audience by ending with Macheath's execution and the Beggar responds that this is easily adjusted, 'for you must allow that in this kind of drama 'tis no matter how absurdly things are brought about. – So, you rabble there, run and cry a reprieve ...' .

Today's audiences may find the nautical jargon that William constantly pours forth ('I'm afraid to throw out a signal – my heart knocks against my timbers, like a jolly-boat in a breeze, alongside a seventy-four') even more preposterous than the play's dénouement but it reflected the real language used by contemporary sailors. A ship's surgeon noted of sailors generally:

> Their pride consists in being reputed a thorough-bred seaman; and they look upon all landsmen, as beings of an inferior order. This is marked, in a singular manner, by applying the language of seamanship to every transaction of life, and sometimes with pedantic ostentation.[13]

Jerrold was certainly not the first dramatist to exploit this trait, while in the novel there is Commodore Hawser Trunnion and his comrades in Smollett's *Peregrine Pickle* and his successors, notably Dickens's Captain Cuttle in *Dombey and Son*. But this elaborately metaphorical style was especially congenial to Jerrold and what he does in *Susan* is what Keats said poets should do, to 'surprise us with a fine excess'.[14] No doubt the fact that he was writing for Cooke, the nonpareil of stage sailors, would also have inspired Jerrold to surpass himself in rendering 'sailor-speak'.

William does indeed have some extremely metaphor-studded speeches, including the famous 'recitative' about the child-swallowing shark San Domingo Billy in Act II, but he does not have a monopoly of linguistic play in *Susan*. Among the original cast was Jerrold's friend from his Sadler's Wells days, J.B. Buckstone, now established as one of the public's favourite comic actors. He played Gnatbrain, an honest rustic who befriends Susan, and Jerrold wrote for him several passages of exuberantly witty sparring with Doggrass and his sidekick, the little bailiff Jacob Twig – and also with his sweetheart Dolly Mayflower, for Jerrold does not forget to supply the good-hearted, squabbling comic lovers called for to support the hero and heroine in every classic melodrama.

Given all its ingredients (not forgetting Dibdin's music and Charles Marshall's excellent scene-painting), it is hardly surprising that *Susan* so quickly became the theatre sensation of the year. Elliston had originally engaged Cooke only for eight nights from Whit Monday, 8 June, and *Susan* was intended, the elaborate staging of the final scenes notwithstanding, only as a supporting piece, the main attraction being *The Pilot*. Such was the enthusiasm aroused by Jerrold's drama, however, that Elliston promoted it to the head of the programme and kept constantly re-engaging Cooke, at £25 per week, for month after month until by 28 November *Susan* had achieved a phenomenal run of 150 performances (and was still, in fact, only half way through its total run at the Surrey). The *Dramatic Magazine* (June 1829) indicates the source of its popularity and gives us an entertaining glimpse of its effect on a real-life William in the audience:

> The plot is extremely simple and natural, for the characters and incidents are founded on every-day occurrences, and yet the most intense interest is excited from the rise to the fall of the curtain. Mr Cooke's acting is inimitable .... We were much amused by the emotion displayed by a young sailor in the pit, who, when William was condemned to die, was so affected that he tried to get out of the theatre; but, when the reprieve arrived, he became enthusi-

astic, and seizing hold with delight of his sweetheart's bonnet, twirled it round his head, notwithstanding her vain struggles to prevent him.

The *London Literary Gazette* also had high praise for Cooke (3 October 1829):

> His hitch, his swing, his back-handed wipe, his roll – in short, his every look, gesture and motion are redolent of the blue water and the lower deck; and all this is qualified by great ability, and a degree of feeling which is far more like truth than acting.

Another critic wrote (in an unidentified cutting held in the Harvard Theatre Collection): 'he identifies himself so completely with our preconceptions of the character of the sailor, that the heart spontaneously fixes on the hero and forgets the actor.'

In true Gag style Davidge attempted to 'trump' Elliston by bringing out at the Coburg *Black Ey'd Susan; or, The Lover's Perils* a week before the opening of Jerrold's drama. In his *Susan* he (or his writer) pulled out all the stops of nautical drama: it had 'views, ballet hornpipe, pressgang, mutiny, storm, shipwreck, cruel separation, pirates' cavern, battle and rescue' with a final 'Nautical Triumph' and 'View of the Victorious British Fleet lying at Anchor' but it could not compete with the result of Jerrold and Cooke's united genius. After a lively war of words between the two managers, conducted on playbills with a good deal of red print, with Elliston contemptuously calling Davidge an 'illustrious Charlatan' and Davidge responding by calling him a 'Vanity-bloated Mountebank', Davidge implicitly conceded defeat and withdrew his *Susan* after only twelve performances.[15]

Meanwhile, Jerrold still had his salary to earn from Elliston since what a Surrey playbill announced on 25 June as 'the extraordinary success and encreasing attraction' of *Susan* brought him nothing beyond the original £60 he was paid for it. No more did he profit from the frequent repetition of several of his other plays with which Elliston regularly filled out his programmes. Indeed, even when *Susan* had been running for no less than 300 nights, Jerrold still did not get to share in the profits but had instead to endure Elliston coolly saying to him, 'My dear boy, why don't you get your friends to present you with a bit of plate?'[16] He had followed *Susan* with a dramatisation of the recently-translated memoirs of François Vidocq, the celebrated Parisian criminal-turned-detective, which had caused quite a stir in London. Jerrold devised from them another vehicle for Cooke's athletic talents. Unlike *Susan*, however, *Vidocq* was pure hackwork, as was the hasty cobbling-together of a different stage version of the legend of the Flying Dutchman when it looked as though Cooke and Elliston were going to be legally prevented from producing the Fitzball version Cooke had earlier starred in at the Adelphi. Jerrold's *Dutchman*, incorporating the 'Optical Illusion of the Spectral Ship in Full Sail' that Cooke 'conducted' using some 'phantasmagoric glasses' specially manufactured for him, followed *Susan* as the second piece on 15 October and the evening was rounded off by the thirtieth performance of *Law and Lions!* Jerrold's work, old and new, provided most of the entire range of dramatic fare offered at the Surrey during the summer and autumn of 1829 but his name appeared nowhere on the bills. Everything of his was billed simply as 'By the Author of Black Eyed Susan', just as *Susan* itself had originally been attributed to 'the author of Ambrose Gwinnet, John Overy, Law and Lions, &c.' Given the tremendous *réclame* now attached to *Susan*, the young dramatist would clearly want it to be known as his work (one journal, at least, thought it was by Buckstone) even if he did not himself set a very high value on it. Duncombe, to whom he sold the right to print it for £10, naturally included it in his series of paperback play-texts with Jerrold named as author but Jerrold would have wanted a more dignified, less ephemeral, form of publication for what was far and away his most successful play to date, and Duncombe could hardly have had the nerve to object to this.

Accordingly, in October a handsome octavo edition of *Susan* appeared, 'printed for the author' by Richardson, and dedicated 'by permission' to the Duke of Clarence, the future 'Sailor King' William IV. In his five-page preface Jerrold poured scorn on 'the usual recipe for the composition of the tar of the theatre' which was 'to make him "shiver his timbers", "bless the king", and swear that one true-born Briton can lick "ten Frenchmen"'. His own endeavour, he wrote, had simply been truly to depict 'an English seaman' based on 'observation made at an early period of life'. His work was too slight 'to earn the smallest share of dramatic, and – though unfortunately the terms have been too long disunited – literary distinction' and he modestly attributed the play's success mainly to Cooke's 'perfect acting'. He also paid tribute to Elliston who 'for the effective representation of *Black Eyed Susan* spared neither pains nor expense'. To him, Jerrold continued,

> the thanks of all tasteful frequenters of the theatre are due. Under his guidance the Surrey has emerged from an almost hopeless condition, to its present 'high and palmy' state of respectability. Mr Elliston has the proudest cause of self-congratulation on his prosperity ... .

Jerrold's relations with his imposing employer were soon to sour but at this point he would have wanted to be on good terms with him since Elliston was shortly going to produce Jerrold's most ambitious play to date, a five-act tragedy on the subject of Thomas à Becket. This work, with its Shakespearian format and its grand English-history theme, was to be Jerrold's second great bid for literary fame and respectability, the first having been the ill-fated *Facts and Fancies* – and perhaps, he may have thought, his *Thomas à Becket* was even destined to inaugurate that 'revival of the drama' so ardently desired by the literati.

By the time the play was premièred on 30 November *Susan* mania was

at its height. Jerrold's play was being produced at Sadler's Wells, at the
Theatre Royal, Bath, and many other theatres both in Britain and America, while Cooke himself, dressed in his William costume, was commuting
nightly by cab over London Bridge after his Surrey performance to perform
again at Covent Garden in a production mounted as an afterpiece to *Romeo
and Juliet* (to the initial discomfort of certain critics who felt that the
'illegitimate' *Susan* was hardly appropriate for performance at one of our
great national theatres). For his Covent Garden appearances Cooke was
paid £10 nightly but when Jerrold enquired whether he as author of the
play might also be entitled to some payment the Covent Garden manager,
said Jerrold later, 'expressed something more than surprise at the request,
and said the representation of that piece at Covent Garden had done me a
great deal of good' ('I have not yet discovered that,' he added drily).[17] One
thing that representation at a Patent Theatre did do for him was to involve
him in unpaid labour for the Lord Chamberlain's Examiner of Plays who
required certain cuts: the boatswain, for example, was not allowed to say
of William, 'He plays the fiddle like an angel.'

Blinded by his adherence to contemporary cultural standards, Jerrold
could not see that in *Susan* he had already written a play that had more
dramatic life in it (both comic *and* tragic) than anything being produced
by the 'legitimate' theatre, and that was also a genuine successor to that
Shakespearian 'national drama', looked back to so longingly by all the
theatre aficionados of the day (wonderfully mocked in Dickens's portrayal
in *Nickleby* of the great critic Mr Curdle). Shakespeare's Tragedies and
Histories, recently illumined by the varied geniuses of Kean and the
Kembles – indeed, Fanny Kemble was making her much-acclaimed début
as Juliet in the very production of *Romeo and Juliet* that was the main
piece at Covent Garden when Cooke took Jerrold's William there – were
universally regarded as the high water mark of English dramatic literature. From this it followed that for any playwright aspiring to 'revive the
drama' what was required was five-act historical tragedies in which all the
principal characters talked in blank verse and all humble, 'comic', folk –
servants, citizens and such-like – would talk in prose. That this model long
remained compelling is shown by Tennyson's adherence to it in the 1870s
when writing *Queen Mary* and his other would-be 'national' dramas.

This iconisation of Shakspeare's Tragedies and Histories led to theatre
managers being inundated with unplayable 'tragedies' full of lofty pseudo-
Elizabethan English and requiring lavish historical settings. The rejection
of such pieces, or the poor reception of them when occasionally one of the
Patent Theatres did risk putting them on, led to a certain snobbery about
the 'unacted drama', the idea that such plays were somehow superior to
the acted drama just because money-grubbing managers and rabble-audi-
ences failed to appreciate them. Jerrold was later, in 'Bajazet Gag', to
make merciless fun of this attitude in the figure of Mr Beaumont Fletcher
Pettichaps, author of that *Prince of Greenland* rejected with disgust by
Gag. Pettichaps is a leading member of the 'Phosphorics', an unacted

authors' club which resolves to press for a substantial Government subsidy to set up a national theatre for the production of their lengthy 'master-pieces'. It is the vanity and incompetence of these writers Jerrold is mocking, not the Shakespearian model itself. In 1829 he certainly believed that the real test of his mettle as a dramatist bidding for lasting fame lay in five-act historical tragedy, not three-act melodrama, however popularly successful. The triumphant progress of *Susan*, together with the staying power shown by several of his other pieces, doubtless made Elliston more receptive than he might otherwise have been when Jerrold presented him with a five-act tragedy set in medieval England, and *Thomas à Becket* was duly produced on 30 November. It had every advantage that lavish costumes, music by Jonathan Blewitt, and Marshall's beautifully-painted scenery (including a 'Gothic Hall in Beckett's Mansion' as well as exterior and interior views of Canterbury Cathedral) could give it. Laman Blanchard supplied a Prologue hailing 'that long-sought absentee, an English Play':

> We offer here – no masque or gaudy dream –
> A native Drama on a native theme!

And Jerrold's 'British bravery' in offering an original piece at a time when 'more than half our plays, like half our fleet, are "taken from the French"' is further commended in Cornelius Webbe's Epilogue which was spoken by Miss Scott, the original Susan. Both Prologue and Epilogue were respectfully printed in the *Dramatic Magazine* on 1 January 1830.

It was not until the fourth night of *Becket* that Jerrold's own name appeared on the bills (previously the author was identified only as 'the author of *John Overy, Black Eyed Susan*') and even then he was upstaged by Elliston's self-advertisement:

> The Proprietor cannot refrain from congratulating himself upon the success-
> ful production of an entirely original Piece from the pen of an Author whose
> merits have been so highly appreciated in his lighter pieces written for this
> Theatre.[18]

Elliston's self-congratulation proved premature, however, as *Becket* ran only for six nights before it was eclipsed by the return of Cooke and *Black Eyed Susan*. It never reappeared in the repertoire, despite the respectful reception it was accorded. Jerrold's weakness in structuring dramas is here far more damaging than in his stage-effective (and much shorter) melodramas: the play, Moncrieff concedes in his generally admiring preface to the printed text in Richardson's New Minor Drama, is 'more a dramatic poem than an acting play' and the *Times* critic noted (2 Dec. 1829) that the events 'hang together too loosely to be called a plot'. Becket himself is, in fact, rather on the sidelines of such plot as there is, which concerns a young Englishman defending his wife 'from the hot grasp of priestcraft' in the shape of a villainous monk whom Becket is protecting (we should remember the strength of anti-Catholic feeling in England in 1829 following Parliament's passing of the Catholic Relief Bill), and Jerrold's own anti-clericalism prevents him from working out a coherent attitude towards his protagonist. As George Daniel noted in his preface to the play in another series, Cumberland's Minor Drama, 'every opportunity is seized to exaggerate the pride, luxury and lasciviousness of the church'. Although Jerrold refrains from blank verse, he does allow his passion for apophthegm, metaphor and elaborate conceits to run riot, laying himself open to *The Times*'s mockery of such 'superfine' writing: 'An unfriendly letter is called "a piece of folded ice"; a person angered by an inferior exclaims, "Despite of us, our lion thoughts will growl at fleas."' Such relentlessly convoluted expression together with such paucity of incident might have strained any audience's tolerance, especially one like the Surrey's which was unused to five-act historical dramas, but it gave its favourite writer's tragedy a respectful hearing and, as Jerrold wrote in the preface to a separate edition of the play, 'There are some auditories from whom even an attentive silence may be received as no mean mark of commendation.'[19] He was shortly to experience far different treatment at the hands of a Patent Theatre audience. Meanwhile, to a friend complimenting him on *Becket* and saying, 'You'll be the Surrey Shakespeare', Jerrold feelingly retorted, 'The sorry Shakespeare, you mean.'[20] His contemptuous response in the preface already quoted to criticisms of the lack of plot was that people who wanted that should stick to French melodramas:

> History is not to be degraded or sported with by an impertinent alloy of invention, or it would have been easy to make King Henry II fall in love with and wed a swineherd's daughter, and the Archbishop of Canterbury to pronounce an oration at the monarch's nuptials ... [the dramatist should aim at] justly delineating the feelings and passions of a great historical character, and ... giving a correct view of his mind ... .

It is noticeable here that he seems to think of plot entirely in terms of 'love-interest' (which is indeed a staple of melodrama) and of 'character' as something seemingly separate from action, something the dramatist 'delineates' through set speeches by and about particular *dramatis personae*. This fundamental failure, shared by most of Jerrold's contemporaries, to grasp that character *in action* is one of the basic essentials of drama is responsible, even more than his 'superfine' writing, for the fact that none of his 'legitimate' plays proved capable of surviving as living theatre.

During the autumn of 1829 the management of Drury Lane showed itself keen to benefit from the lucrative skill of the author of *Black Eyed Susan*. According to Walter Jerrold, he was first asked to adapt a French piece, and indignantly replied, 'I will come into this theatre as an original dramatist or not at all.' He had his wish on 19 December when his two-act historical drama *Matthew Hopkins the Witchfinder* was staged there. His name did not appear on the playbill but the piece was evidently known to be by him. Once again, there was too little action and too much metaphor and this audience would seem to have been a good deal less patient than the Surrey one was with *Thomas à Becket*. *The Times* reported on 21 December:

> The solemn silence which attended the first act was only the fore-runner of the hurricane which burst forth in the second. The cries of 'off! off!' and other marks of disapprobation, were loud and frequent; and when Mr Cooper came forward to announce a repetition of the drama, the opposition was redoubled.

The play was not repeated and, while reviewers gave Jerrold full credit for attempting originality, the *Morning Chronicle* critic pointed out on 21 December that 'if a piece be deficient in the three requisites of incident, character and interest, it cannot be expected that people should be content to listen to it, merely on the score that its dulness is indigenous'. Smarting from the disappointment, Jerrold wrote to Mary Russell Mitford, who had responded flatteringly to the copies of *Susan* and *Becket* he had sent her:

> In the present day a moderately gifted dramatist has a pretty time of it; if he succeed his piece has the immortality of a month – if he fail his name is gibbetted in every journal as a dullard and a coxcomb. French melodramas have ruined us.[21]

Since this claim about the 'immortality of a month' was patently untrue as regards *Susan*, it would seem that Jerrold is here excluding his 'illegitimate' pieces from consideration. He was probably little comforted, therefore, by the success of his next contract piece for Elliston which was another vehicle for Cooke, taking its title, as *Susan* had done, from a popular song (*Sally in Our Alley*, Surrey, 11 January 1830). But in it he struck a more overtly political note than anything in *Susan*. An old peasant bitterly recalls having been turned out of his home into the fields with his wife and children for falling behind with his rent:

> Oh master, when I have heard of great battles – of towns burnt – I have often thought if the pains and sufferings of the poor man's fireside were registered they would show more dismally than the gazette of Trafalgar or Waterloo.

Soon after writing those words Jerrold himself was in financial trouble. He had evidently felt able, on the strength of his salary from Elliston, supplemented by his earnings from the *Weekly Times* and other journalism, to move his household upmarket from Somers Town and by the end of 1829 was living at number 4 Augustus Square, a two-storey cottage or 'villakin', as Hannay calls it, near Regent's Park where Mary Ann was now expecting her fourth child. Despite the *Becket* disappointment and the *Witchfinder* débâcle, it was reasonable for Jerrold to presume that he would not have much difficulty in finding managers ready to take any new plays he might write. Suddenly, however, on 25 January he found himself committed to the King's Bench debtor's prison, along with a man called Booth, 'in discharge of their bail at the suit of Sandford Fox', the sum involved being £23.[22] Walter Jerrold believed that the debt was connected with his newspaper commitments (Jerrold's part-proprietorship of the *Sunday Monitor* perhaps?). Whatever the circumstances, one might have expected Elliston or Cooke to have come to the rescue of a man whose work had profited them so greatly. On the very day that Jerrold went to prison Cooke had a benefit night at the Surrey in which he enacted a 'Melo-Dramatic Scene' called *Lo Studio!* in which he 'attempted various specimens of Antique Sculpture' and which was billed as 'written expressly for Mr. T.P. Cooke by the Author of *Black Eyed Susan*'.[23] Moreover, Cooke and Elliston had begun discussions with Jerrold about a major new Whitsuntide piece suited to Cooke's talents as well as a piece for another benefit night.

Far from arranging Jerrold's release, Elliston sent him 'a most arrogant letter' and in a following visit refused to guarantee him any contract after Whitsun. In a letter to Mrs Cooke describing the interview (Cooke was by this time away acting William in Dublin) Jerrold wrote that he had declined to write anything more for Elliston 'on such an uncertain tenure' whereupon

> Mr E. (just and literal soul!) declared the engagement at an end, and from that period (about a month since) *stopped my salary*. Nay, more, he had the unblushing effrontery to tell me that I had for some time received money without making any adequate return – that he had scarcely made anything by *Black Eyed Susan* – that other pieces of mine, *Law and Lions, John Overy*, etc., had kept money out of the house, and that he had gratified my vanity at the cost of £300 by the production of *Thomas à Becket*.[24]

Elliston subsequently asked Jerrold to state his price for the two pieces for Cooke but broke off negotiations when Jerrold insisted on cash on delivery of manuscript.

It was not until 16 March, just ten days before the birth of his second daughter, that Jerrold was released from the King's Bench, having gone through the Insolvent Debtors' Court. He set to work on the new nautical drama he had had in mind for Cooke, determined now, of course, that it should not be produced under Elliston's management, but he was still harassed by financial worries, as shown by another letter to Mrs Cooke in which, Cooke himself being again out of town, he asks for a short-term loan of £15. He had earlier told her that the sailor he contemplated writing for Cooke to act 'was a peculiar, and yet untouched character' but had not divulged that it was also an historical one. The sailor was, in fact, Richard Parker, the ordinary seaman who became the leader of the Nore mutineers in 1797, displaying remarkable powers of organisation and leadership, and who was court-martialled and hanged at the yard-arm after the quelling of the mutiny. He figured in official English history as a dangerous Radical. In fact, the mutiny had not been primarily politically motivated, despite the use of phrases like 'the Floating Republic' and other rhetoric borrowed from the popular radicalism of the day; the main cause had been the harshness of the sailors' lives and discontent about alleged unequal distribution of prize-money. It was a bold stroke for Jerrold to present Parker as a hero, a man more sinned against than sinning, into whose mouth, as we have seen (above, p. 29), he puts fierce denunciations of the extreme brutality of the (unjust) punishment inflicted on himself and others under the code of naval discipline. In most of his melodramas, Jerrold, perhaps following Buckstone's lead in *Luke the Labourer*, had sought to present the villain of the piece as a man who has *become* an evil-doer as a result of some external circumstances (Doggrass in *Susan* is a notable exception to the rule). In *The Mutiny at the Nore* he goes a stage further and presents the 'villain' as a quasi-tragic hero, William's dark double, for whom there can be no last-minute reprieve. The curtain falls as the noose is being tightened around his neck. The husband/wife relationship is still central to the plot and once again 'the distress of the work' (to borrow Jane Austen's phrase) is promoted by the behaviour of the sailor-hero's officer. But whereas Captain Crosstree's dishonourable conduct was a momentary lapse due to intoxication, Captain Arlington in the *Mutiny* is portrayed as a vicious tyrant, the unacceptable face of authority, which is in keeping with the greater radicalism of this second nautical drama from Jerrold's pen.

To show Parker as a man driven to extremes by his wrongs Jerrold borrows wholesale from the first chapter of Captain Marryat's newly-published nautical novel *The King's Own* in which Marryat had clearly based the character of Peters, the hero's father, on what was known or believed about Parker. Peters is wrongly convicted of theft ('His heart did not break, but it swelled with contending passions, till it was burst and riven with wounds never to be cicatrised'), driven to desertion, recaptured and then subjected to the barbarity of being flogged through the fleet; his 'irritated mind' moving him to join the mutineers, he quickly becomes their ringleader on account of his intelligence, pride and superior education. Jerrold also borrows, as he acknowledges in a footnote to the printed text, from Marryat's novel a sensational incident that climaxes Act 2 (Adams, the doggedly loyal seaman who will not join the mutiny, snatches Peters's child from the muzzle of a gun that Peters is about to fire, unaware that his child has wandered in front of it). Since Jerrold is writing a historical melodrama and not a tragedy, he apparently has no problem with involving historical characters in a fictitious drama of sexual passion (in *Becket* this element was strictly confined to the invented characters): so Captain Arlington is made the disappointed lover of Parker's wife, who is as much the domestic icon of her play as Susan is of hers.

T.P. Cooke, with his rich experience of playing both outlaws and heroic sailors, could certainly have made something sensational of Jerrold's Parker but Elliston's treatment of the outraged dramatist put a Surrey production out of the question. It was not at the Surrey but at an East End house, the Pavilion, Whitechapel, that *The Mutiny at the Nore; or, British*

Sailors in 1797 was first produced on Whit-Monday, 31 May 1830. It was billed as 'an entirely New Historico-Nautical and Domestic Melo-Drama, in Three Acts, written expressly for this Theatre by the Author of *"Black Eyed Susan"*'.[25] The Pavilion was at this time a flourishing neighbourhood theatre (Foote noted in his 1829 *Companion to the Theatres* that 'the people of this populous district are zealous play-goers'). It specialised in a mix of nautical drama, burlettas, dog dramas (the legend at the head of the *Mutiny* bill reads 'The celebrated dog HECTOR will appear every Evening during the Week' and the evening's programme concluded with *The Smuggler's Dog*), and of good old-fashioned Gothic sensation pieces. On 14 April 1828, for example, the bill included *The Sailor's Return*, 'with a quadruple hornpipe', and 'an entirely new Terrific Legendary Recreation called *Romanzoff the Regicide; or, the Hag of the Tombs!!* The great hit of 1829 had been *Fifteen Years of a British Seaman's Life*, a play that paid tribute to Jerrold by copying the format of one of his Coburg successes. 'Indeed the sailors are *all in their element* at this little theatre', commented the *Monthly Theatrical Review* in September 1829.

Clearly the Pavilion was a highly suitable venue to launch the *Mutiny* with its powerful indictment of the excessive harshness of naval discipline and yet also its unquestioned patriotism ('Parker's celebrated farewell' is quoted on the playbill: 'here's health to the King, Confusion to my Enemies, and Peace to my Soul'). Surviving reviews seem scarce – unsurprisingly, since the Pavilion was rather beneath the notice of reviewers – but evidently the *Mutiny* was sufficiently successful for other theatres to be encouraged to mount productions. It was produced at the Coburg on 16 August and at both the Tottenham Street and (rather surprisingly) the Richmond theatres on 27 September. Indeed, the Coburg became very much the home of this particular drama over the next year or so, reviving it several times, and Jerrold, having denied it to Elliston for the Surrey, must have been irritated to see it enriching the treasury of his old enemy Davidge. On 4 January 1831 it was produced at the Theatre Royal, Brighton, perhaps with Jerrold's connivance (and therefore to his profit, however minimally). The blurb on the playbill, a copy of which can still be seen at the theatre, reads as though it were written by him:

> this remarkable point in our naval history took place ... in the year 1797 and was emphatically called by the sailors the BREEZE at the Nore [this sounds as though it might be Jerrold drawing on childhood memories – the Nore Mutiny would certainly have been very much a living memory at Sheerness in the early 1800s]. The extraordinary and masterly organisation of their system struck terror into the stoutest hearts, and called forth characters and situations in themselves so dramatic, that small skill was required in the author to arrange them for representation. The noble use made by the seamen of the mighty power in their hands, is now a subject of astonishment to all, and realizes, more forcibly than any other point in history, the romantic gallantry of a British sailor. ...

Rather different was the blurb used by Davidge for the 1831 revivals at the Coburg. William IV, the 'Sailor King', was now on the throne and the playbill refers to the fleet's now being 'under the august and paternal care of Him, who is the Head and Pride of the British Navy'. William IV was far from universally popular, however, because of his perceived opposition to the cause of Reform and this no doubt was the reason for the hisses that were heard in the theatre when Parker drank the King's health before execution. They were differently interpreted, however, by a playgoer who wrote to Leigh Hunt's *Tatler* on Christmas Eve 1831 to protest against what he saw as the 'brutish tendency' of the piece and the

> insulting public representation of the butchered sailor thus, on the point of death, drinking the health of 'the King'. The man is made actually to glory in being the victim of a naval code, which allows ... a malignant officer to ... order the flogging of a brave 'common' man on mere suspicion of stealing a watch ... .

Jerrold wrote a furious reply on 29 December, quoting several passages from the play in which the degrading brutality of naval discipline is denounced, and asserting the authenticity of Parker's final speech: 'the words are the words of *Parker* himself, – repeated to the author by ear-witnesses, two of whom, former shipmates of the "mutineer", were, in June 1830, in Greenwich Hospital'. He was, he continued, made impatient by a charge

> which accused me of endeavouring to uphold the doctrine of non-resistance, under a most atrocious and tyrannic system of punishment, my abhorrence of which system has been heightened, by having, in my green days, frequently witnessed its cold-blooded and brutalizing operation. My pictures, such as they are, of the lashed seamen are not ideal, but drawn from the quarter-deck, or the launch of the ship's side. It was my aim that these pictures should, however humbly, aid, and not retard, the cause of humanity.

Injustice and official brutality also feature strongly in the piece he did, after all, write for Cooke to perform at the Surrey, *The Press-Gang; or, Archibald of the Wreck* (Surrey, 5 July 1830), the copyright of which for three years was purchased by Elliston.[26] The hero, a merchant seaman called Arthur Bright or Bryght, is press-ganged as he comes from his wedding, escapes and is recaptured and sentenced to be flogged through the fleet. As in *Susan*, the final scene shows preparations for a grim naval ritual:

> The Larboard Broadside of H.M.S. the Trident. Captain Fenton, Lieutenant of Marines, Marines, Sailors, &c, ascend the deck from behind – Arthur Bryght last – Drum rolls behind – Shaking water down to front – a launch to receive the prisoner in C. in front of Ship two sailors in it – one has the Cat o' nine tails.

At the last minute, in an ending clearly intended to be a savagely ironic reprise of the end of *Susan*, the mysterious Archibald of the Wreck comes on in a boat flourishing papers to show that Arthur's mother was niece to 'the much neglected Earl de Wrothesley' and that he has now succeeded to the title. As a peer he cannot be pressed and so is at once set free ('General shout' and curtain). During the play a character called Turnstile turns on a lawyer defending the press-gang system on the grounds that 'the navy must be manned'. The gangs don't seize middle class men, says Turnstile, and continues:

> those rascals that are poor, healthy and strong (never mind the whimpering wives and squalling children) were born for no other purpose than to be kidnapp'd at a moment's notice, and, whether they will or no, sent to sea – for as you say, Sir, the Navy must be mann'd ... Full of this idea you explode into Rule Britannia and roar Britons never shall be slaves – the Press Gang, with their bludgeons, all the while keeping time in the street.

The *Examiner* reviewer (25 July 1830) delighted in this as 'a good piece of irony, and put in a popular shape', wondering greatly that 'the zealous timeserver, Mr Colman [Examiner of Plays for the Lord Chamberlain] did not interdict the whole of [Turnstile's] answer'. Had press-gangs been still operating in 1830 he – or rather the local magistrates, for the Surrey was not yet subject to censorship by the Lord Chamberlain – would almost certainly have done so. The *Examiner* also rammed home the social point made by the abrupt denouement:

> [Bright] is discovered to be heir to the peerage, and *by the laws of the land, no Peer can be pressed to sea.* Oh! 'envy of surrounding nations!' where the laws are open to the poor as well as the rich – when they can pay for them; and where the rich only make the laws.

By now the twenty-seven-year-old Jerrold was generally recognised as being a cut above the general run of writers for the Minor Theatres – Milner, Moncrieff, Fitzball and the rest. Not only was his dialogue better but also his plays were all his own. They might take as their point of departure, as those of the revered Shakespeare himself had often done, some old legend or ballad but they were emphatically *not* adaptations or translations, or merely vehicles for sensational stage effects, performing animals and so on. Moreover, he was always experimenting and not just repeating the same formulae, even in the nautical dramas. Five months after *The Press Gang*, for example, came something very different, an allegorical melodrama in blank verse (prose for the 'low' comic characters, of course, like the cheeky servant played by Buckstone) called *The Devil's Ducat!; or, The Gift of Mammon*. This was produced on 16 December 1830 at the Adelphi, very much a 'West End' theatre, which, being in Westminster, was licensed directly by the Lord Chamberlain. Despite its small size, it had become celebrated for its spectacular melodramas and musical shows such as adaptations of Mozart operas. Mary Jerrold, Douglas's mother, was engaged here in August 1830 and seems to have become primarily associated with this theatre (her obituary in the *Dramatic Register*, 1852, stated that she 'performed the old ladies' here). Its managers were two very popular and enterprising comic actors, Frederick Yates and Charles Mathews the Younger, and its two great melodrama stars were T.P. Cooke (when he was not playing William at the Surrey, that is) and a tall, gaunt actor with a sepulchral voice and great stage presence, known as 'Obi' or 'O' Smith after one of his most celebrated parts. Jerrold's Mammon was certainly a part for this actor to make a great effect in as he threw aside his 'mask and ragged clothing and [appeared] a mass of gold, with a golden crown and sceptre':

> Start not, signor; I am earth's harlequin [i.e., master of transformations]
> I build up palaces, put slaves on thrones,
> Erase the spots from treason's stained coat,
> Manacle warm youth to shivering age,
> Re-christen fools most wise and learned men,
> And trumpet villains, honest.

In his *Tatler* Leigh Hunt praised the piece for its novelty, humour and the ambition of its dialogue. Writing to thank him, Jerrold – ever prickly towards managers – complains that Yates and Mathews had 'slipped out the piece at a time, and in a manner as though they were ashamed of it' but audience response had been good nevertheless. He sends Hunt copies of some of his plays on the strength of 'a long, and I trust, profitable acquaintance with your writings'. Of the plays themselves he writes:

> They were all the hasty work of time stolen from the more arduous duties of newspaper vocation. The piece – *Black-Eyed Susan* – which has commanded the greatest success is, of course, – at least, in my opinion of smallest worth. As far as the *managers* were concerned, it was, however, a lucky accident. Yet though its pretensions are moderate, I send it, as a casual glance at its pages will serve to acquit me of writing *all* the nonsense uttered in it by the actors of Covent Garden.[27]

So ended a two-year period during which Jerrold wrote and had produced at a wide variety of venues all the way from an East End neighbourhood theatre to one of the great Patent Houses, upwards of twenty dramatic pieces – farces, burlettas, melodramas, tragedies – many of them very popular and one a really huge and lasting success. His name as a dramatist was made but he still had a hard daily struggle to maintain himself and his family and had to rely on plenty of journalistic employment to make ends meet. He was as fired up as ever by his two ambitions, both relating to his passion for the English language and his veneration for the great Elizabethan and Jacobean masters of it. He wanted to deploy his literary talents and his hard-won learning in a fierce crusade against all social injustice, abuse of privilege and oppression of the poor. And he wanted to be at the forefront of 'reviving the drama' by writing plays that might be worthy of a permanent place in a national repertoire already glorified by the likes of Shakespeare, Jonson and Massinger. He had not yet abandoned hope of fulfilling both these aims in the theatre world of his day, and was a keen participant (he certainly had motivation enough!) in the ongoing campaign to reform the whole British theatre system, and to assert the 'Rights of Dramatists', to quote the title of an essay he published in the *Monthly* in May 1832. By the time this essay was published he had firmly established himself as 'legitimate' – initially, though, by means of a genre hitherto untried by him, that of 'petite comedy'. He could perhaps be forgiven for thinking that, with the success of *The Bride of Ludgate* (Drury Lane, 8 December 1831) behind him, he could now go forward combining the writing of 'legitimate' drama with expression of his social concerns. And, for a brief while, it did indeed seem that he could do just this.

Chapter Five

The Brownrigg Years (1): Dramas

1831-1841

Three years after Jerrold's death his eldest son collected together for volume publication a score or so of his father's essays and articles which had first appeared in different journals and annuals during the 1830s. Blanchard Jerrold gave the volume the title *The Brownrigg Papers,* many of the pieces having been originally written 'under the *nom de plume* of Henry Brownrigg'. To contemporary readers this surname would have been instantly recognisable as that of a notorious murderess, Elizabeth Brownrigg, a London midwife who barbarously abused her young female apprentices and was hanged for the murder of one of them in 1767. Blanchard Jerrold remarks:

> It has been said that this pen-name was adopted in a moment of bitterness; that the author for a moment regarded apprentices to literature as unfortunates no whit less brutally treated than were the apprentices of Flower-de-Luce Court. But this explanation is one without foundation in fact – so far as I know.

Blanchard was concerned always to present his father as a tender-hearted, essentially sweet-natured, man, quite unlike the bitter jester of popular belief. But it is safe to assume that Jerrold, who shared the age's delight in satirical nomenclature, joined a family name (that of his brother Henry) with the fearful Mrs Brownrigg's to make a sardonic comment on the harshness of his long struggle to establish himself as a writer. Blanchard himself tells us that his father

> always felt that he had *snatched* his reputation from the public. He always bore about him the firm belief that he had been fighting throughout his life under the most galling disadvantages of fortune, and that with his own vehement soul – his iron courage – he had cut his way to success.[1]

In 1831 he had ahead of him a decade of increasing fame but, despite incessant labour both as dramatist and as journalist, very little fortune – indeed, for at least the first six years of it he continued to be dogged by much financial anxiety and ill luck.

The politically tumultuous years 1831-32 (the Reform Bill finally passed the Lords with a majority of just nine on 14 April 1832) saw the production of Jerrold's last social-message 'domestic dramas', *Martha*

Willis, the Servant Maid (Royal Pavilion, 4 April 1831), *The Rent Day* (Drury Lane, 25 January 1832) and *The Factory Girl* (Drury Lane, 6 October 1832) as well as of the first two of the string of 'witty' comedies that constituted his chief dramatic output during this decade, *The Bride of Ludgate* (Drury Lane, 8 December 1831: his first Patent Theatre success), and *The Golden Calf* (Strand Theatre, 30 June 1832). The years 1831-32 also saw the beginning of Jerrold's deeper involvement in Radical journalism with his work for Thomas Wakely's the *Ballot* from January 1831 and, briefly, on Duncombe's short-lived *Punch in London* (January 1832). Privately, there was the sadness of his infant daughter's death on 8 April 1831 and the happiness of the birth of another daughter on 21 September the same year. She was named Mary Ann for her mother and also for her dead sibling, as was often the custom at the time, but always known in the family as Polly. Not long afterwards, during the winter of 1831/32, the family moved from Augustus Square to the more desirable area of Little Chelsea, a hamlet between Kensington and Chelsea on the Fulham Road, which had grown steadily in size since the beginning of the century. Market gardens were gradually yielding place to new rows of houses such as Seymour Terrace, the one into which the Jerrolds moved. Despite such development, it was still felt to be quite rural: Jerrold describes himself in a letter a few years later as 'a simple Arcadian living in the wilds of Fulham'.[2]

On 10 November 1831 Jerrold became a Freemason. There was a great surge, generally, in recruitment to Freemasonry during the 1820s and 1830s[3] but we can only speculate as to why Jerrold was part of this. He may well have seen it as a good networking move in his efforts to establish himself as a respectable dramatist and journalist, given that so many leading figures in those fields were Masons, one example being Edmund Kean. Jerrold was initiated into the Bank of England Lodge 'on the introduction of Brother Crucefix', his fellow-proprietor of the *Sunday Monitor*.[4] A prominent Mason and an MD, Crucefix sat on several Grand Lodge committees and was very much the dominant figure in the Bank of England Lodge, which seems to have consisted mainly of young professional men with some leaning towards journalism and the arts (Crucefix himself wrote at least one play) as well as concern with upward social mobility. Several of the initiates, Jerrold among them, give 'Gentleman' as their occupation. Dr Crucefix campaigned vigorously for the establishment of an asylum for aged and infirm Masons (mockingly referred to by his opponents as 'a Masonic workhouse') and was also the prime mover in founding the *Freemasons' Quarterly* (1834). Jerrold strongly supported both projects; he contributed several articles (presumably unpaid) to the *Quarterly* during the first four years of its existence, and composed some poems, constructed around characteristically elaborate conceits, for recital at gala performances in aid of the planned Asylum. These are reprinted in Blanchard Jerrold's *Life*.

Jerrold's first year in Little Chelsea began auspiciously. *The Bride of*

Ludgate, played as an afterpiece at Drury Lane, had been well received. It had, said *The Times* on 9 December 1831, 'much more respectable claims to public favour than the common run of those [plays] to which we have of late been accustomed' while the *National Omnibus* pronounced that it was 'a clever, spirited, and amusing trifle' (16 December 1831). And now the far more serious and substantial *The Rent Day* was a great hit. William Dunn, the Drury Lane Treasurer, told Bulwer's 1832 Committee on Dramatic Literature that it had been 'the most profitable of anything that was played' at the theatre, including real live lions, over the whole year. Jerrold's total profit, however, as he himself informed the same Committee, was only £150, paid to him on the twenty-fifth night of its run (which lasted over forty nights) and shortly afterwards he told John Payne Collier, a staff reporter on the *Morning Chronicle*, that he 'sadly wanted employment'. He asked Collier for an introduction to the *Morning Herald* and did get work as a theatre critic on this 'grandmotherly' daily, as Vizetelly later called it. Problems continued, however. On 8 March he sold the 'perpetual copyright' of *The Rent Day* to C. Chapple for a mere £10, the same amount he got for the copyright of *Susan*,[5] and any hopes he may have had of *The Rent Day*'s successor, *The Factory Girl*, becoming a money-spinner were brutally dashed at its first night in October. On 17 November 1832 Collier noted in his diary:

> Douglas Jerrold, very much out of heart, tells me that he has recently had two new pieces rejected by the manager of Drury Lane: one he called by the very attractive title of 'Hearts and Diamonds' [this 'burletta' was eventually produced at the Olympic, 23 February 1835]. He wishes he had adhered to his profession of the Navy, where he was a midshipman until he was turned adrift by the peace. He is now above thirty [actually just under], and talks of going on the stage, where his father was an actor; but his face has not sufficient power of expression, and his figure is small, though not bad.[6]

As we shall see, going on the stage (but a stage that he at least partly controlled) was indeed one of the things Jerrold tried in his efforts to achieve some degree of financial security during this decade. Before that, however, he made his last attempts at combining the writing of plays with championship of the poor.

Martha Willis, the Servant Maid; or, Service in London, which opened the 1831 summer season at the newly rebuilt and refurbished Pavilion Theatre in Whitechapel, was in fact conceived more as a thrilling warning to the poor who formed the overwhelming majority of the Pavilion's audiences than as a championing of them. Evidently inspired by the first plate of Hogarth's *Harlot's Progress*, Jerrold's drama took up a theme which, even in its 18th-century dress, would have had an urgent and compelling interest for the Whitechapel playgoers (as also later for their counterparts in Lambeth where Davidge's Coburg soon mounted its own production). This was the 'mysteries of London' theme, dwelling on the complexity, deceptiveness and dangerousness of the huge city that envi-

roned the theatre, a city in which so many of the audience were, like
Martha Willis herself, first-generation immigrants struggling to make a
living:

> This great Metropolis teems with persons and events, which ... beggar
> invention: – every knave has his mystery, every dupe his sorrow, every street
> its romance of real life. It is these scenes of every-day experience – it is these
> characters, which are met in our hourly paths – that will be found in the
> present Drama ... .[7]

The first scene shows Martha's arrival at a London coaching inn, fresh
from the country like Hogarth's Moll Hackabout. She has come to take up
a job as a servant in a house in fashionable Brunswick Square but is
talent-spotted by Joannah, an old Gipsy woman ('A pretty lass this, and
new to the town'). 'Come with me,' she cajoles Martha, 'and I'll introduce
you to one of my friends – one of my most intimate friends.' Joannah is,
however, chased off by honest Tom Scarlet, the stage-coach guard. Jerrold
cannot be any more explicit in indicating that Joannah is a procuress
(when she next appears she seems more intent on stealing the Brunswick
Square spoons than on ruining Martha) but for anyone who knew the
Hogarth print – how large a portion of the Pavilion audience, one wonders?
– Joannah's real trade would have been clear enough. Since he can no more
show Martha becoming a whore than Dickens could, a few years later,
show Nancy in *Oliver Twist* plying her trade as the prostitute he boldly
proclaims her to be in his 1841 preface to the novel, Jerrold focuses on the
moral degeneration of Walter Speed, Martha's village sweetheart. Walter
becomes a thief and highwayman, and is in the toils of the villainous
Nunkey Gruel, outwardly a respectable pawnbroker and a devout Christian but secretly a ruthless manipulator of criminals (Jerrold is evidently
here drawing once more on Gay's *Beggar's Opera*). Through Walter Martha
finds herself innocently in possession of stolen goods, which leads to her
conviction and incarceration in a very 18th-century Newgate ('her ears
assailed by clinking chains, by horrid oaths and hideous ribaldry') waiting
to be hanged. She is, of course, saved after a bravura sequence of melodramatic effects involving a violent on-stage murder, disguise, and the suicide
of the remorseful Speed.

What lifts the play above the level of run-of-the mill melodrama is, as
usual, the liveliness and ingenuity of Jerrold's dialogue in the non-pathetic
parts (his pathos, on the other hand, like much of Dickens's, tends to be
expressed in the standard clichés of contemporary literary discourse) and
the use of 'realistic' detail as in Martha's running commentary on the
contents of her precious box while she is unpacking in the Brunswick
Square kitchen:

> there's the Charm for the Tooth Ache, and there's 'The Babes in the Wood',
> and 'Lady Godiva', and my grandmother's wedding-ring, and the needle-case
> Ralph Thomas would give me, and there's the dream book, and Doctor Watts,

and my sampler when I was a little girl. Oh, those were happy days! and here's the picture of our church and village, that Mr Carmine painted for me, and told me to keep it by me ...

This speech would have struck a chord with many a Wordsworthian Poor Susan in the audience and shows a characteristically Jerroldian 'solidity of specification' (compare William's distribution of gifts to his shipmates before going to execution in *Black Eyed Susan*). Generally, I think, *Martha Willis* would have succeeded in making the members of its working-class audience feel good about themselves as well as making them feel rather thrillingly situated in a wicked city – such glimpses as we get of the upper classes in the play show them as frivolous and self-indulgent and the only representative of the middle classes is a secretly criminal pawnbroker and money-lender. It is the hard-working poor who either survive with vindicated virtue or, if they have chanced to fall into that 'sea of pleasure – which leads to guilt, to infamy and death', die penitent. Jerrold's play presents to its audience a picture of their world as a world of feeling glowing in the brutal darkness of the money-dominated city and casting a beam of light back to that 'innocent' country home from which so many of them (or, if not them, their parents) had come. The Hogarthian-era setting provides a clear moral perspective in a way that a distractingly contemporary one might not have done (Jerrold was furious when he found Farrell, the Pavilion's manager, who played Scarlet, had initially envisaged a modern-dress production and insisted on the use of 18th century costume[8]).

The Patent Theatre play *The Rent Day* also had a pictorial point of reference more pronounced and emphatic than the Hogarthian allusions in *Martha Willis*. In this case it was two famous paintings by Sir David Wilkie which had long been popular as prints, *The Rent Day* (1807) and *Distraining for Rent* (1815). The curtain rose for the first act to show a 'realisation' of the first painting with tenant farmers gathered at the squire's hall to pay their rent to his steward, and the act finished with a tableau representing the second painting. Wilkie himself wept with pleasure at the sight of this translation of his art into another medium and praised Jerrold's 'inventive fancy ... which, like the scenic skill I have heard much admired in Massinger, advances the story step by step and without confusion to the end of the play'.[9] This overpraises the drama's ramshackle structure but the highly melodramatic plot is certainly, to borrow a phrase from Lady Bracknell, 'crowded with incident' – as one might expect of a play originally intended for the Adelphi. Audiences at this theatre, wrote F.G. Tomlins in his *Brief View of the English Drama* (1840), delighted in plays involving 'blue fire and sinking traps ... frenzied fathers, mad daughters and remorseful wives', variegated by the occasional elephant drama. Jerrold refused to agree to certain changes to *The Rent Day* (probably to sensationalise the play further) demanded by the management and took it to Drury Lane where the success of *The Bride of*

Ludgate had made him persona grata (and where he was no doubt de-lighted to find that the scenery was to be painted by his former shipmate, Clarkson Stanfield, now hailed as 'that great master ... who has elevated scene-painting into so honourable a branch of his art'[10]).

How to account for the great success of *The Rent Day*, which remained for the rest of his life Jerrold's most celebrated and enduringly popular play after *Susan*? Its fame as what the *Thespian* called (8 July 1857) 'the very *beau ideal* of a domestic drama' continued well into the second half of the century. In 1867, for example, G.H. Lewes chose it to represent 'Domestic Drama' in his *Selections from Modern British Dramatists*. The meticulously-detailed stage pictures of Wilkie's paintings were evidently a great draw but so also was the excellence of the acting. As in the case of *Susan,* Jerrold wrote his protagonist's part with a particular actor in mind, and James Wallack's Martin Heywood (a sturdy tenant farmer driven desperate after years of struggling against bad harvests, diseased flocks, a rapacious absentee landlord and a threatening taxman) was everything he could have hoped for. In his preface to the printed text, dedicated to Wilkie, Jerrold praised Wallack for his 'tasteful direction' of the production and for the 'pathos, sensibility, and manly power' of his Heywood. Review-ers commented on Wallack's 'muscular energy ... strong bold voice, and freedom of limb' and the 'homespun honesty' of his Heywood[11] (though the *Athenaeum* [28 January 1832] felt that the part was badly written and Wallack's 'admirable' acting 'evidently forced, from his being obliged, at a moment's notice, to throw himself into extremes of feeling, without having had reason or opportunity for working himself up to them'). Heywood passionately wants to continue farming the land his father and grandfa-ther farmed before him and to hand it on to his children. The bitter irony of his being confronted with a choice between destitution and the work-house at home and accepting a post as overseer of slaves on a West Indies plantation would not have been lost upon the audience. Evidently, Wallack powerfully conveyed the man's increasing desperation and his sombre performance was balanced by the lively comedy of J.P. Harley's Bullfrog, the bailiff and auctioneer whose single-minded devotion to business is a running joke throughout the play and who has many of the best and most pointed lines, as in his maladroit wooing of Polly Briggs:

Polly	Well, I'm very poor, Mr Bullfrog.
Bullf.	You are; it's your only fault.
Polly	Fault! Poverty's no crime.
Bullf.	Isn't it? well, it's so like I don't know the difference. It's a pity poor girls have pretty faces; they lead us prudent capitalists into many false reckonings.

The acting and brilliant *mise-en-scène* undoubtedly had a great deal to do with the play's initial success (Heywood became one of Wallack's great parts; after his move to America in 1845 he successfully produced *The Rent Day* at theatres throughout the States), but the drama also had a strong topical appeal. On the one hand it spoke to the anxieties aroused by the agricultural disturbances of the early 1830s, when starving mobs, supposedly under the leadership of the legendary 'Captain Swing', roamed the countryside firing the ricks of wealthy farmers and landowners, and on the other it addressed the hopes of social reconciliation and progress aroused by the Reform Bill. At one point it seems possible that Heywood will, in his despair, turn to violence. His wife, Rachel, urges patience:

Martin	I may sit down and see my little ones pine ... I may feel their wasting limbs, and hear them scream for bread; and I may stare in their white faces and tell them to be patient. Patient!
Rachel	Look not so fiercely at me, Martin ...

Rachel seems on the face of it to be another domestic icon like Susan but, as has recently been argued by Daniel Duffy, she is a more complex figure who takes on 'the role of defender of the family, the role adopted by so many women of the day' while her husband is sunk in bitter despair. Moreover, her brave but 'unwomanly' extra-mural action (breaking into the young squire's bedroom at night to warn him of murderous robbers) leads to economic security for the family, but only after she has had to suffer the agony of harsh rejection by her husband who misinterprets her action.[12] Grantley, the squire, has been an absentee landlord, but has now returned incognito (an echo here from Shakespeare's *Measure for Measure*?) to observe for himself the abuse of his tenants by the unjust steward Crumbs, who is making a very good thing out of what he contrives to make fall from the rich man's table. In the end Grantley reveals his identity, dismisses Crumbs and begs forgiveness from his tenants, promising amends ('I will, henceforth, reside on my lands') and rewards Rachel for her brave deed by granting Martin the freehold of his farm. Many would surely have seen this as a hopeful paradigm of the juster but (as regards distribution of power) still fundamentally unchanged society that might result from the Reform Bill.

The Rent Day has all the hallmarks of Jerrold's earlier Minor Theatre melodramas – an 'angel in the house' threatened by lechery on the part of minor or secondary villains, a chief villain whose nature has been warped by suffering (Crumbs's beautiful young wife was seduced long ago by Grantley's father and he has determined to revenge himself by ruining the son), an authority-figure who repents of his sins of omission or commission and low-comedy characters full of exuberant repartee. It also has a sensational denouement, of more than usual preposterousness (an old arm-chair that belonged to Heywood's grandfather, and which he is struggling to save from being seized by Bullfrog, bursts open and out tumbles a small fortune in gold and money-bags complete with a note from the old man bequeathing the hoard to his grandsons). But its 'realization' of Wilkie's admired paintings (far more elaborate than the echoing of Hogarth in *Martha Willis*) gave it considerable cultural cachet. This, together with its exaltation of the quintessentially backbone-of-England figure of Heywood and of what we would now call 'family values' would have given it, for contemporary audiences, a dignity and seriousness that made it worthy of performance in one of the great national theatres. Jerrold had by this time established a reputation for writing original dramas and many reviewers noted with satisfaction that he continued in this vein in *The Rent Day*. The *Morning Chronicle* wrote on 26 January 1832:

> We always look with more than usual anxiety to the result of Mr Jerrold's dramatic experiments ... They are not merely French kick-shaws – dishes tossed up again for the second day; he draws upon his own resources, and if they are not very great, they are at least his own ... If Mr Jerrold only gives us a stew, there is some solid English meat in it, the vegetables are in just proportion, and there is a good sprinkling, too, both of pepper and salt. He deserves all encouragement ... .

The *Athenaeum* might regret (28 January 1832) Jerrold's introduction of 'some very prosy disquisitions upon the Slave Trade – Emigration – the Game Laws, and sundry other Parliamentary topics, which had been better left to be discussed "in another place"' but Leigh Hunt's *Tatler* applauded him on 26 January for being unafraid to touch on topics 'likely to be voted bores by the coxcombs in St James's Street'. Whatever the critics said, good or bad, the fact was that the play was a decided hit and audiences flocked to Drury Lane to see it; no wonder that David Morris at the Haymarket pilfered it for his theatre later in the year.[13] It may also be said to have established the domestic drama as the dominant form in the theatre of the 1830s and 1840s – 'a poor thing but mine own', Jerrold is supposed to have remarked of this genre.[14]

Encouraged by the reception of *The Rent Day*, Jerrold set to work on another social drama. In *The Factory Girl*, he turned to the sufferings of children working in the factories of the North, responding no doubt to all the publicity this subject was attracting in the wake of the harrowing report, presented in August, of a Parliamentary Committee of Enquiry. (This Committee resulted from a vigorous campaign conducted by its Chairman, the radical Tory MP for Aldborough, Yorkshire, Michael Sadler.) As in *The Rent Day* Jerrold provided a strong domestic centre to the play. Skelton, a poor widower, agonises over the fate of his young children toiling in a factory to keep the family from starvation. The domestic icon role is filled by an older child, his daughter Catherine, and she is duly sexually threatened by the machinations of Husk, the brutal factory-manager, who is the 'unjust steward' figure equivalent to Crumbs in *The Rent Day*. There is a comic part for Harley, that of Wynkyn de Worde, a book-pedlar and 'humble illuminator of the people' which provides the same sort of verbal slapstick comedy as did his Bullfrog role in *The Rent Day*. Like Grantley, the land-owner in that play, Ridley the factory-owner is essentially be-nevolent and dismisses the villainous Husk (who is a straightforward villain, however, not a man warped by an injury done him like Crumbs) at the end promising to be more careful in his choice of manager in future. Skelton and his family, suddenly discovered to be related to wealthy friends of Ridley's, are lifted out of poverty as abruptly, and even more improbably, than the Heywoods, and all ends happily – though the audience is gently reminded in the play's closing words of the continuing 'hard privations' and 'daily sorrows' suffered by child workers in factories and asked to spare 'one pitying thought, one sympathizing tear' for their plight.[15]

Given such similar ingredients, and embellished, as was *The Rent Day*, with Stanfield's beautiful scenery ('A Wild Romantic Scene', 'Another View in the West Riding', etc.[16]), *The Factory Girl* might have been expected to be received as favourably at Drury Lane as the earlier play had been. In fact, it was a catastrophe. Jerrold wrote later, in a note appended to his sketch of 'The Factory Child' in *Heads of the People* (1840), that the play was 'cruelly maimed the first night, and mortally killed on its second representation'. Writing after the publication of Dickens's *Oliver Twist* and Mrs Trollope's factory novel, *Michael Armstrong, the Factory Boy*, he claimed that his drama suffered from being '*before the fashion*': 'it was not then *la mode* to affect an interest for the "coarse and vulgar" details of human life'. This might seem borne out by the *Examiner*'s review of the ill-fated production on 14 October 1832:

> The object of the piece ... is beyond all praise; and it is pursued with characteristic fearlessness; but the means employed are too coarse, and too little relieved by graceful or poetic touches ... Mr JERROLD is, in the drama, what the late Mr CRABBE was in poetry – a bold and faithful copier of some of the least agreeable points of nature .... His nautical dramas ... are more agreeable ... [because] the romance which hovers about a seaman's habits and life, insensibly relieves the pressure of wrongs and sufferings, which also might be found too real.

It is difficult, however, to reconcile these comments with the actual text of *The Factory Girl*. This begins with what the less sympathetic critic of the *National Omnibus* (12 October 1832) thought was altogether too 'poetic' a touch, Skelton's apostrophe to the rising sun and praise of the beauties of nature 'in something like blank verse'. Also, far from finding the presentation of famished factory children too grimly 'real', the audience, according to this same critic, was 'perverse enough to laugh at the gang of half-starved wretches who were collected on the stage at the summons of their "dreadful bell"'.

The trouble would seem to have been that the subject was an impossible one to handle on the legitimate stage because it was altogether *too* topical, too specifically related to an ongoing debate in Parliament. Even when it was presented in the purely sentimental and non-subversive way that Jerrold presents it (and which was partly, no doubt, the result of having to keep the Lord Chamberlain's office happy, but also expressive of Jerrold's own brand of sentimental radicalism), handling the topic at all inevitably called forth conflicting political reponses from the Drury Lane audience, which tended to be more mixed with regard to class than audiences in the minor theatres.[17] When Harley stepped forward to announce the piece for repetition there was, according to *The Times* on 8 October 1832,

> a storm of mingled applause and opposition. Some gentlemen in the dress circle were remarkably violent in their disapprobation, and at one time there was every appearance of an approaching battle royal. This confusion lasted for several minutes ....

These conflicting reponses were reflected in the reviews. The Tory *Times* thought that:

> A more ticklish subject (colonial slavery alone excepted) could not have been selected for scenic representation. A play founded on an exaggeration of factory horrors, however cleverly written, was sure to excite a host of opposition. ...
>   Mr Jerrold seems to have dramatised the well-known speech of 'the great Mr Sadler, of Leeds;' and he is likely to gain very little, either of fame or profit, by his labour.

The Liberal *Morning Chronicle*, on the other hand, pronounced the piece 'decidedly successful' (8 October 1832) and minimised the opposition:

> Some two or three dissentients there were in one of the boxes of the dress circle, but their objections were attributed to personal feelings, and the applause they endeavoured to check by cries of 'Off' were converted by those cries themselves into general cheering.

The Drury Lane management braved the storm for two nights but then withdrew the play, a financial blow to Jerrold as well, of course, as something of a humiliation after the success of *The Rent Day*. Nor, apparently, were they prepared to risk another play by him, even of a very different kind. No wonder Collier found him 'very much out of heart' in November and thinking it might be a better idea to turn actor than to go on struggling for continuity of success as a 'legitimate' dramatist. In the event, he continued to write plays but seems to have recognised that the success he wanted was not compatible with using the domestic drama to express his radicalism. Looking back to the success the previous winter of *The Bride of Ludgate*, he seems to have resolved to concentrate in future on this kind of play and, in place of exposés of particular social injustices, to present the more generalised kind of social criticism of middle and upper class mores associated with the comedies of Sheridan – 'high comedy', as it was often called, to distinguish it from 'low comedy' or farce. 'Let Mr Jerrold ... deal with *human nature generally*,' the *National Omnibus* reviewer of *The Factory Girl* had urged, 'and he will find no lack of sympathy on our parts.' But Jerrold did not abandon his championship of the poor and powerless. More opportunities were opening up for him in the field of Radical or left-wing journalism, and this provided a much less restrictive and volatile outlet for his social criticism than the theatre. He had no less than eighteen plays produced over the next nine years, but they were nearly all comedies, farces or 'burlettas'; and the three exceptions were not social-problem dramas but respectively: a two-act tragedy about a gambler set in the French Revolution, *The Hazard of the Die* (Drury Lane, 17 February 1835); a one-act historical 'Tragic Drama' in which he himself played the leading role, *The Painter of Ghent* (Strand, 25 April 1836); and a domestic-drama vehicle for the French actress Céleste, *The Mother* (Haymarket, 31 May 1838).

All the two or three act comedies proper (as opposed to the two farces and two 'burlettas'[18]) have period settings, either Restoration or 18th-century. The hundred years 1680-1780 was the time during which wit, the life-blood of 'high' comedy, was believed to have flourished most brilliantly both in fashionable life and in literature (notably, of course, in the work of Congreve and other Restoration dramatists). Hence any dramatist in the 1830s who set a play in this period and labelled it a comedy was signalling that witty dialogue was intended to be one of the chief strengths and pleasures of the piece. It was not until the successful productions of Bulwer Lytton's *Money* (Haymarket, 8 December 1840) and Boucicault's *London Assurance* (Covent Garden, 4 March 1841) that there was general acceptance that a 'legitimate' high comedy, or comedy of manners, might have a contemporary setting and not lose its cachet. Meanwhile, the difficulty for Jerrold and other writers was that the great age of the flourishing of wit to which they harked back had had a very different moral climate – most especially, so far as the Restoration period was concerned, with regard to sexual transgressions. Leigh Hunt in a later preface to his novel *Sir Ralph Esher; or, Memoirs of a Gentleman of the Court of Charles II* (first published 1832) said he had originally projected a book entitled *The Wits of the Age of Charles the Second* but had to abandon it because Rochester and his fellows were 'persons not producible in good company'. To make Charles II and Nell Gwynne 'producible' Jerrold has in his two comedies featuring 'the royal libertine'[19] to play down – indeed, almost wholly suppress – Charles's well-documented licentiousness, however directly he may refer to it outside the text of the plays. In his preface to the second of them, *Nell Gwynne* (Covent Garden, 9 January 1833), for example, he calls Charles 'an unprincipled voluptuary'. In the plays themselves the king appears as a shrewd but essentially benevolent figure, not particularly witty, much given to mildly amorous pranks that involve moving among his subjects in disguise; in *The Bride of Ludgate* he shows his good nature and susceptibility to sentiment by bringing about the happy union of the play's young lovers; in *Nell Gwynne* he rescues Nell from marriage to a lecherous old lawyer. The action of the play tactfully predates Nell's becoming Charles's mistress; she appears as a sweet-natured orange-girl who dreams about getting the king to found a hospital for old soldiers at

Chelsea. In *Beau Nash* (Haymarket, 16 July 1834) Jerrold presents the so-called 'King of Bath', the dictatorial arbiter of elegance there from about 1705 to about 1745, and regarded as a type of the 'heartless' frivolity that characterised 18th-century high culture, as yet another essentially good-hearted authority-figure who exposes thieves and hypocrites and brings young lovers together. In his combative prefaces to the published texts of the plays Jerrold parades his historical sources to justify his interpretation of Charles, Nell and Nash whilst also asserting the dramatist's right 'to fix on a historical circumstance as the means of developing imaginary events'.[20]

There is, in fact, scant evidence of historical imagination in these comedies. The characters and plot-situations are for the most part the familiar dramatis personae of the Comedy of Manners – engaging young lovers and their sympathising confidants, arbitrary old fathers, uncles or other guardian figures who want to marry the heroine to some grotesque elderly suitor for his wealth or status, comic servants and/or petty officials, and minor characters representing various social vices and follies. They wear period costumes which grace the actors ('Mrs Nisbett looks charming with her hoop and powder, and black sparkling eyes') and the settings provide opportunities for some of those 'living history' tableaux so beloved by 19th-century audiences – the exterior and interior of Drury Lane in Nell Gwynne's time, a grand ball in the Bath Assembly Rooms, the London Stock Exchange in 1707 (*The White Milliner*, Covent Garden, 9 February 1841). But it is all a matter of costume and scenery and a peppering of historical allusions – references to linkmen and so on. In his long laudatory notice of *Beau Nash* in the *New Monthly Magazine* (August 1834) Forster acclaims Jerrold for bringing Nash back to life 'in his habit as he lived, with his tawdry dress and his white hat ... on the real scene, with the real associates of his life around him' but Jerrold's Nash is, for all his white hat, very much a man of the 1830s – in his amiable old man's eccentricities, sentimental benevolence towards young lovers, and zeal against all rascals a recognisable contemporary of Mr Pickwick's. Nor did Jerrold refrain from obvious contemporary allusion when opportunity served. In *Beau Nash* both Nash himself and Thespis Claptrap, an actor (Jerrold was certainly not one to stint himself when it came to pointedly comic nomenclature) comment in a very 1830s' way on the lamentable state of the theatre. Nash observes, 'A good murder is now the very life of a drama', adding a characteristically Jerroldian conceit: 'Thus, if a playwright would fill his purse, he should take a hint from the sugar-baker and always refine his commodity with blood'; and Claptrap says, 'I know the most refin'd folk who'd not budge a foot to hear Garrick, would give a guinea each, nay, mob for a whole morning, to see a Greenlander eat seal's flesh and swallow whale-oil.'

Some of these comedies were more successful than others but all passed Talfourd's nine nights test[21] and some like *The Housekeeper; or, The White Rose* (Haymarket, 17 July 1835), which centred on Jacobite intrigues in

1722, had long runs and many subsequent revivals (the *Times* obituary of Jerrold ranked *The Housekeeper* next in popularity among all his plays after *Susan* and *The Rent Day*, and Balfe in the 1850s was very keen on turning it into an opera[22]). Jerrold was constantly praised for writing original pieces (in his preface to *The Bride of Ludgate* in Cumberland's British Theatre George Daniel called this 'one step towards dramatic reform most praiseworthy; and to the *ultra translators* intolerable!') and for what one, admittedly friendly, newspaper called the 'very superior tone' of his productions (*Morning Herald*, quoted in the *Examiner* on 20 December 1835). Reviewer after reviewer praised the wittiness of his dialogue, 'wholly distinct from that low humour or coarse ribaldry which is generally put forward as a substitute for wit in the productions of modern playwrights', 'admirable for point, neatness, and appropriateness', full of 'smart hits and sharp allusions, little bits of piquant satire and some excellent *equivoques*', and so on.[23] Here follows an example of the kind of dialogue that elicited such encomia.

In *The Housekeeper* Maynard, the rich young hero, who has become a deeply studious hermit in his own mansion, is reproached by the heroine (disguised as a housekeeper) for the state of his study:

Felicia	But, sir, only look at the cobwebs and spiders.
Maynard	I'm partial to cobwebs – I encourage spiders.
Fel.	But then, the mice – they gallop about like little ponies. Why don't you keep a cat, sir?
May.	A cat! No, even in little things I hope I have the spirit of a philanthropist.
Fel.	Oh! You prefer a trap? But if learning were wisdom, your mice should be too wise to be caught.
May.	Too wise! How?
Fel.	Because 'twould seem, by some of your volumes, that the mice devoured as many books as their master. [*Showing book with its leaves half-destroyed*]
May.	[*Taking book*] Alack, poor Homer! If Pythagoras' creed were true, and every mouse an annotator, they couldn't have used the Iliad more unmercifully.

This scholarly joke against scholars would, of course, both flatter and divert the audience in its assumption that they would know all about Pythagoras and editions of Homer. Jerrold's plays were also celebrated for their satirical one-liners, such as 'Depend on't, there's nothing like a prison pavement to ring our old friends upon' (*Doves in a Cage*) and their 'witty' conceits such as Sneezum's words in *The White Milliner* to a magistrate who had once sentenced him for being a rogue and a vagabond, 'I was found guilty of taking another man's doorstep for my pillow, and burning starlight for rushlight'. He resorts to puns less often in his comedies than in his farces but they do occur, though usually given a witty Jerroldian twist. Having been told that another character is protected 'under the wings of the law', Sneezum replies, 'Oh, the law's a pretty bird, and has charming

wings! 'Twould be quite a bird of paradise, if it didn't carry such a terrible
bill.'

In some respects these 'witty' comedies of Jerrold's resemble the highly
conceited verse-dramas of Christopher Fry that enjoyed a period of popularity during the late 1940s and early 1950s and were praised and blamed
for similar reasons. Reviewers of Jerrold admired his word-play but would
also comment that there was 'a little too much sentence-making among the
characters', that Jerrold, like Congreve, 'made wit too much the business,
instead of the ornament of his comedies', that the one 'great fault' of the
plays was that 'all his characters are *equally witty*', and so on.[24] Also, that
there was too little action in them, no 'startling situations'. To this last
charge Jerrold wrote a furious rebuttal in his preface to Duncombe's
edition of *Beau Nash*:

> ... doubtless a comedy of *manners* would be a much better comedy, were it a
> melodrama. 'Startling situations' have been so frequent, that the public are
> now taught ... to consider mere men and women mere common-places; and
> mere pictures of life, mere every-day dullness ... audiences are to be treated
> not as a body of persons in sound moral health, but as a convocation of
> opium-eaters. A dramatist is now to be 'a dreamer of dreams', and not an
> illustrator of truths.

When noting the success of these comedies of the 1830s we should
always keep in mind that, as had been the case with *Susan* and with *The
Rent Day,* Jerrold was fortunate in having some of the best actors and
actresses of the day (each with his or her own special line of business)
creating his characters. Particularly outstanding were two beautiful come-
diennes, Madame Vestris and Louisa Nisbett, also the unrivalled William
Farren, whose 'crusty old bachelors, jealous old husbands ... or ancient
fops with ghastly pretensions to amiability' won such praise from, among
others, Hazlitt and also Lewes in his *On Actors and the Art of Acting*, and
three consummate broad-comedy actors, Ben Webster, J.B. Buckstone and
Robert Keeley. The latter's drag performance as Orange Moll, Nell's
competitor in *Nell Gwynne*, was particularly relished. So was what George
Daniel called his 'forlorn, simple-hearted, shrewd' Rags, the parsimonious
Pinchbeck's servant in *The Golden Calf* (New Strand Theatre, 30 June
1832), in which he would bring the house down by his handling of such
exchanges as the following (Rags has just told Chrystal, the play's *raison-
neur* figure, that one of his chief enjoyments is seeing his master's pocket
picked):

Chrystal	And these are your pleasures?
Rags	In the day time. At night the mice scamper about the cup-boards, and then I sit in the dark and enjoy their disappointment.

Most of these star actors and actresses seem to have been on good terms with Jerrold despite the harsh things he sometimes wrote about their profession (his satirical 'Full Length' portrait of 'The Actor' in the *Monthly Magazine* for February 1829, for example). Farren seems to have been an exception. Jerrold blamed him for the failure of *The Witch-Finder* at Drury Lane: 'Mr Farren,' he wrote to Mary Russell Mitford, 'first injured it by his extravagant praise, and then made the mischief complete by his utter misconception of the part.'[25] On the eve of the first performance of *The Bride of Ludgate* Farren, who was to play Charles II, walked out and later, despite Jerrold's published expressions of gratitude to him for his fine creation of the 'long and most arduous' title role in *Beau Nash*, he appeared as a witness for the Haymarket manager David Morris when Jerrold sued the latter for more money for that play. In court Farren, as reported by *The Times* on 18 May 1835, did not absolutely deny that he had called *Beau Nash* 'dull as ditchwater' and backed up Morris's claim that it had not attracted audiences; nevertheless, he continued to perform in Jerrold's work, creating several major roles in the more ambitious comedies of the 1840s.

It is surprising that Jerrold's relations with individual actors were not more prickly since he so vociferously resented star actors domineering over the playwrights who provided their scripts and was always infuriated when they wanted to alter the dialogue. In his *Monthly Magazine* piece already cited, Jerrold had castigated actors for this and suggested the reason for it:

> An Actor, in the full enjoyment of his art, must experience the most intense and violent delight. He fairly bathes himself in the plaudits showered around him; he seems saturated with commendation .... The consciousness of self-importance knocks hardly at his heart; his pulses are at full gallop; his very being is multiplied. It is to this cause that an Actor has less admiration for his author than has the uninitiated man. The Actor loses all recollection of the dramatist in self: he is persuaded that he has snatched the unformed lump from the author, and, by his own feelings and emotions, given shape and beauty to the plastic mass! It is *he* who has *made* the part.

Charles Mathews the Younger remembered Jerrold as 'a fearful instance' of the playwright who, the moment an actor suggested 'the slightest alteration, the cutting of a speech here, the insertion of a few words there', would 'tuck his play under his arm and proclaim his intention of taking it elsewhere'.[26] Jerrold also writhed with anger over the gross disproportion between the high earnings of leading actors and actresses and the meagre rewards that accrued to those who provided them with the means to ply their trade. The playwright, he wrote at the end of an article entitled 'The Rights of Dramatists' in the *Monthly Magazine* for May 1832, may 'build a house of gold for the actor, and be himself the Lazarus at its gates'. He lost no opportunity to remind T.P. Cooke of the huge discrepancy between their earnings from *Black Eyed Susan*; hearing that a play of his, *Jack Dolphin* (presumably another nautical-drama vehicle for Cooke – the script seems not to have survived) was to be produced at the Coburg by Davidge by arrangement with Cooke, he wrote the latter a stiff letter demanding some remuneration: 'I have written quite enough for the high profits and popularity of others with but the most paltry pecuniary advantages to myself (I got sixty pounds by *Black-Eyed Susan!*')[27]

As might be expected, Jerrold was pugnaciously in the forefront of the campaign for theatre reform that was waged throughout the 1830s, a campaign focusing mainly on the abolition of the Patent Theatres' asserted but now very threadbare monopoly of the 'legitimate' drama, and the securing of better payment plus some copyright protection for dramatists (censorship was very much a side issue and one doomed to remain unresolved until 1968). He attended meetings during the winter of 1831/32 to consider the petition to Parliament being organised by Thomas J. Serle (who as actor, sometime provincial theatre-manager and minor dramatist had pretty well boxed the compass of the contemporary theatre industry) and in the month that Bulwer presented the petition to Parliament Jerrold wrote the already-cited piece for the *Monthly Magazine* which was a review of T.J. Thackeray's pamphlet *On Theatrical Emancipation, and the Rights of Dramatic Authors.* Thackeray, another Haymarket dramatist and a cousin of the future great novelist, had shown how such things were better ordered in France; there a prolific playwright like Eugène Scribe could earn 'from three to four thousand pounds yearly'. Jerrold, ironically comparing English writers to clergy in the Established Church (he could not leave the bishops alone for long), comments:

we should call the dramatist the poor drudge of a curate in the establishment of letters: the poet, the novelist, the historian, nay, the writer of a *confectioner's oracle*, is secure in the fruits of his see, his deanery, his rectorship, his fat living – but the dramatist, dependent on caprice, is not insured even his 'forty pounds a-year'; he is every now and then stopped on the highways, and the little he may have in his purse, rifled by thieves … it would not be more monstrous were a bill to be passed, exempting robbers from punishment who should attack curates, and hanging the knaves who should rob the higher dignities of the church; than in the present state of the law, which guards poems, novels, histories, cookery books, – and only leaves unregarded, plays.

He was one of the chief witnesses to appear before Bulwer's Select Committee on Dramatic Literature which in the summer of 1832 took evidence from thirty-nine people connected with the theatre industry, and when, as a result of the Committee's investigations, the Dramatic Copyright Act passed into law in June 1833, he and Serle were very active in helping J.R. Planché to form the Dramatic Authors' Society.[28] This was intended to ensure that playwrights would get the fees to which they were now entitled – 'it is only by acting *in a society* that the managers are to be fought', Jerrold wrote to a fellow-dramatist, Joseph Lunn.[29] The Society was founded on 12 July and Jerrold's third son, born a few days earlier, was christened Thomas Serle Jerrold in honour of Serle who was one of his godfathers.

The new Act was intended to benefit dramatists by ending the situation whereby a play, once published, was considered, as David Morris had told Bulwer's Committee, to be in the public domain and available for production by anyone free of charge. It was also intended to put a stop to the illicit copying of a play before publication by shorthand writers taking it down verbatim in the theatre, then selling transcriptions of the text. Jerrold had complained about this to the Committee, mentioning a particular agency office, Mr Kenneth's on the corner of Bow Street, which would 'supply any gentleman with any manuscript on the lowest terms'. A country manager had written to tell him that he would willingly have paid him £5 for a copy of *The Rent Day* had he not already bought one from 'some stranger' for £2. Jerrold had no doubt that this copy had derived ultimately from Kenneth's office.

The intentions of the Act were to a large extent frustrated, however, when in the following year Lord Chief Justice Denman ruled in the case of Cumberland v. Planché that copyrights sold to a publisher conferred performance rights as well as printing ones so that fees went to publishers rather than playwrights which, since the Act applied retrospectively to plays published up to ten years before, proved very profitable for Duncombe, Cumberland, Richardson and Co. New plays by members of the Society were better protected in that they were published for their authors by John Miller of 13 Henrietta Street, Covent Garden, whom the Society appointed as its agent and secretary. The first two titles to appear in 'Miller's Modern Acting Drama' were *Nell Gwynne* and *The Housekeeper* and Jerrold asked Forster to get them noticed in the *True Sun*: 'I publish these dramas on my own account; and of course all publicity – the more especially as they are now being played – helps the sale.'[30] Priced at either one or two shillings, these editions were not commercially published but intended for specialised distribution to theatre professionals. At least two more of Jerrold's plays, *Beau Nash* and *The Wedding Gown*, were included in Miller's series but by 1835 he had evidently decided to try for a more general sale in a joint venture with his old publisher Duncombe. Another two-act comedy *The Schoolfellows* (Queen's Theatre, Tottenham Court Road, 16 February 1835) appeared as the first in a series entitled 'Jerrold's Original Dramas' – Jerrold, one imagines, would have been quite insistent on the qualifying adjective – which formed a sub-section of Duncombe's ongoing 'British Theatre' series. 'This Edition', ran Duncombe's announcement,

will comprise ... a complete Collection of the Acted Dramas of Mr DOUGLAS JERROLD, to be followed (arrangements having been made with the Proprietor to that effect,) by the new Dramas of the same Author, as they may be represented. The price of each number (illustrated by FINDLAY), one to be published monthly, will be Sixpence. A portrait of the Author, with titles, &c. will be given with the last number of the First Volume.[31]

99

The text of *The Schoolfellows* was prefaced by an open letter to Serle reprinted in Blanchard Jerrold's *Life* in which Jerrold, freshly aggrieved by the play's rejection by both Covent Garden and Drury Lane at the hands of the same reader, a veteran hack dramatist called Reynolds, once more bitterly assails the Patent Theatres' monopoly. He fumes that 'a writer who, unassisted by a troop of horse, a conflagration, or a cataract, trusts merely to the conduct of his fable, his words, and his characters, must fail, at least in the treasury sense, at either Drury Lane or Covent Garden'. Prices of admission being 'nearly double' those at the Minor Theatres, who, 'unless it be to see some extraordinary raree-show', would pay the higher charges? As to the minor theatres, they are 'with only two exceptions ... at the mercy of the common informer every night'. With a characteristic Jerroldian flourish, he rebuts the argument that his play has only been successful (it has been performed twenty-seven times) because it has been playing to an unsophisticated, easily-pleased plebeian audience:

> Though little disposed to make the Court Guide the only test of judgment, I might have crowded into the page a long list of lords and ladies of every degree of nobility, who – for their names have gemmed the paragraphs of newspapers – have assisted, to use a French phrase, at the unlawful representation of *The Schoolfellows* at an unlicensed theatre. This is no extravagance; the tyro in heraldry might gain most discursive knowledge from the coach panels that are nightly wedged in Tottenham Street.

At least eight more of Jerrold's plays (including *The Rent Day*, the copyright of which he seems to have been able to buy back) appeared in Duncombe's 'Jerrold's Original Dramas' series, though sometimes, it would appear, he had to goad Duncombe into action. On 26 January 1836 he wrote to ask Duncombe if he intended to publish *Doves in a Cage* (Adelphi, 18 December 1835) 'on the same terms as the others'. If so, he adds, 'there is no time to be lost ... *if not* write immediately as I must publish elsewhere' and concludes, 'That the other plays have not appeared has been, and continues to be, money out of my pocket.'[32] The front wrapper of No. 9 in the series, *The White Milliner*, announces, 'March 1st [1841] will be published, price 4s. 6d., vol. 1 of JERROLD'S PLAYS' but no trace of such a publication has ever been found. We must presume that, like the 'New Work by Mr Douglas Jerrold' called *Stray Papers,* announced as 'In the Press and shortly [to] be published' on the back wrapper of No. 6 of Duncombe's 'Jerrold's Original Dramas' series, *The Painter of Ghent*,[33] this was another of those abortive projects that seemed to haunt Jerrold's early career.

Chapter Six

The Brownrigg Years (2): Journalism

1831-1841

By now Jerrold was certainly earning more from his plays than in his Coburg/Surrey days, both as regards payment by managers (he earned £200 from *Nell Gwynne*, for example) and as regards the sale of printed texts, but being a dramatist was still a penurious business, 'a devil of a trade', as George Colman the Younger once described it. Jerrold had constantly to look to journalism to provide a more reliable source of income. In its 27 December 1834 issue the satirical weekly *Figaro in London* picked up a rumour that Jerrold intended giving up dramatic authorship altogether and, referring to him as 'a great genius', commented

> we can hardly believe that this gentleman, who is the first, if not the most prolific, of comic writers, should be induced to abandon a pursuit from which he does derive so much deserved fame, and from which he ought to derive very considerable emolument ....

The *Figaro*'s concern was premature but economic necessity was compelling Jerrold to develop a more reliable and regular source of income through the extension of his journalistic activities. As noted above, he got work as a drama critic on the *Morning Herald*, but it seems that his joint proprietorship of the *Sunday Monitor* with Dr Crucefix had not worked out well. According to an anonymous but authoritative-sounding memoir of Jerrold published in the *Illustrated Review* on 15 May 1872,

> considerable discomfort and anxiety, to say nothing of the pecuniary losses involved in the undertaking, also resulted from this ill-advised partnership. Happily, however, time arrived full soon for its dissolution. From being part-proprietor, and we may presume for the time being co-editor of the *Monitor* Jerrold became sub-editor of Mr Wakely's *Ballot* newspaper.

Thomas Wakely, the medical reformer and founder of the *Lancet*, was a vigorous campaigner for Parliamentary reform and founded the *Ballot*, a weekly, in January 1831. He proclaimed in its first number, 'We shall attack the boroughmongering Tories on one side, and the boroughmongering Whigs on the other, until their tottering battlements are levelled with the dust' and rejoiced that 'the light of wisdom has at last fallen on the world and man, perceiving the blessings of liberty, is determined to be

101

free'. For all its political preoccupations the paper found room for extensive theatre coverage, a great deal of which was written by Jerrold, who may well have been also responsible for a column of general editorial comment called 'The Easy Chair' which appeared from 30 October 1831 onwards. According to his son, he also wrote at this exciting time when the fate of the Reform Bill hung in the balance, 'a violent political pamphlet that was suppressed'. When in November 1832 the *Ballot* merged with Fonblanque's *Examiner* Jerrold continued as sub-editor on that paper. That he retained Wakeley's affectionate regard is shown by a letter Wakely wrote to him eighteen years later:

> My dear old Jerrold, ... I shan't see you again – God bless your witty old brain – for a long time, as I am going to make the tour of England ... God preserve you, Jerrold. You are one of the bright lights of the day![1]

During 1832-33, and possibly later, Jerrold contributed some brief satirical essays to the *Athenaeum*, writing to its editor, C.W. Dilke, after he had accepted a piece called 'The Poulterer's Hare',

> I should be glad to become one of your poulterers, and serve you with anything that may fall in my way from a white elephant to a welch rarebit, – a roc to a house-sparrow.[2]

He also worked on a new Liberal daily, the *True Sun*, which began publication on 5 March 1832. Laman Blanchard was appointed the literary editor of the new paper and the theatre editor was Forster. Writing about the latter in *Temple Bar* many years later (April 1876), R.H. Horne recalls a scene in the *True Sun* offices that he calls 'worthy of our best school-boy days':

> a dispute arose between Jerrold and Forster on the acting of a certain play, concerning which the latter made some contemptuous remark ... and concluded by pushing Jerrold 'out of his way', in a half-jocose, half-scornful manner. In an instant his slight-made but sinewy opponent, with an equally jocose ejaculation, darted upon the burly critic, threw him face-forward upon the editorial table among the inkstands, 'copy, and proofs', and administered a rapid and ridiculous castigation. With loud execrations the offended critic extricated himself, and, with an inflamed countenance, made headlong towards a large jug on the washing-stand, while Jerrold rushed out of the room and flew down the stairs, pursued by Forster, who discharged the contents of the jug with such force that the jug accompanied the water, leaving the handle in his hand ....

There seems to be something boisterously schoolboyish, too, about the little satirical weekly called *Punch in London*, which Duncombe began publishing with Jerrold as editor on 14 January 1832. Spielmann says this project was proposed to Jerrold by the printing firm of Mills, Jowett and Mills of Bolt Court (the second largest such firm in London, according to the journalistic historian Joseph Hatton) but he seems to be confusing it with another idea for a comic paper using the name Punch which, we learn from Hatton, Jerrold had been exploring with Mills *fils*. Young Mills was a friend of Jerrold's and long afterwards told Hatton that the two of them 'had frequently discussed ideas for new illustrated papers'. One day, having seen a Punch show in the street, Mills suggested *Punch* as a good title for a new comic paper, after which he and Jerrold 'went into the business of the thing, and discussed it at various times for a considerable period'. Mills showed Hatton a letter he had had from Jerrold written from Augustus Square and dated only 'Monday evening' reporting a sudden problem that had arisen:

> Your letter found me engaged on a prospectus for 'Punch'. I sallied out for Bolt Court in the hope of meeting you, but on my way called at Dymock's, the news-vendor's, when in taking up 'The Satirist' what was my horror to discover our idea anticipated in an advertisement, running thus – 'PUNCHINELLO, on FRIDAY NEXT'. I made enquiries and found that it was to be started against the 'Figaro'.
>
> Of course, in this instance, so far as the name of Punch is concerned, our scheme must fall to the ground. ... Cannot another good name be procured?

As *Punchinello* ran for only ten numbers and its demise was reported in *Figaro in London* on 7 April 1832, Jerrold must have seen this advertisement in early to mid January and, as *Punch in London* appeared on 14 January, it seems that he must have almost immediately had second thoughts about whether he could still use the name of Punch. He evidently got his old publisher Duncombe, who could probably move faster than the Mills firm, to rush out *Punch in London* pretty well simultaneously with *Punchinello* as a rival challenger to Gilbert à Beckett's weekly *Figaro in London* which had begun publication on 10 December 1831.[3]

Punch in London was published by Duncombe 'for the proprietors' and cost the same as *Figaro*, one penny, for the same amount of text (though in octavo rather than quarto size), but the crude woodcut illustrations were much inferior to Robert Seymour's in *Figaro*. For the first number Jerrold wrote a bravura editorial manifesto in the character of Mr Punch, conceived as the embodiment of all chicanery and hypocrisy and the great prompter of all human stupidity and cruelty:

> when aiding or acting for the great, I generally give my services under a feigned name; it is enough for me that my acts are fully impressed with the character of *Punch*. For instance, who, think you, planned Buckingham Palace – Nash? Nonsense – it was I, *Punch*! Who writes the speeches for the member for Boroughbridge – WETHERELL? Pooh – *Punch*! Who talks in 'the unknown tongue' – Young barley-meal fed ladies from Scotland? Pshaw – *Punch*! Who writes the 'leading articles' for the Morning Post – Mr. Nokes? No – *Punch, Punch, Punch*! He, in this tricksy world is the grand originator. What! Now-a-days *Punch* can ride in his coach-and-six, whilst a Solon would walk in the gutter.

𝕻𝖚𝖓𝖈𝖍'𝖘 𝕻𝖚𝖓𝖈𝖍-𝕭𝖔𝖜𝖑.

... now I deal in religious tracts, and now I hawk about a petition against Reform, and a prayer for the eternity of Bishops – Now I am seen mounted in Hyde Park, or drinking Burgundy at the Athenaeum ... .[4]

It is evident that nearly every monarch has large dealings with *Punch*. I shall, in a future number, publish some letters of my brother Miguel [Dom Miguel, the violently reactionary King of Portugal, 1828-33] – they are written in the prepared skins of liberals with their own blood (Mig. has always a fresh supply) ... besides these I have some curious papers relative to the Polish campaign, as I, *Punch*, under the name of Glory, (with what fine names I have tricked mankind to be sure) led on the Russians to cut the first throat they could reach. It was *Punch* who, a few days since, joined with [Tsar] Nicholas in the *Te Deum* celebrated at St. Petersburgh in favour of murder!

Compared with the polished irony, baroque flourishes and trenchant wit of Jerrold's writing for *Punch in London*'s great successor, *Punch* itself, this is pretty crude stuff, but it does suggest that if he had been able to settle into this journal he might have gradually found that voice which was to dominate the early years of the later publication and to help so greatly in establishing its popularity. It seems, however, that the proprietors, whoever they were, did not put enough money into *Punch in London* to enable it to compete successfully with *Figaro*, and Jerrold could not afford to write for nothing. He apparently contributed very little beyond the second number and after only fifteen more issues the little weekly ceased publication.

'Magazine work', declared Carlyle in 1831, 'is below street sweeping as a trade': and he was referring to such a notable journal as *Fraser's*. Jerrold's labours were generally in less intellectually exalted periodicals. He dashed off sketches, stories and theatre criticism for all sorts of papers. In addition to those already mentioned, he contributed to the *Freemasons' Quarterly* (from July 1834), and to such obscure and ephemeral publications as the *National Omnibus* and the grandly-named *Cambridge Quarterly Review and Magazine of Literature, Arts, Sciences, &c.*, which lasted for only three issues. The story called 'The Bird of Paradise' in the *National Omnibus* on 20 January 1832 and the sketch called 'Patches and their Penalties' in the *Monthly* for April 1834 may stand for a great deal of this output. In the first, a tale of a 'homely English fireside', newly-wed Mrs Brown's vanity and extravagance in buying a bird of paradise head-dress to attend a ball leads to domestic ruin and in the second a beadle prevents a mother and her children from going into a public park on account of the children's patched pinafores, thereby forcibly impressing on them the idea 'that poverty is a great sin' with the probable result that they will grow up with a sullen sense of social exclusion. All the tales and sketches, whether historical-anecdotal, contemporary-domestic or allegorical-fantastic, are strongly *moralisé*. Later, when he came to launch his *Shilling Magazine*, Jerrold announced his editorial intention 'to make every essay – however brief, and however light and familiar its treatment – breathe WITH A PURPOSE'. So, in these journalistic writings of the 1830s, later collected by his son as *The Brownrigg Papers*, he is always concerned to 'point a moral' about human folly, or to denounce examples of man's inhumanity to man, such as a windowless workhouse set in beautiful countryside 'with its blank dead wall of brick; a cold, blind thing, the work of human perversity and human selfishness, amidst ten thousand thousand evidences of Eternal bounty!' He loses no opportunity to castigate the complacent rich, 'Bully Bottom's Babes', as he calls them in one essay (taking Shakespeare's grotesquely self-satisfied weaver in *A Midsummer Night's Dream* as their great archetype). It is only when he writes about the theatre past or present, or embroiders some romantic legend about the life of his idolised Shakespeare, that he seems willing to relax and aim simply at entertaining his readers. We should always bear in mind, however, that the insistent moralising which we now find tedious and over-predictable (Jerrold may sometimes put us in mind of Carroll's Ugly Duchess and her words, 'Everything's got a moral, if you can only find it'), Jerrold's contemporary admirers would have seen as very much part of his greatness as a writer.

The years 1834 and 1835 were testing ones for him. The eye trouble, attributed to some form of rheumatism, which was to recur for the rest of his life began around this time and seriously affected his ability to work: 'I cannot at all confront the light, and pen this with difficulty,' he writes to Forster in connection with some work for the *Examiner*; 'the doctor has just been with me and pronounced another sentence of leeches with supplementary blister and poultice.' He speaks of fainting while trying to finish some work and of being forbidden 'to make the slightest effort with my eyesight'.[5] For someone dependent entirely on freelance work any kind of illness is always a very serious matter and Jerrold must have redoubled his efforts to get a salaried post. He applied to join the Parliamentary reporting staff of the *Morning Chronicle* (where he would have had the young Dickens for a colleague) and wrote on 15 January 1835 to thank J.P. Collier for supporting him:

> I could not expect ... that Mr Black [Editor of the *Chronicle*] would accept an untried, and consequently unskilful person, over a gentleman long practised in his craft. I shall, however, be further obliged to you for a line to the editor of *The Mirror* [the *Mirror of Parliament*, a rival to Hansard, edited by an uncle of Dickens's]; for as he is compelled to enlist new recruits I may stand a fairer chance among the raw volunteers. I can only wish that I were as intimate with St. Stephens Gallery, as I have unhappily been with the galleries of Drury and Covent-garden.[6]

Jerrold would certainly have found Parliamentary reporting even more uncongenial than grinding out plays for Davidge or Elliston and, judging by Dickens's account of the conditions of the work involved, it would have been quite disastrous for his eyesight.

Another job-searching letter of Jerrold's, dated only '21 April', probably belongs to this time. It is evidently a reply to an advertisement for an editor for a projected new paper and he offers 'the experience of eight years (on two of the most respectable Sunday journals) in the joint departments of sub-editor co-editor and editor'. He is, he says, 'fully acquainted with all the practical details of a newspaper' though he has 'quitted the press for the last three years'.[7] But this also came to nothing and Jerrold had to continue wholly dependent on freelance work for his journalistic income. He went upmarket, culturally speaking, in April 1835 when he began contributing a series of rather laboured and prolix farcical tales about satirical types to the prestigious literary monthly *Blackwood's Edinburgh Magazine* where, as Margaret Oliphant somewhat loftily remarks in her history of Blackwood's publishing firm, 'he scarcely can have found himself at home'.[8] No doubt she had in mind the strongly Tory politics of the journal as well as its decidedly 'high-culture' contributors (De Quincey, Professor John Wilson, alias 'Christopher North', Mrs Hemans, the historian Archibald Alison, and so on). Jerrold's 'Silas Fleshpots; a "Respectable Man"' and subsequent similar offerings certainly do sit rather oddly alongside heavyweight articles on Pitt, Spenser, the 'Conversations of M. de

Chateaubriand' or 'The Canada Question'. Oliphant claims that Jerrold's contributions were 'vigorously denounced' by the lawyer-novelist Samuel Warren who wrote to Blackwood imploring him 'to put an end to contributions which were impairing the tone of the Magazine and disgusting its readers' but no such letter is to be found in the Blackwood Papers at the National Library of Scotland. From Jerrold's (very polite and respectful) letters to Blackwood it seems, on the contrary, clear that the publisher actually encouraged him to develop a series and the reason why Jerrold wrote no more such pieces after 'Isaac Cheek, the "man of wax"' (July and September 1836) probably had more to do with the fact that Blackwood's rates of pay were, as Mary Russell Mitford complained, rather on the low side than with any blackballing by Warren.

During the winter of 1835/36 Jerrold's impulsive generosity towards anyone in need led to his having to leave the country to avoid arrest. He had backed a bill for a friend or acquaintance who proved unable to pay his debts – or perhaps just vanished and left Jerrold to deal with them. This marked the beginning of a period of even greater financial strain than before. Blanchard Jerrold notes that his father was 'fettered for some years by the treachery or the misfortune of friends' and it was not until February 1838 that he could write to Laman Blanchard:

> I have had a very narrow escape of being knocked to pieces by usurers and lawyers – for nearly three years I have been their bondsman, compelled to turn half my income 'to villainy and parchment'. However, I am now, I trust – but only within these few days – *free of them*. 'To-morrow to fresh ink, and half-crowns new'.[9]

In December 1835 Jerrold had to flee to Paris with his wife and baby daughter, leaving the other children, including two-year-old Tom, in the care of (presumably) their paternal grandmother. Forster was at this time connected with the *New Monthly Magazine* and Jerrold wrote that he hoped to be able to send him 'a few tolerable pages of gossip' for the journal on a monthly basis if the editor, Samuel Carter Hall, favoured such an arrangement – evidently Hall did not do so since no such gossip column appeared. Jerrold went on to say that he hoped to get a play produced at the Théâtre Français 'in conjunction with a French author who will translate my piece, and share profits' ('It may appear a fiction,' he adds, 'but dramatists here eat, drink, dress and dwell like gentlemen'). He continues:

> [I] am now at work upon my novel (should goose-quills rise in Paris, you will know to *whom* to attribute the advance). By-the-way, will you, in your literary news in the N.M. give a line on that fact (I mean the novel) – a circumstance so important to the world of letters? I have, however, a reason for wishing certain people to know that I am about to publish – that I am not idle.[10]

No such information appeared in the *New Monthly*'s literary gossip-column to reassure Jerrold's creditors, however, nor did Hall accept the substantial article Jerrold said he would be sending for publication in the journal's next issue; and some time before 25 January 1836, when he wrote to Duncombe from 4 Cecil Street, his wife's illness (the winter of 1835/36 was a bitterly cold one and Mary Ann was again pregnant) compelled Jerrold to return to London. The necessity of coming to some arrangement about his debts no doubt added urgency to his pressing Duncombe, as noted above (p. 100), to get on with the publication of *Doves in a Cage* which had opened to good notices at the Adelphi on 18 December and which he hoped – vainly as it turned out – would be produced at other theatres.

The hardships of Jerrold's brief Parisian exile were alleviated by the jolly companionship provided by the singer and composer John Barnett, his elder by one year, and two younger men who were to play very important parts in his subsequent life, William Makepeace Thackeray and Henry Mayhew. Thackeray, Jerrold told Forster, hearing he had arrived, had called on him and given him 'a most cordial greeting; with offers of introductions, &c'. The future author of *Vanity Fair* had had to abandon ideas of succeeding as a painter and was living frugally in cheap lodgings, earning what he could from hackwork for *Galignani's Messenger* and wallowing in love for a portionless young Irish girl living in a boarding-house with her difficult mother. The future author of *London Labour and the London Poor* was living as a remittance man on a pound a week, having been banished from the family home in London by his wealthy old tyrant of a father who also just happened to be the solicitor retained by Jerrold's creditor. Jerrold had a nasty turn, therefore, when he first met young Mayhew, assuming, naturally enough, that he was pursuing him about the bills that had not been honoured; but he was quickly reassured by the admiring young man, who eventually became his son-in-law. Jerrold was already 'one of the gods of young Mayhew's literary idolatry', according to Athol Mayhew, Henry's son and Jerrold's grandson, writing sixty years later. Athol quotes his father's recollection of Jerrold's vivid charm at the time he first met him: he

> had been greatly prepossessed by the extreme boyishness and rare comeliness of Jerrold's appearance. The freshness of his complexion, the dapperness of his figure, reminded my father more of some young daredevil of a middy than a man who had been accustomed to earn his living for many years by the sweat of his brain. At this period his hair was the colour of ripe corn, and his large full eyes blue and brilliant to a degree ... the wonderful play of the nostrils, which seemed to work like a stallion's with the least excitement ... .

Thackeray, Henry Mayhew and Jerrold would gather 'night after night' in Barnett's lodging in the Rue d'Amboise and find that nearly always they ended up arguing about which was the greatest art, music, painting or drama:

Jerrold took up the cudgels for the drama, and belaboured away at the others in right good earnest – his final knock-down blow invariably being a reference to Hamlet's celebrated soliloquy, 'To be or not to be'.

'There, Master Thackeray!' the little man would cry, triumphantly, 'could *you* or your Michael Angelo, or your Rubens or your Rembrandt, ever put *that* upon canvas? And you, Master Barnett! Could you, or any Beethoven or Mozart that ever lived, set *that* to music?'[11]

One hopes that Mary Ann, nursing her baby daughter in strange and probably not very luxurious lodgings, found similarly congenial company with whom to pass her evenings before her illness, probably connected with the early stages of a new pregnancy, necessitated the family's return to London.

Apparently Henry Mayhew was able to intervene with his father to help Jerrold come to some arrangement with his creditors but the terms, if we are to believe what Jerrold wrote in 1838, were harsh and the necessity to increase his income correspondingly urgent. Once more he looked to the theatre to help him in the struggle for solvency but this time he meant to be his own manager, or at least to keep that aspect of the business in the family. His favourite sister Jane's husband, William James Hammond (1799-1848), was strong in broad comedy and burlesque (in 1838 the fanzine *Actors by Daylight* called him 'this favourite son of Momus' and praised his 'agreeable quaintness'). Jerrold and Hammond agreed to take over the lease of the little New Strand Theatre which stood on the site of the present-day Aldwych tube station and which had for some years been, as Jerrold put it in his evidence to Bulwer's 1832 Committee, 'playing at bo-peep with the law' by finding ingenious ways to subvert the Patent Theatres' cartel regarding legitimate drama. More than once the Strand had been summarily closed down by the Lord Chamberlain. Early in 1836, after public meetings and petitions in Parliament, he granted it a licence on the same terms as the Aldwych and the Olympic: it could perform 'burlettas' but not straight drama. Jerrold and Hammond got round this simply by calling everything a burletta, including *The Rent Day* (billed for performance on 30 May 1836 as 'Mr. Douglas Jerrold's Original Domestic "Burletta"'). They opened the theatre on 25 April (eleven days after Hammond had also joined the Bank of England Freemasons' Lodge) with 'an ENTIRELY ORIGINAL BURLETTA OF SERIOUS INTEREST, in One Act (written by Mr. Douglas Jerrold)' as the main attraction. This 'burletta' was called *The Painter of Ghent* and Jerrold himself played the leading role ('His First Appearance on any Stage' – his infant appearances on his father's humble provincial stage in the arms of Kean were not to be allowed to interfere with this fetching announcement, it seems). The *Painter* is a sort of truncated tragedy, on the age's favourite father/daughter theme, which seems to have been a misjudgement of his audience on Jerrold's part (*The Times* mockingly called it on 26 April 1836 'very serious but ... wholly devoid of interest') Sending the dedication copy to Talfourd Jerrold struck an apologetic note:

The state of the theatres – declining every day from bad to worse – has ... compelled me to limit my endeavours to sketches of dramas, forbidding me, under a penalty which I *must not* incur, the *attempt* of higher and severer compositions. I have thus made a poor offering ... .

He adds a postscript to 'excuse the squalid coat in which the bookseller has habited the *Painter*'. 'Acted plays not being looked upon as literature', he writes, publishers will not pay for 'extrinsic refinements' and playwrights 'must now sue to be read – *in forma pauperis*'.[12]

What the Strand audiences wanted was a rather more light-hearted bill of fare and Jerrold turned to in an effort to provide this, either in the form of revivals of earlier comedies or else as new 'burlettas', mostly founded on his *Blackwood's* pieces and billed as having been written by 'Henry Brownrigg Esq.' The great money-spinner, however, was not one of Jerrold's pieces but an 'Operatic Burlesque Burletta' by Maurice Dowling called *Othello (according to Act of Parliament)* which was a vehicle for Hammond who had first played this Othello ('Moor of Venice, formerly an independent nigger from the republic of Hayti') in Liverpool in 1834. That inveterate London theatre-goer of the 1830s Charles Rice saw its seventy-seventh successive representation on 13 August 1836 and noted that it 'drew an excellent crowd half price, the house being, towards the end of the evening, crowded in every part'. He also noted that the Strand was 'the most comfortable theatre in London'.[13] It was small but Hammond and Jerrold increased its capacity by converting the upper circle boxes into a gallery, which also made it available to less well-heeled playgoers (instead of two shillings and sixpence for an upper box gallery admission was one shilling), and altogether the leasing of the New Strand would seem to have been a profitable venture. Jerrold wrote to Charles Cowden Clarke nearly a year later that the little theatre, 'the only national playhouse', was 'going up-up-up'[14]). Apart from once apparently playing Heywood, a role for which he hardly seemed suited physically, in the revival of *The Rent Day*, Jerrold himself does not seem to have acted again after the short-lived *Painter*, perhaps because of health troubles but most likely because burlesque was not his line. By 1838 Hammond's name appears alone as manager. Barton Baker believed 'the partnership lasted only a few months' and Jerrold's share in it probably 'did not extend beyond the productions of his pen',[15] but the letters to Clarke suggest otherwise. It would, anyway, have been rather odd for Jerrold to have withdrawn from the enterprise when things were going so well. The burlesque *Othello* and similar fare continued to draw audiences and in April 1837 the theatre began cashing in on the sensational success of Dickens's *Pickwick Papers* by staging a dramatisation (by the indefatigable Moncrieff) called *The Pickwickians* in which Hammond scored a great personal success as Sam Weller.

Whatever the extent and duration of Jerrold's financial investment in the Strand – and it is possible that this consisted essentially in his lending his name and in providing quantities of stage-fodder – he was still working hard at his journalism and concerned to establish himself as writer. 'Oh!' said 'one of the most popular of the blood and murder school' of dramatists when Jerrold told him he was now writing for the magazines, 'then you have cut *us*, and are going to take to *literature*'.[16]

He became involved with Thackeray and Laman Blanchard in a project for a new 'gentlemanly-Radical' morning newspaper, the *Constitutional and Public Ledger,* largely funded by Thackeray's stepfather Major Carmichael-Smyth. The Government had just repealed the old newspaper stamp duty, substituting instead a penny stamp which guaranteed free postage, so it seemed a propitious time to start a new journal. Laman Blanchard was appointed Editor, Thackeray the paper's Paris correspondent, and Jerrold its theatre critic. Thackeray wrote elatedly to his wife that he was to have 'three or four hundred a year'[17] and it seems reasonable to assume that Jerrold would have been hired on comparable terms. The first issue appeared on 15 September 1836 and boldly announced the paper's politics, its support for extending the suffrage, vote by ballot, reform of the House of Lords, the restoration to Labour of 'the rights and rewards of which Property has despoiled it', the 'redress of the manifold wrongs and miseries [of the Many] which they have suffered by the Usurpation of the Few', and more in the same vein. All this, it was careful to stress, was to be accomplished by strictly constitutional means. Jerrold, if not Thackeray, would have found himself at home in this atmosphere, and his column gave him an excellent platform from which to carry on his campaign against the degradation of the Patent Theatres under unworthy managers. The egregious showman Alfred Bunn, who as 'the Poet Bunn' was later to be one of Jerrold's chief butts in *Punch,* had had the lease of both Covent Garden and Drury Lane since 1833 but in October 1835 the actor David Osbaldiston, celebrated for his heavy villains in melodrama and a former manager of the Surrey, took over Covent Garden. In the *Constitutional* Jerrold campaigned against him relentlessly, declaring on 9 January 1837 that 'his tastes, his habits, his meanness and his ignorance [render] him incapable of the conduct of anything above the dignity of a booth' and ridiculing 'the phantasmagoric productions of his stock scribe, his hack porcupine of all work'. On 17 January 1837 Jerrold writes that Osbaldiston has been fortunate in having Charles Kemble as a 'golden wing' for his management but 'if, in lieu of making pounds by Mr. Kemble, the manager could have made guineas by a rhinoceros, is there any doubt, from his previously developed taste, which of the two animals he would have preferred?'

Jerrold did not, apparently, continue as a *Constitutional* contributor for long, probably because from January 1837 he began writing regularly for the *New Monthly Magazine* under its new editor Theodore Hook. The publisher Henry Colburn had recruited Hook to help the journal compete with the new monthly just launched by his great rival Bentley, called simply *Bentley's Miscellany* (it was originally to have been called *The Wits'*

Miscellany and Jerrold is one of two or three people on whom was fathered the quip about there having been no need for Bentley, when changing the title, to go to the other extreme). Bentley had secured the rising young literary star Charles Dickens as his first editor so it is hardly surprising that Colburn should have felt the need of a livelier and more distinguished editor for his organ than the drearily self-important Samuel Carter (alias 'Shirt Collar') Hall, later the model for Dickens's Pecksniff, who had succeeded Bulwer Lytton in the post in 1833. In Hook, widely celebrated as a practical joker, a witty improviser of comic songs and verses, and a prolific author of farcical tales (Thackeray put him into *Vanity Fair* as Mr Wagg and Disraeli into *Vivian Grey* as Stanislaus Hoax), Colburn found just the man for the job and Hook lost no time in encouraging Jerrold, whom Hall seems to have disliked, to increase his contributions. Dickens sought to recruit Jerrold for *Bentley's* also, writing to him in early November 1836,

> Although I have not the pleasure of knowing you personally, I am on such intimate terms with your writings that I almost feel an apology to be unnecessary when I say that I intend calling on you tomorrow afternoon ... in the hope that I may be able to obtain your promise of a paper for the first number of Mr. Bentley's 'Wits Miscellany'.

Jerrold had probably committed himself to Hook and Colburn before Dickens presented himself in Chelsea. At any rate, nothing from his pen appeared in *Bentley's* until long after Dickens had angrily severed his connection with the journal. Nor did anything come of the agreement Jerrold had signed with Bentley on 17 October 1836 to write a three-volume novel about Nell Gwynne (for £200 with a further £100 if sales exceeded 900 – hardly princely terms, compared to £50 an act for a play) with Bentley to have first option on two more historical novels following the Nell Gwynne one.[18]

Dickens's Chelsea visit, although he failed to recruit Jerrold as a contributor, did mark the beginning of a close and important friendship between these two writers who were in such profound sympathy in their social and political outlook (their later sharp disagreement over public executions only emphasised how much they thought alike on most social questions), and who were seen by contemporary readers and critics as forming, together with Thackeray, the supreme triad of English comic and satiric writing. Many years later Dickens recalled his first meeting with Jerrold for the benefit of Blanchard Jerrold's *Memoir* of his father:

> I remember very well that when I first saw him ... when I went into his sick room, ... and found him propped up in a great chair, bright-eyed, and quick, and eager in spirit, but very lame in body, he gave me an impression of tenderness. It never became dissociated from him. There was nothing cynical or sour in his heart, as I knew it.

The Jerrolds' last child, Bessy, born in August, was either already dead or dying when Dickens made his visit and it seems likely that some reference would have been made to this; all the evidence is that Jerrold loved his children deeply, and the 'impression of tenderness' Dickens received may well have had something to do with the sad domestic situation at the time of his visit.

Dickens's words remind us that by the later 1830s Jerrold's life was becoming a continual struggle against ill-health, the rheumatism that bowed his figure and attacked his eyesight. According to the anonymous friend who wrote his obituary in the *Sunday Times* (14 June 1857) this originated with a fast walk on a wet night, 'closely buttoned up in a mackintosh', from Drury Lane Theatre to a newspaper office in Fleet Street to deliver copy for a review. The 'excessive perspiration' that this produced was followed by 'a fit of cold shivering' and led to his being prostrated for many weeks by a 'fearful attack' of life-threatening rheumatic fever which 'left behind it the malignancy to which he ultimately succumbed, and which for nearly twenty years previously gave him the care-worn aspect and bent body of extreme old age'.

Whether it was this attack that he was recovering from when Dickens saw him we do not know, nor whether this was the occasion when he dramatically rejected Dr Wigan's gloomy prognosis ("'What!" said the patient, "die, and leave my wife and five helpless children! By − , I won't die!" ... [he] got better from that hour'[19]). But it is certainly the case that the years 1837-41, the first of the new queen's reign, saw him vigorously developing his career as a literary journalist. Between January 1837 and May 1839 few issues of the *New Monthly* appeared without a comic or satiric tale from Jerrold's pen. Though he still used the 'Henry Brownrigg' signature from time to time, Jerrold must nevertheless have felt that he was at last beginning to emerge from his harsh apprenticeship to literature. Many of these sketches and stories, including 'The Manager's Pig' (see above p. 63), were later collected up in his two-volume *Cakes and Ale,* published in 1842 with a dedication to Thomas Hood, by then Editor of the *New Monthly*, and some excellent illustrations by Cruikshank. Meanwhile, in 1838, Colburn published *Men of Character*, a three-volume collection of Jerrold's *Blackwood's* pieces. For this Jerrold supplied five more 'men' in the same vein (one at least of which had been declined by Blackwood) and one of those satirical prefaces that were becoming a hallmark of his. The formula to which these pieces are written is not a happy one since 'character' is just what these farcical figures lack, as the *Athenaeum* observed in a severe review on 24 February 1838. This also pointed to their 'vagueness of plot' as a reason why the stories could not be dramatised, even though their readers will be constantly 'tantalized ... with the vision of [what] this or that popular actor or actress ... could make of some racy extravagance, or prominent opportunity for buffoonery'. In fact, as we have seen, Jerrold *was* able to turn some of them into farcical 'burlettas' for the Strand where they seem to have met with moderate success. The *Athenaeum* regretted that, despite many 'shrewd, fanciful

and witty observations', the stories exhibited 'such a constancy of extravagance, such a laboured struggling after tinsel effect, and so bitter a spleen
against theatres, managers and actors', and justly castigated the dozen
etchings *after* Cruikshank' anonymously supplied by Thackeray that were
remarkable only 'for the badness of the drawing, and the total absence of
humour'.[20] *Men of Character* must have found some appreciative readers,
however, as that enterprising German publisher Baron Tauchnitz found it
worthwhile to bring out a continental edition of the book fourteen years
later.

His regular income from the *New Monthly* perhaps encouraged Jerrold
to leave 'the wilds of Fulham' and move closer to town. Early in 1837 the
family moved into a market-gardener's house at Sinton's Nursery on
Haverstock Hill in Hampstead where, Mayhew noted, Jerrold with his
acute sense of smell revelled 'in the perfume of the acres of roses in which
his new homestead was literally embedded'.[21] Jerrold still had to watch the
pennies ('I have some doubts of my present purse-ability for the Piazza
Coffee House', he wrote to Laman Blanchard on 15 February 1838, about
a proposed Shakespeare Club jaunt to Covent Garden; 'I fear me, "four-
penny *goes*" do not abound there … are pewter pots extant?'[22]) but at least
he was no longer mainly dependent for his living on the caprices and
prejudices of managers and star actors. The family visit or visits to France
in the summer of 1838 were not to escape creditors but partly for recupera-
tive and holiday purposes (Jerrold had been ill again in the spring) and
partly to settle his two older boys, twelve-year-old William Blanchard and
ten-year-old Douglas Edmund, as boarders in the school of the amiable M.
Bonnefoy in Boulogne.[23] In the autumn the family moved to Kentish Town,
a new outer suburb half-way between Hampstead and London, where their
immediate neighbours in Lower Craven Place included a girls' school, an
attorney, a station master, a painter and several people listed in the 1841
census as having 'Independent Means'.

In November 1838 the publisher Robert Tyas began issuing the monthly
parts of a series called *Heads of the People Taken Off by Quizfizz*. This was
built around a series of woodcuts of contemporary occupational and social
types executed by the convivial artist Kenny Meadows (1790-1874) whom
Jerrold had met through Duncombe and whose 'quaint way of viewing
things', as Vizetelly called it, would surely have been highly congenial to
him (Meadows was also a fellow-sufferer from severe attacks of rheumatism). Tyas turned to Jerrold for letterpress to accompany the etchings in
the form of 4000-word essays descriptive of the type illustrated. Jerrold
recruited others to the enterprise and *Heads* included contributions from
Thackeray, Leigh Hunt and his son Thornton, R.H. Horne, William Howitt
and Laman Blanchard. Jerrold also wrote to invite Mary Russell Mitford
to 'enrich' the series (which, he tells her, 'has been much praised for its
strength and straightforwardness of purpose') with 'sundry English pictures of female life' but though she readily promised to do so, nothing from
her pen appeared.[24] Jerrold published the first five of his own contributions

under his Brownrigg pseudonym but thereafter used his own name, perhaps because the series proved successful (it did well enough to justify the issue of a second series); Kenny Meadows, too, soon drops his 'Quizfizz' pseudonym. *Heads of the People* was finally published in two volumes (with a few changes in content from the monthly parts) in 1840 and 1841.

Altogether, Jerrold wrote nineteen 'Heads', some predominantly in his ornately ironic style, some predominantly in his social-melodramatic vein. A good example of the first is 'The Pew Opener' which begins as follows:

> Even in the temple – at the very shrine – where meekness, self-humiliation, contrition of heart, and remorse of spirit, kneel, and make sweet sacrifice; yea, even there, plies the Pew-Opener; the busy servitor of pride; the watchful handmaid of distinction; the soft-spoken waiter upon Mammon: yes, in the temple, the hopeful looker-out for sixpences.

His 'Dress-Maker', on the other hand, uses the idiom of melodrama to present the social reality behind all the 'poor but honest' heroines of the contemporary stage and novel (Kate Nickleby at Madame Mantalini's in Dickens's *Nicholas Nickleby*, for example):

> How many bleak, savage winter mornings does she rise, and, with half-frozen fingers, put on her scanty clothes, – all insufficient to guard her shrinking limbs from the frost, the wind, and the rain, – and with noiseless feet, that she may not disturb 'any of the lodgers', creep down three-pair of stairs, and, at six o'clock, pick her timid way through mud, and cold, and darkness, to the distant 'work-room'.

Throughout all his contributions as throughout most of the others, though never so unremittingly as in Jerrold's pieces, runs a strong sympathy for the physical and mental miseries of the poor and a bitter scorn for those who exploit or prey on them, like the Common Informer who does not meddle with the upper classes but 'snuffs his prey afar' in the poorer quarters of London, the City Road or 'the Borough' (Southwark):

> His quarry is at some 'Goat and Compasses' in an alley – some 'Bag o'Nails' in a back street: for there he has had good intelligence of social iniquity; there, at both hostelries, the landlords have – music!

Prolix as many of these pieces are – eight pages had to be filled with text for each monthly part, and Jerrold was a past master of repetition with variations – his contributions include some highly effective vignettes of common scenes in contemporary London such as description of the brutal revelry surrounding a public execution ('The Hangman'). We can clearly see emerging in these pieces the fierce joker of *Punch*, scourge of well-fed moralising magistrates and prosperous pontificating bishops, callous petty officials, uncaring politicians and the grossly self-indulgent wealthy (not excluding Royalty).

The Jerrold of *Punch* is also foreshadowed, more surprisingly, in the pages of the *Morning Herald*. Although Jerrold assured Leigh Hunt that he wrote only theatre reviews for this pre-eminently family newspaper and had nothing to do with its 'foolish politics', Vizetelly notes that it was 'an open secret' that Jerrold also contributed to the *Herald* 'some biting comments on the justice's justice of the day and kindred topics'.[25] Scanning the pages of the paper in the light of this remark, we may easily spot items that, if we were to find them (to borrow Coleridge's famous comment on some highly characteristic lines of Wordsworth's) 'galloping wild in the deserts of Arabia', would make us cry out 'Jerrold!' Two such appear on the same page of the issue for 24 February 1840, for example. The first, in his satirical-fantastic vein, was evidently inspired by Barry's medievalising design for the new Palace of Westminster. It announces the Government's decision to add to the building 'a DONJON KEEP ... provided with numerous cells for the solitary confinement of parliamentary prisoners' ('The present aspect of the privilege question renders it probable that *accommodation* may be required for 500 or 600 prisoners ...') and a 'HALL OF INQUISITION ... suitable for ... six hundred and odd inquisitors'. The paintings in this hall ('in *chiaro'scuro* only') should be appropriately allegorical: 'Privilege trampling on *Magna Charta*, the Bill of Rights, and *Habeas Corpus* Act; Legislative Wisdom bidding adieu to Shame, &c.' The second item, headed '*POVERTY IS INFAMY!*', is a ferociously indignant report of a recent police-court case. An unemployed man named Wilton with a starving wife and children at home, was trying to earn a few pennies by selling wash-leathers in the street, unaware that he needed a hawker's licence for this. Convicted of this 'enormity', he had no money to pay the £10 fine nor any goods that could be distrained (even the leathers belonged to someone else who had been trying to help him) and the magistrate had no option but to send him to gaol for three months. This sentence, says Jerrold (for it is surely he), is

> an insult wreaked in the name of justice, on the crying wants, the crushing necessities of hungry thousands. At this moment how many hundreds throughout the metropolis are honestly seeking a bitter morsel of bread for themselves and their children in the very teeth of the law that has condemned Wilton! Is he, then, to remain a solitary victim, or are our gaols to be thronged with wretches not permitted to work? When the doom was passed that 'man should live by the sweat of his brow' there was surely no after-meaning, 'if *duly licensed* thereto'.

In other columns of the *Herald* Jerrold continued, with equal ferocity, his battle for the regeneration of the drama. He was still smarting from Macready's rejection, at the beginning of 1839, of his five-act historical drama *The Spendthrift* (this was during Macready's managership of Covent Garden). Macready had found the play, on which he had advanced Jerrold £50, 'too didactic ... very heavy ... hopeless affair' and spoke to Jerrold about its 'want of action and purpose'.[26] Jerrold may, as Macready noted, have 'assented to much that I urged' but he made no secret of his belief that Macready would have accepted the play if it had been the work of a baronet. He was alluding to Bulwer Lytton, whose romantic melo-drama *The Lady of Lyons* featuring a preposterously high-minded and super-intelligent gardener's-son hero, played by Macready, had been the great Covent Garden hit of 1838.[27] The success of yet another Bul-wer/Macready collaboration, *The Sea Captain; or, the Birth-Right* (Haymarket, 31 October 1839) rubbed salt into Jerrold's wounds, espe-cially as Bulwer was giving himself the airs of a regenerator of the English drama. On 22 January 1840 Jerrold prefaced a fine, detailed appreciation of Macready's new Macbeth at Drury Lane ('... a perfect creation of the very highest order of the art. We never saw any other actor so completely possess himself of the secret of *Macbeth*'s apparent superstition') with some disobliging comments about Macready's self-indulgent vanity and abuse of the power that the star system and the Patent Theatre cartel gave him. He compares Macready's migration from the Haymarket to Drury Lane to that of 'the royal elephant' moving off after a fair to another site: 'in this mode [Macready] comes to Drury-lane, carrying with him two or three actors to *feed him with words*, and a sort of stage-valet to see the sawdust properly strewed for him.' Those actors who had been with him at the Haymarket and are now left without work and those who find them-selves turned out at Drury Lane can only blame 'the dignified professor of the art, who, wrapt in the incessant contemplation of his own vast conse-quence, makes to the very utmost of his power, managers and actors bow down and worship it'.

On 31 January, reviewing Macready's performance as Ruthven in James Haynes's tragedy *Mary Stuart*, Jerrold took the opportunity to attack Bulwer again and in his most waspish vein. Haynes's play, he declares, is at least 'the writing of a man, and not of a man-milliner' and will prove more enduringly attractive to audiences than

> such fantastic yet laboured experiments on human nature, as those of late put forth by the self-dubbed regenerator of the stage (Sir Lytton Bulwer), who ... month after month, in the sweet serenity of his vast conceit, pro-claimed the modern drama dead, graciously intimating that a wizard – a very near and dear acquaintance of his own – would, in due season, walk forth and work its resurrection. We are happy to meet Mr Macready on ground more worthy of his powers than that unprofitably occupied by him for weeks past. Any one speech of his *Ruthven* is worth all the copper-gilt sentiment of his *Sea Captain*; aye, though we add thereto all the funereal lightness of its comedy – most grim hilarity – all the churchyard joyousness that brightened and enriched it.

There is certainly not much to be said in defence of Bulwer's play but it seems clear that the venom of this attack has more to do with spleen than with literary judgement. Bulwer, of all people, ought to have been a hero to British dramatists at this time. It was he, after all, who had caused Parliament to set up the 1832 Select Committee on Dramatic Literature which, although it had not succeeded in persuading the House of Lords, so over-protective of the Royal Prerogative, to end the cartel operated by the Patent Theatres, had at least tried to improve the playwrights' lot. But the subsequent great successes of plays by him at those very theatres, strongly helped by Macready both as manager and as actor, was evidently too much for Jerrold, after all his troubles and frustrations, and the fact that Bulwer was, into the bargain, a member of the aristocracy brought his class antagonism into play as well. Yet it was to be Bulwer's example, and that of the equally objectionable (though on different grounds) Boucicault that would shortly show Jerrold the pathway to the kind of success in full-scale 'legitimate' comedy that he so craved.

Chapter Seven

Triumphing with Mr Punch

1841-1843

In late May 1841 Jerrold and his wife, accompanied by a maidservant, returned to Boulogne to be near their children, now all at school there, establishing themselves for the summer first in a cottage formerly occupied by William IV's discarded mistress Mrs Jordan and then in a 'snug little villa' in the recently much-improved suburb of Capecure, considered by the *Boulogne Gazette* (15 July 1840) as 'one of the most desirable spots about Boulogne'.[1] A young journalist friend of Henry Mayhew's, the 'mild, meek, kind-hearted' George Hodder,[2] later Jerrold's right-hand man in various editorial enterprises, came to spend a fortnight's holiday. He later painted an idyllic picture of the Jerrolds in Boulogne, 'surrounded by every comfort, not to say luxury, which could be desired by a contented and united English family abroad'. Hodder was struck by Jerrold's 'pride and pleasure' in his children and his 'amiable predeliction for giving juvenile parties' involving the acting of charades with himself and M. Bonnefoy playing major roles. He noted also Jerrold's passion for the sea and sea-bathing. Walking on the beach with Hodder one beautiful evening, Jerrold

> suddenly exclaimed: 'How lovely the water looks! Egad, I'll have a dip!' and in scarcely more time than is occupied by the pantomime clown in making his inevitable 'change', he stuck his stick in the sand, placed his hat upon the top and his clothes around it, and ran into the water with a nimbleness which he could hardly have surpassed in the midshipman days of his youth.[3]

It was during the Jerrolds' Boulogne sojourn that there appeared in London the first number of an illustrated comic and satiric weekly which was hugely to increase Jerrold's fame and his popularity with middle-class and artisan class readers, whilst at the same time guaranteeing him a certain regular income (it was, as Hannay somewhat exuberantly put it in his *Atlantic Monthly* memoir, 'the Argo which conveyed him to the Golden Fleece'). The paper was *Punch, or the London Charivari*, the first number of which was published on 17 July 1841, price 3d. The well-known engraver Ebenezer Landells, a former pupil of Bewick's, and Henry Mayhew had got together with a prolific scribbler of farces and 'burlettas' called Mark Lemon, and with a printer called Joseph Last, to make yet another effort (initially financed by Landells to the modest tune of £25) to produce a London equivalent of the immensely successful Parisian satirical paper

119

Le Charivari, founded by Charles Philipon in 1832 with Daumier as one of its leading artists. During the convivial evenings Jerrold, Mayhew and Thackeray had spent together in the course of Jerrold's enforced Paris sojourn of 1835 the young men had canvassed the idea of setting up a London *Charivari* and Mayhew had already been much involved with the nearest thing to date, *Figaro in London*.[4] *Figaro* had ceased publication in 1838, however, so the field was clear for further new ventures.

Mayhew, Landells and Lemon at once recruited the young lawyer and seemingly indefatigable scribbler of facetious journalism Gilbert à Beckett and naturally turned also to Jerrold with his by now well-established reputation for caustic wit directed against the follies and misdeeds of the nation's rulers. For Jerrold it must have been a very attractive prospect. It provided the same sort of stimulus for quick-fire, up-to-the-minute satirical comment that his dramatic criticism in the newspapers had hitherto done but was not restricted to one theme. At the same time it allowed him greater freedom of expression and more scope for fanciful treatment than had been available to him when writing his social sketches and moral tales for *Blackwood's*, the *New Monthly* and so on. 'No man', Spielmann writes of Jerrold,

> ever gained so much from the paper in which he worked. He simply frolicked in its pages, that fitted his talent as accurately as his genius suited the times in which he lived. It is doubtful whether he would have made the same mark in it were he alive today ....[5]

Jerrold was at this time producing in his 'Bajazet Gag' series some of his best 'monthly' work to date, and so was in good form to respond to the challenge of this new outlet. His first *Punch* contribution, 'Punch and Peel', appeared in the second number in the form of a comic dialogue between naïve 'Reader' and ironic 'Mr Punch' relating to the so-called 'Bedchamber Crisis' (caused by the Tory premier Sir Robert Peel's insistence, on coming into office, that the young Queen should dismiss her Whig ladies-in-waiting and replace them with Tory ones, a demand initially resisted by Victoria). Mr Punch instructs his questioner:

> the ropes of the state rudder are nothing more than cap-ribbons; if the minister hav'n't hold of them, what can he do with the ship? As for the debates in parliament, they have no more to do with the real affairs of the country than the gossip of the apple-women in Palace-yard. They're made, like the maccaroni in Naples, for the poor to swallow; and so that they gulp down length, they think, poor fellows, they get strength. But for the real affairs of the country! Who shall tell what correspondence can be conveyed in a warming-pan ...? What subtle, sinister advice may, by a crafty disposition of royal pins, be given on the royal pincushion? What minister shall answer for the sound repose of Royalty, if he be not permitted to make Royalty's bed? How shall he answer for the comely appearance of Royalty, if he do not, by his own delegated hands, lace Royalty's stays? ...

In this dialogue, shot through with characteristic scornful contempt for Parliamentary windbaggery and for the backstage manoeuvring of party politics in a constitutional monarchy, Jerrold was helping to build up, very much as he had earlier done in his editorial for the first number of *Punch in London*, the figure of 'Mr Punch' (the traditionally anarchic figure of the puppet Punch made into a respectable, but still potentially subversive, citizen by that 'Mr') as the personification or embodiment of the new journal, its mouthpiece, all contributions being published anonymously and so subsumed into the utterance of 'Mr Punch'. The creation of this figure, together with the careful avoidance of the sort of scurrility and obscene innuendoes usually associated with comic papers at this time, was one of the most important factors in the rapid establishment of *Punch's* popularity and public image, rather as the mythical proprietorial figure of 'Lord Gnome' helped to give the newly-founded *Private Eye* such a distinctive personality in the 1960s.

Jerrold's fourth contribution, 'Peel "Regularly Called In"', in *Punch's* ninth number (11 September 1841), was, however, signed – not with his name but simply with the letter Q (short, perhaps, for 'Quiz', i.e., a mocking or satirical person) and was the first of the celebrated 'Q Papers' that he was to write for the journal over the next four years, a total of sixty-seven articles.[6] 'Q' became, as it were, Mr Punch's formidable alter ego and his diatribes, often complemented pictorially by the week's 'big cut' or full-page cartoon, functioned in the paper rather in the manner of editorials or leading articles. More than anything else, they established the strongly democratic, even at times Radical, tone that was the dominant one in *Punch* during its first lustrum, the earlier years of the 'Hungry Forties'. They did this through their relentless, ferocious detailing of examples of inhumanity, injustice, insensitivity, hypocrisy, abuse of power and privilege, and downright stupidity perpetrated by members of what we should now call 'the Establishment': the great landowners, aristocrats, prelates, capitalists, MPs and magistrates who held all the power in Britain. Jerrold's authorship of these 'Q' pieces was an open secret and it is not surprising, therefore, that many should have supposed him, rather than the more low-profile Mark Lemon, to have been *Punch's* actual editor or at any rate its moving spirit. Macready, galled by the journal's 'paltry impertinence', abused its writers 'who rejoice in the miserable Jerrold as their captain' and as late as 1844 Elizabeth Barrett, recommending the journal to Mary Russell Mitford, wrote, 'Douglas Jerrold is the editor I fancy; & he has a troop of wits ... to support him.' And still today, on the rare occasions when Jerrold is remembered at all, he is often mistakenly identified as having been the Editor of *Punch*.[7]

Leaving their boys to the care of M. Bonnefoy and their girls to that of the 'Dames Frévilliez',[8] Jerrold and his wife returned from Boulogne in the early autumn. He went to lodge with his brother-in-law Hammond in Essex Street, just off the Strand, writing to Leigh Hunt that 'horrors of the rheumatism' had driven him from Kentish Town but that he had made

a very tolerable compromise between my love of green grass and my necessity of flag-stones. I am studded about by lawyers – 'A young lamb's heart
amid the full-grown flocks!' *Hem*! Nevertheless, I look at one side on the
pastoral Inner Temple and at another on the Thames.[9]

He continued until February 1842 writing 'Gag' for the *New Monthly* and
contributed one or two other items to this journal (now under Hood's
editorship, Hook having died in August) but his main journalistic output
was now directed towards *Punch* and, for the present, mainly in the form
of 'Q' papers. He was, however, far from ready to abandon the theatre,
notwithstanding all the disappointments, injustices and vexations he had
encountered in that field. In hand were two new 'legitimate' comedies
intended for the Patent Theatres, one of them a full-scale five-act comedy
of manners. Nevertheless, it was to be his *Punch* work that was destined
to bring him a far greater and more enduring audience than any future
dramatic works, and it was the 'Q' papers that laid the foundation of this
success.

These papers are suffused, as Dickens's first two 'Christmas Books', *A
Christmas Carol* (1843) and *The Chimes* (1844), were also to be, with a
passionate sympathy for the poor and downtrodden, the sufferers under
the harshness of the New Poor Law and other inhumane legislation.
Jerrold raged, in his own densely and vividly metaphorical style, against
the cruel treatment meted out to the workhouse mother whose five-week-
old baby was taken from her and only 'occasionally brought to her for the
breast' ('The "Milk" of Poor-Law "Kindness"', 28 January 1843), or to the
wretched William Simmons, 'a starving tailor, in a perishing condition',
who was sentenced by Sir Peter Laurie to a month on the treadmill as 'a
rogue and a vagabond' for attempted suicide. Sir Peter was a saddler who
had made a fortune out of Government contracts and had become a City
alderman and Lord Mayor. He prided himself on his worldly wisdom ('The
Pig-skin Solomon' was one of Jerrold's titles for him and Dickens lampoons
him in *The Chimes* as 'Alderman Cute'). He announced from the bench his
determination to 'put down' suicide, provoking Jerrold into writing one of
his most stinging 'Q' papers, 'Sir Peter Laurie on Human Life' (13 November 1841). It begins:

SIR PETER LAURIE has set his awful face against suicide! He will in no way
'encourage' *felo-de-se*. Fatal as the aldermanic determination may be to the
interests of the shareholders of Waterloo, Vauxhall, and Southwark Bridges
[all toll-bridges and favourite sites for would-be suicides], Sir PETER has
resolved that no man – not even in the suicidal season of November – shall
drown, hang, or otherwise destroy himself, under any pretence soever! Sir
PETER, with a very proper admiration of the pleasures of life, philosophises
with a full stomach on the ignorance and wickedness of empty-bellied
humanity ... [He] henceforth stands sentinel at the gate of death, and any
hungry pauper who shall recklessly attempt to touch the knocker will be
sentenced to 'the treadmill for a month as a rogue and a vagabond!'

It is a rare Jerrold article that contains no allusion to his idolised Shakespeare and it is not long before one appears here, prompted by the fact that Laurie was a Scotsman by origin:

> Had the cautious Sir PETER been in the kilt of his countryman *Macbeth*, he would never have exhibited an 'admired disorder' on the appearance of *Banquo*, with his larynx severed in two; not he – he would have called the wound a slight scratch ... and immediately ordered the ghost to the guard-house.

Jerrold ends by suggesting that there might be a better remedy for such desperation as William Simmons's than the treadmill: 'The surest way for the rich and powerful of this world to make the poor man more careful of his life is to render it of greater value to him.'

Another news item that 'Q' notices is the report that Parliament is to be asked to vote £3000 a year to be paid, if she should be widowed, to the Princess Augusta, daughter of the Queen's uncle, the Duke of Cambridge, as part of her marriage settlement when she weds the Hereditary Duke of Mecklenburgh Strelitz. In his 'A Royal Wife of –£3000!' (24 June 1843; the article is accompanied by a wonderfully effective cartoon by John Gilbert) Jerrold comments:

> ... £3,000 a year from the taxes. This is moderate – very moderate indeed. How the young couple will be able to get on we know not. To be sure, the court of STRELITZ is not quite so dear as that of St James's, and so they may get pudding for dinner all the year round. Again, when we remember that the immense sum of £10,000 was voted only for the education of the poor of all England, we are surprised at the magnanimity which contents itself with something less than a third of that amount. If Stockport and Paisley do not, with all their rushlights, illuminate when they hear the glad tidings then is the spirit of manufacture dead to gratitude – then have weavers no bowels. (By the way, it would save them much inconvenience if they never had.)

Although he was far from being a Chartist, Jerrold, like Gaskell in *Mary Barton* later, shows both sympathy and understanding towards those many thousands of men and women in the working classes driven by glaring social injustice and inequality to demand radical constitutional reform in the shape of 'The People's Charter'. Taking very much the same line as had Carlyle in his *Chartism* (1840) but, like Gaskell and also Dickens, putting far more emphasis on the need for sympathetic understanding, Jerrold writes in 'The Charter – The House of Commons "Hushed and Still"' (21 May 1842):

> Chartism is born of defeated hope, of disappointment of the fruits of the Reform Act; it has been fostered ... by a sordid, remorseless contempt of the inalienable rights of humanity. The vice of the age is want of sympathy with the condition of the great mass of the people. They are looked upon as mere instruments of wealth – the mere machines with eyes to direct them, and

limbs to labour for the privileged classes; whose money-bags are to them as the Great Wall of China, shutting them out from the barbarian poor. In England, the test of a man's social worth is to be found only at his banker's. Property is the Mumbo Jumbo of the high-minded, intelligent John Bull.

Particular concerns of Jerrold feature prominently in these 'Q' papers. His militant anti-militarism finds vigorous expression in many of the articles, as does his unwavering opposition to capital punishment, and his constant sniping at Church of England prelates for their very comfortable life-style, remoteness from the poor and apparently questionable adherence to Christian doctrine ('there is not any body of men', commented the *Examiner* on Anglican bishops on 25 March 1848, 'who exhibit more unambiguous signs of living at ease'). Two of these themes fused dramatically together when Jerrold happened upon a report of an announcement made by the Duke of Wellington that some new regimental colours he was presenting had been consecrated 'by one of the highest dignitaries of the church'. 'Q' is eager to know (on 5 February 1842)

> who was the prelate whose orthodox breath hath given the odour of sanctity to the bloody flag of homicide and rapine; and next we desire ... to learn the exact ceremony performed on the now consecrated silk. ... Did the blessing bishop watch and pray all night, calling on the Lord of Hosts to pour down his grace upon the banners of death – invoking the spirit of JESUS to bless and make holy the flag of slaughter? ... Will the supplication appear in the next *Gazette*, to be forthwith inserted in the Book of Common Prayer?[10]

And, always, 'Q' is quick to seize upon instances of sheer, crass class blindness on the part of Britain's rulers. Thus he pillories Lord Brougham, the former Lord Chancellor, in 'Lord Brougham on Wet-Nurses' (6 April 1844) after Brougham argued in the Lords against a factory bill which sought to limit women factory-workers' hours to ten per day. Supporters of the bill had argued that children suffered from malnutrition because their mothers had no time to feed them but Brougham replied that peeresses and MPs' wives were also often prevented 'by their various avocations' from breast-feeding their children but he 'had never heard that any mischief resulted from that practice'. This is one of the comparatively infrequent 'Q' papers that appeared during 1844 (Laurie gets another lambasting in one of them) and only two more followed in 1845. The last to be published (15 March 1845) strikes an optimistic note about a future end to class antagonism. It faces a 'large cut' by Leech entitled 'The Reconciliation; or, As It Ought To Be', showing an aristocrat in full Garter robes doffing his hat to a respectfully forelock-tugging farm labourer. The aristocrat treads underfoot such hated class legislation as the Poor Laws and the Game Laws, the farm labourer likewise treads underfoot a smouldering brand, indicating renunciation of rick-burning and violent protest, and in the background the aristocrat's child teaches the alphabet to the labourer's. Accompanying the cartoon is the 'Q' piece written by Jerrold very much in his sentimental-Utopian vein:

> Surely there will come a time when the Rich and the Poor will fairly meet ... will hold a parliament of the heart, and pass acts that no after selfishness and wrong – on either side! – shall repeal! [W]hen the Rich shall have cast away the arrogance of wealth, their pride, their wicked and irreligious sense of exclusiveness – and the Poor shall have quenched all heart-burnings, all thoughts of revengeful wrong – then will it be a glorious sight ... to see man reconciled to man.

Until that time shall come, however, Jerrold, both in his 'Q' papers and in many of his numerous anonymous contributions (often mere squibs but also full-page pieces), continues to keep *Punch*'s predominantly middle-class readers vividly aware of the follies and misdeeds of the rich and powerful and the harshness of life for the poor.

During the latter part of 1841, while he was so vigorously making his mark in the new journal, Jerrold was smarting from the (as it seemed to him) malicious treatment afforded to his last historical comedy, *The White Milliner*, at Covent Garden in February of that year. According to his son's memoir, he believed that its condemnation by reviewers stemmed from the hostility inevitably incurred by any contemporary dramatist who 'kept aloof from a small faction'. Blanchard Jerrold does not indentify this 'faction' but it perhaps included the *Morning Chronicle* critic who conde-scendingly (but with deadly accuracy) asserted on 9 February 1841 that this play, and others of Jerrold's 'in the light vein of the drama' (comedy) merely showed how little talent he had in this genre and recommended him to 'stick to the little farcical line in which he first introduced himself to the public, and in which he has at present no rival'.

The resounding triumph in the same great national theatre of Dion Boucicault's breezy five-act comedy *London Assurance*, which followed hard upon the *Milliner*'s failure, and the first night of which Jerrold attended on 4 March 1841, would surely have rubbed salt into his wound.[11] Now he himself was seeking a double theatrical triumph. He submitted a 'light' three-act comedy, *The Prisoner of War*, to Macready, now at Drury Lane, and the full-scale five-act comedy of manners, *Bubbles of the Day*, to Madame Vestris and Charles Mathews at Covent Garden. The length of this last was a somewhat defiant gesture. A few years earlier Jerrold had said in the dedicatory epistle to T.J. Serle prefixed to *The Schoolfellows* (1835) that he had really wanted that comedy to be in five acts – 'but five acts in these days!'[12] He had perhaps been encouraged to go for a five-acter now by Boucicault's success or, more likely, by the earlier success of Bulwer's *Money* at the Haymarket (8 December 1840). *Money* was a five-act comedy like *London Assurance* but its elaborate satirising of contemporary mammon-worship gave it a literary status that would not have been accorded to Boucicault's piece, though the latter is certainly a better acting play. As regards *The Prisoner of War*, Jerrold told a lady who praised it that he had written it 'for success – for *mere* success':

> It is not exactly my notion of what a comedy *ought* to be ... [I] am, I own, as pleased as astonished that the piece has obtained the good word of higher minds than ordinarily sit in judgment upon modern dramas.[13]

Bubbles was first produced on 25 February 1842 at Covent Garden, where it seems to have been overshadowed by the great success of *London Assurance*. Jerrold later complained to Benjamin Webster, manager of the Haymarket, that Vestris and Mathews ran it for only eighteen nights, netting him only £270, whereas Boucicault's play had been allowed 'a long, uninterrupted run'. *Bubbles* was merely 'suffered to glisten between the shakes of a prima donna' and

> the author, with his tobacco-pipe and soap-dish, is on the eighteenth night of his blowing – *only* the eighteenth, my masters – of his blowing, compelled to make way for what? why – the German Flute![14]

Jerrold clearly feels that the play was not given a fair chance to establish itself but Charles Kemble's reported remark that *Bubbles* had 'wit enough for three comedies' points us to what was most probably a major reason for the play's failure. The very thing that contributed so strongly to the success of the 'Q' papers in *Punch*, the density and intensity of ingenious similes and metaphors, 'metaphysical' conceits, literary allusions and epigrammatic phrases – all this, when kept up throughout five acts, becomes, as the *Athenaeum*'s critic put it (5 March 1842), mere 'redundancy of vivacity' and 'fatiguing at last'. When, later, John Hollingshead was commenting on W.S. Gilbert's first serious effort as a playwright, (*An Old Score*, Gaiety Theatre, 1869), he compared its reception to that of many of Jerrold's comedies – 'a success with a first night and critical audience, but not an enduring success with the public'.[15]

Eight years before *Figaro in London* had pointed (1 February 1834) to 'one great fault' in Jerrold's dramas, namely that 'all his characters are *equally witty*', and this is still the case in *Bubbles*. This characteristic description of a perfidious love letter, for example, could have been spoken by just about any one of the numerous *dramatis personae*: 'every flourish [is] a mortal serpent to a woman's heart. The whole alphabet is here no less than six-and-twenty black assassins, marshalled to stab a woman's peace!' The play's extensive cast includes several paper-thin satirical sketches of various contemporary metropolitan political and literary types, like Lord Skindeep, an MP who wants to be thought a great philanthropist, mingled with older stock types, derived ultimately from Jonsonian comedy, like the corrupt City magnate Sir Phenix Clearcake, and no less than two pairs of young lovers in 18th-century comedy mode. But the play did not, as Horne remarked in his *New Spirit of the Age*, 'have story enough, nor action enough, for a good one-act drama'. Unlike Boucicault and

Bulwer, Jerrold did not have the art of developing a one-dimensional satirical type into a quirky comic character – with, as we shall see, one notable exception, but that was in another genre – nor of structuring a full-length comedy so as to build up dramatic tension towards a satisfying fifth-act dénouement. Even favourable reviews commented on this last failing. The *Era*, for example, after rhapsodising about the play's 'brilliancy of dialogue, sparkling wit, and caustic satire' ('The selfishness of the human heart is laid bare as an anatomical preparation ...'), criticises the comedy's 'want of construction, and meagreness of plot' (27 February 1842). *London Assurance* and *Money*, both well structured and containing some excellent comic characterisation, have shown themselves to be eminently capable, despite much strained 'witty' language, of successful revival in the modern theatre. *Bubbles*, however, though it may still be *read* with some enjoyment, rather as one might read Jerrold's better *Punch* pieces, was – after an enthusiastic first-night reception with a reluctant Jerrold having to be almost dragged across the stage by Mathews to acknowledge the plaudits of the audience – pretty well moribund as a piece of live theatre.

The slighter piece, *The Prisoner of War* which opened at Drury Lane on 1 March 1842, fared much better. It is set in Verdun in 1803, among a group of English tourists who, visiting France after the Peace of Amiens, now find themselves detained when war breaks out again. Its plot and love-interest are tritely conventional but the first production had other things going for it. Macready, according to his Diaries, 'bestowed much pains' on its production and Jerrold, having written it with his eye very much on the leading players in the Drury Lane company, had supplied each of them with a role that gave ample scope for the display of his or her special talents. Jerrold's old sparring-partner from his printer's-apprentice days, Samuel Phelps, 'astonished everybody' (so he later boasted to John Coleman[16]) as the crusty old sea-dog Captain Channel, and the Keeleys revelled in the roles of Peter and Polly Pallmall, a Cockney brother and sister. Peter's mania, or 'humour' as Ben Jonson would have termed it, is an extreme patriotism and G.H. Lewes wrote that what he calls Keeley's 'idealism'

> preserved the real comedy of the type from degenerating into gross caricature or unpleasant truthfulness. One recognised the national failing; but one liked the good-natured Briton. .... [I]t was the manner that gave the joke its *bouquet*; and when he vindicated the superiority of the air of England over the air of France, on the ground that it 'goes twice as far – it's twice as thick' the pit screamed with delight.

Lewes thought Mrs Keeley's part less well written but acknowledged that by her make up and acting, above all by 'the inimitable manner in which she read a letter interrupted by sobs', she 'raised the part into first-rate importance'.[17] Jerrold himself was delighted, telling her, she later recalled, 'You've topped your author!' (a very rare instance of his allowing the actor to be exalted above the playwright), and dedicating the published version of the play to her and her husband.[18] The *Prisoner*'s popularity (it ran until

127

mid-April) led to its later revival by Charles Kean for performance before the Queen, and to its being chosen as one of the two Jerrold plays to be performed with Phelps and the Keeleys in their original parts during the 'funeral games' Dickens organised after Jerrold's death, (the other play, was, naturally, *Black Eyed Susan*).

No matter how pleased Jerrold was by the success of the *Prisoner*, the failure of the far more ambitious *Bubbles* was a severe blow for him. In spite of the new source of steady weekly income provided by his *Punch* salary and casual earnings, such as the five guineas paid him on 14 April for a sketch for *Bentley's Miscellany*,[19] he was again in financial difficulty – hence, probably, the long periods he and his wife spent in Boulogne this year. In a letter of 2 July he offers *Bubbles* to Webster 'for £30 for all past and future representations for present season' but, if this is not acceptable, he apologetically tells Webster that he must still 'intrude upon' him for £15 (for three performances already given[20]) 'as just now the villainy of a scoundrel makes every pound 40s to me'.[21] We do not know what lies behind this somewhat melodramatic allusion, though it may well have something to do with the 'Proclamation of Outlawry' that had just been pronounced against Jerrold in the Middlesex County Court (on 30 June, when he was en route back to London from Boulogne), presumably in connection with some outstanding debt he was now legally obliged to pay. Further evidence of Jerrold's need to raise money at this time is provided by his agreement, dated the same day as his request to Webster, to write for *Punch* a series entitled 'Punch's Letters to his Son'. For this he received from Bradbury and Evans (who were in the process of taking over the proprietorship of *Punch* and easing Landells out) the sum of £52 10s[22] and the first 'Letter' duly appeared in the issue for July.

The Letters are a prolonged exercise in irony, like the little *Handbook of Swindling*, purportedly written by the 'scamp and cur' Captain Barabbas Whitefeather, that Jerrold had published anonymously in 1839. As Thackeray's later *Punch* series, 'Mr Brown's letters to a Young man about Town' (1849), was also to do, Jerrold's 'Punch's Letters' parody (but much more savagely) Lord Chesterfield's mentoring letters to his illegitimate son, written in 1774. Like Dickens, who was contemporaneously caricaturing Chesterfield in the figure of the thoroughly black-hearted polished hypocrite Mr Chester in his novel *Barnaby Rudge*, Jerrold sees these letters as the very epitome of elegant 18th-century heartlessness and cynicism. Each of his Punch's letters, like those of C.S. Lewis's Screwtape, supports some blatantly amoral or immoral rule of conduct ('Choose your friend as you would choose an orange; for his golden outside, and for the promise of yielding much, when well squeezed') and then illustrates it by the kind of allegorical anecdote that was very much one of Jerrold's trademarks. In Letter XI ('On the Necessity of Hypocrisy') Jerrold takes the opportunity to hit back at those critics who accuse him of bitterness, 'painting human thoughts and motives more darkly than nature formed them', and 'dipping his pen in his own bile':[23]

My son, never see the meanness of mankind. Let men hedge, and shirk, and shift, and lie, and with faces of unwrinkled adamant tell you the most monstrous falsehoods, either in their self-glorification, or to disguise some habitual paltriness, still never detect the truth ... . By these means ... you will be deemed a sociable, a most good-natured fellow. ... To have an insight – or at least to show you have – into the dirty evasions of life, is to have a moral squint. To lay your finger upon a plague-spot, is to be infected with malice.

... When you have seen something more of the world, you will know that men rarely attribute an exposure of a social evil to an inherent indignation of the evil itself, but to an unhealthy appetite for moral foulness. ... The wrestlers of old, says Plutarch, threw dirt on one another that they might get a better grasp, and more successfully trip up each other's heels. In the like way, does ignorance and hypocrisy, in the name of virtue, cast dirt upon him who would trip up the giant wrong. There were, doubtless, those among the Philistines – particular and most virtuous friends of Goliath – who called David a very bitter, ill-natured little fellow.

Jerrold manages, in fact, to have it both ways as regards his satire on fashionable amorality. Punch's instructions, strictly adhered to by his son, lead the latter not to the worldly profit and success that Lord Chesterfield hoped for his son, but to the condemned cell at Newgate following a conviction for theft ('It is a case of mutton and I am to be hanged on Monday'). Jerrold being so profoundly in tune with the essentially melo-dramatic and optimistic nature of the dominant ideology of his day, it is axiomatic that in these Letters, as in the majority of his works, evil must in the end be seen to be defeated or, better still, self-defeating.

Not long after 'Punch's Letters to His Son' had begun their run in *Punch*, Jerrold's disappointment over *Bubbles of the Day* must have been further assuaged by the success of another 'light' comedy (only two acts this time) brought out at Covent Garden on 30 August and called *Gertrude's Cherries; or Waterloo in 1835*. It played nightly until 17 September and then twice a week until 4 October. Jerrold used the same formula as he had used for *The Prisoner of War* mixing traditional romantic comedy with Dickensian-style characters whose 'humour' or whose occupation colours their every word and action. Such is Mr Crossbone, the newly-married Houndsditch undertaker, who, 'having an eye to business', has determined to 'spend the honeymoon in the principal churchyards on the Continent'. Like many British tourists of the day (Dickens's Mr Meagles in *Little Dorrit* is another literary example), he is an avid souvenir-hunter and the field of Waterloo promises rich pickings: 'If I can only get the skeleton of a French dragoon for my summer house I shall be happy.' He meets his match in Aristide Blague, an infinitely resourceful and plausible Belgian vendor of fake souvenirs, a role that was the making of Alfred Wigan, a young actor Jerrold had befriended and who had stayed with him in Boulogne. The *Theatrical Journal*, always well disposed towards Jerrold, eagerly anticipated the production of this new comedy by 'the "freshest" and most original writer, in his terse and quaint style, of our day' (3 September 1842) and was delighted by the play in performance: 'It has all the writer's rich peculiarity, biting sarcasm, strong contrast of light and shade, sparkling wit, and startling antithesis' (17 September 1842). The *Examiner* review of the same day, probably by Forster, admitted that there was some truth in the charge made by other reviewers that Jerrold was repeating, less successfully, effects from *The Prisoner of War* but contended that this did not matter as 'the thoughts are not repeated' and went on to attribute the play's success to the sheer power of Jerrold's witty satirical writing, his '*hard hitting*':

> Actors may completely fail this writer, his story desert him, his audience begin to yawn; and even under these ribs of death his wit shall create a soul. Some such dangers beset the little comedy more than once, but the rescue was efficient and complete, and all Mr Jerrold's own.

There was a sour after-note to this little triumph, however, in that Macready evidently complained to Forster that by taking *Gertrude* to Covent Garden Jerrold had broken a pledge to write his next piece for Drury Lane. This clearly stung Jerrold to judge by the unusual length of his letter of indignant repudiation, written to Forster from Boulogne, where he had returned after *Gertrude*'s production. He had, he asserted, been treated earlier at Drury Lane like 'a dealer and chapman – a mere seller of sentences' and had therefore subsequently felt free to take his wares 'to the highest bidder'. 'No one', he added, will rejoice more heartily than myself when the atmosphere of a theatre may enable the dramatist to feel that he is pursuing an art, and not a handicraft – and that all the cordialities of the profession are not summed up in l.s.d.[24]

The jovial fellowship of the weekly dinners of *Punch*'s proprietors and its 'staffers' round their beloved 'mahogany tree' as Thackeray had dubbed their dining-table in *Punch*, 9 January 1847 (in fact it was deal), and the way in which he had so quickly established himself as the new magazine's star writer, must surely have contrasted strongly in Jerrold's mind with all the manifold vexations, difficult personal relationships and disappointments that seemed perpetually to dog his career as a dramatist. Being a downright trading journalist, paid at so much per week or per column, might have seemed preferable to the uneasy tension between, on the one hand, the desire for artistic achievement and recognition as a not unworthy heir to the great English dramatists of the past (above all, of course, to his adored Shakespeare) and, on the other, the urgent need for commercial success as well as *succès d'éstime*. Nevertheless, he still tenaciously pursued his ambition to make a permanent addition to the nation's dramatic literature and in the summer of 1841 began work on another full-length comedy. This was intended for Webster to produce at the Haymarket where, as we have seen, *Bubbles* had briefly appeared after its Covent Garden production. During the autumn however, a severe bout of rheumatism interposed, as he later told Dickens, 'like a despotic editor' and forced him to write on his manuscript the words 'to be continued'.[25] He had caught a chill as he sat one evening reading on the Boulogne pier-head, his son tells us, 'and in a few days the old enemy, rheumatism, attacked his eyes':

a French doctor came to him and treated him as a horse might be treated. He was blistered, and again blistered. He shrieked if the light of the smallest candle reached him; yet he could, if the chord were touched, say a sharp thing. This French doctor had just been operating on the patient. The patient had winced a little, and the operator had said, 'Tut! tut! It's nothing – nothing at all!' Presently some hot water was brought in. The doctor put his fingers in it, and sharply withdrew them with an oath. The patient, who was now lying, faint, upon the sofa, said, 'Tut! tut! It's nothing – nothing at all!'

A quick visit to London in early November to see a specialist seems to have brought further relief even though 'thick spots' still came before his eyes when he read or wrote for any length of time. Somehow he still managed to keep the 'Punch's Letters' series going (or maybe had stockpiled enough instalments in advance) but work on a projected review-article on Rabelais, one of his most cherished literary idols, had to be suspended. Blanchard Jerrold quotes his letter to Forster, to whom the article had been promised for the *Foreign Quarterly Review* (of which Forster had just become Editor), 'I might still eke out sight enough for it without any permanent evil, yet the nervous irritability which besets me, weakens every mental faculty.' In this state he had to undergo a further shock when a much-loved fourteen-year-old niece ('a lovable, affectionate creature, little less to me than a daughter' he told Forster), died suddenly of typhus at her school; cutting short his London visit and returning to France, Jerrold found his wife 'almost frantic with what she felt to be a terrible responsibility; for we had brought the child only last April from her heart-broken mother, to Boulogne'.[26]

Whether it was because of all the troubles that came upon them in Boulogne or because the financial situation had eased somewhat, the Jerrolds returned to London for good in December. On top of his regular *Punch* salary (two very spirited 'Q' papers appeared this month) and the money already received for the serial rights of 'Punch's Letters' Jerrold received at this time a further £50 for the copyright of the series which Bradbury and Evans proposed to reprint in volume form,[27] as they would do with all successful *Punch* series in the future.

After a short time in lodgings in the Vale of Health, Hampstead, the Jerrolds moved into a small but picturesque new house close to Regent's Park. This was Number 3 Gothic Cottages, Park Village East, where, in a study 'bowered by trees', Jerrold gradually got back to regular work – though for a while he was unable to write by candlelight. He embarked on what was to become his first novel, *The Story of a Feather*,which was serialised in *Punch* during 1843, and 'on account' of which he received a payment of £25 from Bradbury and Evans on 4 January,[28] a payment presumably over and above his regular salary. From March onwards he added greatly to his workload, but also presumably to his income, first by writing for a new weekly called the *Pictorial Times* and then by accepting the editorship of Herbert Ingram's new monthly journal the *Illuminated Magazine* (see Chapter 8 for details). None of this prevented him from continuing to supply a steady stream of miscellaneous contributions to *Punch*. Sometimes these were mere two- or three-line squibs, such as the one headed 'An "Insane" Question' which asks, 'As there can be no doubt that *Hamlet* has in his character a considerable touch of *insanity*, ought not Mr Charles Kean, when appearing in the part, be allowed to *murder* Shakespear [*sic*] with impunity?'. Frequently, however, they were whole-page articles including sixteen 'Q' papers. The only *Punch* staffer who was more prolific was Gilbert à Beckett.

The Story of a Feather, which was very popular, introduced a new note into *Punch*, one of sentiment and of that tragic-heroic presentation of the poor which reached its apogee with the publication of Thomas Hood's harrowing poem about a starving seamstress, 'The Song of the Shirt', in the Christmas number for 1843. Patty Butler, Jerrold's heroine, is a gentle, sweet-natured fifteen-year-old, whose creation may owe something to memories of his recently-dead little niece and perhaps also to Dickens's Little Nell. The story begins in 1762, the last year in which a Prince of Wales had been born before the birth of Victoria's first male child in November 1841. Patty lives with her dying mother in 'a long, dark lane' off the north side of the Strand, 'one of those noisome, pestilent retreats, abutting on, yet hidden by, the wealth and splendour of the metropolis', where, in 'an almost empty garret', she toils for a pittance at her trade of feather-dressing. By choosing the bizarre device, one well suited to his taste for quaintness and grotesquerie, of having the story narrated by an ostrich-feather (he may have been imitating the device used by Charles Johnstone in his mid-18th-century satire *Chrysal, or the Adventures of a Guinea*), Jerrold is able to make a link between the highest and the lowest echelons of society. The feather, groomed and dressed by starving Patty in her garret, finds itself in Buckingham Palace waving above the cot of the future George IV. Jerrold had already seized the opportunity in one of his 'Q' papers (20 November 1841) for some ironic reflections on the two 'happy events' of 1762 and 1841 in relation to the lives of the poor and finds ample scope to develop them in this story.

Notwithstanding the awkward fantasy of the feather-narrator device, Jerrold manages to sustain a lively, if highly episodic, narrative, which introduces a rich variety of character-types, in his *Heads of the People* vein, one of the most effective being a Hogarthian procuress called Mrs Gaptooth. There are also some vividly-drawn sketches of London street-life and of backstage life in Garrick's theatre, as well as some good sensation scenes at the Old Bailey and in Newgate, where the innocent and terrified Patty is at one point unjustly confined just as Martha Willis had been before her (like Martha, Patty is constantly, and thrillingly, threatened by an evil old woman and various predatory males). Jerrold further enlivens his story with farcical episodes of lower-middle-class, conventionally misogynistic, domestic comedy involving domineering or jealous wives, a hypocritical preacher (a Muggletonian called Uriah Cloudy), and a foolish Frenchman who trains poodles to dance and is driven to drunkenness by his shrewish wife, much to the disgust of his fellow-topers at the Horse and Anchor:

These true-hearted Britons ... considered it something like impertinence, conceit, in a Frenchman to get beastly drunk; it was very like a liberty in a foreigner. Therefore, they manfully marked their censure of the circumstance by filling the offender's pockets with soot, by blackening his face with the same substance – whilst an indignant wag emptied the mustard-pot upon the Frenchman's skull telling him, to the glee of the party, that yellow hair became him beautifully. (ch.19)

The mid-18th-century setting of the story is merely a thin historical veneer, allowing the introduction of Kitty Clive and other real-life figures from the Georgian stage, a highwayman (like the one in *Martha Willis*), and various other picturesque details. Jerrold clearly has his eye on the contemporary world in such passages as his scathing condemnation of the mercenary nature of many Society marriages made in 'the slave-markets of St James's' (ch.12), and in his exaltation of the moral virtue and spiritual value to be found in the poorest of the poor:

Unseen, unknown, are the divinities that – descending from garrets – tread the loud, foul, sordid crowding highways of London. Spiritual presences, suffering all things, and in the injustice – most hard to turn to right – of our social purpose, living and smiling, daily martyrs to their creed of good. Young children, widowed age, and withered singleness – the ardent student, flushed and fed with little else but hope – the disappointed, yet brave, good old man, a long, long loser in the worldly fight … all of these in their thousand shades of character and spirit – the army of martyrs to fortune, and the social iniquities that, dressed and spangled for truths, man passes off on man – all of this bright band have, and *do*, and will consecrate the garrets of London, and make a holy thing of poverty … .(ch.5)

But *Punch*'s respectable readers had no need to fear any revolutionary propaganda nor any flouting of the rules of melodrama, the age's dominant mode of understanding and interpreting human existence, through the pure young heroine's coming to a bad end. No matter how stridently he inveighed against social injustice and the harsh fate of the poor, and no matter how much he mocked the treatment of misery in novels where it is 'generally hung with golden fringe at the end' (ch.33), Jerrold was far too much at one with the mass of his readers, politically and aesthetically, to disconcert or disappoint them. Rescued from the dark and wicked city by two wealthy but unworldly old maids, Patty is taken, like Oliver Twist before her, to live and thrive in the healthy, happy countryside (Jerrold, thoroughly and deplorably participating – even at the expense of the moral coherence of his characters – in *Punch*'s fondness for what we would now call blatantly sexist jokes calls the old spinsters' home 'Mantrap Park'). And her happy marriage with a virtuous young clergyman called Inglewood (his name evoking both domesticity and rurality) is made possible by the paternalistic benevolence of a nobleman whose chaplain Inglewood had once been.

Besides *The Story of a Feather* and all the miscellaneous pieces contributed to *Punch* in 1843, Jerrold, aided by Leech's vivid depictions of the character, also introduced into the magazine the richly comic figure of a snobbish and culturally pretentious footman called by the generic servant-name of Jenkins. Jenkins, whose ludicrously affected language foreshadows the 'Pseuds' Corner' column in today's *Private Eye*, was based on the *Morning Post*'s opera critic (this paper, forerunner of the *Daily Telegraph*, was very much aimed at a self-consciously fashionable readership of the 'nobility and gentry', or those who wished to be thought such). Jerrold would joyfully seize on a paragraph like the following in the *Post*'s opera column and quote it, supplying some mischievous italicisation and capitalisation:

Ever since the Italian lyrical drama crossed the Alps in the suite of the tasteful Medicis, its *vogue* has daily increased … it is *the quintessence of all civilised pleasures*, and *wherever* its principal *virtuosi* hoist their standard, *there for the time is* THE CAPITAL OF EUROPE where the *most illustrious, noble, elegant, and tasteful* members of society *assemble*.

'We do earnestly hope', Jerrold comments,

> that Jenkins ... will keep this profound truth from the knowledge of the
> singers and the dancers. Only ... imagine them in a fit of the sulks to take
> ship for Sidney, or Adelaide, or Macquarrie Harbour; there immediately
> would be 'the capital of Europe'. Jenkins, be an Englishman. Would you
> destroy your country? Would you deprive us at once of the 'most illustrious –
> noble – elegant – and tasteful?' For the sake of the nation scatter not these
> firebrand truths.

The *Post*'s critic deplores the presence of 'objectionable spectators' at the
Opera in the shape of 'valets, tailors and shoemakers' who get into the pit
through tickets provided by actors or singers for whom they have worked
and who are accompanied by 'their frowsy dames'. Jerrold has a field day
with such blatant snobbery, which would be, of course, deeply offensive to
Punch's extensive readership of small tradesmen and artisans:

> Now, reader, can you not sympathise with the sufferings that have produced
> this horror of tailors and shoemakers in the breast of Jenkins! See him in the
> pit. He rises – looks airily about him, then falls, as though shot, upon his seat.
> And wherefore? Alas! he has caught the eye of his tailor in the pit – his
> long-suffering unpaid tailor: he turns him round – ha! – dreadful apparition!
> there is the very shoemaker whose trusted cordovan of three years' wear still
> protects the feet of Jenkins![29]

It was not long after Jenkins had made his bow in *Punch* that both Mary
Ann Jerrold and one of her daughters, Jane or Mary, fell ill, and in spring
Jerrold decided to move his family to the more bracing air of the Kentish
resort of Herne Bay for the summer. On a jaunt there the previous summer
with Landells and Mayhew he had been attracted by the way its quietness
contrasted with its 'flaunty neighbours, Ramsgate and Margate' and by the
beautiful countryside, 'unpolluted by the innovations of fashionable taste',
in which it was set.[30] He hired what he described to Dickens as 'a little
cabin, built up of ivy and woodbine, and almost within sound of the sea'
and his son paints an idyllic picture of this summer of 1843 with his father
enjoying the countryside 'like a boy':

> He was in the orchard when the dew was on the grass; he played upon the
> haycocks. He was known in the Bay for his lively talk with the bathing folk.
> In the villages round about he would watch the sports, and laugh as though
> he had just come out of school. Every minute the beauty of the country
> enraptured him. He would pick a beetle from a rose-bush, and laying it on
> the back of his hand would watch it for half an hour, and then put it upon
> the flower again.

According to Hodder, the Jerrolds hospitably received many visitors at
Herne Bay. The hours of hard grind that Jerrold had to get through every
day to meet his heavy commitments to both *Punch* and the *Illuminated*

were dealt with in the very early morning (no lingering in that dewy orchard, it seems), so that Jerrold 'never seemed absent from his guests', and could busy himself with organising jolly excursions, such as a jaunt to Whitstable to eat oysters 'fresh from the sea' and washed down with 'some obviously-smuggled Schiedam'.[31] His companions on this expedition were Hodder, Leech, Henry Mayhew and Kenny Meadows. Mayhew was deep into one of his great projects, this time an English dictionary ('on a very elaborate scale', says Hodder) and was living in a neighbouring farmhouse from whence he would, Blanchard Jerrold recalls, come striding across the fields at sunset, pipe in mouth, to spend the evening in 'talk of books and men'. It was during these talks, perhaps, that a mutual attraction began between Mayhew and Jerrold's elder daughter, Jane Matilda, which, notwithstanding the big age-difference (Mayhew was at this time thirty-two years old and Jane was just eighteen), was to lead to their marriage in the following year.

Once again, Jerrold tried hard, as he had done in Boulogne, to get Laman Blanchard to come and stay with him:

> I am down here ... in quiet and *greenery* again, to the which I wish I could stir you; but all such endeavours seem as fruitless as 'twould be to fling one's glove in the face of Charles at Charing Cross; the statue wouldn't move – but remain fixed and dignified in London smoke.

He adds: 'I never get to London without an increasing wish to get out of it. I think, after all, I shall die in a smockfrock.'[32]

The idyllic summer was succeeded by a distressing autumn back in London when Jerrold's 'foul fiend of rheumatism', as he called it[33] attacked him again and this time so severely that he had to suspend both *The Story of a Feather* and – what probably upset him more as being much closer to his heart and more central to his literary ambitions – the 'Chronicles of Clovernook' series that he was publishing in the *Illuminated*. He decided, or was advised, to try the fashionable cold water cure at Malvern and went there in December. He put himself under the direction of Dr James Gully, the great pioneer of hydropathic treatment, and reported to Lemon in a letter dated simply 'Sunday':

> I am getting on well; but find such invigorating good from the *douche* bath, that I may (Gully says I ought) to stay here until Saturday week. I was on the hills this morning in *such* a frosty wind! I have no doubt that the treatment will set me up for life; especially as I shall continue its principal points – cold bathing, water-drinking, and *no* grog; and that I may do all this, I shall certainly live out of town. I may have time enough *yet* to do some-thing.[34]

The last sentence is a poignant reminder of Jerrold's constantly-frustrated Miltonic yearning to leave 'something so written to after-time' that people would not willingly let it die. Now, however, as throughout so much of his career, he was beset both by illness and by urgent financial necessity and had to ask Lemon for help in raising some ready cash. He has not, he tells Lemon, yet paid Gully anything and will have school fees to pay when he gets back to London. Calculating that he will need another £30 ('The £10', he writes, 'has gone to clothe the women, who were really fast approaching a state of Evedom'), he asks Lemon to send a quick response 'as I shall be on tenterhooks'. 'I'm afraid that this will bother you,' he adds apologetically.

On 31 December Jerrold wrote to Bradbury and Evans that his 'late idleness' lay heavily on his conscience 'but it has been a part of the penalty of my illness that when I would have worked with the most pleasure, there I have been useless'. He had, in fact, been working on some copy for the New Year number but a relapse had prevented his finishing it. Gully had reassured him, however, that such set-backs were 'part of the system' and he was now gaining strength again and expecting to 'altogether crush down the malady'. Bradbury and Evans had perhaps been less than happy about his editing of the *Illuminated* and he assures them that this would soon end so that he could devote all his energies to *Punch*: 'I quite agree with you that *Punch* is worthy of the best efforts of anybody.'[35] By 23 January Dickens had heard from Forster that Jerrold had been 'discharged cured'. The 'bent immovable figure' that had left Number 3 Gothic Cottages for Malvern returned home, his son remembered, 'with a light easy step' and plunged once more into regular work for *Punch*. During the first half of 1844 he contributed dozens of columns'-worth of squibs and articles to the magazine, exceeded in total amount only, and as always, by Gilbert à Beckett.

He also revised *The Story of a Feather* for volume publication in May 1844, dedicating the little book to his two daughters 'from their affectionate father' and noting in a preface that he had endeavoured to render the later chapters 'less imperfect than when they originally appeared; written, as they then were, under severe illness'. He sent a copy to Dickens whose enthusiastic response is quoted by Blanchard Jerrold:

> I am truly proud of your remembrance, and have put the 'Story of a Feather' on a shelf (not an obscure one) where some other feathers are, which it shall help to show mankind which way the wind blows, long after *we* know where the wind comes from. I am quite delighted to find that you have touched the latter part again, and touched it with such a delicate and tender hand. It is a wise and beautiful book. I am sure I may venture to say so to you, for nobody consulted it more regularly and earnestly than I did, as it came out in *Punch*.

By this time a notable new recruit had also become a *Punch* 'staffer'. Thackeray, Jerrold's old journalist-artist friend from his Paris days nine years before, had succeeded to the place vacated by the bounderish showman Albert Smith whose boisterous flamboyance had very much grated on Jerrold (once, noticing Smith's initials, he had asked, 'Why does that man only ever tell two thirds of the truth?'). Conscious of his own gentlemanly background, Thackeray evidently felt that he had to excuse himself for being involved with what he described to his pious and high-minded mother as 'a very low paper called Punch'. It paid well, he told her, and gave him 'a great opportunity for unrestrained laughter sneering kicking and gambadoing'.[36] Between January 1844 and June 1848 he was to contribute, on average, roughly half of the amount of copy that Jerrold did, and less than half of the amount à Beckett did.[37] He also supplied many deliciously comic illustrations for his own pieces. Thackeray quickly became the third great mainstay of *Punch*'s writing staff and his advent, as we shall see, considerably altered the dynamics of the group, particularly in relation to Jerrold.

On 9 September 1844 Jerrold wrote to Hodder that he had been 'worked to death for *Punch*, having it all on my shoulders, Mark [Lemon], à Beckett, and Thackeray being away'.[38] 'Nevertheless,' he adds, 'last week it went up 1500.' During the last six months of this year he was regularly contributing half a dozen or more items, of varying length, to each number. Included was a new weekly epistolary series, 'Punch's Complete Letter-Writer', parodying the letter-writing manuals that had become popular. These *Punch* letters are mostly exercises in the sort of domestic humour for which the early Victorian middle classes seemed to have an inexhaustible appetite ('From a Young Gentleman, soliciting his Father to pay his Debts' is a characteristic title), but there are some that have rather more bite, such as those that show the exploitation and harsh treatment of governesses by wealthy employers such as 'the Hon. Mrs Flint' and 'Lady Honoria Asphalt'. In his miscellaneous pieces Jerrold continued to deride and lampoon such oppressors of the poor as Sir Peter Laurie as he bore down heavily on yet another desperate would-be suicide, or the Marquess of Londonderry threatening to evict miners on his land for joining a trades-union. He attacked, too, all those who interfered with individual liberty, whether in England like the Home Secretary, Sir James Graham, who had authorised the opening of private letters on anti-espionage grounds, or – far more appallingly – abroad, like the Czar driving thousands of Jews into internal exile in 'the deserts of the interior of Russia'. Recalling the rapturous welcome given to the Czar the previous summer by 'high-born ladies of England – wives and mothers – conveniently oblivious of the women of Poland, of their every domestic tie torn by the autocrat asunder', Jerrold pretends to regret that the Czar had not postponed his visit until 'the wrongs and sorrows of another *one-hundred-and-fifty-thousand* of his fellow-creatures would, if possible, have made him more lustrous in the eyes of his worshippers'. Victoria and Albert's participation in blood sports also draws his fire ('"Sporting" at Blair Atholl' and 'The Queen and the Otter'), as does such political showmanship as Disraeli's smoking a peace pipe with some native Americans on exhibition in London ('Ben Sidonia smoking the Calumet with the Ioways'). But some of his fiercest invective is, as always, directed against militarism, whether

138

French (in Algeria) or British ('Sons of Glory! Recruiting at Birmingham').[39] From the moment the 'homicidal shilling' is slipped into the raw recruit's hand, Jerrold writes in the latter piece, he is

> at Her Majesty's service to cut, stab, burn and destroy, as though all human will and human conscience were suddenly stricken dead within him, and he was left no other than a machine of bone and muscle ....

In August 1844 Jerrold acted as a special correspondent to report for *Punch* on a great Burns Festival in Ayr, and seized the opportunity to expose what he saw as the humbug of official Scottish penitence for allowing Burns to die in near-poverty whilst Willy Thom the 'weaver-poet' of Inverurie, whose book *Rhymes and Recollections* was about to be published, had received no help from any institutional or governmental source. Only the generous patronage of a local landowner, Jerrold told Forster, had stood between Thom and 'the direst wretchedness'.[40] Thanks to Jerrold's comments in *Punch* and a favourable notice of *Rhymes* by Forster in the *Examiner*, Thom's financial situation improved greatly though Walter Jerrold quotes Jerrold as writing to another correspondent on 10 October,

> almost all the assistance has been from the south. Scotland has kept her purse-strings with a double-knot in 'em, even though it seems that half-far-things have been expressly issued to tempt her liberality.

By the time he was writing this letter Jerrold and his family had moved to West Lodge, Putney Common, a pleasant-looking, white-walled, somewhat rambling structure, shaded by lime-trees and entirely surrounded by gipsy-haunted common land (the site is now covered by Putney Hospital). According to the 1851 census (which gives the address as 32, Lower Common, Putney) Jerrold's nearest neighbours included a carter and several gardeners. Writing to Laman Blanchard on 6 October to urge him to become a regular contributor to *Punch*, Jerrold describes himself as having moved 'into the desert' but adds, 'there is an oasis, in the shape of an excellent garden; out of which I hope to dig two or three plays and books of better quality than any yet from the same hand.' He urges his beloved friend to come and visit him ('There are lots of Fulham omnibuses – and a boat leaves the Essex-st. (Strand) wharf at 20 minutes to every hour. My house lies about one third of a mile from the bridge') and gives his reasons for the move:

> I was determined not to risk another winter on the clay of Regent's Park. Besides I was too near London – and the convivial calls of the *Punch* club tho' pleasant, were neither healthful nor profitable.[41]

Jerrold was to remain at West Lodge for seven very productive years and it is the address most regularly associated with him by 19th-century literary chroniclers. When he moved there in the autumn of 1844 his family consisted of himself, his wife, his three sons William Blanchard, Douglas Edmund and Thomas Serle, respectively aged eighteen, sixteen and eleven, and his younger daughter, the thirteen-year-old Mary Ann, always known as 'Polly'. William Blanchard was a student at the Royal Academy Life School but was soon to abandon art in favour of journalism because of his weak eyes, and the two other boys were still at school. Jerrold's older daughter Jane had been six months married to Henry Mayhew, 'a blasted philosopher not worth a straw', according to Jerrold's boon-companion Harry Baylis who made up some 'chaffing' verses for the wedding, including this broad allusion to the poor pecuniary outlook for the happy couple.[42] Quite apart from the precariousness of Jane's situation, Jerrold had at this stage, as we have seen, five mouths to feed beside his own, so it was just as well that he was now on the verge of achieving his greatest popular success since *Black Eyed Susan* and that, this time, it would be one from which he himself would profit as well as others.

Chapter Eight

Editing the *Illuminated* and Chronicling Clovernook

1843-1844

In May 1842 Herbert Ingram, a friend of Mark Lemon's from his boyhood days in Boston, Lincolnshire, launched a remarkable new weekly paper, the *Illustrated London News*. Ingram, a former printer's apprentice, had worked as a bookseller and newsagent in Nottingham where, in partnership with his brother-in-law Nathaniel Cooke, he made a fortune from patent medicine.[1] Ingram came to London with the idea of starting a magazine that should help publicise his wares. It was to be very much an illustrated journal because he had noticed that, whenever a newspaper happened to feature an illustration, its sales shot up, and the development of the art of the woodcut meant that such illustrations could now be produced much more cheaply than by the old method of engraving on steel. According to Joseph Hatton, who was a good friend of Lemon's, *Punch*'s editor was Ingram's 'chief adviser' in the early days of the *Illustrated London News*. The wood-engraver Henry Vizetelly, whom Ingram recruited to work on the paper, asserts in his memoirs that Lemon 'knew nothing about the matter', but Hatton is surely closer to the truth. It seems most unlikely that Ingram would have failed to seek advice and help in his new venture from an old friend who was already editing an illustrated London weekly, albeit one of a rather different nature from the paper he himself was planning.[2] There is also the testimony of Charles Mackay, who became editor of the *Illustrated London News* in 1852, in his *Forty Years' Recollections*. He records that Lemon himself and other 'Punchites' – the Mayhew brothers, Albert Smith and Jerrold – all 'habitually contributed' to the *Illustrated London News*, while Kenny Meadows, Landells, Leech, and H.G. Hine all contributed on the pictorial side, though the magazine's mainstay here was John (later Sir John) Gilbert, whose employment on *Punch* Jerrold had opposed on the grounds that his style was too artistic. Spielmann reports him as having objected, 'We don't want Rubens on *Punch!*'

The *Illustrated London News* was an immediate success, reaching a circulation of 25,000 by the end of its first year[3], but early in 1843, Vizetelly fell out with Ingram and set up a rival publication in partnership with the Queen's printer, Andrew Spottiswoode. It was called the *Pictorial Times. A Weekly Journal of News, Literature, Fine Arts and the Drama* and the first issue appeared on 18 March. Ingram's *Illustrated London News* had declared that it would eschew party politics and be 'earnestly domestic'. It had also proclaimed, however, that it would be 'above all' concerned with 'the English poor' and that three 'essential elements of discussion' in its pages would be the Poor Laws, the Factory Laws, and conditions of work in the mines. It would support Lord Ashley in his campaign to ameliorate the lot of factory workers and miners, it would attack the Poor Laws – not wholesale but only 'in their clauses of cruelty and of wrong' – and it would keep a close eye on the nature of the justice meted out by magistrates, judges, and coroners. This all sounds very close to the stance of Jerrold's *Punch* and, indeed, in the early numbers Kenny Meadows supplied several comic little courtroom sketches that could equally well have appeared in *Punch*. The *Pictorial Times*, on the other hand, might have been expected to keep a much greater distance between itself and anything political or critical of authority. Spottiswoode was an arch Tory, who, wrote Vizetelly, 'if he could have had his own way, would certainly have transported every chartist in the kingdom', and he probably saw the *Illustrated London News* as a dangerously radical rag.

This being so, it seems surprising, on the face of it, that Vizetelly should have invited Jerrold, of all people, to write leading articles for the *Pictorial Times* – even if they were to be 'confined exclusively to social topics', and equally surprising that Jerrold should have agreed to do so. Perhaps Spottiswoode was a generous paymaster and this enabled Vizetelly to recruit also the other leading 'Punchites' – Lemon to act as drama critic, as recommended by Jerrold; Thackeray to write on art (as 'Michael Angelo Titmarsh'); and à Beckett to contribute 'humorous columns'. Vizetelly describes the 'curious' meeting between Jerrold, 'the aggressive radical with a professed contempt for titled folks', and Spottiswoode the 'uncompromising tory'. The two men

> vied with each other in displaying their urbanity. Jerrold, who was at once deferential and genial, soon saw an opening for an inoffensive jest ... Spottiswoode's habitual austerity at once relaxed; he laughed appreciatively, and the conversation drifted into a pleasant channel.[4]

However 'urbane' Jerrold might have been at this meeting, a glance at his leaders in the *Pictorial Times* (they can be identified only by internal evidence but Jerrold's hand is unmistakable) shows that he did not modify his 'Q' style or alter his 'Q' themes for the new paper. A leader in the first issue, commenting on the recent Chartist trials, argues that 'another means' exists of dealing with the social threat posed by Chartism:

> We must prove that we have quickened sympathies towards the condition of the labouring class. There is a cold, calculating philosophy, the result of enormous wealth, that lays down an iron line of demarcation between the well-to-do in this world and those whose sole capital (the only capital of ADAM) is labour. We cannot, must not blink our eyes to this fact – that ... a

country which towers above the world in its political greatness ... that sends its thousands of missionaries from pole to pole ... has, like ulcers in its bosom, hordes of its own children, whose social darkness and whose physical privations, are not less dark and terrible than the condition of the most forlorn savage life ... .

Let us send missionaries among the poor of our own country and we shall hear less of Chartism. Let us send sympathy to do its glorious mission at the quenched hearth, the loafless cupboard, of the artisan. ...

Over the next few months Jerrold wrote many other vigorous leading articles denouncing such social evils as prize-fighting (comparing the fighters to the 'self-mortifying' fakirs of the East with their 'maimed joints' and 'slashed flesh'[5]) corrupt elections, public executions, the expensive and obfuscatory 'word-mongering' of the legal profession, the plight of the young lace-workers in Nottingham who were forced into prostitution in order to survive, and the national disgrace of allowing the East India Company to continue its lucrative opium trade despite strong protests from the Chinese government. Quintessentially Jerroldian is one leader (24 April) headed 'Beauties of the Police'. It was inspired by the case of Henry Bull, an elderly man sentenced to ten days' imprisonment for begging in the streets with his little daughter; he had voluntarily left the shelter of the workhouse because he could no longer bear to be kept separate from his child – 'like cattle in the pens at Smithfield', as Jerrold puts it. Bull was in anguish at being once more forcibly separated from his child but, comments Jerrold,

He ought to have known the penalty of his poverty. He should have remembered that he was a pauper; a human weed; so much human offal; a foul noisome creature, the modern leper; the blotched Lazarus of our highway; the nuisance to be put down, got rid of, swept aside like the ordure of beasts ... .

The wholesale inveiglement of the Punchites by a rival paper must have been viewed with some anxiety by Ingram, and it seems more likely than not that he decided to woo them back by launching yet another illustrated magazine but one different from both the *Illustrated London News* and the *Pictorial*. It was to be a monthly, more artistic in its orientation, and involving some experimentation with colour printing. The name settled on was *The Illuminated Magazine*, which, because all the woodcuts inside the magazine were black and white, gave a handle to hostile reviewers ('there is nothing of an illuminated nature, except that a portion of the illustrated title-page is printed in *red*'[6]) even though Jerrold had explicitly stated in the Prospectus published in the *Athenaeum* on 1 April 1843 that people who were expecting the magazine to be 'a thing like a cardinal's missal, enriched and adorned with painted figures' were on the wrong track.

Figures and objects of every kind there assuredly will be, ILLUSTRATIVE OF THE TEXT IN ITS EVERY VARIETY OF ESSAY – NARRATIVE –

HISTORY OF SOCIAL RIGHT AND WRONG OF THE TRAGEDY OF REAL LIFE, AS OF ITS FOLLY, ITS WHIM, ITS MERE BURLESQUE. These 'Illuminations' – for we use the word in its original, and not in its conventional sense – though colourless, will be so placed and scattered, that Literature may, it is hoped, reveal new graces by the pure light of Art.

Each issue was to have sixty-four copiously illustrated, double-columned quarto pages, 'such size being considered best adapted to an illustrated text',[7] and yet it was to be published at the modest price of one shilling. This also provoked some scorn: 'Here is a monthly periodical preposterously professing to give *sixty-four quarto pages of letter-press, in double columns,* for ONE SHILLING! The notion is perfectly ridiculous ...'[8] For the *Theatrical Journal*, on the other hand, the fact that 'all this 'illuminated' dazzling casket of high art [could] be had for one shilling' made the magazine 'really the magazine for the million' (13 May 1843).

Lemon could hardly take on the editorship of this new journal in addition to that of *Punch* and so the post went to Jerrold, who composed the above-quoted Prospectus which also promised 'ample reviews of the literature of the day'. And any Spottiswoodes among potential readers were warned, 'We shall not shrink from any subject with a social wrong at its core.' Ebenezer Landells, probably still aggrieved about the way he had been eased out of the proprietorship of *Punch*, became a part-proprietor of the new magazine and took responsibility for everything to do with the illustrations, a fact impressively announced on every contents page.

In his preface to the first volume of the *Illuminated* (May-October 1843) Jerrold restated the magazine's mission:

> It has been the wish of the proprietors of this work to speak to the MASSES of the people; and whilst sympathizing with their deeper and sterner wants, to offer them those graces of art and literature which have too long been held the exclusive right of those of happier fortunes.

Each number contained a wealth of woodcut illustrations, some of them, as Brian Maidment says, 'startlingly varied in shape and composition'[9] and was lavishly decorated by Kenny Meadows, from its contents page on, with numerous column-headings, borders and endpieces featuring playful cherub-like creatures such as those he had already been using to ornament the pages of the *Illustrated London News* and the *Pictorial Times*. Besides these 'graces of art', the purchaser of the *Illuminated* also received for his or her shilling a rich mix of social commentary, fanciful sketches, historical anecdotes and legends, travel pieces, and poems and stories, plus several pages of literary and artistic reviews. The *Theatrical Journal* commented:

> The contents combine every variety of subject – 'from grave to gay, from lively to severe'. It is what a magazine ought to be – a thing of 'shreds and patches;' – an article of the utile – a column of the dulce, and a text for everybody.

Judging by the cuttings in the British Library's Moran Collection, the *Illuminated* found a welcome from others besides the *Theatrical Journal* reviewer. Jerrold's name was a powerful talisman. One of the cuttings asserts that 'the magic words "edited by Douglas Jerrold" imprinted on the title-page in dainty characters give sure token there is healthful food within'. Jerrold himself was disappointed with its actual appearance, however. Walter Jerrold quotes from a letter of his to Dickens:

> As for 'illuminations', – you have, of course, seen the dying lamps on a royal birthday-night; with the R burnt down to a P, and the W's very dingy W's indeed, even for the time of the morning. The 'illuminations' in my *Mag* were very like these. No enthusiastic lamplighter was ever more deceived by cotton-wicks and train-oil, than I by the printer. However, I hope in another month we shall be able to burn *gas*.

The 'gaslight' or colour printing never did amount to much and was in any case confined to the title-page until after Jerrold had relinquished the editorship. But, apart from the one comment already quoted, the hostile reviews included in the Moran Collection do not focus on this aspect of the publication but rather on its personnel. One cutting, a column headed 'The Magazines' and dated May 1843, jeers at 'the Jerrold clique' who were responsible for the journal (another clipping in Moran also says the magazine is 'evidently got up by a clique') and at their 'overweening confidence' in their own powers. Jerrold himself is mocked as a pedlar of 'stale Byronism and second-hand bitterness'; he is, says the writer, 'a man of very scanty powers, and unbounded audacity in appropriation' with 'commonplace Timonism and vulgar Radicalism' forming 'the intellectual staple of his literary labour'.

There was some justice in the 'clique' accusation because Jerrold did turn for contributions to old friends such as Lemon, who supplied a series illustrated by Meadows called 'The Boys of London', and Laman Blanchard, one of whose poems, 'Nell Gwynne's Looking Glass', appeared in the first number. But he was also receptive to offerings from young or untried writers – and 'what is more', says Hodder in his *Memories of My Time*, allowed them

> to affix their names to the articles if they were so disposed, for he could not see the justice of one all-powerful writer keeping his own name prominently forward while those of his *collaborateurs* were suppressed.

It was in the *Illuminated*, for example, that Wilkie Collins made his literary debut with 'The Last Stage Coachman', a fanciful piece published under his name and splendidly illustrated by Hine.[10] Later, when reviewing Blanchard Jerrold's biography in *Household Words* on 5 February 1859) Collins described Jerrold as 'one of the first and dearest of my literary friends'. In the *Illuminated* Jerrold also welcomed the work of one of the newest stars in the literary firmament, the 'Farthing Poet' Richard Hengist Horne, whose recently-published allegorical epic *Orion* had been a huge success, helped no doubt by Horne's stunt of setting the publication price at one farthing (as an ironic comment on the value placed on epic poetry by the general reading public). Jerrold, like many of his contemporaries including Carlyle, was hugely impressed by *Orion*, seeing it in terms of the sublime, full of 'glorious thoughts' and with 'a massiveness of power ... as far apart from the pretty timidity of much of the poetry of our day ... as Prometheus from Punch'.[11] He published another example of Hornian blank-verse sublimity, seven whole pages of it, in the August *Illuminated* ('The Old Problem [i.e., of how to live]. Discussed by the Poet, the Stoic, and the Fool') but, already in the magazine's first number he had featured a very different piece by Horne, an illustrated nine-page account of the harrowing Report of the Children's Employment Commission (Horne had been on the Commission). Jerrold told Horne that he could make two articles of the subject if he wished but that there could not be more than one sheet (eight pages) on it in any one issue: 'People are apt to think human misery "heavy matter" and to succeed we must be various.'[12]

Contributing to the variety Jerrold sought were a number of Oriental travel sketches by a naval officer's wife, Marianne Postans, affording good opportunities for illustration, also a comic serial about a jobbing painter entitled 'Pictorial Passages from the Life of Theophilus Smudge. Edited by Cimabue Briggs, Esq.', illustrated by Leech and possibly written by à Beckett.

Jerrold himself contributed six of his most strongly-written essays to the first six numbers of the *Illuminated*. The first number opened with what the *Theatrical Journal* called 'a national glowing subject', a lively piece entitled 'Elizabeth and Victoria' mocking those who look back nostalgically to what they call 'the merry golden days of Good Queen Bess' by sharply contrasting the discomforts, brutalities, political tyranny and class oppression of Elizabethan England with the hugely increased daily comforts and conveniences, as well as the far greater civil liberties, enjoyed by Victoria's subjects. The essay, illustrated with numerous little dropped-in woodcuts wittily integrated with Jerrold's text, was, Dickens wrote to him on 3 May, 'written with the finest end of that iron pen of yours; witty, much needed, and full of Truth'. In the other essays Jerrold hymns the endurance and long-suffering of the poor, denounces militarism ('The Folly of the Sword'), laments the truckling of great talent to rank and wealth as seen in the career of Theodore Hook, or meditates on the beauty and rich historical associations of the Kentish countryside as contrasted with the money-grubbing preoccupations of so many in the present commercial age ('A Gossip at the Reculvers'). He also wrote for the first number six columns of editorial paragraphs entitled 'The Button Holder', consisting of characteristically fierce satirical comment on news items of the day (the £1,921 spent on the costumes of the nation's state trumpeters, for instance, or the refusal of the Marylebone workhouse authorities to allow a pauper to visit his dying wife in another part of the workhouse). These paragraphs are pretty much indistinguishable from the kind of thing he was regularly contributing to *Punch* ('We shrink from the sneering, sarcastic, bitter spirit of "The Button Holder"' says one commentator represented in the Moran Collection), and it was consciousness of this, perhaps, that caused him to drop the feature – it appeared only once more after the first number in the course of these first six issues.

Jerrold continued to fret about the pictorial aspect of the magazine, writing to Laman Blanchard on 1 August, 'I share your horror of all illustrations – but in the case of the Illum:Mag it was made a necessary evil.' He concedes, however, that Kenny Meadows has done 'some admirable things', especially in the latest number, and reports that the magazine was 'steadily rising – and is now safe'.[13] Six days later he wrote to Dickens:

These are dull months: nevertheless it [the *Illuminated*] moves and well; especially the last two numbers. The first two were, however, so atrociously put forth, that it will take a month or two more to wipe out their blots. Unfortunately, the people, of whom we have got rid were too great apes not

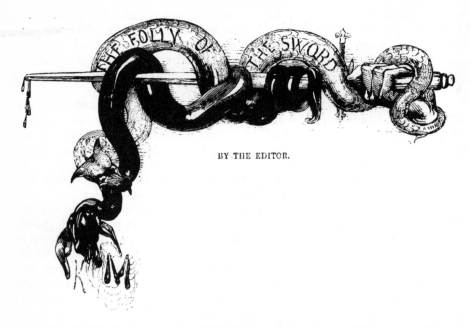

BY THE EDITOR.

to have money and when they relieved us of their braying they took their cash. Still, we have rallied, so much so, that I think the Mag will be a good property.[14]

There is no clue as to who the rich 'apes' were but, presumably, they were backers who had joined Ingram in floating the *Illuminated*.

Perhaps one of the reasons for Jerrold's feeling so positive about the magazine in August was that the latest number contained the first instalment of a serial that he himself would certainly have considered his most notable prose work to date. The serial was called 'The Chronicles of Clovernook' and was an ambitiously-conceived satirical Utopian fantasy, clearly much influenced by his recent revisiting of his beloved Rabelais, whose wit, 'Xtianity in its finest sense' and 'wonderful moral courage' he had praised to Forster the previous autumn when he was still hoping to write a review-article on him for the *Foreign Quarterly*.[15] Jerrold intended 'Clovernook' to convey, in fanciful form, his most cherished beliefs and ideals about both personal and social morality. Despite its imperfect execution, the writing of it having been much interrupted by illness, he 'often declared' says Hodder, 'his belief that it had a better chance of reaching the hands of future generations than the rest of his books'. Blanchard Jerrold, too, writes that his father told him 'Clovernook' 'contained more of his true self, as he would like to be known and remembered, than any other of his writings'. But the high value Jerrold placed on his 'Chronicles' did not exempt them from suffering, like his full-length plays and longer narratives, from his inability to structure a literary work. The very idea of 'Chronicles' encouraged his strong tendency towards digressiveness, something to which he makes a playful reference within the work itself when he makes its protagonist say – with much truth – 'to wander is a besetting sin of mine'. Jerrold was a brilliant, if often somewhat undisciplined, satirical journalist, and a sharply perceptive critic of contemporary theatre, but the 'Chronicles of Clovernook' is in quite a different vein. It testifies to those 'high aspirations' that Hannay tells us, in his *Atlantic Monthly* memoir, Jerrold 'sacredly cherished': 'he disliked being talked of as "a wit" because he thought (with justice) that he had something better in him than most wits.' Jerrold wished to be remembered not for jokes but for his ideas (his 'philosophy') and for what he saw as the truly 'witty' creations of his imagination. His ambition was, in other words, very similar, however ephemeral in its literary results, to that of a great Romantic poet like Keats. He wanted to be among the English writers when he died.

The modern reader, confronted with the 'Chronicles', will be less troubled by the work's digressiveness than by that excess of fancy to which Hannay drew attention when commenting on 'Clovernook'. Jerrold, he wrote, had 'let his fancy run riot like honeysuckle and overgrow everything'. Beginning with an elaborately allegorical account of the creation of the idyllic village of Clovernook by means of goosequill, paper and ink, Jerrold proceeds to introduce the stout and hearty sub-Rabelaisian figure of 'the Hermit of Bellyfulle' in his 'Cell of the Corkscrew'. The Hermit, who is found frying a heroic number of eggs in a huge pan, is surrounded with lavish amounts of appetising food (the Cell's walls are 'tapestried with sides of bacon, with hams smoked over fires of cedar and sandal-wood', while 'festoons of sausages' hang from the roof, dazzling the eyes and melting the hearts of the beholders). His cellar holds thousands of bottles containing the ales and wines of the world arranged in geographical order ('At the present time I am in Hungary, drinking Tokay'). He tells Jerrold, with intense nostalgia, of his magic sojourn in the kingdom of 'As-You-Like'. This is Jerrold's sentimental-Radical vision of a hierarchical but wholly benevolent society, a glorified mirror-image of contemporary England, where 'the state with paternal love watched ... at the very cradles of the poor', where bishops 'from their tenderness, their piety, their affection towards their flocks, were looked upon as the very porters to heaven', where all tradesmen were honest and not obsequious, where the rich were not envied but 'looked upon as men, who having put into a lottery, had had the luck to draw a prize', and the poor 'were always treated with a softness of manner that surprised me'. The characters of the nobility of As-You-Like are expressed by their titles – the Duke of Lovingkindness, the Marquis of Sensibility, the Earl of Tenderheart, and so on.

Less than four months after Jerrold had begun publishing the 'Chronicles' Dickens wrote his *Christmas Carol* which is so exactly similar in its vision of a world of joyous abundance (the presentation of the jovial Ghost of Christmas Present seated upon heaps of 'turkeys, geese, game, poultry, brawn ... long wreaths of sausages', etc., may well owe something to Jerrold's gastronomic Hermit), and of the replacement of harsh political-economic attitudes to the poor by a loving and benevolent paternalism. The strong appeal that this aspect of both 'Clovernook' and the *Carol* had for all those hundreds of thousands struggling for their daily bread in the Britain of the 'Hungry Forties' is vividly expressed by the great Radical George Holyoake reviewing the volume publication of 'Clovernook' in the short-lived *People's Press* (1847). After commenting that in this century 'Starvation has been for the first time in Europe, reduced to a regular science, and elevated into notice and fashion by the ... legislature', Holyoake continues:

> Immortal Oliver Twist, famished and ragged, begging with his empty basin for one bowl more, has carried consternation into the camps of the Bumbles, but it has been reserved for Jerrold, to run up [*sic*] with his own scorching contempt, every rag of argument, by which the miserable dietetics of poverty, has been erected, either by folly or parsimony, into a national principle. The 'Hermit of Bellyfulle' looks down with quiet, unctuous, and glorious disdain on the wretched progeny of the voluntarily lean, and the wilfully wan. I speak ... of our streets where the outcast perishes for the sake of a moral example – of our poor-law unions where joy and plenty are banished from those whose bones have been wasted in building up our commercial greatness, and who are penned up to perish as a flattering stimulus to the industry of their children – of our manufactories, those congregations of pallid faces, where phantoms of gauntness stalk about like the galvanised inmates of a vast dead house: – as you emerge from the industrial prisons of these semi-living, you bless yourself that genius is not yet all servile, and that in this *lean* as well as iron age, it has created the Hermit of Bellyfulle, to shake the hungry world with his mellow hand, and inspire it with the love of richness, of plenty, of content, and jollity.[16]

In later instalments of the 'Chronicles' Jerrold develops his image of Clovernook with its beautiful surroundings, inspired by the Kentish countryside (both as remembered from his childhood years in Cranbrook and as most recently experienced at Herne Bay) and its snug 'hostlery' the Gratis, which is reached from the Hermit's cell by 'Velvet Path'. There are also some overdetermined fantasies about the villagers as 'purified' versions of their earlier, worldly selves, and about the Gilbertian-sounding 'Land of Turveytop', which is inhabited by benevolent giants evidently derived from Rabelais via Swift's Brobdingnag. These creatures remove 'weak and wicked' people from the world and rear them again as from infancy, a peculiarly Jerroldian take on that New Testament text so dear to the Victorians, 'Except ye ... become as little children, ye shall not enter into the kingdom of heaven':

> 'Oh! The men I have seen there', cried the Hermit with a laugh – 'the kings, lords, bishops, lawmakers I have seen, all put into second swaddling clothes, and brought up again as gentle, wise, charitable, sagacious folk, doing great

credit to the beautiful earth, which, in their former days, they so grievously scandalised.'

Included in all this are digressions on many of Jerrold's most regular themes such as anti-militarism and the harshness of life in the poorer quarters of London 'where the hard realities of life [knock] daily, hourly at people's hearts', as well as more personal ones such as the miseries of authors and the injustice of charges of 'bitterness' against those who seek to expose the truth about social evils. We have occasional glimpses of effective Jerroldian wit as in this passage:

> 'Kings, queens, knights, bishops, and castles!' cried the Hermit. 'How few the syllables! Yet in this world what an uproar have they made! How much wickedness and suffering, and violence, and stone-blind bigotry ... Kings, queens, knights, bishops, castles! What a significant short-hand is here, my master'.

But for the most part one must agree that Hannay was right and Jerrold has indeed let his fancy 'run riot over everything'. And for the modern reader, one of the most striking aspects of these 'Chronicles' is likely to be their relentless sexism, which is very much in the established *Punch* tradition. The pretty serving-maid at the Gratis is called 'Sweetlips', and the Hermit is jocose about 'old maids', bachelors having to get married in order to ensure their buttons are looked after,[17] 'fatally industrious' women writers, female lack of humour ('woman is rarely a joke-making animal'), domineering wives, and so on. Mrs Caudle, one feels, is just around the corner.

Jerrold was perhaps encouraged to think that 'Clovernook' would prove to be one of his most lasting works because Holyoake's was not the only voice according it great acclaim. The author of one of the Moran cuttings likens the 'Chronicles' to 'that fine old specimen of allegorical writing, the "Pilgrim's Progress", and a reviewer in the *Examiner* (5 August 1843), possibly Forster, places Clovernook 'in a snug and durable valley between More's *Utopia* and Rabelais's *Home of the Bottle*'. When Bradbury and Evans published it in volume form together with his other *Illuminated* papers, the *Daily News* devoted a whole column of praise to it (1 May 1846), delighting in the figure of the Hermit, 'a jewel of a man':

> Conceive the peremptoriness of Boswell's Johnson purged of the Doctor's ill humours ... combined with the riotous, wilful imagination of a Rabelais, purified from its grossness; and this mind lodged in the body of a Friar Tuck – that is, a Friar Tuck grown old, abstaining from rough exercises, and eating and drinking for a dozen. The *tout-ensemble* is the Hermit of Bellyfulle.

This reviewer then quotes the description of the contents of the Hermit's cell – 'glowing and beautiful were a hundred vitreous jars of pungent pickle ... the olive in its mild immortal green, for Bacchus in his after-dinner hour to dally with', etc. – and judges the place 'worthy the pencil of a Turner'. A specimen of the narrator's philosophical reflections is given and highly praised, as are the tales of the Hermit's fantastical adventures, and, finally, the whole of 'this witty and thoughtful little volume' is 'heartily' commended to the reader.

The *Chronicles* were later praised by *Eliza Cook's Journal* (28 December 1850) for their 'unctuous humour, quaint and delicate sarcasm, deep insight into the heart of man', and were eulogised at some length in the *Athenaeum* (23 October 1854) as being, beneath all the 'exquisite foolery', the 'most serious of Mr Jerrold's works'. Such later acclaim is comparatively rare, however, and it is noticeable that the stock of the 'Chronicles' had fallen by the time of Jerrold's death. The book features very little in the many appraisals of his work that followed his death. It was, as I have already suggested, very much a product of the early 1840s like Dickens's *Carol* – but, unlike the *Carol*, it could not transcend its time.

Jerrold had barely got under way with the 'Chronicles' in the *Illuminated* when his severe illness and retreat to Malvern compelled him to suspend them, but this does not seem to have unduly damaged the journal. *Bell's Life in London* noted (3 December 1843) that, 'notwithstanding the continued illness of its editor', the *Illuminated* continued to 'support its position as one of the most talented of our monthlies': 'It is full of stuff of the right sort, and displays great tact and judgment in its selection.' For Jerrold himself, however, editing the journal seems to have become by this stage a somewhat uncongenial labour. Landells's ceasing about this time to be one of the *Illuminated*'s proprietors left Jerrold free, he felt, to cut down on his own commitment to the journal. When he formally severed his connection with it the following autumn, at the end of its third volume, Walter Jerrold records that he told Mrs Newton Crosland that working on it had kept him 'from higher and better labour' (which seems rather to contradict reports of the high value he placed on the 'Chronicles'), and that he was 'constantly tramelled by indecision and ignorance'. Ingram, he wrote to Blanchard about the same time, was 'in his way a very literal, ignorant person or money grubber, but nevertheless liberal'.[18] At the end of 1843, he had promised Bradbury and Evans that he would 'merely *see*' the *Illuminated* 'to the end of the volume', till May 1844, and then drop it. In the event, however, he continued as editor, at least in name, until October 1844 and published four more discursive instalments of 'Clovernook' between March and July. He wrote nothing else for it, however, apart from an attack on the inhumanity revealed even in the very architecture of workhouses ('The Two Windows', June 1844) – the sharpness of which provoked *Bell's Life in London* to comment on 9 June, 'Jerrold's cynicism injures his best efforts'. His 1844 contributions certainly stood out from their context more than his 1843 ones had done, since the bulk of the magazine was now less concerned with social justice and morality. The emphasis was more on stories, notably Irish folklore tales, poems, travel writings, and so on. That the journal was not, however, prospering with this new mix is indicated in a letter from Horne to Edgar Allan Poe written in April 1844 and quoted by Walter Jerrold. Horne says that he could probably help to get something by Poe published in the *Illuminated* ('Jerrold has always spoken and written very handsomely about me') but

> I fear this magazine is not doing at all well. I tell you this *in confidence*. They have a large but inadequate circulation. The remuneration would be scarce worth having – ten guineas a sheet is poor pay for such a page! And now, perhaps they do not even give that.

After Jerrold left the editorship the *Illuminated* carried on for a few more months under the editorship of the engraver W.J. Linton but finally ceased publication in 1845.[19]

Jerrold, meanwhile, had been promised his own monthly journal by those 'truly printer princes', as he called them, Bradbury and Evans. They were evidently anxious to keep their great *Punch* star loyal and happy, and he was about to reward them for their princeliness with the most success-ful *Punch* series to date, one that would be instrumental in driving up its circulation and that would also prove to be an altogether better passport to posterity for Jerrold himself than his cherished 'Chronicles of Clover-nook'.

Chapter Nine

At The Summit

1845

Walter Jerrold rightly sees 1845 as the *annus mirabilis* of Jerrold's career, 'from the point of view of work accomplished'. Throughout most of the year, from 4 January onwards, Jerrold was writing his hugely popular series, 'Mrs Caudle's Curtain Lectures', in *Punch* whilst at the same time contributing a weekly average of four or five other items to the magazine, many of them, like the last two 'Q' papers,[1] quite substantial ones. Also from January onwards, he edited his own monthly journal, *Douglas Jerrold's Shilling Magazine*, in which he serialised his second novel, *St Giles and St James*, and contributed numerous articles including a column of satirical comment on current affairs called 'The Hedgehog Letters' ('containing the opinions and adventures of Juniper Hedgehog, cabman, London; and written to his relatives and acquaintance, in various parts of the world'). In addition to all this, *Time Works Wonders*, his most ambitious 'legitimate' comedy to date, was produced at the Haymarket on 26 April 1845 where it ran for ninety nights. And at the end of the year came another major new commitment when he accepted Dickens's invitation to become a sub-editor and leader-writer on the new national newspaper the Liberal *Daily News*, scheduled to begin publication, with Dickens as editor, in January 1846.

It was not only in terms of output, however, that 1845 may be seen as a high point in Jerrold's career. This year also saw some striking expressions of the grateful affection and admiration that was by this time felt for him by thousands of people, particularly among the artisan classes. Presiding at the Birmingham Polytechnic Institute's Annual Conversazione on 7 May, he was, said the *Manchester and Salford Advertiser*, 'worthily lionised' and ceremonially presented with a ring by 'the Operative Committee of the Fancy Trades of Birmingham'. At the Anniversary Soirée of the Manchester Athenaeum in the great Free Trade Hall on 23 October, chaired by Talfourd and attended by three thousand people, Jerrold was greeted when he rose to speak (following John Bright) with 'several rounds of applause', and was loudly cheered at several points during the speech.[2] He would certainly have received similar treatment at Sheffield had he been well enough to attend and preside at the Mechanics' Institute festival there on 30 October. As things were, he had to be eulogised *in absentia* and wrote on 3 November to John Fowler, the Institute's secretary, to express his appreciation of the 'kind and cordial spirit of the people of Sheffield as manifested towards me at the meeting':

> I assure you in all sincerity that I feel unworthy of the fullness of such acknowledgment. It is an extravagant over-payment for the little in my career, I have been able to accomplish; but if I know anything of myself, I know that such approving sympathy must quicken me to greater exertion for the future.[3]

Our wonder at all the things that Jerrold managed to achieve in 1845 can only increase when we remember how precarious his health continued to be, and remember also that he had to sustain the shock of a terrible bereavement early on in the year. There are several references to his afflictions from sciatica ('very lame in bed the whole of two days') and from what he calls 'my old fiend rheumatism' in such of his letters as have survived from, or can be definitely dated to, this year. And on 15 February his deeply loved friend of more than twenty years, Laman Blanchard, whom he was supposed to meet that very afternoon,[4] cut his own throat in a fit of despair. Ann Blanchard had died in the previous December after a long and harrowing illness which had caused her husband much stress and anxiety. Only a few days before her death he and Jerrold had sat side by side listening entranced to Dickens giving a private reading of his new Christmas Book, *The Chimes* (containing a lampoon of Sir Peter Laurie making that egregious declaration about 'putting down' suicide that Jerrold had already satirised in *Punch*). And now this gentle, loveable friend of friends, called by the *Examiner* (22 February 1845; most probably written by Forster) 'the very impersonation of kindness and goodness of heart', was dead, having cut his own throat in a fit of madness brought on by his intense grief. Blanchard Jerrold describes finding his father alone in a room at the *Punch* office soon afterwards with his face 'white as any paper', trying to maintain his composure but quickly breaking down into a fit of helpless weeping. At the funeral he collapsed and had to be carried from the ground. Blanchard and he had made a solemn pact, Walter Jerrold was told long afterwards, that 'if it were given to the dead to appear to the living the one who died first should revisit the other' and an affrighted Mary Ann Jerrold could hear her husband alone in his study at night 'calling aloud in a voice nearly choked by tears' for his dead friend to come to him: "'I've called him. No, no: he can't come, my boy", he said wildly to a friend who happened to drop in on one of those sad evenings.'[5]

It was not surprising that there was no 'Mrs Caudle' in the issue of *Punch* for 22 February (though there were other Jerrold items). Indeed, if there is anything in the suggestion I make below that Ann Blanchard's marital behaviour may have helped to inspire the composition of Mrs Caudle's nightly monologues, the surprise must rather be that her death, and Laman Blanchard's subsequent frantic suicide, did not put paid to the series altogether. By mid-February, however, the Caudle Lectures had already so firmly established themselves as *Punch*'s greatest success to date that there would have been considerable pressure on Jerrold, both internal and external, to keep the series going.

Margaret Caudle, the wife – 'the lawful wedded wife, as she would ever and anon impress upon him, for she was not a woman to wear chains without shaking them'[6] – of Job Caudle, London 'toyman and doll-merchant' – lectures him remorselessly night after night as they lie in bed. She reviews the domestic events of the day, complains volubly about Caudle's sins of omission and commission, and expresses her constant anxieties about the family's future. Her name ('caudle' is a hot sweet drink of spiced wine and was much favoured as a nightcap in the 19th century) is a contemporary joke, as is the description of her monologues as 'curtain lectures', a sort of pun on bed-curtains and the stage-curtain that normally formed a backdrop to the speaker at public lectures. Mrs Caudle herself, however, exemplifies a perennial comic type, the scolding wife, that dates back at least to Mrs Noah in medieval mystery plays and doubtless much further back than that, as Jerrold himself playfully imagines: 'Eve herself may now and then have been guilty of a lecture, murmuring it balmily amongst the rose-leaves.' Jerrold presents himself as editor of the records of Mrs Caudle's nightly harangues, reconstructed by Job as an act of exorcism, to lay 'the Ghost of her Tongue' that still haunted him ('a dreadful thing that her tongue should walk in this manner'), after he had been 'left in this briary world without his daily guide and nocturnal monitress ... in the ripe fulness of fifty-two ['fifty-seven' in the original *Punch* serialisation]'. Jerrold explains that Mrs Caudle knew

> her husband was too much distracted by his business ... to digest her lessons in the broad day. Besides, she could never make sure of him: he was always liable to be summoned to the shop. Now from eleven at night until seven in the morning, there was no retreat for him. He was compelled to lie and listen. ... Besides, Mrs Caudle copied very ancient and classic authority. Minerva's bird, the very wisest thing in feathers, is silent all the day. So was Mrs Caudle. Like the owl, she hooted only at night.

She hooted 36 times in *Punch* between 4 January and 8 November 1845. The first lecture, 'Mr Caudle Has Lent Five Pounds to a Friend', sets the pattern:

> ... Do you hear that shutter, how it's banging to and fro? Yes – I know what it wants as well as you; it wants a new fastening. I was going to send for the blacksmith today, but now it's out of the question: *now* it must bang of nights, since you've thrown away five pounds.
>
> Ha! there's the soot falling down the chimney. If I hate the smell of anything, it's the smell of soot. And you know it; but what are my feelings to you? *Sweep the chimney!* Yes, it's very fine to say, sweep the chimney – but how are chimneys to be swept – how are they to be paid for by people who don't take care of their five pounds? ...

Mrs Caudle does not always scold, however. She is equally adept at wheedling and successfully campaigns for such desired outcomes as a trip to Boulogne (marred by Mr Caudle's 'unmanly cruelty' in refusing to 'smuggle a few things' for her on the return journey), a country cottage ('The Turtle-Dovery'), a gig (that Carlylean emblem of respectability), and a well-to-do godfather for the new baby. Only twice is she defeated – once when she tries to discover Job's Masonic secrets (how often had Jerrold himself been maritally interrogated on this subject, one wonders?), and again when she proposes that her mother should come and live with them:

> I'm sure, the money she'd save us in housekeeping. Ha! What an eye she has for a joint! the butcher doesn't walk that could deceive dear mother. And then again for poultry; what a finger and thumb she has for a chicken! I never could market like her: it's a gift – quite a gift!

MRS. CAUDLE'S DEAR MOTHER.

We hear only Mrs Caudle's voice but in her monologues she often scorn-
fully echoes her sleepy husband's feeble protests and interjections which
serve to fuel her own rhetoric and his every movement is strictly moni-
tored: 'What are you sneering at, Mr Caudle? *How do I know you're
sneering?* Don't tell me; I know well enough by the movement of the pillow.'
By this means, similar to Browning's in his great dramatic monologues,
the listener who does not speak directly is made very much a presence in
these 'lectures'. Other characters, too, emerge in the course of Mrs Caudle's
tirades, notably Job's boon companion, the jocund Mr Prettyman and his
good-looking young sister whom Mrs Caudle suspects of planning to
become her successor:

> ... she must be a nice person to come unasked to a woman's house. But I
> know why she came. Oh yes; she came to look about her. *What do I mean?*
> Oh, the meaning's plain enough. She came to see how she should like the
> rooms ...

The series was a tremendous hit. It fitted in absolutely with that vein of
jokey misogyny that permeates early Victorian *Punch* (the famous joke,
'Advice to persons about to marry: Don't', which appears in the *Punch
Almanack* for 1845 is aimed at men rather than women) and points to a
predominantly male readership.[7] Jerrold's account of the origin of Mrs
Caudle, literally true or not, is itself part of that cherished Victorian
gender-myth that joyous male freedom comes to an abrupt end with
marriage, into which it is the business of charming and resourceful young
women to ensnare hapless, romantic young men (Jerrold tells the newly-
wed Hodder, for example, that he looks forward to seeing him in his
'bran-new fetters'[8]). With regard to Mrs Caudle Jerrold says that he
happened to be watching a crowd of happy schoolboys ('unconscious men
in miniature') at play and musing 'on the robust jollity of those little
fellows, to whom the tax-gatherer was as yet a rarer animal than a baby
hippopotamus' when 'there struck upon him, like notes of sudden household music, these words – CURTAIN LECTURES':

> One moment there was no living object save those racing, shouting boys; and
> the next, as though a white dove had alighted on the pen-hand of the writer,
> there was – MRS CAUDLE.

Mrs Caudle, in other words, embodies all the constricting cares and
troubles of the grown-up married life that will be the fate of most of these
carefree boys, so enviously watched by an 'old, old man of forty' (Gray's *Ode
on a Distant Prospect of Eton College* with its line 'Alas, regardless of their
doom the little victims play' may have been hovering in his mind perhaps).
   What, one inevitably wonders, did Mary Ann Jerrold think about Mrs
Caudle? We know so little about her and her marital relationship that we
can only speculate. Hodder's description of Mary Ann as 'the most thoughtful and considerate of housewives'[9] might suggest that she had Mrs

159

Caudle-like preoccupations but the only suggestion that she might have had Mrs Caudle-like propensities came sixty years after her death when Lemon's daughter was reported in the *Daily News* (17 August 1926) as remembering an occasion during the time that the Caudle Lectures were appearing in *Punch* when Jerrold went off to a luncheon party 'but Mrs Jerrold got to hear about it and the irate wife gave chase in a pony chaise'. It is not at all clear why she should have been so moved, however, and since this anecdote does not seem to fit with anything else we know about Mary Ann (which, as already said, is very little) we should perhaps take it with a pinch of the proverbial salt. Similarly, we should not perhaps take at face value Jerrold's assertion to Ludwig Kalisch, whose 1855 report of an interview with Jerrold has already been quoted, that the Caudle Lectures derived directly from his own marital experiences. It seems at least possible that he was at this point indulging in leg-pulling at the expense of his somewhat solemn and self-opinionated young interviewer. When Kalisch asked him about the origin of the Caudle Lectures he said that he had

> quite simply conveyed to the public his own wife's lectures, but adapted somewhat for literary purposes. Without any thought of publication, he said, his wife had delivered these lectures behind the [bed]curtains, in the way other wives did; his only merit lay in a skilful piece of plagiarism.

We have no record of Mary Ann's domestic talk with which to compare the curtain lectures but a specimen of Ann Blanchard's speech, as reported by her husband to Jerrold in a letter of 1842 and quoted by Blanchard Jerrold, does certainly sound as though she might have posthumously assisted in the creation of Mrs Caudle. Jerrold had pressed Laman Blanchard to bring his wife on a visit to the Jerrolds in Boulogne but for Mrs Blanchard such an expedition was evidently no simple matter. Laman Blanchard wrote to Jerrold:

> with a consistency marvellous in women, she continues to the close of the month in the same way of speech, saying, 'Ah! it's all very nice talking', and 'It's easy enough for you', and 'Nothing I should like so much, *but*' – and 'Suppose Edmund were to get down to the ditch' – and 'What do you think? *that* Miss Mary had the porkbutcher down in the kitchen last night' – and five thousand other objections rung upon such changes as the house on fire, the necessary new bonnetings, the inevitable sea-sickness, and the perils of the ocean – to say nothing of a reserved force brought up when all other objections are routed, in the shape of a presentiment that *something* will happen – God knows what, but something – directly her back is turned upon old England (what *can* she mean?) ....

Identifying a real-life model for Mrs Caudle's monologues is bound to be a speculative business, however. What can be said with certainty is that, as Richard Kelly long ago pointed out,[10] Jerrold in developing this character has his eye very much on the books of one of Mr Punch's recurring targets in his earliest years, Mrs Sarah Stickney Ellis. Ellis was the author of a whole series of advice manuals or conduct books for women, beginning with *The Women of England, Their Social Duties and Domestic Habits* (1839) and running to three sequels on the Daughters, Wives and Mothers of England, each with a sub-title stressing the duties and responsibilities incumbent on women in their various relationships (the sub-title of the 'Wives' volume reads: *Their Relative Duties, Domestic Influence, and Social Obligations*). Ellis was the happily married wife and co-worker of a distinguished Nonconformist missionary and she exhorted her female readers in every way to support and uplift their menfolk, to cultivate patience, unselfishness, tender solicitude, and a high moral tone, and to see their role very much as regenerators of society through the exercise of their spiritually beneficent influence on fathers, sons and husbands. *Punch* had on several occasions made fun of Ellis's high-flown sentiments and her exalted concept of 'Woman's Mission'.[11] Now in the voluble Mrs Caudle Jerrold has great fun in presenting the polar opposite of the 'Mrs Ellis wife' in the shape of a woman whose ideas about wifely, housewifely and maternal duties and responsibilities are equally strong but stridently practical and emphatically materialistic. She is also comically self-regarding (when Job in desperation at being denied sleep, takes up a book – *Paradise Lost*, of course – Mrs Caudle exclaims, 'If that isn't insulting a wife to bring a book to bed, I don't know what wedlock is' adding, 'But you shan't read, Caudle; no you shan't; not while I've strength to get up and put out a candle').

If Jerrold had portrayed Mrs Caudle merely as a ripe specimen of a nagging wife his series could not possibly have had the impact or achieved the tremendous popularity that it did. Just one more version of such a time-honoured joke would have quickly worn thin. It is because he develops her into the kind of humorous character especially prized by readers of the day (and abundantly provided for them by Dickens) that she so seized the public's imagination. Those comically eccentric or extreme characters whose heart is yet in the right place, who show some complexity of feeling, who are presented with all the trappings of realism but who live, in Chesterton's wonderful phrase, 'in a perpetual summer of being themselves' – those were the ones in whom the Victorian middle-class reading public delighted. Thackeray expressed it beautifully in his *Morning Chronicle* review (26 December 1845) of the volume publication of the Caudle series:

> Almost all the events and perplexities of Cockney domestic economy pass before [Mrs Caudle]. ... a foreigner, or a student in the twentieth century, may get out of her lectures as accurate pictures of London life as we can out of the pictures of Hogarth. Caudle's friends, and habits, and predilections; his cozy evenings with the Skylarks – his attachment to punch – his struggles for a latch-key – his natural and manly hatred for cold mutton – the manner in which the odious habit of smoking grows upon and masters him, are here exposed with the most frightful distinctness. There must be thousands of

161

Caudles in this town who drank punch and annoyed their wives with tobacco-smoke last night. The couple have become real living personages in history, like Queen Elizabeth, or Sancho Panza, or Parson Adams, or any other past character, who, false or real once, is only imaginary now, and for whose existence we have only the word of a book. And surely to create these realities is the greatest triumph of a fictitious writer – a serious or humorous poet. Mr Dickens has created a whole gallery of these ... .

Spielmann says that the Caudle series 'created a national *furore*, and set the whole country laughing and talking'; Mrs Caudle 'passed into the popular mind and took a permanent place in the language in an incredibly short space of time'. As always with any literary hit, there was a flurry of dramatic adaptations. In at least two of them Mrs Caudle was played by favourite male comic actors in drag – William Oxberry in a 'laughable interlude' at the Princess's Theatre (30 June 1845)[12] and Robert Keeley at the Lyceum (2 July 1845). Jerrold's own dramatisation appeared at the Haymarket on 30 July, and on 31 August *Bell's Weekly Messenger* reported that 'the Caudle mania has at last reached the Adelphi and Mr Selby has cleverly adapted the immortal lectures of Jerrold to the purposes of the theatre'. This adaptation, entitled *Mrs Caudle Abroad and At Home and Adventures in France*,[13] was, the *Bell's* reviewer claimed, the best adaptation to date, all previous ones having tended to present Mr Caudle as an 'unseemly compound of sot and snob'. Maybe it changed the mind of the *Illustrated London News* reviewer who had written of the Lectures on 9 August: 'Never was a greater mistake made than in imagining they would prove attractive on the stage. Every atom of their spirit; every trace of their humour, is entirely lost in their theatrical representation.'

The provincial press freely pirated the Lectures as a matter of course – 'I have seen at least 6 country papers with "*Caudles Lectures*" but no *acknowledgment* from Punch,' Jerrold wrote to Lemon, 'Ought they not to have a line?'[14] He protested vigorously in *Punch* on 19 July 1845 in a three-quarter page piece called 'Punch and the "Pickers and Stealers"'[15] against those 'newspaper thieves who weekly crown themselves with our CAUDLE cup, and, in their forlorness of intellect, hope the cup will be taken as a thing of their own family'. He also denounced, recycling an image he had already used once in 'Bajazet Gag' (above, p. 59) the 'stage-thief' who 'scissors in hand, and his eye twinkling on the paste-pot, watches the birth of a new book, clothing and feeding himself, Hottentot-like, with its intestines'. 'By this man,' he writes, 'is chaste and decorous MRS CAUDLE – one lump of propriety as she is! – belied and slandered at a playhouse in Oxford Street.'

On 26 July *Punch* sought and obtained, amidst much merriment in court, an injunction against the *Hereford Times* for blatant piracy of the eighth and ninth lectures. The barrister acting for *Punch* declared that 'the fame of Mr and Mrs Caudle was universal' and 'in every kind of shop these imitations were to be seen'[16] and *Punch* hoped to abate them by this particular prosecution. But 'Caudle mania' raged on. The copy of the crude plagiarism entitled *Mrs Cuddle's Bed-Room Lectures* to be found in the British Library (announcing itself as 'NEW EDITION') doubtless represents the tip of a very considerable iceberg. John Sharp, the Musical Director of Vauxhall Gardens, recited a sequence of Mrs Caudle's soliloquies, interspersed with sung interpolations (always ending with the refrain, 'Sure I'm almost broken-hearted / Caudle, it is time we parted'), for fifty nights, according to his *Vauxhall Comic Song Book, First Series.*[17] On 31 July at the notorious 'Judge and Jury Society', which met at the Garrick's Head Tavern in Bow Street and held mock trials involving lots of dirty jokes and indecent *double entendres* under the presidency of 'Baron' Renton Nicholson, there was a 'Special Case' of Caudle v. Prettyman. A handbill announced, 'Mrs Caudle will appear to prosecute Mr Prettyman for a breach of etiquette and decorum' (drunkenly relieving himself over the flowers in the Caudles' back garden – 'Why couldn't he go to the front door or upstairs, instead of destroying my hyacinth and poppyflower? *It was only a little sweet pea?* Caudle, you are getting aggravating, keep your jokes to yourself ...'). A broadsheet was published for street sale called 'Victoria's Caudle Lectures' in which the Queen is represented as nightly berating Albert:

> when you came from Germany you had not got as much as would bait a mouse-trap. I made a gentleman of you, put money in your pockets and now you have the impudence to ask for more pocket-money. You help with the children? Well, I am sure. You may help to get them Al., and that is all you care about the matter ....[18]

James Hannay remembered the fame of the Caudle Lectures 'being bruited about the Mediterranean' in his midshipman days in 1845. The Radical leader George Harney, writing to Engels in Brussels in March 1846, could assume that his correspondent would know all about Mrs Caudle (his wife, says Harney, hearing that Engels's wife had worked with him well into the small hours, was proposing that wives should form an 'Anti-3- or 4 o'clock-in-the-morning-Association' and had suggested that '*Mrs Caudle* might also be induced to join the sisterhood'.[19] There were innumerable Caudle merchandising 'spin-offs' as we should now call them, like a charming pair of Royal Worcester candle-extinguishers in the shape of the heads of Mr and Mrs Caudle,[20] or the 'Caudle Bottle' marketed by Doulton and illustrated in Walter Jerrold's biography. Perhaps the most engaging of all the manifestations of 'Caudle Mania' was that discovered in 1850 by Henry Mayhew during the course of his field-work for *London Labour and the London Poor*. An exhibitor of performing birds and mice told him

> My birds are nearly all canaries ... I have names for them all. I have Mr and Mrs Caudle, dressed quite in character: they quarrel at times and that's self-taught with them. Mrs Caudle is not noisy and is quite amusing. They

ride out in a chariot drawn by another bird, a goldfinch mule. ... Mr and Mrs Caudle is very much admired by people of taste.[21]

It was for 'people of taste' also, one presumes, that Bradbury and Evans brought out a very handsome edition of the Caudle Lectures nine years after Jerrold's death. It was elegantly printed on tinted paper and splendidly illustrated by Charles Keene. It should be added that Leech's original cartoon-type illustrations in *Punch* are also very fine in their different way, however much they may later have offended Alice Meynell.[22]

Meynell, writing in the 1890s, strongly objected to the Caudle Lectures for their (as she saw it) relentless 'vulgarising of the married woman'. But there seems to have been little overt female protest at the time. A notable exception was the popular novelist Anne Marsh who wrote in her best-selling *Emilia Wyndham* (1846):

> Any vulgar penny-a-liner can draw a Mrs Caudle, and publish her in a popular journal; and with such success that she shall become a by-word in families, and serve as an additional reason for that rudeness and incivility, that negligent contempt, with which too many Englishmen still think it their prerogative, as men and true-born Britons to treat their wives.

For her pains she was ridiculed in *Punch* (not by Jerrold personally, however).[23] There was also the protest made directly to Jerrold himself, as reported by Mrs Newton Crosland (who wrote for Jerrold's periodicals under her maiden name of Camilla Toulmin). She recalls that she was Jerrold's guest at 'a friendly midday dinner' in Putney:

> Towards the close of the meal a packet arrived – proofs, I fancy – at any rate Douglas Jerrold opened a letter which visibly disturbed him. 'Hark at this,' he said, after a little while, and he then proceeded to read a really pathetic, though not very well-expressed letter from an aggrieved matron who appealed to him to discontinue or modify the Caudle Lectures. She declared they were bringing discord into families, and making a multitude of women miserable.

Mrs Crosland, who refers to the Lectures as 'those coarse papers ... unworthy of his pen', believed that this letter, with its strong allegation of a wide hinterland of real female distress behind all the male chuckling and guffawing, gave Jerrold 'great pain'[24] but this may have been wishful thinking on her part. At any rate the protest did not cause him to either to stop or change the basic plan of the series. And his (very well received) ironic apologia for the series in his Birmingham speech in May, quoted by Walter Jerrold, hardly sounds penitent:

> Your honourable member has said he does not believe there is a Mrs Caudle in all Birmingham. I will even venture to go further than he: I do not think there is a Mrs Caudle in the whole world. I really think the whole matter is a fiction – a wicked fiction, intended merely to throw into finer contrast the trustingness, the beauty, the confidence, and the taciturnity of the sex.

The fiercest published criticism of the Caudle Lectures came not from a female source but later from the highbrow, conservative *Saturday Review*, nicknamed 'The Saturday Reviler'. In the course of a terrific onslaught on Jerrold in general and Mrs Caudle in particular the *Saturday*'s writer disdainfully asserted (1 November 1856) that Mrs Caudle had 'no individual character' but was 'simply a collection of six capital letters prefixed to a string of ill-natured and unreasonable complaints' ('We rise from reading [the lectures],' the writer says later, 'with the sensation of having dined for a week on mouldy wedding-cake'). So much for what Jerrold's obituarist in *The Times* was later to call 'those specimens of life-painting that scarcely can be surpassed'!

The *Saturday* scorned 'Mrs Caudle's Curtain Lectures' as 'a manufactured article ... a mere inorganic mass of fun divided into weekly portions', and it does seem that Jerrold himself put a low value on them, at least at the outset. According to Spielmann, he told Landells, after the first one or two instalments had appeared, that he could write 'such rubbish as that by the yard'. But as the series took hold of readers' imaginations, Jerrold perhaps began to think differently about it. Even though he would certainly have preferred that it might have been 'The Chronicles of Clovernook' that had such success rather than the Caudle Lectures, he was nevertheless delighted, his son records, 'to see the circulation of *Punch* grow even under the nightcap of Mrs Caudle' and during this period went 'radiant' to the weekly *Punch* dinners. Whether he realised it himself or not, Jerrold had hit upon a form, the dramatic monologue, that precisely fitted his remarkable talent, shown in his 'Q' papers, and in his leading articles, for working up an impressive head of steam through the vehement repetition of some main theme or argument variegated with a dazzling richness of witty illustrations. Jerrold's 'Q' papers, Altick comments, 'depend for their impact on a process of elaboration', adding:

> More than one impatient reader may have concluded, perhaps unfairly, that Jerrold's rhetoric consisted largely of finding twenty or thirty different and arresting ways of saying the same thing.[25]

In the case of Mrs Caudle, however, this technique was the very basis of the comic effect but was made genuinely humorous by being suited to the real-life vocabulary and limited allusive powers of a contemporary London housewife. What Altick calls Jerrold's 'deep reservoir of familiar tropes and literary and scriptural allusions' is only partially available to Mrs Caudle, and only rarely does he allow her shafts of quintesssentially Jerroldian wit, as when she reproaches Mr Caudle for taking up billiards:

> Billiard-balls indeed! Well, in my time, I've been over Woolwich Arsenal ... and saw all sorts of balls; mountains of 'em, to be shot away at churches, and into people's peacable habitations, breaking the china, and nobody knows what ... and there's not one of 'em, iron as they are, that could do half the mischief of a billiard-ball. That's a ball, Caudle, that's gone through many a wife's heart, to say nothing of her children.

That detail of broken household china as a powerful image of the horrors of war is, of course, wonderfully in character for Mrs Caudle, the kind of touch one associates more with George Eliot than with Jerrold.

No *Punch* serial was intended to be open-ended. Each would run only for one volume (six months) or, at most, one year. In the case of the Curtain

Lectures there must have been a temptation, given the immense popularity of the series, to prolong it into a second year but Lemon and Jerrold prudently resisted this. And there may have been other signs of public satiety besides the comments of the *Era*'s critic, reviewing on 10 August 1845, Sterling Coyne's Haymarket adaptation: 'the curtain lectures themselves are becoming tedious as a twice-told tale, and the sooner the worthy couple are "tucked up" the better, both in the periodical and on the stage.' Feeling perhaps that it might be inappropriate for a character as popular as Mrs Caudle to be killed off just before Christmas, Jerrold presented her final lecture in November. It is a splendidly comic version of the Victorian deathbed scene to set against all the solemn and pathetic ones. No mystic shining light or fluttering angel-wings attend her valedictory oration. 'Though Mrs Caudle had her faults,' wrote Thackeray, entering into the fun of the thing, 'perhaps there was no woman who died more universally lamented than she.' Jerrold certainly takes care that she dies in character. To the last she maintains that her fatal chill is not the result of wearing thin shoes in wet weather but was caught by her one night ten years before as a result of sitting in a draught when waiting up for Caudle to come home from a jolly evening with his fellow-Skylarks.

> I fell asleep, and the fire went out, and when I woke I found I was sitting right in the draught of the key-hole. That was my death, Caudle, though don't let that make you uneasy, love; for I don't think you meant to do it.

This is indeed the end of Mrs Caudle but in the *Punch* Almanack for 1846 there appear twelve brief chapters entitled 'Mr Caudle's Breakfast Talk', hectoring monologues delivered by Job to his second wife (née Prettyman) but it is thin stuff, and basically unfunny in that there is really nothing intrinsically comic about a tyrannical husband.

Jerrold subsequently wrote several other series for *Punch*, in addition, of course, to his regular prolific supply of free-standing columns and paragraphs, amounting, he told the young educationalist W.B. Hodgson visiting him in the summer of 1854, to three *Punch* pages weekly. Many of these series had a dramatised speaker, such as 'The Life and Adventures of Miss Robinson Crusoe' and 'The English in Little By General Tom Thumb' (both 1846), 'Miss Benimble's Tea and Toast' (1849), and 'A Bit of My Mind By Mrs Mouser' (1850) but none of them had anything like the success of the Caudle Lectures, a success that was soon overshadowed by the enormous popularity of Thackeray's 'Snobs of England By One of Themselves' (1846-47; published in volume form as *The Book of Snobs* 1848). For today's readers the most entertaining of these later Jerrold series is likely to be 'The English in Little' (which for a while ran alongside Thackeray's 'Snobs') in which Jerrold ventriloquises the Yankee voice of 'General Tom Thumb', the American midget, Charles Stratton, who, under the management of that great maestro of publicity P.T. Barnum, took London by storm and attracted far more Royal patronage than the 'legiti-

mate' theatre ever could do. Writing as General Tom Thumb enabled
Jerrold to satirise two things at once, British (especially Royal British)
ceremoniousness and philistinism and American dollar-worship and jin-
goism. Barnum and the General are offended at having to enter
Buckingham Palace by the back stairs. They arrive in a cab 'to show
American independence':

> we ... hadn't need to ring the bell; for the door was opened in a minute, and
> a dozen critturs in crimson – with railroads of gold running up and down
> their coats, and their heads as if they'd come out of a snow-storm, were
> waitin for us. I hadn't then time to make a meditation; or I should have said
> something about happy Columbia, where our helps are free citizens, and not
> tatooed by the tailors, as they are among the Britishers. However, I did say
> to GOVERNOR BARNUM very softly, 'I'd rather be a Red Man than a Man
> in Crimson.' Whereupon the Governor half-shut his eye, like a slit in a
> money-box, and held up his finger.[26]

Returning to Jerrold's miscellaneous *Punch* contributions in 1845, we
might note that, like the bishops or Alfred Bunn, the vulgarian showman-
manager of Drury Lane, Royalty is a recurrent target, as it was to be in
'The English in Little'. 'The Queen and the Corn Laws' (19 July 1845), for
example, comments satirically on Victoria's blacklisting of Covent Garden
Theatre because it had been used for a meeting of the Anti-Corn Law
League, and Jerrold mounts quite a campaign against her for presiding
over a mass slaughter of deer by Prince Albert and his fellow-hunters at a
battue in Saxe-Coburg-Gotha. One of Jerrold's responses to this event,
which was fully and gruesomely reported in *The Times*, parodies an old
nursery rhyme:

> Sing a song of Gotha – a pocket full of rye,
> Eight-and-forty timid deer driven in to die;
> When the sport was open'd, all bleeding they were seen –
> Wasn't that a dainty dish to set before a Queen!
>
> The QUEEN sat in her easy chair, and looked as sweet as honey;
> The PRINCE was shooting at the deer in weather bright and sunny;
> The bands were playing Polkas, dress'd in green and golden clothes;
> The Nobles cut the poor deers' throats, and that is all *Punch* knows![27]

Another article, 'Queen Victoria's Statue of Shakespeare' (13 September
1845) mocks her lack of interest in England's national poet, and in the
national drama generally (the Italian Opera was much more in her line).
No wonder Jerrold kept his hat firmly on his head when the Queen and
Albert passed him, riding through Putney village in a *'char-à-banc'* attended by several courtiers. This was during W.B. Hodgson's visit to him
and the young principal of Liverpool Mechanics' Institute, recorded the
scene and Jerrold's subsequent comments to him:

D.J. told me she had turned 'Punch' out of the Palace, though at first she liked it very well; that she is extremely indifferent to the claims of literary men; that she would not go to see the Belgian Company at Covent Garden on account of the Anti Corn Law League's connection with that house ... that she would not go to the theatre to see his play, though she went the very night after its performance was discontinued.[28]

PUNCH PRESENTING YE TENTH VOLUME TO YE QUEENE.

The play Victoria neglected to see was the one Jerrold himself and many of his admirers like Dickens and Wilkie Collins considered to be the best of his dramas to date, the five-act comedy *Time Works Wonders* which Webster produced, very handsomely, at the Haymarket on 26 April 1845. It had a decidedly starry cast including Farren, Mathews, Buckstone and Madame Vestris, and it opened to a chorus of approval from both audience and the press. The first act deals with an intercepted runaway love-match between young Clarence Norman, heir to a baronetcy, and Florentine, a mere baker's daughter (a Florentine was the name for a certain kind of meat pie baked in a dish with a cover of pastry). The lovers try to elope from Miss Tucker's school but are caught in the act. Clarence is sent abroad for five years by his outraged father, Sir Gilbert, for whom rank is all-important, and Act 2 begins after this time has passed. By this time Sir Gilbert has himself fallen in love with Florentine and, coming to feel that 'nature has her holiest claims' that must prevail over all considerations of rank and wealth, proposes marriage to her. As a result of mutual misunderstandings, Clarence and Florentine each believes that the other has forsaken their previous love but an *éclaircissement* puts all right, and Sir

Gilbert (whose situation and change of heart seem to owe something to Sir Harcourt Courtly in the despised Boucicault's *London Assurance*) releases the suppliant Florentine from her promise of marriage ('Rise, madam, you are free. I sought a wife and not a victim') and blesses the union of his son with the baker's daughter. To this Jerrold adds a secondary plot (the *Examiner* commented that the two plots 'do not very artfully cohere') of another runaway love-match between Felix Goldthumb, heir to a fortune accumulated by his trunk-maker father, and Bessy Tulip, a penniless schoolfellow of Florentine's. Felix and Bessy fulfil the role of the comic lovers, and were played, of course, by Mathews and Vestris. The fifteen-strong cast is filled up with comic servants (one played by Buckstone) and sub-Jonsonian 'comedy of humours' characters like Old Goldthumb (Farren), the querulous schoolmistress (Mrs Glover, a popular character actress) and Professor Truffles, a wandering con-man passing himself off as an expert lecturer on matters scientific ("Twould have done your heart good to see him exhaust a mouse in an air pump', Bessy tells Florentine).

In this play Jerrold does seem to be trying harder to match dialogue to character, and to individualise his characters (at least as comic 'humours' like the ultra-patriotic Peter Pallmall in *The Prisoner of War*) than he did in *Bubbles of the Day*, and there are fewer 'bitter' jibes at contemporary social follies and injustices. Certainly, the play was perceived by the critics as a notable consolation of a great and beneficial change in his dramatic writings. For *The Times* (28 April 1845) he was, happily, following 'Congrevian wit less and nature more': while 'the tone and temper of the man remain the same ... the same talent for flashing wit ... the same spirit of humanity, and restlessness under conventionalism', he was now drawing his characters 'with more truthfulness and simplicity'. He was, continues *The Times*, still deficient in 'that constructive tact which belongs to many authors not worthy to be named in the same day with him' and sometimes this leads to 'too great prolixity of dialogue' but the reviewer seems to see these as minor faults, and they evidently did not much worry the first-night audience either: 'there was a perfect roar of approbation at the fall of the curtain.'

The *Illustrated London News* (3 May 1845) also welcomed Jerrold's abandonment of 'the school of Congreve' (which had involved trusting to 'a string of smart repartees, and ceaseless flashes of wit and epigram' to carry the play through, with 'little display of character or natural feeling to interest') and his abandonment also of his 'bitter sneers at social conventionalities, which ... are still good in their way for preserving the proper balance of society'. The dialogue in *Time Works Wonders* is as brilliant as ever 'but it is natural and kindly', the hearts of the characters 'are all well placed'. In the *Era* advertisements for the play were headed 'The Legitimate Theatre Triumphant' and the paper's critic hailed it (4 May 1845) as 'a triumph from the beginning to the end, which bravely gives the lie to the dormancy of British genius':

Not a character presents itself, even down to the landlord or the *Postboy*, but has a definite cause assigned for his exit or his entrance; the interest never flags for an instant, and a sterling modern five-act Comedy has been triumphantly achieved.

This first night was evidently a major triumph for Jerrold, bowing from one of the side boxes as the audience (which, according to the *Illustrated London News*, included 'an unusual number of literary men') roared its applause. Hodder, who shared Jerrold's box that evening, and walked with him afterwards to a celebratory dinner at the Bedford Hotel in Covent Garden, remembered his response when he, Hodder, renewed his congratulations on the play's success as they were entering the hotel:

> Jerrold, turning his eye full on me, and smacking his chest with his hand, exclaimed, with a degree of exultation which was most natural under the circumstances, 'Yes; and here's the little man that's done it!'[29]

The play settled in for a long run and was revisited by the *Examiner* on its 46th performance, by which time, it seems, it was being 'very carelessly played' by some of the actors. The play itself still triumphed, however:

> exuberant, liberal, unrestrained even by the flatness of dull interpreters, it subsists by a vitality of its own ... the knowledge, the humour and the wise irony of this excellent critic strike home notwithstanding.

Jerrold, says the *Examiner* critic (21 June 1845), writes in the cause of 'wit and sense against folly and pretension, and [the audience is] proud to take part' with him.

A few days later W.B. Hodgson saw the play and found that it acted even better than it read: 'There is a never-failing life about it; the dialogue is a continual sparkle, and nature is not outraged in any way.' On his subsequent visit to the author he found Jerrold complaining 'grievously' of the acting and expressing himself 'surprised' that the play's 'great purpose' had been overlooked: 'while the Tory papers had abused his former plays as radical and revolutionary, they had praised this, which in his opinion was the most radical of all.'[30] It is difficult to know what the author of plays like *The Mutiny at the Nore* and *The Rent Day* could have meant by this if it was not simply a reference to the theme of true love and nature's 'holiest claims' triumphing over pride of rank, the baronet's son marrying the baker's daughter with his previously disdainful father's full blessing. This perennial theme of comedy, the triumph of love and 'natural' feeling over rank and wealth, was in full bloom in the 'legitimate' drama of the early Victorian period. It was especially relished by audiences when Macready, known for his rugged anti-monarchical beliefs, played the plebeian-lover role, e.g., Bulwer's ever-popular *Lady of Lyons* (1838) and Westland Marston's blank-verse *The Patrician's Daughter* (1841), for which Dickens wrote a prologue. It was a kind of romantic 'radicalism' perfectly acceptable on the 'legitimate' stage, and perhaps the reason why the reviewers of *Time Works Wonders* did not pick up on it more was because here it is the *female* lover rather than the male one who is of humble rank. This would make it, in fact, somewhat less socially 'radical' even than Bulwer's and Westland Marston's plays. Once again, as with the 'Chronicles of Clovernook', Jerrold seems to have wanted to put a different value on his more ambitious work from what the public did, even when, as in the case of this play, it was enthusiastically received.

Time Works Wonders ran for ninety nights, and the printed text sold some 6,000 copies as a result of being published (by Bradbury and Evans) at one shilling instead of the more usual price for play-scripts of half a crown (had it been sold at that price, Jerrold told Hodgson, he thought 'not more copies might have been sold than might be required for the circulating libraries') but it then disappeared from the national repertory until 1873 when, as noted below, it was briefly revived at the Globe Theatre. The genre of 'High Comedy' or comedy of wit, which Jerrold struggled so hard – *too* hard – to revive, had to wait for the advent of Wilde to re-assert its place in the British theatre.

What, then, does survive of Jerrold's *annus mirabilis*? Neither *St Giles and St James* nor the full-length 'high comedy' that earned him such acclaim. How chagrined he would have been could he have known that of all he wrote in 1845 it is only the Caudle Lectures, to which he attached so little value, that still have any kind of continuing life.

Chapter Ten

Jerrold, Dickens, Thackeray

A favourite literary-critical game of the mid-19th-century was to compare and contrast the writings of Jerrold, Dickens and Thackeray. 'When viewed in the general as humorists and men of inventive talent,' wrote David Masson in 1851, 'the three do form a triad so that it is hardly possible to discuss the merits of any one of them without referring to the other two.'[1] Here is the *British Quarterly Review* reviewing Jerrold's satirical novel, *A Man Made of Money* in August 1849 and striving to identify its uniquely Jerroldian flavour:

> ... difficult would it be to describe in words [as opposed to providing examples] in what consists the peculiar raciness of the Jerroldian as compared with the Dickensian, or of this, again, as compared with the Thackeristic humour. A judicious use of such words as fruity, sweet, tart, sparkling, astringent, might, indeed, convey some vague sense of the thing, but not sufficient for critical purposes .... Were we to say that [Jerrold's] humour is less kindly and genial than that of Mr Dickens, but more tart and hearty than that of Mr Thackeray, we should probably be nearer the truth. Mr Jerrold's comic writing, is, in fact, ... more like a *liqueur* than a wine; one discerns the alcoholic ingredients of strong personal feeling in it, drugging and firing the true juice of the grape. Hence, probably, it is that one can read less of him at a time than of either Dickens or Thackeray ... the moralist too strong in him, soon heats and chafes you with his bitter sentiments.

This exercise of comparing the comic gifts of the three writers was part of the early Victorian debate about wit versus humour to which we will return in Chapter 13.[2] Leigh Hunt's introduction to his anthology *Wit and Humour Selected from the English Poets* (1846) is a *locus classicus* for this debate and in a later essay, 'On the Combination of Grave and Gay', Hunt grouped the three writers together as wits with a purpose (as R.B. Martin observes, 'There were few things the Victorians feared more than the useless'[3]). Jerrold, Dickens and Thackeray were, wrote Hunt,

> remarkable for their combination of grave and gay; for the vein of tenderness which forms so beautiful an undercurrent to their satire; and for that love of the general good, and that freedom from personality for its own sake,[4] which has exalted the character of satire itself, and shown how it can be rendered a true instrument of reformation.[5]

That Jerrold should have since dropped so completely out of the equation would have surprised not only Leigh Hunt but also Dickens, always generous in his praise of Jerrold's work, and Thackeray who was reported to have said when he was seeking to establish his literary reputation that Jerrold was 'the only rival whom he feared'.[6]

As we have seen, Dickens's personal acquaintance with Jerrold began in 1837 but the two writers had no professional relationship until nine years later during Dickens's brief reign as editor on the *Daily News* when Jerrold was, for a few months, one of the new paper's leader-writers, campaigning against the Corn Laws. Later in the same year (1846) Dickens, responding no doubt to an invitation from Jerrold, wrote an article boosting his friend Maclise for the August number of *Douglas Jerrold's Shilling Magazine*.[7] Jerrold did not return the compliment in *Household Words*, perhaps, as Anne Lohrli suggests, because of Dickens's policy of anonymous publication (Jerrold is reported to have said, when he saw that the journal carried the name of Dickens, its 'Conductor', at the top of every page, 'Ah, *mon*onymous throughout, I see!') but Blanchard Jerrold, who was beginning to make his name in journalistic circles, was a regular contributor from the outset.[8]

Dickens would have welcomed contributions from Jerrold whose views and social ideas often chimed closely with his own. We have already noted his admiration for Jerrold's *Illuminated* essay, 'Elizabeth and Victoria' and for *The Story of a Feather*. Since he was deeply concerned about the way that individual lives could be ruined, and society damaged, by the wrong kind of education, he was also strongly responsive to Jerrold's rather heavy-going moral tale 'The Lives of Brown, Jones and Robinson' in his 1842 collection *Cakes and Ale*, a book which Dickens said he read 'with perfect delight' when Jerrold sent him a copy in the spring of 1843. Nearly a year later it was Dickens's turn to send Jerrold a book. This was the *Christmas Carol* and Dickens wrote in a covering letter:

> I can't tell you how often I read, Brown, Jones, and Robinson, whereunto I solemnly called Horne's attention t'other day. It is full of melancholy and pain to me, but its truth and wisdom are prodigious.[9]

Responding on 30 January 1844, Jerrold congratulated Dickens on the *Carol* ('You have done nothing more beautiful, more full of heart. It must last so long as English Xmas and English holly') and regretted that it came to hand too late in the month for him to write about it in his 'nothing of a Magazine'. He also responded to Dickens's comments on the Brown, Jones and Robinson story, comments which had evidently stirred bitter memories of his Brownrigg days:

> There *is* pain – there is melancholy in the papers you speak of. I have just so much impression of them – and shall never have any other for I shall never look at them again. There are certain scribblings of mine the recollection of which sometimes gives my whole moral man *a wrench* bringing as it does the memory of circumstances under which they were racked from me.[10]

When Dickens was working on the *Carol*'s successor, *The Chimes*, in Italy in the autumn of 1844, he re-read *The Story of a Feather* and praised it to Forster, dwelling on the 'masterly' portrayal of the old actor Gauntwolf, a degenerate parent who has profited from conniving in his daughter's becoming a nobleman's mistress. Dickens even borrowed a dramatic repentant-prostitute scene from Jerrold's story for his own tale.[11] Jerrold meanwhile had delighted Dickens by the way in which he had referred to the *Carol* in Letter No. 27 in his 'Punch's Complete Letter Writer' series, 'From a Lady in Want of a Governess, to an Acquaintance' where the writer is indignant at finding her governess, who has just returned from taking the children for a three-hour walk, reading a book instead of amusing her charges:

> What book, think you, was it? *A Christmas Carol.* I have never read the thing; but knowing it to be aimed at [against] the best interests of society, all the feelings of a mother rushed upon me, and I believe I *did* read her a pretty lesson … I [reproached] her for her ingratitude, her baseness in bringing such books into my family … .

'It was very good and hearty of you, Jerrold,' wrote Dickens to him, 'to make that affectionate mention of the Carol, in Punch; and I assure you it was not lost upon the distant object of your manly regard, but touched him as you wished and meant it should.'

Jerrold's 'hearty' appreciation of the message of the *Carol*, and *The Chimes*'s indebtedness to the *Story of a Feather*, no doubt accounted for Dickens's keenness that Jerrold should be of the party assembled in Forster's rooms to hear him read *The Chimes* on 3 December, two weeks ahead of publication. 'I have tried', he wrote to Jerrold,

> to strike a blow upon that part of the brass countenance of Wicked Cant, where such a compliment is sorely needed at this time. … If *you* should think at the end of the four rounds (there are no more) that the said Cant … 'comes up piping' [boxing slang for 'panting with exhaustion'], I shall be very much the better for it.[12]

As to Jerrold's great popular hits, *Black Eyed Susan* and Mrs Caudle, Dickens's very funny, but also very affectionate, recalling of T.P. Cooke's William, and his inspired parody of William's nautical lingo, in an 1844 letter to Clarkson Stanfield,[13] shows his unfailing delight in Jerrold's evergreen sailor-drama as does an anonymous review he wrote for the *Examiner* on 12 May 1849 of a production at the Marylebone Theatre. The audience, he reported 'laughed and wept with all their hearts', the play being 'a remarkable illustration of what a man of genius may do with a common-enough theme'.[14] He had quickly caught the spirit of the Caudle Lectures when they began appearing in *Punch* and wrote to Forster from Italy, 'I wish you would suggest to Jerrold for me as a Caudle subject (if he pursue that idea), "Mr Caudle has incidentally remarked that the house-maid is good-looking".[15]

Dickens's richest response to Mrs Caudle, however, came a bit later when he recruited Jerrold's celebrated character to the ranks of the off-stage friends of one of his own greatest comic creations, Sairey Gamp. Meanwhile, he had high praise for *Time Works Wonders*, writing that he was 'greatly struck by the whole idea of the piece':

> The elopement in the beginning, and the consequences that flow from it, and their delicate and masterly exposition, are of the freshest, truest and most vigorous kind – the characters (especially the Governess[16]) among the best I know – and the wit and the wisdom of it are never asunder. ... I agree with you in thinking it incomparably the best of your dramatic writings.[17]

All these enthusiastic responses by Dickens to Jerrold's work date, like Jerrold's 'affectionate mention' of the *Carol* in *Punch*, from the middle 1840s when the two men's personal friendship was at its height. Such letters as have survived from this period are written with great warmth on both sides, Jerrold's being full of humorous references to their overbear-ing mutual friend Forster ('whose growing magnitude of all effects moral and physical has now convinced me that he is, at least, the Sub-Editor of Providence, and to be treated accordingly'[18]) and more waspish jokes about the bumptious Albert Smith. 'Take care of yourself for all our sakes', Jerrold adjures Dickens, as he responds 'most delightedly' to an invitation to 'snatch a holiday' with him,[19] and Dickens issues pressing invitations to Jerrold to visit him in Switzerland ('what sort of welcome you would find, I will say nothing about, for I have vanity enough to believe that you would be willing to feel yourself as much at home in my household as in any man's'[20]) and later at Paris ('*Do* arrange to run over at Christmas time, and let us be as English and as merry as we can'[21]). Jerrold could not get away to Lausanne or to Paris but a year earlier had gone with Maclise and Forster to rendezvous with the Dickenses in Belgium in 1845, returning from their Italian sojourn. Later, in the reminiscences he wrote for Blanchard Jerrold's *Life* Dickens fondly recalled that Jerrold was on that occasion 'the delight of the children all the time, and they were his delight ... I doubt if he were ever more humorous in his life.'

Dickens, Jerrold once said, 'had the showman instinct so strongly developed that if you only gave him three square yards of carpet, he would tumble on that (like a street-acrobat)'.[22] The remark was prompted by Dickens's energetic organisation of some elaborate amateur theatricals between 1845 and 1848, initially for fun but later for charitable purposes. Jerrold was one of the leading participants and might even have had the pleasure of seeing his illustrious friend playing Heywood in *The Rent Day*, one of the plays considered by the group before their choice settled on Jonson's *Every Man in His Humour*.

Dickens and Jerrold were the undoubted stars of this production. Vizetelly thought Jerrold's appearance

so peculiar that it seemed scarcely possible he could make up well for the stage and thoroughly lose his own identity, yet he did so most effectively ... With the exception of the acting of Dickens ... and Mark Lemon's clever presentation of Brainworm, I thought Jerrold's studied rendering of Master Stephen alone displayed real histrionic power.[23]

This was confirmed by *The Times* on 15 November 1845. Jerrold became the foolish country gull to perfection: 'His by-play is masterly. During the whole time he remains upon the stage he never forgets to further the exhibition of character – he is always doing.' Browning found his performance 'very amusing and clever' while for Jane Carlyle Jerrold's performance outshone all the others (not even excepting 'poor little Dickens, all painted in black and red'). The 'oddity' of Jerrold's appearance, she told Carlyle, 'greatly help[ed] him'.[24] Forster, also in the company, was obstreperously vain of his Macready-style performance as Kitely and Jerrold wrote to Dickens that he believed Madame Tussaud was going to advertise him in character as Kitely as 'Another Magnificent Addition' to her collection: 'he is to stand between Hume and Burke [the body-snatcher] fronting the "Chamber of Horrors".'[25]

It was in the summer of 1847, when the Amateur Players travelled north to perform in Manchester and Liverpool, that Dickens decided to do some fund-raising by writing an account of the expedition using his Mrs Gamp from *Martin Chuzzlewit*. She accompanies the Players with an eye to business, having heard that 'several of the ladies concerned are in an interesting condition' and sends regular bulletins to Mrs Harris. When Jerrold is pointed out to her ('There's him as wrote the life of Mrs Caudle!') it gives her a turn, and Dickens an occasion for a vivid thumbnail sketch:

Oh the bragian little traitor! right among the ladies, Mrs Harris ... laughing at his own jokes as loud as you please; holding his hat in one hand to cool hisself, and tossing back his iron-grey mop of a head of hair with the other, as if it was so much shavings – there, Mrs Harris, I see him getting encouragement from the pretty delooded creeturs, which never know'd that sweet saint, Mrs C, as I did, and being treated with as much confidence as if he'd never wiolated none of the domestic ties, and never showed up nothing! Oh the aggrawation of that Dougladge![26]

Underlying the rapport between Jerrold and Dickens during these years was a shared outlook on life and contemporary social problems, exemplified in a much-quoted exchange of letters about *Punch* in late October 1846. Jerrold wrote to Dickens in Switzerland to congratulate him on *Dombey and Son* ('Your book has spoken like a trumpet to the nation. ... You have rallied your old thousands again'), and to report the success of his own new weekly paper. He mentions that Thackeray is 'big with twenty parts' (of *Vanity Fair*, to be published in twenty monthly numbers) and expecting the first instalment at Christmas and remarks, '*Punch*, I believe, holds its course' but that he does not 'very cordially agree with its new spirit':

> I am convinced that the world will get tired (at least I hope so) of this eternal guffaw at all things. After all, life has something serious in it. It cannot all be a comic history of humanity. Some men would, I believe, write the Comic Sermon on the Mount. Think of a Comic History of England; the drollery of Alfred; the fun of Sir Thomas More in the Tower; the farce of his daughter begging the dead head, and clasping it in her coffin on her bosom. Surely the world will be sick of this blasphemy. I can only say for myself, at times I am ashamed of my literary companionship and its perpetrators. And therefore do I rejoice in this newspaper [*Douglas Jerrold's Weekly Newspaper*].

This may allude to Thackeray's 'Snobs of England' series, begun in the issue for 28 February 1846, which was enjoying an even greater success than the Caudle Lectures, and quite eclipsing Jerrold's recent series, the short-lived 'Mrs Bib's Baby' and 'The Life and Adventures of Miss Robinson Crusoe'[27] It seems clear from his reply that Dickens believed Jerrold was referring to the 'Snobs' series; but there can be no doubt that Jerrold's primary target is *Punch*'s other leading contributor Gilbert à Beckett, whose long-running legal satire, the 'Comic Blackstone' (21 October 1843 – 21 December 1844), had been highly popular, and who was now publishing his *Comic History of England* in monthly parts, and, in *Punch* itself, a facetious occasional series called 'Punch's Historical Portrait Gallery', which had begun on 29 August 1846, with a splendid caricature of Richard III and the little Princes by Richard Doyle. When the public's taste for this sort of thing changes, writes Jerrold

> unless *Punch* goes a little back to his occasional gravities, he'll be sure to suffer. And this I preach, now and then, at Whitefriars; and am I have no doubt duly laughed at when 'I leave my character behind me'.[28]

Dickens replied,

> Anent the Comic History of England and similar comicalities (Snobs in general included) I feel exactly as you do. Their effect upon me is very disagreeable. Such joking is like the sorrow of an undertaker's mute, reversed – and is applied to serious things with the like propriety and force.[29]

It is hard to resist the idea that Jerrold's discontent with what he sees as *Punch*'s 'new spirit' is mainly a matter of resentment at the runaway success of Thackeray's 'Snobs', especially after the clear attack on himself and his friend Wakely in 'On Radical Snobs' (8 August 1846). Earlier in the year, after the abrupt disappearance of Baby Bib, rumours seem to have begun circulating to the effect Jerrold was 'off *Punch*' and he felt obliged to deny this (1 June 1846).[30] Perhaps *Punch*, with Thackeray's

'Snobs' series now so prominent in every issue, had begun to be perceived as less 'Jerroldian' (but one distinguished reader, at least, assumed that the 'Snob' papers came from Jerrold's pen[31]) yet Jerrold's assertion about the magazine's being pervaded by a new and inferior 'spirit' is hardly borne out by a look through the issues for the summer and autumn of 1846. Mr Punch is having one of his periodic fits of obsession (in this case, with a controversy about the best place to locate a large equestrian statue of the Duke of Wellington) but on the whole the mixture is much the same as it has been from the beginning. There is plenty of satire – much of it contributed by Jerrold – directed at such favourite targets as the devious foreign policy of King Louis Philippe, upper-class philistinism, the lifestyle and social attitudes of Church of England bishops, the evils of hanging and flogging, and the insensitivity of the Royal Family. To the 22 August issue Jerrold contributed a scathing half-column entitled 'Dreadful Destitution in Buckingham Palace', inspired by a Royal request for a costly remodelling of the Palace, and an item headed 'Crime and Ignorance' that could have been written by Dickens himself. Four young agricultural labourers had been convicted of gang rape and sentenced to transportation for life. Jerrold comments on the fact that the State allows 'thousands and tens of thousands to grow up, with no more self-respect taught them than is taught their contemporary cattle':

> ... disgust of the culprits must not make us forgetful of the terrible truth that, had the State fulfilled its first duty to them, they might not have so grievously failed in their duties to a fellow-creature. They were brought up as brutes, and society reaps the terrible fruit of their rearing.[32]

As for mere 'guffawing', it is Jerrold's own male-chauvinist serial, 'The Life and Adventures of Miss Robinson Crusoe', that is the most extensive example to be found in this particular stretch of *Punch*.

Jerrold seems at this time to have been as happy as ever in the society of his *Punch* colleagues. In his journal for 13 August 1846 Thackeray writes about having been on a jolly river outing ('Champagne began the instant we got on board') with his fellow-Punchites and others including Forster: 'Jerrold chirped and laughed & made laugh with all his might, and little Evans had his hat knocked off.'[33] And yet this was only a few days after the appearance in the journal of Thackeray's essay on 'Radical Snobs' which would seem to have pointed reference to Jerrold:

> Perhaps, after all, there is no better friend to Conservatism than your outrageous Radical Snob. When a man preaches to you that all noblemen are tyrants, that all clergymen are hypocrites and liars, that all capitalists are scoundrels banded together in an infamous conspiracy to deprive the people of their rights, he creates a wholesome revulsion of feeling in favour of the abused parties, and a sense of fair play leads the generous heart to take a side with the object of unjust oppression. (8 August 1846)

Perhaps by October it was simply the runaway success of the 'Snobs' that had got under Jerrold's skin – that, and the fact that, from late August onwards, the nature of the 'Snob' sketches had changed[34] so that they could possibly be seen as no longer having much purpose beyond that of merely 'guffawing' at middle-class pretentiousness.

Whatever it is that accounts for Jerrold's remarks in his autumn 1846 letter, it seems clear that both he and Dickens shared a general uneasiness about Thackeray, his consciousness of being a born gentleman, and his ambivalent comic irony. It belonged very much to the general outlook on life that Jerrold and Dickens shared. In November 1849, however, they found themselves in sharp disagreement on one particular issue, a burning one following the furore over the public hanging of Frederick and Marie Manning for the cold-blooded murder of Mrs Manning's lover Patrick O'Connor. Dickens was present at the execution and was utterly horrified, as he had been on a previous similar occasion (the Courvoisier hanging in 1840), by the carnivalesque behaviour of the huge crowd that swarmed round the double gallows in Horsemonger Lane. He made his feelings public in letters to *The Times* vividly describing the 'wickedness and levity' of the crowd and urging support for a proposal to have future executions carried out as 'a private solemnity within the prison walls'.[35] He declined an invitation from the Quaker Charles Gilpin, a leading opponent of capital punishment (whom Jerrold thought 'a noble fellow'), to attend a public meeting calling for the total abolition of the death penalty. Three years before Dickens had written a series of five powerfully argued letters in the *Daily News* advocating the abolitionist cause. Now he felt that the public mind, inflamed by the horror of the Manning murder, was not ready for such a measure, and that meanwhile a stop had to be put to the macabre, scandalous and demoralising spectacle of public hangings. Jerrold, however, as a supporter of the abolitionist movement, wrote to Gilpin deploring the idea of private executions; they would make a fearful 'mystery' out of capital punishment and so cause its indefinite continuance. Gilpin communicated this view to Dickens, who promptly wrote to Jerrold, beseeching him to leave such words as 'mystery' to 'the Platform-people' and to remember the squalid brutality of the days when there was no mystery about any form of judicial punishment and 'all was as open as Bridewell when Ned Ward went to see the women whipped'.[36] Dickens also wrote a second letter to *The Times* reiterating at greater length his objections to public executions and ending with an aggressive dismissal (right after invoking Ned Ward in Bridewell again) of total abolitionists, a dismissal which seems to glance at Jerrold. There were, Dickens wrote, a class of objectors to private hangings who,

> desiring the total abolition of capital punishment, will have nothing less; and who, not doubting the fearful influence of public executions, would have it protracted for an indefinite term, rather than spare the demoralization they do not dispute, at the risk of losing sight for a while of their final end. But of

The young Douglas Jerrold. Anonymous watercolour,
The Fales Library, New York University.

T.P. Cooke as William
in *Black Eyed Susan*,
1829.

T.P. Cooke as William ~ in Black Ey'd Susan.

London. Published Sept.ʳ 2ᵈ 1829, by W.West. at his Theatrical Print Warehouse, 57. Wych Street.Opposite the Olympic Theatre.Strand.

Jersey. Pubᵈ by G.SKELT, 29, Clearview Sᵗ Saint Helier.

Samuel Laman Blanchard.
From a miniature by Louisa
Stuart Costello.

Duncombe's Edition.

MORE FRIGHTENED
THAN HURT;

A FARCE,

IN TWO ACTS;

By D. W. Jerrold.

THE ONLY EDITION EXTANT WHICH IS CORRECTLY MARKED
WITH THE STAGE BUSINESS, SITUATIONS, AND
DIRECTIONS,

AS IT IS PERFORMED AT

Sadler's Wells Theatre.

London:

PUBLISHED BY DUNCOMBE, 19, LITTLE QUEEN STREET,
And Sold by all Booksellers.

1821.

Title page of *More Frightened Than Hurt.*

J.P. Wilkinson as Popeseye in *More Frightened Than Hurt*.
From the hand-coloured etched frontispiece
to Duncombe's edition, by Cruikshank.

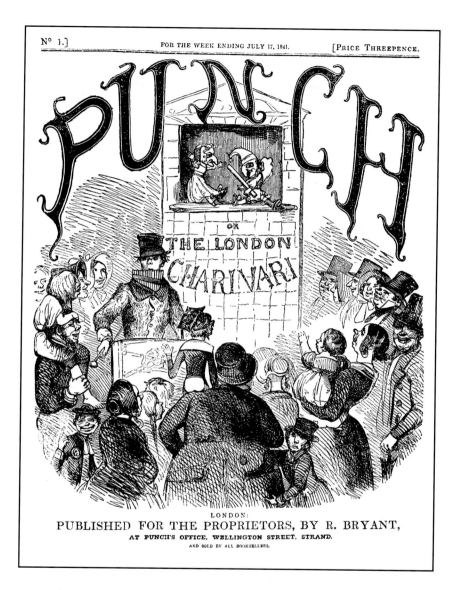

PUNCH

OR

THE LONDON CHARIVARI

LONDON:
PUBLISHED FOR THE PROPRIETORS, BY R. BRYANT,
AT PUNCH'S OFFICE, WELLINGTON STREET, STRAND.
AND SOLD BY ALL BOOKSELLERS.

Cover of the first number of *Punch*. By Archibald S. Henning
from a rough sketch by Ebenezer Landells.

DEATH
AND THE DRAWING ROOM
OR
THE YOUNG DRESS MAKERS
OF
ENGLAND

T is very certain that if our hearts were as tender as nature made them, and had not gone through a sort of macadamizing process by the hard knocks they encounter in the world, we should scarcely ever enjoy an hour's peace, far less indulge in a joyous laugh, or sleep a quiet sleep, so great is the sum of human suffering that exists at every moment of time. If we gave to misery out of our sight a tenth part of the sympathy which we give to that which comes home to ourselves, or even accidentally falls under our eyes, we should never be at rest; and it is a merciful dispensation we are so made that we can forget it. The funeral bells toll daily, while men go to wedding feasts, and the multitude hurries on regardless. "Death is common," and we are used to it. But, even when any unusual occurrence forces some new consciousness of human pain upon us, we devise all manner of expedients to drive it away. Some people have even gone so far as to turn all that misery which *will* force itself upon their sight into a source of luxury and self-complacency, on the principle of enjoying the sounds of wind, and rain, and driving sleet outside our doors, while we sit snug by our own fireside. Into this species of luxury the childish mind is initiated in such moral songs as the following:—

> "How many children in the street
> Half naked I behold,
> While *I* am cloth'd from head to foot,
> And cover'd from the cold."—Watts.

The class who thus luxuriate will only read the description of the young dress-makers which we are about to give, to hug themselves in their own comfortable state, and to look round at their own blooming daughters and "Thank God." In this complacent feeling they will rest, let us do or say what we will; so there we leave them, and turn to those who, so far from taking any pleasure in such things, may put themselves to considerable trouble to drive them out of their memories; for, let it frankly be confessed, this paper is written with no purpose of affording mere information or the gratification of curiosity, but with an earnest wish to drive people out of their strongholds of indifference and calculating policies, and, by bringing home to their feelings the suffering which is now remote and hidden, to make them rouse themselves and say, "These things shall exist no longer."

Among the lulling expedients to which we resort to hush the cry of pain that begins to sound in our hearts, few are more successful than the plea of distance. When we hear of the hard toil

Page of the *Illuminated Magazine* for June 1843
'illuminated' by Kenny Meadows.

Henry Mayhew caricatured in Punch in 1841 (vol. 1, p.98). `There was an article about hats and Punch gave a portrait of Mr Henry Mayhew with the hat he wore, with the inscription "The (s) tile four and nine" '. F. Eason to M. Spielmann, 7 August 1895 (MS. Punch Library).

THIS (S)TILE——FOUR-AND-NINE.

The Hermit of Bellyfulle (*Chronicles of Clovernook*).
By Kenny Meadows (*Illuminated Magazine* for August 1843).

PRINCESS'S THEATRE,
OXFORD STREET.

Lessee, Mr. J. M. MADDOX, Oxford-Street.

☞ LAST NIGHT BUT SIX OF THE SEASON.

Mr. WALLACK

Will perform Jacques, THIS EVENING.

43rd TIME.

A COURT BALL IN 1740

Which was most gloriously received, it increases nightly in attraction, and will be performed EVERY EVENING until further notice.

MR. COLLINS,

Will make his Fifth Appearance at this Theatre, TO-NIGHT, as McShane, in the NERVOUS MAN.

" So, Mr. Caudle, they've made a brother of you—
" What would you say, if I was to go and get made a sister of ?"

🖘 Mrs. CAUDLE

Delivered her **CURTAIN LECTURES**

For the 81st TIME,

To a House crowded in every part, amidst shouts of laughter and applause. Mrs. C. will therefore have the honor of repeating them EVERY EVENING until further notice.

Section of a playbill for Princess's Theatre, 4 August 1845.
Mrs Caudle was played in this production by William Oxberry.

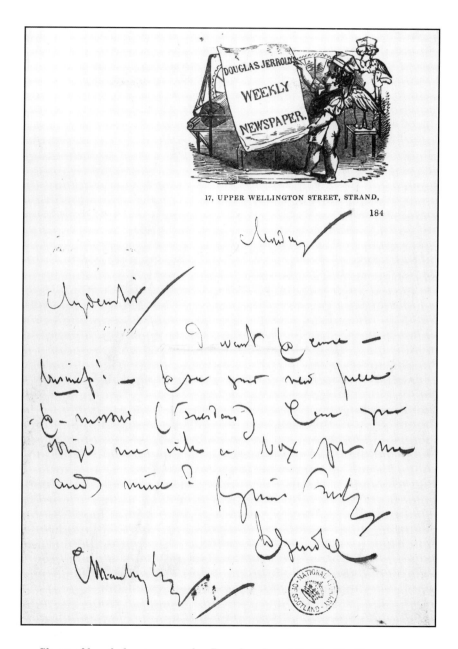

Sheet of headed notepaper for *Douglas Jerrold's Weekly Newspaper*.
National Library of Scotland (MS. 966, ff.188).

The Amateur Players in *Every Man In His Humour*, 1845,
by Kenny Meadows. The players are (clockwise)
Forster, Leech, Dickens, Jerrold.

Punch cartoon showing Jerrold and himself by Thackeray. Vol. 15, p.198 (4 November 1848).

AUTHOR'S MISERIES

Old Gentleman. Miss Wiggets. Two Authors

Old Gentleman: "I AM SORRY TO SEE YOU OCCUPIED, MY DEAR MISS WIGGETS, WITH THAT TRIVIAL PAPER 'PUNCH.' A RAILWAY IS NOT A PLACE, IN MY OPINION, FOR JOKES. I NEVER JOKE—NEVER."

Miss W: "SO I SHOULD THINK, SIR."

Old Gentleman: "AND BESIDES, ARE YOU AWARE WHO ARE THE CONDUCTORS OF THAT PAPER. AND THAT THEY ARE CHARTISTS, DEISTS, ATHEISTS, ANARCHISTS, AND SOCIALISTS, TO A MAN? I HAVE IT FROM THE BEST AUTHORITY, THAT THEY MEET TOGETHER ONCE A WEEK IN A TAVERN IN SAINT GILE'S, WHERE THEY CONCOCT THEIR INFAMOUS PRINT. THE CHIEF PART OF THEIR INCOME IS DERIVED FROM THREATENING LETTERS WHICH THEY SEND TO THE NOBILITY AND GENTRY. THE PRINCIPAL WRITER IS A RETURNED CONVICT. TWO HAVE BEEN TRIED AT THE OLD BAILEY: AND THEIR ARTIST—AS FOR THEIR ARTIST. . . . ."

Guard: SWIN-DUN! STA-TION!"

(1848)

(*Exeunt two Authors*)

Douglas Jerrold in middle age. *Carte de visite*, published in
the 1860s by the United Association of Photographers Ltd
using an earlier photograph.

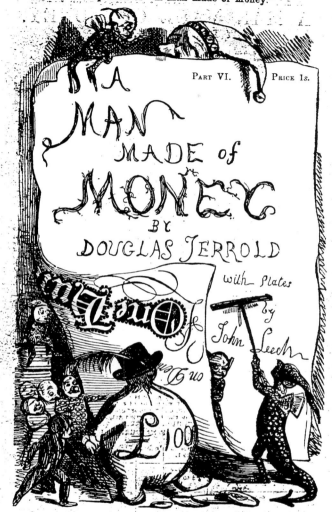

Monthly part cover for *A Man Made of Money* by John Leech.

Advertisement for *Lloyd's Weekly Newspaper* from B. Darwin,
The Dickens Advertiser, 1930.

William Blanchard Jerrold, *The Illustrated Review*, 13 March 1873. From a photograph by Elliott & Fry.

'The Manager's Pig' by Lewis C. Daniel (*The Whimsical Tales of Douglas Jerrold*, Roedale Press, Allentown, Pa., 1948).

Douglas Jerrold in May 1857, photographed by
Dr Hugh Welch Diamond.

these I say nothing, considering them, however good and pure in intention, unreasonable, and not to be argued with.[37]

Given this blustering public dismissal of his deeply-felt opposition to hanging, Jerrold's response, in a private letter to Dickens of 20 November quoted by Walter Jerrold, seems moderate and reasonable:

... what I sincerely lament in your letter of yesterday is that, in its advocacy of private executions, it implies their continued necessity. The sturdy anti-abolitionist may count upon it as on his side. I am grieved that the weight of your name, and the influence of your reputation, should be claimed by such a party.

Grant private hanging, and you perpetuate the punishment .... As to the folly and wickedness of the infliction of death as a punishment, possibly I may consider them from a too transcendental point. I believe, notwithstanding, that society will rise to it. In the meantime my Tom Thumb voice must be raised against any compromise that, in the sincerity of my opinion, shall tend to continue the hangman amongst us, whether in the Old Bailey street, or in the prison press-yard.

Sorry am I, my dear Dickens, to differ from any opinion of yours – most sorry upon an opinion so grave; but both of us are only the instruments of our convictions.

We do not know if Dickens replied to what he probably saw as this 'unreasonable, and not to be argued with' letter but we do know that Jerrold's views were strongly pitted against his at Gilpin's meeting, as reported in the *Illustrated London News* on 24 November. After alluding to Dickens's letters to *The Times*, Gilpin went on to quote from Jerrold's letter to him, describing Jerrold as 'a writer who held as influential a place in public estimation as Mr Dickens'. Jerrold, said Gilpin, believed that 'the genius of England would never permit private hanging: the brutality of the mob was even preferable to the darkness of secrecy'. Gilpin also quoted letters from two prominent reformist MPs, Cobden and Bright, supporting the abolitionist position; the 'new dodge' of a private hanging was, wrote Cobden, 'simply assassination'.[38]

Walter Jerrold surmised that it was this disagreement (in which Dickens seems to have been determined to shout down all opposition) that led to the temporary 'estrangement' between himself and Jerrold to which he referred in the reminiscent letter he sent Blanchard Jerrold for use in his *Life*. Writing in 1857, Dickens refers to the estrangement having taken place 'within these two or three years', which suggests a later date than 1849. Even in early 1852, when Dickens was furious with Jerrold for pulling out of another Amateur Players venture at very short notice, seems too far back, yet this may have been what Dickens was referring to. If so, he was putting a particular gloss on the incident (something at which he was adept) when he wrote that the coolness was 'not on any personal subject' and did not involve 'an angry word'. In the Players' production of Bulwer Lytton's *Not So Bad As We Seem*[39] Jerrold, well suited to the part of Shadowly Softhead, a foppish young gentleman,[40] had again been one of the stars of the show, amusing even Queen Victoria who described him in her journal as 'a funny little man who writes in *Punch*' and thought he acted 'extremely well'.[41] His character was supposed to be the double of Dickens's (Lord Wilmot, the lead) so his defection had serious consequences for Dickens's own performance. Even before his withdrawal he had irritated Dickens by 'wet-blanketing the proceedings', together with Forster, which was the result, Dickens wrote to Bulwer, of Jerrold's being 'constitutionally inconstant and unsettled' and when he did withdraw six months later Dickens wrote angrily to Bulwer,

> Jerrold – who never in his life was true to Anything – has deserted us! When the walls of Manchester and Liverpool had been for days covered with bills announcing him for next week in his part! ... I immediately called the Company together, and they unanimously passed a severe censure upon him, discarding all private considerations (as men must in such a matter if they have any good faith in them) and heavily reflecting on his conduct.[42]

This seems to me more likely than the disagreement over capital punishment to have caused the estrangement which was ended, as Dickens later remembered, by a generous gesture on Jerrold's part. Both he and Jerrold happened to be dining in the Stranger's Room of a club, each with a separate party of guests:

> Our chairs were almost back to back, and I took mine after he was seated and at dinner. I said not a word (I am sorry to remember) and did not look that way. Before we had sat so long, he openly wheeled his chair round, stretched out both his hands in a most engaging manner, and said aloud, with a bright and loving face that I can see as I write to you, 'For God's sake, let us be friends again! A life's not long enough for this!'[43]

Whatever the date of the estrangement, Jerrold and Dickens were on good terms again by the beginning of 1855 when Dickens warmly invited Jerrold to join him at Greenwich to celebrate his birthday as they had once done, years before, in Rochester. Later on, he tells the reformist MP Austen Layard ('Layard of Nineveh') that he has recruited Jerrold ('whom I can trust') to support the Administrative Reform Association in his capacity as editor of *Lloyd's Weekly Newspaper*.[44] Dickens's last meeting with his friend was just a week or so before Jerrold's untimely death, and he recalled it with tender affection, in a letter written for Blanchard Jerrold to publish in the memoir he was preparing (see below, p. 266f.). It seems clear from the tone of this piece that the warm friendship he and Jerrold had enjoyed in the 1840s had long been re-established.

Jerrold's relationship with Thackeray, the other member of Masson's triad, was more complex than that with Dickens. Marked differences of temperament, social background, artistic beliefs, and outlook on life all contributed to this complexity, as, no doubt, did Thackeray's rapid rise to fame in his mid-thirties with *The Book of Snobs* and *Vanity Fair*. Five months or so after he had stopped contributing to *Punch* he wrote to Bradbury and Evans (10 May 1852) with a characteristic touch of that self-mocking humour so different from Jerrold's sardonic jibing at others, 'I fancied myself too big to pull in the boat.' He added, 'It wasn't in the nature of things that Lemon and Jerrold should like me,'[45] referring primarily, I take it, to the class differences between himself with his public school and Cambridge background and the other two, one the child of strolling players and the other the product of a solidly bourgeois background.[46]

Unlike Jerrold and Dickens, Jerrold and Thackeray were above all work-associates – most intensively so on *Punch* from 1842 onwards, though their social-professional relations went back many years before this, to those jolly disputatious evenings in the Rue d'Amboise, and to subsequent work together on the short-lived *Constitutional* and other journalistic projects. Their relationship was essentially a colleaguely one, involving, as such relationships often do, tensions and competitiveness as well as cameraderie. And competitiveness was inevitably sharpened in early 1846 when Thackeray began emerging as the second star in *Punch*'s literary firmament where Jerrold had previously shone alone. When Thackeray asked, 'What is the use of quarreling with a man if you have to meet him every Wednesday at dinner?'[47] he was acknowledging the fact that Jerrold and he had to contrive to rub along together despite occasional flare-ups like the one he referred to as the 'Parson-Snob' controversy,[48] and their differences in table manners ('M[ark] L[emon] afterwards tells that D.J. and W.M.T. quarreled because T. said D.J. ate peas with his knife and therefore was not fit company for him'[49]). The mutual banter or 'chaff' that was routine at the weekly *Punch* dinners seems often to have had an edge to it, as it did when some of the same characters came together with others at other Bradbury and Evans dinners. Thackeray alluded to this in a letter written to Mrs Sartoris (Adelaide Kemble) in 1850:

> ... a dinner at Bradbury and Evans's yesterday; when the literary wags were assembled and where Dickens, Jerrold, Forster and your humble servant sate sparring at each other. Would any of us, I wonder, have liked Laertes's foil?[50]

Jerrold's fiery temper, once he had become chafed, would sometimes carry him too far. Speaking of him at a *Punch* dinner eighteen months after his death, Thackeray recalled that Jerrold had once 'talked treason at this table and M[ark] L[emon] charged him with it and for once made him blush'.[51] As to Jerrold's writings in *Punch*, Thackeray was, as we have seen, a delighted admirer of Mrs Caudle and, if Vizetelly is to be believed, always eager to see what Jerrold had written:

> I was several times present when the early number of 'Punch' reached Young-street [Thackeray's home], and well remember how, as Thackeray

nervously tore off the wrapper, he would exclaim, 'Now let's see what young Douglas has to say this week'. For some little while he would remain absorbed in the chapter of the 'Caudle lectures', or of 'Miss Robinson Crusoe', or whatever Jerrold's contribution may then chance to have been ... .[52]

What Thackeray thought about Jerrold's more political and polemical contributions we may learn from what he wrote after the latter's death, in a *Times* article on Leech's sketches in oil (2 June 1862). He remarks that Leech 'surveys society from the gentleman's point of view' whereas Jerrold had taken 'the other side':

> he looked up at the rich and great with a fierce, a sarcastic aspect, and a threatening posture, and his outcry, or challenge was: 'Ye rich and great, look out! We, the people, are as good as you. Have a care, ye priests, wallowing on a tithe pig and rolling in carriages and four; ye landlords grinding the poor; ye vulgar fine ladies, bullying innocent governesses, and what not – we will expose your vulgarity; we will put down your oppression; we will vindicate the nobility of our common nature,' and so forth. A great deal was to be said on the Jerrold side, a great deal was said – perhaps even a great deal too much.

While no less pointed than Jerrold in his satire on the vices and follies of contemporary society,[53] Thackeray eschewed melodrama, seldom presenting figures of unadulterated evil (*Vanity Fair*'s Lord Steyne is a grand exception here), or of spotless virtue carefully protected from authorial irony. Nor, certainly, did he align virtue with poverty and vice with rank, power and wealth like Jerrold and also Dickens in his earlier fiction. Reviewing Lever's comic novel *St Patrick's Eve*, Thackeray deplored the fact that 'the chief of our pleasant writers – Mr Jerrold, Mr Dickens, Mr Lever' were so addicted to 'comic philosophy', or moralising social criticism, in their writings, always 'rushing forward' to tell us 'that society is diseased, the laws unjust, the rich ruthless, the poor martyrs, the world lop-sided'. If, he wrote, the moral of Lever's novel were to be accepted, all property might be declared iniquitous and 'all capital criminal': 'Let fund-holders and manufacturers look out – Judge Jerrold will show them no favour, Chief Baron Boz has charged dead against them.'[54]

He would sometimes tease Jerrold, even in *Punch*, calling him 'the chivalrous advocate of Toryism and Church and State' (20 June 1846) but he always gave him credit for honesty, believing, as he wrote to Lemon in 1847, that his opinions were 'wrong on many points, but I'm sure he believes them honestly, and I don't think that he or any man *has* hit a foul blow in Punch'.[55]

There came an occasion in the summer of 1850, however, when Thackeray thought Jerrold had gone outrageously too far in *Punch*. He read a piece that he believed to have been written by 'poor Jerrold' ('poor' here meaning 'deluded', I assume) and that was, he wrote to Jane Brookfield, 'so wicked ... that upon my word I don't think I ought to pull any longer in the same boat with such a savage little Robespierre'.[56] In consequence, he tells her, he has resigned from the journal. However, the article (perhaps another of *Punch*'s anti-Church sallies) seems to have been withdrawn before publication (Thackeray must have seen an advance proof) – because there is nothing in the issue of the magazine following the date of his letter that could fit his description – and he remained one of the *Punch* team. His last contribution did not appear until the issue for 22 November 1851 ('The Last Irish Grievance') but he continued to attend the weekly dinners from time to time.

Thackeray's mocking humour got him into trouble with Jerrold again in 1854, and indeed with the whole *Punch* table, when he wrote in a review of Leech's *Pictures of Life and Character* that it was only Leech's wonderful cartoons that made people buy the magazine:

> Fancy a number of Punch without Leech's pictures! What would you give for it? The learned gentlemen who write the work must feel that, without him, it were as well left alone.[57]

When it became clear that he had given great offence, Thackeray quickly acknowledged to Whitwell Elwin that, however good-naturedly he had been writing, he should not have let slip this joking reference to his 'dear kind old comrades'. Jerrold, he told his publisher George Smith, had attacked him about it, 'with perfect reason, calling me snob and flunkey', but, when writing to apologise for the gaffe to his old friend, Percival Leigh, *Punch*'s much-loved 'Professor', he said, 'Jerrold has had his fire into me and do you know I am rather comforted', which suggests a certain pleasure in needling his fiery former colleague.[58]

Jerrold was, I believe, baffled by Thackeray's humour and his easy-going mockery, which included self-mockery. Even in the heat of the 'Parson-Snob Controversy', he could enter into the fun of Thackeray's 'Snobs of England', though with a touch of Jerroldian overkill, as shown by his spoof letter to Mr Punch from the *Morning Post*-reading, peerage-worshipping 'Slavery Fitztoady', who protests against Thackeray's 'unhallowed attacks on all that is good and gracious in this free and happy country'.[59] But the effect of the twist that Thackeray gives to the original title of the series 'The Snobs of England' with the by-line 'By One of Themselves', was completely lost on him.[60] And he would have furiously rejected Thackeray's charge, recorded in the following anecdote of Vizetelly's, that he himself was no more free of all taint of 'Snobbism' than any of his compatriots:

> I remember him [Thackeray] mentioning to me his having noticed at the Earl of Carlisle's a presentation copy of one of Jerrold's books, the inscription in which ran: 'To the Right Honourable the Earl of Carlisle, K.G., K.C.B., &c., &c.' 'Ah!' said Thackeray, 'this is the sort of style in which your rigid, uncompromising radical always toadies the great'.[61]

When responding to Thackeray's work Jerrold was always happier when he felt that Thackeray was writing with what Chaucer called 'ful devout corage'. He could praise the *Irish Sketch Book* for its 'fine observation, ... fine sympathy for the suffering, and a happy ... expression of indignation towards injustice', and the first instalment of *Vanity Fair* for its 'hearty, healthy, natural' tone and avoidance of superfine, sugary unreality ('We have people who really live, and the world as it is').[62] But it was the continual uncertainty about the degree of earnestness exhibited by Thackeray in his talk and in his writing that defeated Jerrold; causing him to say things like, 'I have known Thackeray for eighteen years, and I don't know him yet', or, in answer to J.H. Stirling's question 'What like was Thackeray?', 'He's just a big fellow with a broken nose, and, though I meet him weekly at the *Punch* dinner, I don't know him so well as I know you'.[63] When Charles Mackay suggested getting Thackeray's support for his candidature for the Reform Club in 1857 Jerrold wrote that he felt his former *Punch* fellow-staffer to be 'so full of crotchets, that, as a favour, I would hardly ask him to pass me the salt' – only to have to eat his words when Thackeray responded warmly to the proposal: 'I suppose that *I* at least must henceforth say nothing of "crotchets".'[64]

FLY LEAVES, No. 3.

A TRIO OF PUNCHITES.

1st " Eminent Writer." I say, Douglas, what do you think of this Puppet-Show?

2nd " Eminent Writer." Why, I think we ought to put down all rival publications.

3rd " Eminent Writer." Otherwise we shall be sold at the butter shops free, gratis, and for nothing.

'A big fellow with a broken nose.' This aspect of Thackeray's appearance was the subject of one of Jerrold's most celebrated impromptus, 'They should have begun with his nose', made after he had been told that someone had been trying to convert Thackeray to Romanism.[65] Thackeray's allusions to Jerrold's diminutive stature are more affectionately humorous, which, again, points us to the great difference between their powers as comic writers. Thackeray would refer to Jerrold as 'Master Douglas', 'Young Douglas' or 'the little man'. Hodder reports Thackeray delightedly calling out to him, 'We've got the little man in!' after Jerrold's election to the Reform Club,[66] and Thackeray told Dr Diamond when congratulating him on one of the photographs he had taken of Jerrold shortly before his sudden death, that 'no one had such a head as that dear little man! & that is his head'.[67] He drew a delicious cartoon of himself and Jerrold as a sort of 'Little and Large' double act for his 'Author's Miseries' series (1848) which shows them in a railway carriage eavesdropping, in a spirit of what Spielmann calls 'fraternal shamefacedness and disgust', on an old gentleman denouncing the Punchites as 'Chartists, Deists, Atheists, Anarchists and Socialists' who derive most of their income from blackmailing 'the nobility and gentry' (see plate). A real-life occasion when the two performed a double act was at a dinner given to Thackeray in 1855 on the eve of his departure for an American lecture-tour. Walter Jerrold quotes an eye-witness account:

> the Chairman (Charles Dickens) quitted, and ... Thackeray was on the move with the Chairman, when, inspired by the moment, Jerrold took the chair, and Thackeray remained. Who is to chronicle what now passed? – What passages of wit – what neat and pleasant sarcastic speeches in proposing healths – what varied and pleasant, ay, and at times sarcastic acknowledgments ...: There were words too nimble and full of flame for a dozen Gurneys [i.e. expert shorthand-writers], all ears, to catch and preserve. Few will forget that night. There was an 'air of wit' about the room for three days after.[68]

This is a swooning sort of account but it does capture what I take to have been the essence of the relationship – a very jokey one but with much mutual appreciation, having also a distinct edginess and a strongly competitive element. It was not a free-standing and intimate friendship like Jerrold's relationship with Dickens. Jerrold and Thackeray met at the *Punch* table, and at gatherings like the 1855 dinner or Dickens's private theatricals at Tavistock House, but we never hear of Thackeray visiting Putney or of Jerrold in Thackeray's home in Young Street.[69] The two were not close friends, but neither were they always at daggers drawn and we have no reason to believe that it was merely out of duty or a sense of decorum that Thackeray acted as one of the pall-bearers at Jerrold's funeral or participated in the memorial fund-raising organised by Dickens. In his memorial lecture, 'Charity and Humour' Thackeray expatiated on Jerrold's wit but dwelt still more on that intrinsic benevolence of his character which was ignored by those who saw in the brillant utterer of repartee the severe satirist only. To illustrate this part of his subject Mr Thackeray read an apologue by Mr Jerrold which shows how a fruit merchant who had dealt in lemons during the greater part of his life found an insuperable difficulty in making the world believe that he had abandoned his old trade and taken to the sale of sweet oranges.[70]

For the last word on the Jerrold/Thackeray relationship we might turn to an earlier, private, comment made by Thackeray in a letter to the *Quarterly*'s editor Whitwell Elwin after the row over his injudicious comments on Leech's role in the success of *Punch*. He wrote that he had tried to repair the damage by 'speaking very politely of my old comrades in a lecture' (the same 'Charity and Humour' one he repeated for the Jerrold Fund) and that 'all of them'

> have quite forgiven me I think except Jerrold who would immediately if any misfortune happened to me but Success is naturally odious to him and the conduct of a gentleman somehow puzzles him and other men who are not of that sort.[71]

The deep-seated class and temperamental differences that prevented any real deep friendship between these two *Punch* colleagues could hardly be made more apparent.

Chapter Eleven

Trading on the Name: *Douglas Jerrold's Shilling Magazine* and *Douglas Jerrold's Weekly Newspaper*

1845-1847

While he was writing the 'Caudle Lectures' Jerrold was also busy launching the new monthly magazine that Bradbury and Evans had agreed to establish with him as editor. As its title indicates, *Douglas Jerrold's Shilling Magazine* was published at the same price as the *Illuminated* had been but was smaller in size (small octavo) and unillustrated, with the sole exception of a fine series of steel engravings done by Leech to illustrate Jerrold's opening serial story *St Giles and St James*. As the normal price for monthlies was half a crown, or two shillings and sixpence, the new journal, like its predecessor, was certainly competitively priced and Bradbury and Evans seem, generally, to have committed themselves to it whole-heartedly. Jerrold exulted to Leigh Hunt that it had 'everything on its side in the proprietorship – so far, as in these commercial times, spirit and money will go. The proprietors are the owners of *Punch* – truly printer princes'.[1]

The magazine's title reflected how bankable his name had by this time become, primarily as a result of his *Punch* writings. He now followed the example set by Ainsworth and Hood in using his name, or having it used, as a sort of trademark to promote a periodical (*Ainsworth's Magazine* began publication in 1842 and *Hood's Magazine* in 1844).

The half-page advertisement for the new journal in the *Athenaeum* (14 December 1844) featured the shilling coin with the young Queen's head on it (that 'stamp of respectability', one contributor called it[2]) which was to feature on the title-page of each issue. It announced that the work was intended to 'appeal to the hearts of the Masses of England' and to be 'mainly devoted to a consideration of the social wants and rightful claims of the PEOPLE'. Jerrold proclaimed his belief that 'the present social contest' between the classes, a 'righteous and bloodless struggle', must necessarily end in a more equitable distribution of 'the good provided for all men', and pledged his journal to work towards this. Party politics as such would be eschewed but every essay, however light, should be made to 'breathe WITH A PURPOSE', and would be also 'exclusively British in its

189

subject'. Sketches, tales and romances would not be excluded so that 'light readers' should not be put off – however, such tales and romances would all be 'illustrating and working out some wholesome principle'. 'Mere stories', made 'like Twelfth-night heroes, of mere sugar', would be taboo.

The contents of the first number set the liberal reformist tone and gave a fair indication of the kind of material the reader might expect to find in future issues. The first instalment of Jerrold's lead story centres on the discovery of a baby, 'a lovely human bud', under the shawl of a drunken woman who has collapsed in the street and been frozen half to death. A poor but good-hearted couple want to adopt the waif but it is almost immediately reclaimed by its mother, another 'wretched, ragged woman', who had loaned it to the first one to use as a sympathy-inducing prop to beg with. The hapless infant is swiftly re-submerged in the hopeless lower depths of society. This opening instalment is followed by a long, fancifully written piece by the reformist writer John Saunders (a contributor to the *Illuminated* and later founder of the *People's Journal*) offering an optimistic interpretation of 'the Spirit of the Age' as one of transition to 'a new, more harmonious, and infinitely nobler state' of society; an anti-militarist essay by another *Illuminated* contributor, the multifarious scribbler Angus B. Reach; some reminiscences of Hazlitt by Peter Patmore (father of Coventry, who was to contribute a few of his early poems to the journal); a Jerrold-style moralised fantasy about a cheating Jewish diamond merchant; a denunciation of the 'slavery' suffered by shop assistants who are made to toil for 'needlessly long' hours; a satirical poem; the first of Jerrold's 'Hedgehog Letters' (satirical observations on current events, supposedly written by a London cabman, Juniper Hedgehog, to his relatives overseas); another poem; and the first instalment of a 'History for Young England', intended to ridicule the Tory version of the nation's past. The last half-dozen pages of the ninety-two that make up the issue are devoted to book reviews.

This last section was the responsibility of the journalist and dramatist F.G. Tomlins, founder of the Shakespeare Society and a great admirer of Jerrold's; according to John Hollingshead, he 'cultivated literature on a City clerkship'.[3] Tomlins's choice of books for review over the years shows that the *Shilling Magazine* was aimed at people interested in serious and 'improving' reading. Most attention was paid to historical and biographical works, along with a fair admixture of travel writing and high-class poetry and fiction, including Browning's *Bells and Pomegranates*, Disraeli's *Sybil* and *Tancred* and Charlotte Brontë's *Jane Eyre* ('a work of considerable merit'). Reviews of handbooks for such activities as angling, singing and learning French assume readers with some leisure and social or cultural aspirations. This is born out by the sort of books and goods offered for sale in the advertising section (handbooks of gardening, fishing rods, shooting jackets, etc.).[4] Jerrold may have wanted the journal to appeal, as he said, to the hearts of 'the Masses of England' and he certainly opened its columns to working-class contributors, but his primary readership was evidently the upwardly-mobile lower and middle middle classes, liberal-reformist but not Radical in politics, progressive and optimistic in their social views but troubled by the abysmal poverty and ignorance in which so vast a portion of the British populace was sunk, and by the harshness with which the law bore down upon them. Brian Maidment groups Jerrold's new venture with certain other journals of the 1830s and 1840s such as the weekly *Howitt's Journal* and *People's Journal*, *Tait's Edinburgh Magazine* and the bi-weekly *Eliza Cook's Journal* in which 'artizan self-expression was aligned with London journalism as a distinct selling element in magazines self-consciously directed towards provincial, industrial readers'. He notes that it differs from these others, however, through being at the point on the spectrum 'where the "artisan" magazine cuts across the "family" magazine like *Household Words* [not started till 1850]'.[5] He might also have noted that the *Shilling Magazine*, like *Punch*, appears to address itself primarily to a metropolitan rather than a provincial readership.

Jerrold set himself to gather the kind of contributions he wanted for the magazine, asking Hodder, for example, to contact 'Mr. H. (I forget his name), the surgeon of Sanatorium' and ask him if he will supply an article 'of the same nature to his last'. 'The matter,' he specifies, 'must be of the *present day*, and social in its application.'[6] To Leigh Hunt he suggests a fanciful literary variation on this prescription – 'Shakespeare in France, by the Ghost of Voltaire'

> making [the ghost] marvel at the wondrous influence of Shakespeare over his countrymen, especially after he had pronounced him so *barbaric* – contrasting the Louis Quatorze public with the present generation, – and re-criticizing *Hamlet*, doubting whether Shakespeare was really so *barbaric* as he at first appeared.[7]

In the event, nothing was forthcoming from Hunt but Jerrold was delighted to receive an unsolicited article called 'The Novelist and the Milliner' from a young Scottish surgeon working in Pontypool, and wrote encouraging him to send more contributions. This young man was James Hutchison Stirling who later achieved great fame as a philosopher, and his article was just the kind of thing to appeal to Jerrold, being a convoluted and long-drawn-out exercise in irony, intended to convey intense sympathy for the 'thin, wry-shouldered Milliner' solacing her miserable existence with escapist romantic stories from a cheap circulating library. Writing to Stirling two months later, Jerrold said he had been 'very much struck with the peculiar vigour and freshness' of this paper which had 'thought and sinew' in it, and would welcome the follow-up articles on the influence of novels that Stirling was proposing but hoped he would vary the titles:

> I feel it necessary to the increasing influence of the Magazine (and it *is* increasing) to give as great a variety as possible to the contents. A reader will be attracted to a paper – with a new title – which, if carrying the same heading from month to month, he might turn from as monotonous. The "to

be continued" is, in my opinion, the worst line a magazine can have, if more than once in the same number. We, too, are limited for space; and must fight as much as possible, with *short swords*.[8]

He had always a very clear idea of the kind of material he wanted for the journal, turning down one offering, for instance, with the words, 'This is a very good Magazine paper – *very good* – but not *Shillingish*.'[9]

The new journal seems to have been well received and in prefacing the first volume (January–June 1845)[10] Jerrold felt able to write, 'We have now to acknowledge the success that has firmly established the "SHILLING MAGAZINE" as a public organ.' The only circulation figure we have for the journal is 9,000, cited by Blanchard Jerrold as having been attained by it 'at one time'. This was respectable, like the 7,000 claimed by *Ainsworth's* in 1842, but very far short of the 40,000 claimed by *Chambers's Journal* in 1845.[11] Fryckstedt quotes several favourable reviews in the provincial press that were proudly cited in the journal itself. Some others are quoted by Walter Jerrold but unsourced. Reviewers tended, naturally enough, to focus on Jerrold himself, his name being seen by the *Liverpool Standard*, for example, as a guarantee of excellence. An unnamed Yorkshire paper quoted by Walter Jerrold commented:

> We have long admired the writings of Douglas Jerrold. He is a hearty and sincere writer. Earnestness is his leading characteristic. He exposes class selfishness with a pen of fire; and loves to strip off the mask of hypocrisy and fraud. And when he has laid hold of some hollow windbag of cant, with what infinite gusto he rips it up. Meanwhile, he sympathises most keenly with the poor, the suffering and the struggling classes.

There is praise too for Jerrold's style, characterised, said the *Waterford Mail*, by 'a playfulness, mingled with its caustic satire which gives a piquancy to every page'.[12] But not everyone felt he was using his literary gifts to the best advantage. In its 'Magazines' column for 6 April 1845 the *Era* grumbled:

> The more we admire the talent of Mr Jerrold, the more do we regret the pernicious tendency of his writings, and that he does not devote that talent to the remedy for poverty, rather than by stirring up the discontents of the poor. To read Mr Jerrold one would imagine all the vice, as well as the poverty of St Giles's emanated from St James's. Virtue, in his opinion, seems quite incompatible with competence [i.e., with having enough money to live on].

This critic's main target is Jerrold's serial story, four months old and destined to ramble on through another twenty-one numbers, the plot (such as it is) being constantly interrupted for various digressions. It is worth noting that the periodicals reviewer of the Chartist *Northern Star* was an admirer of this story, welcoming, on 25 April 1846, its re-appearance in the

April number of the *Shilling Magazine* after a gap of a couple of months ('the other articles are, as usual, very good').

St Giles and St James derives its title, as Robert Colby has pointed out, from Dickens's 1841 preface to *Oliver Twist* in which he uses the names of these two sharply contrasting localities to represent the social extremes of the metropolis.[13] Here Jerrold uses them to name his two leading characters, the slum child and the aristocratic one. The whole story reads, as Jerrold's fiction so often does, like the work of a sort of second-rate Dickens (if that is not a contradiction in terms). It is crowded with farcical types and 'humour' characters like Capstick the misanthropic but soft-hearted muffin-maker, shrewish wives like Mrs Whitlow ('a face as sharp as a penknife, and lips that cut her words like scissors'), and vulnerable waifs exploited by criminals. The villainous Tom Blast, who 'blasts' St Giles's childhood, reminds us of both Fagin and Bill Sikes. A beautiful young girl marries a horrible old usurer called Ebenezer Snipeton (echoing 'Ebenezer Scrooge', no doubt) to save her father from beggary, the very fate from which Nicholas Nickleby's beloved Madeline is saved by the sudden death of her father.

Jerrold's overall purpose in this narrative is to enforce a contention that he, like Dickens, never tired of repeating, namely, that the state's gross neglect of the children of the poor inevitably pushed them towards the criminal world. At that point only would the state then intervene, to punish with imprisonment, flogging or hanging those whom it had previously taken no care of. From the moment he is reclaimed by his wretched mother St Giles never has a chance to live a decent life whereas St James, brought up in the lap of luxury, has no problem in avoiding crime. Various creaking plot-contrivances bring the two characters together at various points, each time so that St James can demonstrate benevolence towards St Giles (he twice saves him from the gallows). From within this shaky framework Jerrold fires away at some of his perennial targets such as electoral corruption, the obscenity of capital punishment, the luxurious lives of the higher Anglican clergy (represented here by the Rev. Dr Gilead of Lazarus Hall), and the glorification of war. Tom Blast is described at one point as 'prepared for robbery, and as it might be, bloodshed' and looking

> as horribly animated, as ferociously happy, as though he had mounted some Indian rampart, then and there graciously commissioned to slay man, woman and child; to pillage and to burn, and all for glory .... (ch.22)

As before in the *Story of a Feather*, Jerrold seems not to see how his plot undermines his message when St Giles returns from transportation to Botany Bay as a reformed character. He is still under the threat of the gallows since, like a later character, Dickens's Magwitch, he was transported for life and has therefore returned illegally. He strives to save his little half-brother, Jingo, from corruption at the hands of Blast rather as Nancy tries to save Oliver. It seems odd, also, given Jerrold's insistence in

193

that letter to Hodder quoted above that everything published in the *Shilling Magazine* should deal with 'the *present day*', that he should set his story in the previous century, just as he had done with the *Story of a Feather*. He was probably still not ready, despite the blazing example of Dickens, to break the approved Bulwerian and Ainsworthian mould of historical settings for works of fiction, a mould first formed by that great forefather of the Victorian novel Sir Walter Scott.

The preface Jerrold wrote when the story was published in volume form (as Volume I of his *Collected Writings*, 1851) shows that he was sensitive to the kind of class-bias criticism expressed by the *Era*. He changed the ending of the story so as to soften down any hint of class asperity ('St James made noble amends in his maturer years for the harmful vanities of his earlier life', etc., etc.). In his *Alton Locke* (1850) Charles Kingsley had already praised *St Giles and St James* as a 'fearless and life-like novel' and the *Athenaeum* applauded 'the playful wit, quaint wisdom, true characterization, and thoughtful philosophy which enliven and sustain this story of high and low life' (19 July 1861). It was perhaps just as well that Jerrold did not see the verdict of the Irish patriot John Mitchel. Mitchel ridiculed Jerrold for what he saw as the soft-headedness of his

> never-ending 'Serial' stories, purporting to be a kind of moral satires (only the satire has no wit and the moral no morality) showing clearly that poor children ... neglected in their education by Society have a good right to commit reprisals by picking Society's pockets, or the pockets of any member thereof. Think of this cruel society, omitting to train up its children in the way they should go, yet having the unnatural barbarity to maintain constables and gaols for the punishment of those very children when they go wrong! But nothing so horribly disgusts this poor snivelling jackass as capital punishments. Hanging by the neck he considers every way unpleasant, and unworthy of the nineteenth century. How would he have liked stoning with stones – or crucifying, head downward?[14]

This bad-tempered travesty of Jerrold's views is interesting in that it shows the passionately negative response his work could evoke, sometimes in unexpected quarters. Mitchel would have found something to applaud elsewhere in the *Shilling Magazine* had he read Jerrold's ferocious attacks, in his 'Hedgehog Letters', on the rabid opposition by ultra-Protestants ('who seem to read their Bibles by the blue light of brimstone') to any increase in the modest Parliamentary subsidy to Maynooth College, an Irish seminary for the training of Catholic priests. Later in the series, too, Jerrold pillories those religious extremists, admittedly an easy target, who claimed to see in the Irish potato blight God's punishment on Britain for aiding and abetting Roman Catholicism.[15]

Jerrold was definitely 'of the present day' in his 'Hedgehog Letters', however much he might conform to the fashionable historicising formula in his serialised novel. These Letters, which appeared at irregular intervals for the first eighteen months of the *Shilling Magazine*'s existence, could just as well have appeared in *Punch*, for which Jerrold was all the while continuing to supply a seemingly inexhaustible stream of contributions ranging from single paragraphs to whole pages (during 1845/46, for example, he contributed an average of about eighty-three columns per six-monthly volume to *Punch*, inclusive of the Caudle Lectures and other series[16]). Thus, Jerroldian onslaughts on the Anglican episcopate (especially on Henry Philpotts, the notoriously litigious Bishop of Exeter) and on the form of 'judicial murder' known as capital punishment feature regularly in both *Punch* and the 'Hedgehog Letters'. In one of the last letters, number 28 (May 1846), Juniper Hedgehog savagely mocks British triumphalism following the victorious campaign against the Sikhs (Hedgehog is writing to 'John Robinson, Private of the 91st Foot, India'):

> Of course there's been a pretty hurrah here in England about your putting down the Sikhs. One quiet gentleman with a goose-quill is very pious indeed upon the matter; and thinks the war was expressly ordered to destroy 'the scum of Asia' .... It's droll to think of your pious Christian ... talking of some twenty thousand slaughtered men as the 'scum', the refuse of creatures; as animals, just a little above apes, of no account at all to the God who made 'em. He – good John! – thinks of 'em as no more than the vermin that once or twice a-year is cleaned out of his bedsteads, that decent respectable people may take their rest all the cosier for the cleaning. Easy Christianity, isn't it?

Compare with this his half-column on 'War and Women' in *Punch*[17] with its satirical comment on one of the 'many speeches ... fired off in glorification of the slaughter' at celebration dinners held by the British in India 'in honour of the late victories'.

Among the original contributors to the *Shilling Magazine* had been, as we have seen, several colleagues from the *Illuminated*. To them Jerrold added some old friends like Mark Lemon and Percival Leigh of *Punch* and some newer ones like R.H. Horne. In the autumn of 1845 he had been instrumental in finding a publisher for the Chartist writer Thomas Cooper's egregious prison poem *The Purgatory of Suicides* (ten books long and written in, of all things, Spenserian stanzas) and in the following year (during which Cooper was expelled from the Chartist movement) Cooper became a contributor to the *Shilling Magazine*. Among other contributors were the Radical *littérateur* William Howitt who wrote for Jerrold on 'English Scenes and Characters', the irrepressible Goodwyn Barmby, a young middle-class convert to Radicalism and Utopianism, who in 1841 had founded the Central Communist Propaganda Society, and William Thom, the weaver-poet of Inverurie, whom Jerrold, as we have noted, had vigorously championed in *Punch* four years earlier.[18]

As the *Shilling Magazine* progressed through its third volume in the first half of 1846, the most notable newcomer to its pages was the Carlyles' friend Geraldine Jewsbury. 'Douglas Jerrold has behaved like a Briton in printing the little paper I sent him,' she wrote to Jane Carlyle, '... Whether he will behave like a brick and pay me, I cannot speculate ....'[19] Since several more articles from her pen followed, she did presumably get paid, and stopped worrying about publishing with such a populist editor as Jerrold (she had sought Jane Carlyle's explicit approval for this[20]).

Already established in the journal's pages was another female contributor, a writer of short stories with a moral or social purpose called Caroline White, and in the December 1846 number appeared the first contribution by a struggling young writer, Eliza Meteyard, future biographer of Josiah Wedgwood. Meteyard was, in fact, already established as a contributor to *Douglas Jerrold's Weekly Newspaper*, the first issue of which had appeared on 18 July. It had included an article by her championing the Early Closing Movement. This piece was signed 'Silverpen', a pen-name apparently bestowed on her by Jerrold and used by her thereafter, however inappropriate it might have seemed to the exceedingly grim subjects she often chose for the *Shilling Magazine*. Her first article for the journal is a highly sensational one centring on juvenile depravity in the heart of London, and her description, in a later piece, of the filthy habitations adjoining Smithfield and their squalid and brutalised population must surely rank as one of the most sheerly nauseating and horrific pieces in all Victorian journalism.[21] Another notable female contributor during the last six months of the magazine's existence (January–June 1848), was the redoubtable Eliza Lynn Linton, who later liked to claim that she was the first fully professional (regularly salaried) woman journalist of the 19th century. Under the name of 'the Author of "Azeth the Egyptian"', she wrote for the *Shilling Magazine* a series of articles on the Greek gods, Jerrold having apparently somewhat relaxed his insistence that all matter in the journal should be 'of the present day'.

Clearly, he was open to contributions from women writers, even if sometimes, out of deference to what he took to be his readers' prejudices, he disguised just how much 'dimity' (as he apparently put it[22]), there was in the journal by having some of his female contributors sign only with their initials, like Jewsbury, or use some such formula as Lynn Linton did. One woman who must have been a contributor was Camilla Toulmin (Mrs Newton Crosland) but her contributions cannot be identified. She was a literary protégée and ardent admirer of Jerrold's and later painted an idealistic portrait of him in her novel *Mrs Blake* (1862). He appears there as the kindly and inspiring 'Horace Jerrard', editor of *Jerrard's Magazine*, making a personal visit of encouragement to the young journalistic novice, Millie Farrell. Toulmin represents Jerrard as calling Millie 'child' and treating her 'with a sort of half-fatherly tenderness, just dashed by the proper chivalrous respect of man towards woman' (whether this tells us more about Jerrold's demeanour towards women or about Toulmin's preferred model of masculine behaviour is difficult to determine). Millie is amazed at her own audacity in having sent her 'wretched writings' to such a 'well-printed, well-got-up magazine, with the stamp of respectability on the cover, and which was conducted by an author of eminence'. But she is quickly reassured by Horace Jerrard and still more encouraged to find, when she goes to the publishers to collect payment, that he has listed her for 'second-class payment – since only the very great dons received a higher remuneration'.[23]

From January 1846 Jerrold added to his regular workload for *Punch* and the *Shilling Magazine* another major commitment. Together with his son Blanchard, now set on a journalistic career, he joined the staff of the *Daily News*, the new Liberal newspaper being launched by Bradbury and Evans with no less a personage than Charles Dickens as its editor.[24] Jerrold now had three major outlets for propagating his beliefs. When his anti-militarism was roused by public excitement over the Oregon Question (a territorial dispute with the United States), he wrote to a correspondent that he intended

> to follow up the subjects of soldiering and war and judicial man-killing in Punch – in my Magazine – and in the Daily News. In the latter paper it is my design to write about the Peace Movement on Monday – the subject is as suggestive as it is noble ... . The fact of anti-war meetings taking place in what may be called the arsenal of England is, indeed, encouraging. ...[25]

One modern commentator has noted a 'deep, pervasive, and intense hostility towards the landed classes and their privileges' underlying the *Daily News*'s attacks on the Corn Laws. Jerrold, as one of a team of leader-writers that also included Forster and W.J. Fox, contributed to the *News* 'five biting satires' savaging agricultural grandees like the Duke of Richmond, who was also a regular butt of *Punch*.[26] Dickens's editorship of the new paper was very brief. He quickly realised the impossibility, even for such a super-energetic man as himself, of editing a great national daily newspaper on top of all his other commitments and resigned, with Forster succeeding him in the editorial chair. That Jerrold's contributions had by the spring fallen off both in quality and quantity seems evident from a letter of his to Forster dated 17 April:

> Why did you not – ere this – inform me that my contributions were (with 'some exceptions') feeble, and therefore valueless? Such opinion given as it arose would in no way have checked our friendly intercourse, that I yet hope will be life-long. At the same time, it is only due to myself, on such expression of editorial opinion, to *immediately* close my connexion with the Daily News. I will no longer bestow my tediousness upon it, whatever may prove its vitality.[27]

Jerrold's comparatively unaggrieved tone perhaps indicates that he was not sorry to have this occasion given him to sever his connection with the *News*. This may have been because he was now actively planning to edit a newspaper of his very own (a weekly rather than a daily, however), a project that he found himself compelled, for some unspecified reason, to bring forward to the summer of 1846 whereas he had had, he told Dickens, not 'the *least* idea of producing it before October – perhaps not until Christmas'.

As already noted, the first number of *Douglas Jerrold's Weekly Newspaper* appeared on 18 July 1846 and for almost two years Jerrold edited it in harness with the *Shilling Magazine*. His main motive in setting up the new paper was financial but it also enabled him to deal with topics as they arose in a different, more conventionally journalistic, format from that of *Punch* while the *Shilling Magazine* could continue as a vehicle for satirical essays like his exercise in savage Swiftian irony, 'Slavery. The Only Remedy for the Miseries of the English Poor. By a Philanthropist' (February 1845), or pieces of a more reflective and generalising nature like 'The Price of a Garter and the Price of a Life' (November 1845). The editing of the two periodicals, together with his unremitting labours for *Punch*, must have imposed a tremendous strain on Jerrold. And on top of it all he had to deal with a distressing family crisis.

Jerrold's son-in-law Henry Mayhew was declared a bankrupt in July 1846, having contracted debts amounting to over £2,000 since September 1845, mainly as a result of moving into a large house called The Shrubbery at Parson's Green and 'furnishing and ornamenting the premises in a way that was not warranted by his position.'[28] He was on a salary of £300 a year only but had been hoping to make money from a new daily paper devoted to railway matters called the *Iron Times*. He had established this together with a man called T.H. Holt, who had previously been involved with him on *Figaro in London*, and the intention was to cash in on the railway boom but this was already coming to a spectacular end and the paper failed. This precipitated Mayhew into the bankruptcy courts. Jerrold, suffering for his daughter, wrote to Lemon about the 'mingled pity and disgust' that Mayhew's 'insane conduct' had aroused in him[29] and later poured out his woe to Dickens in his long October letter:

> And indeed, my dear Dickens, I have been much worried ... by one of those grave evils of life which I hope you may be spared. I have found that to marry a daughter is to bury her, – at least to her father. My eldest girl was gentle as gentlest womanhood – and her lot is to marry one of those terrible beings whose [? business] absorbs their hearts. However, in his wild, unscrupulous way, he 'at least behaves well to her' – people say: that is, does not beat her, – although, in the most reckless manner he sacrificed her home, and brought bailiffs prowling about her child-bed.[30]

He had been compelled, he told Dickens, 'by something very like congestion of the brain, to abscond for ten days' health and idleness' in Jersey. It was perhaps after this restorative break that he took part in the *Punch* river-party at which Thackeray noticed his 'chirruping' high spirits. Towards the end of the year he was again afflicted, this time by his old enemy, rheumatism, and returned to endure once more the rigours of the Malvern water-cure (earlier, he had ruefully ended a letter to R.J. Lane, the author of *Life at a Water Cure*, as follows: 'Human bliss may, for what

I know, haunt the bottom of a sitz-bath; but it was never found there, by Yours faithfully, Douglas Jerrold'[31]).

In the long letter to Dickens of October 1846 previously quoted Jerrold admits that his new weekly paper 'with *other* allotments, is hard work' but, he adds,

> it is *independence*. And it was the hope of this that stirred me to the doing. I have a feeling of dread – a something almost insane in its abhorrence of the condition of the old, worn-out literary man; the squeezed orange (*lemons* in my case, sing some sweet critics) … flung upon literary funds while alive, with the hat to be sent round for his coffin and his widow. And I therefore set up this newspaper, which … is a large success. Its first number went off 18,000: it is now 9,000 (at the original outlay of £1,500) and is within a fraction three fourths my *own*. It was started at the dullest of dull times, but every week it is steadily advancing. I hope to make it an engine of some good … .

To Mark Lemon he had not been quite so fully explanatory about his motivation when he wrote to him before the paper had appeared;

> of course you know it will come out. It is nothing but a strong conviction that I can make it a powerful instrument that induces me to the undertaking. It will, I hope, be something away from the other papers, and certainly equally away from Punch.[32]

The implication here is that *Punch* will not at all suffer as a result of the new periodical Jerrold is about to launch. The *Shilling Magazine* could not be so protected, however, and Jerrold inevitably found that he now had less and less time for it. The 'Hedgehog Letters' came to an end. And, as he could no longer write so much for the magazine, he had to lower the rate of payment to contributors (Bradbury and Evans fixed the rate at eight shillings a page and Jerrold made it up to ten, at least for some contributors, out of the payment received for his own work).[33]

Horne, however, being in dire financial straits at this time, was only too happy to accept a commission to write a new twelve-month serial to follow *St Giles and St James* when that ended in December 1846. Unfortunately, *The Dreamer and the Worker* (as his story was rather uninvitingly titled) was a turgid attempt to dramatise its author's theories about the 'twin faculty' of genius – hardly a subject to make the *Shilling Magazine*'s readers eager to buy the next issue. To fill out the rest of each issue Jerrold relied heavily on the uninspiring *Athenaeum* journalist Henry Fothergill Chorley. Chorley's lucubrations, together with such things as a series of articles expounding the philosophy of Auguste Comte by G.H. Lewes, amateur psychologising by Mayhew ('What is the Cause of Surprise? And What Connection has it with the Laws of Suggestion?' [December 1847]), and quite a lot of seriously awful poetry seem, unsurprisingly, to have sent the circulation down. 'I fear we have been a little *too* didactic and must amend the fault,' Jerrold wrote to Chorley in a letter of 6 December 1847 quoted by Walter Jerrold. He defers a series of 'Education Papers' proposed by Chorley and begins a new story for the journal 'unwillingly enough' but 'when a man's name is over the door, people expect to have him now and then serving in the bar'. This new story, 'Twiddlethumb Town', was, as its name indicates, very much in the whimsical-satirical vein of 'Clovernook'. Leigh Hunt, addressing him as 'Jerroldo Mio', wrote that he thought the idea of 'Twiddlethumb' was 'admirable ... but how for any length of time will you be able to vary the faces of that monstrous family? I suppose by diversity of circumstances'.[34] Unsuited to a would-be crusading journal like the *Shilling Magazine*, this story seems to have done nothing to stop the slide in circulation. By the summer of 1848, therefore, it was clear that this journal, which Jerrold had started, Blanchard tells us, with such ambitious hopes of making a great impact in 'high places, where action for the good of the people might be the result', was doomed, and it closed with the June issue. A paper called the *Puppet Show*, which was seeking to challenge *Punch*'s supremacy in the comic-journalism market (see illustration, p. 186) seized the opportunity to mock, not scrupling to allude to Jerrold's reputation for excessive drinking. The *Shilling Magazine*, it declared on 8 July, 'has proved too heavy to be carried on any further, and has consequently been dropped' and goes on to quote some verses that an 'aspiring young libeller' has written attacking Jerrold 'and the whole of the Whitefriars clique' (i.e. Bradbury and Evans and the *Punch* set):

> The Douglas at the blush of day
>   From his tenth tumbler started –
> 'My magazine, 'tis said, don't pay
>   Success from it has parted ...'
>
> The publishers – too fond of cash
>   To be forever striving
> To make men swallow Jerrold's hash
>   Declared its end arriving;
> And all the town rejoiced and sang
> Because St Giles's vulgar slang
> With much low cant and whining
>   Would soon become trunk-lining.

By the time the *Shilling Magazine* folded *Douglas Jerrold's Weekly Newspaper* was also losing ground. Back in July 1846 it had made, as Jerrold told Dickens in his October letter, a very good beginning. The battle for the repeal of the Corn Laws had finally been won and in the front-page leader he wrote for his first issue Jerrold rejoices that his paper

comes before the country at a time of holiday and hope: for present victory gives us the assurance of future good. That giant iniquity, the Corn Laws, numbered with the wickedness of the past, the heart of England beats with a new health. All men must feel their natures elevated by the conviction that from the present time we start, as a nation, in a new career of glory ...

This 'glory' would be to teach the nations the virtues and great rewards of Free Trade. With his Liberal colours nailed thus firmly to the mast, Jerrold makes clear from a leader entitled 'The People and Their Rulers' that the paper will be primarily concerned with the progressive improvement of the condition of the British working classes. This will be achieved by such things as the promotion of Free Trade and of State education, a more equitable distribution of national wealth (involving, among other things, the ending of large farms and tenancies at will), sanitary reform, support for the Early Closing Movement, and so on. Another subject close to his heart that featured prominently in this first number was the abolition of corporal punishment in the armed services. It was made highly topical by the fact that a soldier named Frederick White had recently been flogged to death (when Jerrold first introduces a chat-column called 'The Barber's Chair' in the third issue of the paper, he has his barber comment, 'I shall never see the ribbands in the hat of a recruiting soldier again – the bright blue and red – that I shan't think of the weals and cuts in poor White's back').

Given the nature of the paper, its strenuously serious commitment to serious issues, and so forth, it seems extraordinary that Jerrold should think it appropriate to carry over the fanciful cherub-like figures with which Kenny Meadows had ornamented the *Illuminated* into this new, and very different enterprise. They do not appear in the paper itself, it is true, but are used to embellish Jerrold's editorial notepaper (see plate). They remind us how greatly he participated in a certain kind of sentimental Victorian whimsy that was in the next century to blossom so abundantly in the studios of Walt Disney.

The new paper's quintessentially Liberal agenda was reported to Marx and Engels with some disdain by Julian Harney (one wonders if he was aware of the cherubs):

> Douglas Jerrold's new paper is announced on Saturday. Contains a good deal of 'Free Trade', and glorification of the 'League' [Anti Corn Law League]. He is for the 'sovereignty of the people', not defined. He is for National Education as a benefit to Universal Suffrage. He is 'not for the impractical' and therefore dismisses as a *mischievous delusion* the doctrine of *perfect equality*. Instead he is for various 'social improvements', 'shorter hours', 'sanatory reforms', 'small farms', 'perpetual leases' &c. Let me add that he *refused insertion to the Address of the F[raternal] D[emocrats] to the people of the U.S., &c.* !!!! [35]

Jerrold was not setting out to appeal to Communists such as Harney but to that large section of the newspaper-buying public, members of the artisan and lower-middle or middle-middle classes, who were Liberal rather than Radical in their politics. Among these readers his name had, according to *Mitchell's Newspaper Press Directory* for 1847, 'become so decidedly popular in the first order of periodical literature' that it might seem merely 'superfluous to dwell more particularly upon the character of this undertaking [i.e., *Douglas Jerrold's Weekly Newspaper*]'. Jerrold's admirers would have thoroughly endorsed the political programme set out in his first issue. But they would have wanted something else from a weekly paper besides politics. In their respectability they would have drawn the line at anything like the crudely sensational *feuilleton*, *The Mysteries of London*, with which G.W.M. Reynolds was titillating the tens of thousands of readers of his penny *London Journal*, nor would they have been happy with the republican propaganda that he mixed in with his lurid fiction. But, just as much as their social superiors reading *The Times* or the *Morning Chronicle*, they would have looked for dramatic police reports, and Jerrold provided them with full measure of 'Crimes and Casualties', as this part of the paper was titled (paragraphs with headings like 'Alleged Murder in Shoreditch. – Penny Show of the Corpse', 'A Desperate Pair', 'Blinded by a Snowball', 'The Strange Charge of Arson Against a Young Lady', etc., etc.). The paper also featured extensive theatre and book reviews (F.G. Tomlins acted as literary editor just as he did for the *Shilling Magazine*), as well as frequent notices of music and fine art publications (sheet music, song collections, prints) clearly designed for family consumption. Reports on the proceedings of institutions and learned societies also appeared regularly as does a feature called 'Magaziniana', sometimes extending to over three pages, which summarised the contents of the latest issues of a remarkable range of periodicals. Parliamentary debates were very fully reported and in the coverage given to national and international news a notable amount of space (including several leaders evidently written by Jerrold himself) was devoted to the Irish question, quoting first-hand reports of the horrors of the famine and strongly urging the need for reform of land tenure.

Jerrold also based a number of leaders, like many of his *Punch* articles, on court cases that had caught his eye involving harsh or unjust treatment of the poor. A brilliant and devastating parody of this Jerroldian speciality appeared in the seventh number of a little satirical monthly, the *Man in the Moon*, that began publication in January 1847. Edited by Albert Smith and Angus B. Reach, its chief target was *Punch* (one sketch of a stupefied-looking man is captioned 'Portrait of a Gentleman finding a Joke in *Punch*') but Jerrold's other journalism did not escape. This parody headed 'A leader for Douglas Jerrold's Newspaper' purports to be from the pen of a 'poor devil author' seeking work as a ghost writer from Jerrold and offering a specimen leader entitled 'The Knout and the Cherub' protesting against an urchin's being sentenced to be whipped for stealing some grapes:

> ... His white and tender back is to be scarred with crimson bands: the *lash* is to enter his soul for a pennyworth of raisins. The blood of the pauper child is less precious than the blood of the blushing grape he pilfered. ... He is the infant of a poor man – a serf, a thing of clay, a pipkin, a Pariah, a mere animal ....

It says something for Jerrold, I think, that he continued to employ Reach on his newspaper after the appearance of this merciless mockery of his style in a periodical co-edited by Reach. When the *Man in the Moon* also derided Dickens's Amateur Players for merely indulging their vanity in their project, Jerrold did, however, write to Dickens drawing his attention to the 'dirty and scandal-like paragraph' and enclosing a letter (presumably of self-exculpation) from Reach, 'to whom I gave his first start in periodical literature, and in whose pocket I have put (for him) much money'.[36]

Among the regular features of *Douglas Jerrold's Weekly Newspaper* was a column signed 'Church Mouse' which dealt with ecclesiastical affairs. Hardly an issue appeared in which those favourite Aunt Sallies of Jerrold's, the bishops, did not come under fire (e.g., a series of satirical songs called 'The Bishop's Little Warbler' that ran for several weeks during 1847) and the Ecclesiastical Commissioners were mocked as 'The Society for the Diffusion and Aggrandisement of Bishops' (5 June 1847). Other regular whole-page features like 'Town Talk' and 'The Button-holder' (the latter column-title carried over from the old *Illuminated*) comprised, as *Mitchell's* put it, 'a vast quantity of foreign and domestic news, well selected, and concisely narrated'. Letters from readers, including some spoof ones, were scattered throughout, and there was the 'Answers to Correspondents' column that was so important a feature in 19th-century popular journalism.[37] Further variety was achieved by occasional satirical sketches purportedly written by 'The Hermit of Pall Mall', or cast in the form of gossip about City affairs between the Guildhall giants Gog and Magog, or of more general gossip about the news of the day in a barber's shop in Seven Dials. This last series, entitled 'The Barber's Chair', was written by Jerrold himself, as the other sketches may also have been, and proved immensely popular. It was, wrote Dickens, 'a capital idea, and capable of the best and readiest adaptation to things as they arise'[38] and *Mitchell's* thought it 'conducted with considerable skill, exhibiting striking contrasts in the characters and opinions of the interlocutors'. The *Graphic* obituarist of Blanchard Jerrold, writing on 19 April 1884, paid tribute to it, though he misremembered the paper in which the series appeared: Douglas Jerrold's name, he wrote 'was a tower of strength to readers of *Lloyd's Weekly Newspaper* (middle-aged working men will remember how eagerly they used to look for 'The Barber's Chair', a weekly epitome of political and other conversation)'.

According to his son, Jerrold's imaginary barber, Oliver Cromwell Nutts, was probably inspired by a real-life one who was 'something of a humourist', and had a little shop by Temple Bar. His mind perhaps 'sharpened by the distinguished men from the Temple, and from the Fleet Street newspaper offices, whom he had shaved', Nutts had 'more than a smattering of literary and forensic gossip', and was very blasé when it came to news stories ('I've had so much news in my time, I've lost the flavour of it. Couldn't relish anything weaker than a battle of Waterloo now. Even murders don't move me ...'³⁹). Jerrold gives Nutts a wife in the Mrs Caudle mode, only not so funny, and a group of regular customers including a policeman, an ex-schoolteacher and a diehard old Tory called Slowgoe, who is constantly shocked by Nutts's irreverent attitude towards royalty, leading politicians, bishops, and so on.

Contributors to the paper are rarely identified. One who was named in the first issue was the American pacifist Elihu Burritt, writing on 'The Last Hour of the [Anti Corn Law] League'. Jerrold appended an editorial note to his piece promising further contributions from Burritt and expressing his gladness at 'the good fortune that makes "the learned blacksmith" our fellow labourer in our first sheet, enriching it with his first printed impressions of England and Englishmen'.⁴⁰ In the second issue appeared the first instalment of a series signed 'By an Eye-Witness'. This was Thomas Cooper whom Jerrold had commissioned to investigate the 'Condition of the People of England'. The editorial introduction to the series read as follows:

> What is the *real* life of 'the masses'? – how are people fed, clothed, housed? – what is the nature and kind of their labours? – how long are their hours of work, and how frequent their holidays? ... What, in a word, is the real social state of our people? – not of the privileged few, but of the many? ... That these questions may be faithfully answered to our mind, and to the minds of our readers, we have sent forth our own commissioner, – or, rather, our own inquisitor-plenipotentiary ....

For the next few months Cooper sent in a series of graphic reports, unsparing of grim detail, of working-class life in Leicestershire, Sheffield, Lincolnshire, Hull, Sunderland, the Coal Trade, Carlisle, Preston, Manchester and Bradford. It may well have been these reports that gave the proprietors of the *Morning Chronicle* their idea for the very large-scale project they announced three years later: an investigation into the condition of the working classes and of the poor throughout England with different correspondents (including Reach) reporting from different parts of the country. This was the series that was to bring fame and (temporary) prosperity to Jerrold's improvident son-in-law, the *Chronicle*'s 'Metropolitan Correspondent', whose reports formed the basis of *London Labour and the London Poor*.

The rich variety of news, comment and what we should now call 'feature-articles', crammed into twenty-six pages must have seemed very good value for sixpence, and would help to explain how 'Jerrold soon got a circulation of 20,000' according to G.H. Lewes.⁴¹ 'The thing has struck deep root,' Jerrold told W.J. Fox when he wrote to him on 3 November 1846 expressing the hope that Fox, his former colleague on the *Daily News*, might write something for the paper, and on 6 April 1847, writing to one Charles Dennet, he expresses his pleasure that the paper 'has already many readers in America', adding that he feels sure 'from correspondence already entered upon, that the circulation will, in a short time, be greatly increased'.[42] The fact that there were never less than four pages of advertisements in each issue (among the most regular advertisers were the makers of something called 'an Itrobolic Hat') may be seen as further proof of the paper's success. On 9 January 1847 there appeared on the front page an announcement that in two weeks' time the size of the paper would be increased to thirty-two pages, the maximum size permitted by the Stamp Law:

> The Editor and Proprietor having, in his determinate appeal to those desirous of progressive movements, been responded to in a manner far beyond his most sanguine expectations, has determined to testify his sense of such support by ADDING, GRATUITOUSLY, ONE-THIRD TO HIS PAPER.

The paper, Jerrold's announcement continues, will increase its news coverage and be made

> equally interesting to all portions of a family, and all classes! and those more curious for news than original dissertations will thus be gratified, as well as those who consider a newspaper not a mere vehicle for the record of passing events, but as one of the great engines for improving the condition of society.

Among the new things that Jerrold promises the readers of his *Weekly Newspaper*, alongside the continuation of some established favourite features like 'The Barber's Chair' and the expansion of others such as the literary reviews, was one that he would later have cause to regret. This was a 'Series of Papers entitled MONEY, THE KEY OF SOCIAL POLITICS' which, as we shall see, was to swell to enormous proportions and, in the opinion of Blanchard, be partly responsible for the paper's decline.

Chapter Twelve

The Whittington Club and Other Projects

1847-1851

One undoubted achievement of *Douglas Jerrold's Weekly Newspaper* was the realisation of a scheme dear to Jerrold's heart. It was inspired by what he saw of the Manchester Athenaeum in October 1845, and was adumbrated in the first issue of the new paper. This was the establishment of an institution in central London which should serve as a club for young clerks and other City workers, a place where they could have access to a library and reading-room, hear lectures and hold soirées, and also be able to get decent meals at reasonable prices. The idea for the Whittington Club, as Jerrold christened it (not altogether happily, at least in the opinion of Sutherland Edwards[1]) was developed in a series of articles written for Jerrold's paper by Reach. Not the least striking aspect of the project was that women should be admitted to full membership of the club, something Jerrold hailed in a speech (quoted by Walter Jerrold) as

> a triumphant refutation of a very old, respectable, but no less foolish fallacy
> ... that female society in such an institution is incompatible with domestic
> dignity. Hitherto, Englishmen have made their club-houses as Mahomet
> made his Paradise – a place where women are not admitted on any pretext
> whatever. Thus considered, the Englishman may be a very good Christian
> sort of a person at home, and at the same time little better than a Turk at
> his club.

Widespread interest was quickly aroused, a committee was established, the paper carried full reports of the business meetings and the Club itself had come into being by the date of the paper's sixteenth number. Its first soirée was held on 17 January 1847 at the London Tavern, attended by between 1,300 and 1,400 people, according to the full report published in Jerrold's paper (20 February 1846). Membership stood at 1,200 and the premises taken for the Club at 7 Gresham Street, on the old Whittington Estate, were being got ready for the opening, which took place on 21 June. As the Club's first President Jerrold was in the chair on 17 February, supported by a notable list of distinguished literati and reformers including John Bright, the Cowden Clarkes, George Cruikshank, William and Mary Howitt, Charles Knight, Eliza Meteyard, Joseph Mazzini and Dr Southwood Smith (the Howitts, Knight and Mazzini had all accepted the office of Vice-President). This is one of the rare public occasions involving Jerrold when Mrs Jerrold is reported as having been present, also Mary, their younger daughter. Overcoming his discomfort with regard to public speaking, Jerrold made a long and eloquent oration in which he mocked those to whom the foundation of the Club seemed an 'impertinence ... almost a revolutionary movement, disrespectful to the vested interests of worshipful society' and made characteristic play with the fact that members would be able to 'obtain meals and refreshments at the lowest remunerating prices':

> Well, surely men threaten no danger to the state by dining. On the contrary, the greater danger sometimes is, when men can get no dinner. In the most troublous times, knives are never to be made so harmless as when coupled with forks. Hence, I do not see why the mutton-chop of a Duke at the western Athenaeum might not be imagined to hold a very affable colloquy with the chop of a clerk, cooked at the Whittington. ...

He goes on to mention the Club's library, reading-room, lecture-programme and planned classes in 'languages, mathematics, music, painting', and to recommend it to employers as 'the exercise of a great social duty – namely, to assist in a work that shall still tend to dignify the employed with a sense of self-respect', though for 'a flourishing vitality' the Whittington would need to depend on the energy of its own members. Finally, he evokes the figure of 'the little outcast boy,' Whittington himself, who came back into the city and 'drudged and drudged' to achieve a 'golden end'. Jerrold presents him as a quintessentially English Liberal hero in whose story may be seen 'that Saxon energy which has made this City of London what it is ... that commercial glory that wins the noblest conquests for the family of man; for the victories are bloodless'. Speeches by Charles Knight and others followed, terminating in a vote of thanks to Jerrold which 'was carried unanimously, amidst deafening applause'.[2]

The Club flourished in spite of sneering jibes from such publications hostile to Jerrold as the *Puppet Show*, which dubbed the Whittington 'the seedy-eating house in the Strand', a place where City clerks got 'an eighteenpenny plate of sodden meat and a glass of table-beer for dinner' and swaggered about the ill-savoured premises trying to delude visitors into thinking it was the Carlton 'or some other gentlemanly association'.[3] As its first President, Jerrold was initially quite active, attending the Club's second soirée on 12 May and recruiting as Vice-Presidents, among others, Dickens, Macready and the literary Liberal peer Lord Nugent, with whom he had been on very friendly terms since Nugent had sought an introduction to him in the autumn of 1846. (Sending Nugent details about the Club Jerrold wrote, 'You will perceive that there is no gunpowder in the conspiracy and that you will not be called upon to draw lots to take your place in the vaults of Parliament next opening day ...'[4]) His involvement seems to have lessened somewhat after a few months, however, and a young solicitor called W.H. Shaen, a prominent supporter of women's rights and education for women, became the guiding spirit.[5] One of the few traces of Jerrold's continuing association with the Club after 1847 is a playbill advertising a production by the Whittingtonians of *The Rent Day* at the New Strand Theatre on 11 October 1848; very large letters proclaim that this event is 'Under the Patronage of Douglas Jerrold, Esq. President of the Whittington Club'.[6]

During the first half of 1847 Jerrold contributed some of his most effective leaders to his newspaper, including five brilliant columns on 27 March satirising the absurdity and hypocrisy of the Public Fast Day ordained by Royal Proclamation for 24 March as an act of national atonement for sin (including, in the eyes of some fanatic Protestant politicians, government support of the Catholic Church in Ireland through the Maynooth Grant) and as a national intercession with the Almighty for the alleviation of the terrible Irish famine. In lighter vein was his mockery of the aged Poet Laureate, William Wordsworth's writing to order a poem to celebrate Prince Albert's accession to the Chancellorship of the University of Cambridge ('Mr Wordsworth's Cambridge Flam', 5 June). For Jerrold it is simply grotesque that a poet such as Wordsworth, who 'in his mountain-home had interpreted the sweetest and most solemn utterances of nature, making them the world's music ... triumphing in the heart of man by their simple grandeur', should have consented to become 'a flunkey sinecurist in bardic plush'. As this last phrase suggests, he objects altogether to the conception of such an office as that of Poet Laureate:

> There is, we learn, a disease among the Brazilian slaves that urges them to devour earth. Now royalty would seem born and nurtured with a taste for untruth; the grosser the falsification, the more palatable. Royalty feeds upon lying, like humming-birds upon honey. Sophistication tends it at its cradle; walks with it through life, and consistent to the last writes its epitaph; though Time may spit upon it.

(Three years later, after Wordsworth's death, we learn from Walter Jerrold, Jerrold wrote to *The Times* suggesting that the Laureateship should be abolished and the post's salary applied to a new national appointment, that of 'Warden of the house of Shakespeare', this property in Stratford having just recently been bought for the nation.)

The spring and early summer of 1847 seem to have been a busy time socially for Jerrold. Besides the Whittington soirées, the weekly *Punch* dinners and evenings at the Museum Club (see below, p. 222), we find him attending a Macready evening party (30 May) and dinner-party at the Dickenses (8 June). Then came renewed anxiety about his daughter Jane Mayhew who was living with her husband on Guernsey, no doubt a prudent retreat for Mayhew in seeking to avoid his creditors (he had been granted protection from arrest for two months only by the Bankruptcy Commissioner in February). In a letter dated simply 'Wednesday' Jerrold wrote to Dickens,

I have this morning received a letter that leaves me little hope of the life of my dear child in Guernsey. 'A sad change for the worse took place on Saturday. She is sinking rapidly' so writes her husband. Had he written before – on Sunday – her mother and myself might have been in Guernsey this morning. As it is we are compelled to wait in misery – until tomorrow at 7 there being no other boat. ... My wife is in a frightful state.[7]

The Amateur Players were scheduled to act in Manchester and Liverpool in late July but Lewes could stand in for him, Jerrold told Dickens.

Happily, Jane recovered ('by a miracle', Jerrold wrote later, 'for she had three doctors; none of whom knew anything of her case, and told me – on my arrival – she might die in an hour') and Jerrold and his wife were able to return to London in time for the marriage on 25 June of their eldest son William Blanchard to Lavinia Lillie, the daughter of Laman Blanchard, at Kensington Church (with both Blanchard Jerrold and Jerrold himself describing their 'rank or profession' on the marriage certificate as 'Gent.'). Thanking Dickens for his 'nuptial congratulations' in the same letter in which he reports Jane's recovery, Jerrold says he believes the marriage would have pleased 'poor Blanchard'. He goes on:

I could have wished the bridegroom more ballast ere he ventured, yet there is no vice in him, and early marriage after all commonly saves men much pollution. I have been annoyed somewhat at his early misdoing in print [Blanchard had begun publishing a novel in six monthly parts called *The Disgrace to the Family*], – but as it was for money wherewith to rush into furniture and the other impedimenta of marriage I cannot be very wrathful ... .[8]

A month later, on 24 July, Jerrold and his wife gave a dinner-party with a distinguished guest-list at West Lodge. Macready recorded in his diary:

Went with Forster to Putney Heath to dine with Jerrold. He was *very glad* to see me. His family and young Blanchard, a Mr Hill, Leigh Hunt, Maclise and the Dickenses were the party. Leigh Hunt I thought *particularly disagreeable* ...[9]

The very next day Jerrold and Dickens with the rest of the Amateur Players left for Manchester and Liverpool to perform Jonson in order to raise funds for a pension for Leigh Hunt.

Jerrold must have been ready for a holiday after all this activity and decided to return to the Channel Islands. No doubt he saw Jane again but his main object was this time to escape deep into nature by fixing his abode on Sark (which he may have visited from Guernsey or Jersey the previous year[10]). His references to Sark make it clear that the place had a strong romantic appeal for him. 'I shall don my goat's-skin and play Robinson Crusoe for some weeks', he tells Leigh Hunt, and to Chorley he writes: 'I go to solitude in Sark, "far amid the melancholy main". Such a place for a man to lie upon his back, and hear "the waves moan for sleep that never comes".'[11] Having got there, he reports to Forster in a letter quoted by Walter Jerrold:

> I am here in this most wild, most solitary and most beautiful place. No dress – no fashion – no 'respectability' – nothing *but* beauty and grandeur; with the sea rolling, and roaring at times, 'twixt me and Fleet Street, as though I should never walk there again.

To Lord Nugent (now addressed as 'Dear Nugent'), who was a keen yachtsman, he writes with a touch of that 'boyish' enthusiasm that friends found so attractive, 'What a retreat this might be made for half-a-dozen real fellows, – with a yacht like a sea-gull to take a flight now and then, and again home to the rocks!'[12]

According to Blanchard Jerrold, his father returned to London to find that his newspaper was in trouble, 'dwindled to a concern that hardly paid its expenses' and an agreement dated 9 August 1847 whereby the whole-sale stationers who supplied the paper for the journal agreed to an extension of time for the payment of a debt of £2,000 certainly suggests that there were difficulties.[13] Blanchard suggests that the cessation of the 'Barber's Chair' series, and the enormous amount of space allowed to the economist writing under the name of 'Aladdin' on bullionism, the paper money debate and other currency matters (often in great technical detail), were factors contributing strongly to the decline in circulation (there seems to have been no falling-off in advertisements, however). The 'Barber's Chair' series was revived in November and a signed series by the campaigner for Australian emigration Caroline Chisholm entitled 'Home in the Bush – Advice to Emigrants' which ran from 23 October to 2 February 1848, added a new interest to the paper, though one necessarily limited in its appeal.[14] Another attempt to boost sales came in March 1848 when Jerrold, accompanied by Hodder, went to Paris with the idea of acting as a sort of 'special correspondent' sending back on-the-spot reports of the tumultuous political events there, following the fall of Louis Philippe. He proved totally unsuited to this work. Such reports as he did file gave, in Hodder's words, 'little or no proof that he was writing from the scene of action' and he himself 'more than once exclaimed, "I might just as well do this in Cheapside or Fleet Street".' He quickly lost all heart for the enterprise and, having made a bonfire of his letters of introduction to Lamartine and other members of the 'Provisional Government', returned to London.[15] His dramatic criticism apart, Jerrold's most effective journalism was always print-inspired. A newspaper report that caught his eye of some flagrant example of social injustice, some Parliamentary shenanigans, 'flunkeyism', abuse of power, gross inequality, etc., would be the inspiration for a satirical piece in *Punch* or one of his leaders in his newspapers. He was a columnist, not a reporter (in contrast to Dickens who was a superb reporter and investigative journalist) and thus very much a fish out of water on this Paris expedition.

Ironically, at the very time when Jerrold was deciding that it was better for him to get back to his study rather than trying to mingle in the action in Paris, Charlotte Brontë was writing to her publisher W.S. Williams about events in the French capital.

> How strange it appears to see literary and scientific names figuring in the list of members of a Provisional Government! How would it sound if Carlyle and Sir John Herschel and Tennyson and Mr Thackeray and Douglas Jerrold were selected to manufacture a new constitution for England? Whether do such men sway the public mind most effectually from their quiet studies or from a council-chamber?[16]

Her inclusion of Jerrold in such an august list of names is a salutary reminder to us of the kind of status this writer now so much forgotten enjoyed in his own time.

Even his name, however, could not keep his journals afloat. As we have seen, Jerrold's *Shilling Magazine* closed in the summer. He remained, how nominally we do not know, editor of his *Weekly Newspaper* until the end of 1848 when he sold it, apparently at a considerable loss.[17] It continued to trade on his name as *Jerrold's Weekly News and Financial Economist* until July 1849. Then it became simply the *Weekly News and Financial Economist* and in 1851 was united with the *Weekly Chronicle*.

Temporarily disillusioned, perhaps, with editing, Jerrold next tried to emulate Dickens and Thackeray (it must have seemed a natural move to make since he was so constantly linked with them by literary journalists and reviewers) by publishing a novel in shilling monthly numbers as they had both so prosperously done. Borrowing an idea from Balzac's *Peau de Chagrin* to give a basic structure to his narrative, he embarked on a story entitled *A Man Made of Money* which was published at the *Punch* office by Bradbury and Evans in six monthly parts from October 1848. Each part was accompanied by two plates by Leech, who also designed a very effective illustrated monthly-part cover. Jerrold clearly intended the story to be his fiercest satire yet on that Mammon-worship that, like Carlyle, he saw as one of the greatest evils afflicting contemporary Britain, and that Dickens was also to target in the Merdle part of *Little Dorrit* (1857). Indeed, Jerrold's Mr and Mrs Jericho can be seen as, in some respects forerunners of Dickens's (of course, infinitely more subtly-imagined and depicted) Mr and Mrs Merdle. Solomon Jericho, a City merchant, apparently not intended to be Jewish despite his name, covets wealth and is driven to distraction by his wife's demands for money (they have married each other from mercenary motives, each deceiving the other into expecting riches as a result of the marriage). His desperate wish that he were 'made of money' is mysteriously granted, his heart being replaced by a wad of banknotes. Each time he draws on himself, so to speak, his flesh shrinks until, after an orgy of auto-cannibalistic spending, he has become 'brown, thin and withered as the last year's leaf'. Terrified, he desperately seeks to keep alive, and also to enjoy what he now believes to be the true value of wealth, that is, *power* rather than display, by becoming an extreme miser living in a bare attic of his sumptuous mansion 'like a rat in hole' and dying at last by a species of spontaneous combustion. At that point everything he has bought with his sinister wealth crumbles into dust and ashes.

The story is bulked out with some fairly standard farcical-satirical social comedy centred on Mrs Jericho, her daughters and their suitors and the activities of an opposing group of good characters, full of domestic virtues and morally correct attitudes to money. At the end these virtuous ones all set off, no doubt as a result of Jerrold's friendship with Caroline Chisholm and support for her emigration scheme, for a wonderful new pioneering life in Australia, just the Peggottys and Micawbers were to do soon afterwards in the closing numbers of *David Copperfield*. Scattered throughout the book are specimens of characteristic Jerroldian 'wit' that were to rank among his most celebrated apophthegms, such as 'earth [in Australia] is so kind that just tickle her with a hoe, she laughs with a harvest' and 'dogmatism is puppyism come to maturity'.

A Man Made of Money met with praise from the critics, and also from some non-professional readers like William Powell Frith who read it when researching his biography of Leech: 'I tried "skimming" but the power of the book, and the brilliancy of the wit in it, so attracted me that I read the whole of it'.[18] 'No man alive can say more bitter or more witty things than Douglas Jerrold,' commented the *Morning Chronicle*, 'and in none of his works has brilliant wit and tingling sarcasm been more profusely poured forth.' For the *Sunday Times* reviewer it was 'without comparison, his greatest [work]':

It displays a rare combination of fancy, philosophy and kindliness, which will cause it to be kept warm in the memory of the public when many a production now at the summit of popularity shall be swept into the gulf of oblivion. We should be glad to see the work, where it will ultimately be, by every fireside in the kingdom; because it is calculated to effect unmixed good ....[19]

When the story appeared in volume form in the spring of 1849 Forster gave it four and a half columns in the *Examiner,* supplying long excerpts but questioning whether the book could really be considered as a true novel; Jerrold, he suggested (assuming Forster himself was the reviewer) should be classed with a great satirist like Rabelais rather than with Fielding ('the cap and bells are shaken too much [for a novelist], though with wise laughter'). An unidentified reviewer in the *British Quarterly Review*, judging it the best of all his work to date, made it the occasion for a sixteen-page critical assessment of his literary achievement to date. Eight years later, James Hannay, summing up Jerrold's life-work in the *Atlantic Monthly* (November 1857) also considered *A Man Made of Money* (which he classed with Bulwer's *Zanoni* as 'a kind of bastard-allegory') to be 'Jerrold's best book – the one which contains most of his mind ... the completest as a creation, and the most characteristic in point of style ... the most original in imaginativeness, and the best sustained in point and neatness'.[20] It would, Hannay thought, be read longer than anything else Jerrold had written (the Caudle Lectures he merely mentioned in passing as 'social drolleries' which 'just hit' English readers' penchant for the domestic).

Forster was not the only reviewer to comment on the way in which Jerrold the satirical moralist tended to overwhelm Jerrold the story-teller and in this, his third attempt at a novel, the imbalance was extreme. There was nothing for the fiction-reading public to set off against Jerrold's unremitting moralising, no matter how 'wittily' it was expressed. *The Story of a Feather* had centred on an 'interesting' and pathetic little heroine, and *St Giles and St James* had had a strong 'Newgate' and revelation-of-the-lowest-depths-of-society appeal but *A Man Made of Money* offered no such attractions. Instead, its chief purely literary attraction consisted in the sort of Gothic-supernatural story that by this time would have been more associated in readers' minds with old-fashioned melodramas like Jerrold's own *The Devil's Ducat*.

We do not have any sales figures for either the monthly parts or the volume form of *A Man Made of Money*, but it would seem that, critical plaudits notwithstanding, it failed to achieve a very wide circulation. This is borne out by the fact that the first number carries a twelve-page advertising section which shrinks to four pages in the next three parts and has vanished altogether in Parts 5 and 6.[21] (For purposes of comparison we may note that the first number of Dickens's *David Copperfield* had a thirty-two-page advertising section, and subsequently a steady eight pages.) Most probably, then, Jerrold was greatly disappointed by this venture of his into the Dickens/Thackeray mode of publication. It may have been particularly galling for him that Bradbury and Evans so vigorously advertised works by Dickens and Thackeray in the parts of *A Man Made of Money* (the back cover of each part, for instance, was occupied by an advertisement for *Pendennis* featuring one of Thackeray's illustrations for the work, and coloured flyers were inserted advertising Dickens's 1849 Christmas Book *The Haunted Man*, and his forthcoming new twenty-monthly-number novel, *David Copperfield*).

During the summer of 1849 Jerrold's eyes were causing him great distress. Apologising to Cowden Clarke for taking so long to answer a letter, he wrote, 'I have been in darkness with acute inflammation of the eye; something like toothache in the eye – and very fit to test a man's philosophy'. He had, he told Henry Holl on 25 June, 'almost lost one of my eyes with severe inflammation' and had been ordered a change of air by his doctor.[22] Accompanied by Charles Knight, he took advantage of the Great Southern and Western Railway Company's offer of a special excursion rate from London to the Lakes of Killarney. They left London on 26 June and the trip made him, he wrote to Mark Lemon 'wonderfully better, strong as ten lions':

Such scenery! Was never so near heaven. Lakes, mountains, mists, barefoot women, with eyes black as death, teeth that bite your soul out – Irish pipes that make the bagpipe a greater *blast*-phemy than ever, and a hundred other glories not to be put upon paper. There is, however, one drawback. Beggary scabs the beauty. I never saw so much human misery – so much degradation moral and physical, as in my ride from Mallow to Killarney. A decent baboon would feel degraded to be put in the same cage with some of these creatures that put out their hands, and gibber their wants.[23]

The dismaying brutality of these remarks is all the more startling coming from a man who was always so strongly moved to pity and indignation by the plight of English paupers and who, moreover, until six months or so before this had been in charge of a weekly newspaper that had consistently given extensive coverage to the terrible state of Ireland and its famine-struck people, and that had campaigned so strongly for the situation to be ameliorated. It forcibly reminds us that Jerrold, for all his reasonableness over the Maynooth Grant and enlightened comment on the Irish problem in his *Weekly Newspaper*, was, like Lemon, a thorough-going *Punch* man and fully shared in the magazine's schizophrenic racism as regards the Irish (no doubt faithfully reflecting the attitude of the majority of its readers), a racism that is most blatant in the cartoons of Leech and others. In *Punch* the Irish are invariably shown either as pretty, barefoot peasant lasses in cloaks (an image later skilfully exploited by Dion Boucicault in *The Colleen Bawn* and his other Irish plays) or as a sort of ape-like sub-species of humanity, evoking a mixture of laughter and contempt, tinged with a certain horror also.[24]

The sight of the terrible reality that lay behind this caricature was clearly too much for both Jerrold and Knight. 'We used to read of Irish beggary as a compound of misery and fun', the latter wrote in his journal, 'but even with them [the professional beggars] the fun was gone', and worse still was the case with those whom 'the Great Hunger' had reduced to beggary, 'pallid girls, boys prematurely old, tall skeletons of men ... mothers with unsmiling infants vainly stretching towards the fevered breast'.[25] How was it that Jerrold, whose capacity for tenderness Knight refers to in this very same account of their trip (Jerrold sat up all night 'in a wretched inn' watching over him when he was suspected of having contracted cholera), could write so harshly of the famine victims he saw? How was it that he could apparently be so little affected by them that, once they were not actually 'gibbering their wants' in his face, he could luxuriate in the 'glorious scenery', write jocosely to Mrs Knight about how naughtily her husband was behaving,[26] and enjoy bantering with the boatmen hired to row him and Knight about the lakes? ('A friend,' Knight records, 'who visited Killarney some ten years after us, wrote to me that Jerrold, and Jerrold's jokes, were still remembered and retailed by these good-tempered fellows.') No doubt the opportunity he and Knight were given to put the blame for the extreme misery they saw on the sufferers themselves ('the workhouses, we were told, were open to all, and they were

215

not filled') helped greatly in letting these English tourists off the hook — that and the fact that 'a humane law' was keeping the famine victims just about alive with a hand-out of a pound of Indian meal per day.

Jerrold did not forget his *Punch* commitment on the trip ('I find it impossible to send anything from here,' he wrote in his letter to Lemon from Killarney, 'but I hope to bring much with me. I am secreting a great quantity of ink ...'). *Punch* was his main source of income but he had still not wholly despaired of the theatre. Earlier in the summer he had resumed work on the long-promised new comedy for Webster. Walter Jerrold quotes a facetious letter about it to Sabilla Novello written on 9 June. He promises that the play will feature a perfect heroine, 'woven of moonbeams', as 'a set-off to the many sins imputed to me as committed against woman, whom I have always considered to be an admirable idea imperfectly worked out'.

Illness and the Irish trip intervened to delay work on the drama and Jerrold played truant again in August when he went, with Bradbury and Evans and others, up to Chatsworth to visit Paxton. Earlier in the year Jerrold had been very pleased when Paxton had acceded to his request to find a place at Chatsworth for his third son, Tom, now sixteen, 'of a very open and innocent disposition' and keen on a career in gardening.[27] This was a chance to see how Tom was doing and happened also to give Jerrold an opportunity of gratifying Paxton. Little Annie Paxton, dressed as a fairy, was placed on one of the great leaves of the stupendous 'Victoria Regia' water-lily that her father had got to bloom in England for the first time whereupon Jerrold composed 'a happy impromptu', as Walter Jerrold calls it ('On unbent leaf, in fairy guise, / Reflected in the water, / Beloved, admired, by hearts and eyes, / Stands Annie, Paxton's daughter. ...'). Jerrold's other Chatsworth activity was more unexpected: 'it may surprise you', Walter Jerrold quotes him as writing to Forster, '(it does *me*) to know that I have committed bloodshed on the moors!'

Returning home, Jerrold found his wife and daughter unwell and shortly afterwards took them to Boulogne from where he was able to report to Lemon, when sending him some *Punch* copy on 11 September, 'my folk have so picked up that I shall stay another week'. (He seems surprisingly unconcerned about the sudden reappearance – which he also reports – of cholera in the town.) He was, he assured Lemon, 'harder at work than when at home', adding, 'Should you see Webster, tell him this.'[28]

Evidently, work on the new play, which had now been promised to Webster for about four years, was going slowly. On 14 December 1845 Jerrold had excused himself from non-completion on the grounds of 'severe illness and many perplexities of occupation', also 'at times that sickness of the brain that arises from over-occupation', and had promised to make the comedy 'the first purpose of my literary life until [it] is done' but shrunk from 'hampering myself with further promise that should tie me to a week or two'.[29] Since then, one very major distraction from work on the play had been his *Weekly Newspaper* and one wonders how Webster would have felt if he had known that Jerrold was once again contemplating starting a journal. At the end of October he proposed to Bradbury and Evans a new weekly twopenny periodical, evidently quite unaware that he had been forestalled by Dickens (we should remember that there was an *éloignement* between himself and Dickens about this time as a result of their disagreement over capital punishment and this may well account for his knowing nothing of Dickens's plans). Evans wrote to Jerrold on 1 November to tell him that 'title, price, form, and time of publication' of the new periodical (*Household Words*) were now all agreed between Dickens and Bradbury and Evans and that 'the whole thing has been for some time in active progress, both on our parts and on that of Mr Dickens'.[30]

Jerrold had, therefore, no choice but to give up the idea of a new weekly. He seems, however, to have put forward another proposal, this time for a new monthly, rather than weekly, publication. Preserved in the Bodleian Library, together with Evans's letter just cited, is a prospectus written in characteristic style by Jerrold for a projected 'monthly monitor'. This was to be called *The Capitol Goose* after the Capitoline geese of ancient Rome whose alarmed cackling, according to Pliny, once saved the citadel from conquest through a surprise attack:

> ... for the GOOSE to chronicle its descent from the Roman Capitol to the Capitol of London – a London Printing-Office – would be pleasant to the modern pride of quills: but this is not permitted. Enough that the GOOSE of 1850 may hope for the ancestral watchfulness of the GOOSE of antiquity – that the GOOSE of present London may aspire to a like vigilance with the GOOSE of early Rome. Nor shall the excelling quality of the bird of our day be dwelt upon; for the GEESE of Rome were, by comparison, mere poultry. Now the GOOSE of our time may carry greatness in its wings; may be a GOOSE ennobled by its Pen Feathers. ...[31]

It was evidently a satirical journal that Jerrold had in mind and it may be that he did not at first share the idea with Bradbury and Evans (the fact that the prospectus is preserved with Evans's letter suggests that it must have come to them at some point). The matter is further confused by some gossip at the *Punch* table ten years later. Under the date of 26 January 1859 Henry Silver noted that Jerrold was criticised for disloyalty. Silver records Thackeray as saying that Jerrold

> Was about setting up 'The Pen' a rival to Punch while he drew his salary and dined and did no work. At same time was writing Dickens his disapproval of Punch. Evans says they debated whether his salary should continue and resolved it should – although he did no work.[32]

It seems probable that 'The Pen' and 'The Capitol Goose' were one and the same project (cf. the joke about goosequill pens in the prospectus) but it was three years before this 'Goose' idea that Jerrold had criticised *Punch* to Dickens and at no stage from 1843 onwards did his *Punch* contributions dwindle to nothing. The evidence of the *Punch* ledgers clearly shows that there were hardly any issues between the beginning of the magazine and Jerrold's death in 1857 that contained nothing from his pen, and during the last six months of 1849 his contributions averaged between two and three columns per issue. He contributed two and a half columns to *Punch's* Almanack for 1850 and wrote the Preface for the half-yearly volume July–December 1849. Evans's memory was evidently very much at fault. Clearly, however, there was still, two years after Jerrold's death, some rankling resentment among the Punchites about his abortive project for establishing another satirical journal.

The failure of these journalistic projects probably concentrated Jerrold's mind more firmly on the theatre as a source of additional income. Many of his plays, besides the evergreen *Black Eyed Susan*, were regularly revived. Just recently, in July, there had been a successful revival of *The House-keeper* at the Haymarket with the Keeleys and Webster playing the roles they had first created in 1833 and a few weeks later this had been followed at the same theatre by a revival of *The Rent Day*. With the disappointment of the failure of *Time Works Wonders* now four and a half years in the past and his editorial career apparently at a standstill, it seemed a natural moment for Jerrold to turn purposefully back to his first love, the drama, and seek once again to achieve the kind of big success in the 'legitimate' theatre that had eluded him since *The Rent Day* packed them in at Drury Lane.

Chapter Thirteen

The Public and the Private Man

'Douglas Jerrold,' wrote G.H. Lewes in 1867, 'was held to be the wittiest man in all England.' Hannay thought he 'was one of the few who in their conversation entirely come up to their renown'. It was this quality of Jerrold's, together with his striking physical presence, that is highlighted by nearly all those who recorded their impressions of seeing him in public. Sala's memories of Jerrold lounging in a theatre green room can stand for a mass of such testimony:

> ... a strange-looking, high-cheek-boned man, with long hair thrown care-lessly away from his forehead, and a piercing eye, that seemed to laugh to scorn the *lorgnon* dangling from its ribbon. I have seen him so, his spare form leaning against the mantel, and he showering – yes, showering is the word – arrowy *bon mots* and corruscating repartees around him.[1]

People will generally then go on to say that they were so dazzled by all the corruscation that they cannot remember much, if anything, of what Jer-rold actually *said*; Elizabeth Gaskell was delighted by his flow of bon-mots which she had expected to remember but they 'now have quite slipped out of my head'. And, even if they can remember, people despair of being able to convey any sense of what William Howard Russell called Jerrold's 'quickness, terseness, and "unexpectedness"'. An isolated impromptu may be remembered as when Alfred Ainger recalls Jerrold watching, with Landseer and others, as the schoolroom at Dickens's home was being cleared for dancing following some private theatricals. He picked up a horse's head overlooked by the property-man and, 'holding it up before the greatest living animal painter', said, 'Looks as if it knew *you*, Edwin!'[2] Or, some sustained flight of satirical fancy may be remembered in a general sort of way, as when Edward Bradley, alias 'Cuthbert Bede' the author of *Mr Verdant Green*, describes a revealing fantasy elaborated by Jerrold on a visit to Oxford as honoured guest of the Mayor in November 1854. A statue of Cain and Abel seen in Brasenose inspired such a 'torrent of witty remarks' that his companions 'fairly roared with laughter as [they] paced the streets'. Jerrold said that

> literary men should establish in London a new club, to be called 'The Cain and Abel Club' in which the members should be allowed to vent all their spiteful jealousies, and to murder each other's reputations in the most truculent and savage way. ... In the reading-room of the club a book was to be kept, in which it should be the duty of the secretary or librarian to paste

all the abusive and offensive reviews that were printed concerning the books and productions of the members of the club. Any engraved caricatures of the members were also to be collected and hung upon the walls of the club. This idea [he] developed very rapidly and at much length … also giving imaginary dialogues far from complimentary in their nature between distinguished members of the club. I can call to mind a few scraps of these; but the gentlemen in question would not thank me for reproducing them.[3]

Generally, however, those who had undergone 'the Jerrold experience' would find the same thing as Mrs Gaskell. They would remember his wit playing, as William Howard Russell put it, 'below or above or around' the conversation 'like summer lightning', but little in the way of particular 'hits'.[4]

Many of his sallies were nevertheless remembered, at least long enough to be repeated and to get into general circulation ('his last bon mot', said the *Times* obituarist, 'was one of those items of news that everybody was glad to hear'). Sometimes, it seems, this circulation could be pretty wide, as was exemplified, in Jerroldian style, by a writer in the *National Magazine*:

> One joke of his was found lately beating about the coasts of Sweden, seeking in vain for a competent Swedish translator; and the other day, a tourist from London, seeing two brawny North Britons laughing together immoderately on a rock near Cape Wrath, with a heavy sea dashing at their feet, discovered that the cause of their mirth was a joke of Mr Jerrold's which they had intercepted on its way to the Shetlands.[5]

A store of Jerroldisms accumulated in the public domain, so to speak, and this was always available to those who could not remember any of the repartee they had heard from his own lips. A favourite in this respect was his retort to one of his victims who protested that he and Jerrold 'rowed in the same boat'. 'But not with the same skulls' was the instant response. This particular repartee is reported in many different ways, e.g., the painter Sydney Cooper's version which had 'two conceited young authors' boasting in Jerrold's presence that they '"rowed in the same boat" with some celebrated literary oar of the day, when he said: "Aye, but not with the same skulls!"' The joke was still going the rounds in 1878 as we can see from G.H. Lewes's diary entry for 9 June that year: 'Neville the actor told Jerrold's repartee of rowing in the same boat but not with the same skulls – as "not with the same oars". On being laughed at for his mistake he said, "Well, a boat *is* rowed with oars, who ever heard of its being rowed with *skulls?*"'[6]

Down in London from Edinburgh to catch up on metropolitan literary gossip, the publisher Robert Chambers noted in his memorandum book (25 January 1852), 'Douglas Jerrold is now the prince of wits in England. No man says such brilliant things,' and proceeds to list a few of these including, 'There is no God, and Harriet Martineau is his prophet', the suggestion that a collection of cockney Mark Lemon's writings entitled *Prose and Verse* ought more properly to be called *Prose and Worse*, and the joke about Romanising Thackeray's nose. Later, he jots down one or two more, e.g.,

> Mr Redford, an old dozy bore, meeting Jerrold in Regent Street, posed himself into a button-holding attitude, saying, 'Well Jerrold, my dear boy, what is going on?' 'I am' said the wag, and rushed off.[7]

What perhaps strikes us most about Chambers's examples is their apparent sheer rudeness – and yet they are mild compared with jokes like the one Jerrold made about a fellow-Punchite called Sterling Coyne: 'Referring to his not very clean appearance Douglas Jerrold said, "Stirling Coyne? *I call him Filthy Lucre!*"', or with the rough fun he would often poke at Forster. Once, for example, when Stanfield had left a scene-painter's pencil on a chair during one of the Amateur Players' rehearsals, Jerrold 'took it up, and looking at it in his arch way exclaimed, "Hallo, here is the exact counterpart of John Forster, short, thick, and full of lead"'. Also, Forster notoriously aped Macready in his acting and once when the amateurs were dispersing at end of a rehearsal Jerrold called out after Forster 'Stop him, he'll be off to Mrs Macready!'[8] Well might Ronald Pearsall comment in his book on Victorian wit and humour, *Collapse of Stout Party* (1975), that Jerrold's recorded witticisms 'make one wonder why no one laid him out'. Shirley Brooks offers an explanation as to why this did not happen in a novel which contains a thinly-disguised sketch of Jerrold as 'the great wit and humourist' Mr Jasper Beryl. One of Brooks's characters quotes a joke of Beryl's at the expense of a fellow-member of his club and is asked how the victim responded. He answers,

> O, all right ... Jasper Beryl makes you feel that he says things of that kind out of an overflow of wit, not to hurt you. He declares, too, that it is bad fellowship for anybody who has got a joke to bottle it up and carry it away instead of giving it out to the people about him. And I think he is right.[9]

There were occasional murmurs, however, that Jerrold did not always 'converse in good humour' and that there was 'frequently a want of courtesy in his manner'.[10] The young journalist H. Sutherland Edwards, having accompanied Jerrold to another festive gathering following a *Punch* dinner, was distinctly underwhelmed:

> Waiting for him were his habitual butt George Hodder, and his occasional bully, Harry Baylis.[11] Everything then pointed to a lively night, but I came away an hour or two afterwards by no means impressed with the wit of the leading personages. Jerrold often uttered witticisms which were to wit what a truism is to truth; and he indulged at every opportunity in repartee which, sometimes facetious, generally sarcastic, was too often in bad taste. When he had made what seemed to him a smart speech he closed his lips with a sort of snap, exclaiming on particular occasions, when he had made a palpable hit: 'I had him there!'[12]

Some people deliberately avoided meeting Jerrold through fear of his tongue. One such was William Powell Frith. Those who knew Jerrold personally assured him that he was 'one of the kindest-hearted men living' but Frith remained unconvinced and 'always avoided an introduction'. He took some pleasure, we may think, in recording one occasion he had heard of when Jerrold was worsted by a barmaid he had been subjecting to a 'torrent of chaff' and who paid him back in his own coin as she served him his drink in a large old-fashioned 'rummer':

> 'There', said the girl as she placed the big glass before Jerrold, 'there's your grog, and mind you don't fall into it'. Jerrold was a very little man, and the hit told to the extent of dulling him for the rest of the evening.[13]

Many of the anecdotes about Jerrold and his wit have one of his clubs for their setting. When trying to account for the immense vogue for his *bon mots* we need some idea of the ambience of such places, and the way in which they reflected contemporary mores and social customs. These clubs were, of course, quite different from the grand established gentlemen's clubs like the Athenaeum or the Reform. They were more like poor relations, or ephemeral versions, of the Garrick, which Jerrold did once apply to join but changed his mind after hearing that candidates were judged 'a little too *politically*'.[14] One such club was the Museum, about which Jerrold wrote to Dickens in 1847 when urging him to join ('The men hunger for your name'). The Museum, Jerrold explains, had been started by Forster, Macready and others 'for literary and artistic men who, not having yet won their golden spurs, have not too much of that hideous metal (as the moral Boucicault would call it) in their pockets'.[15] The avowed basic aim of these clubs was to promote good fellowship and social mirth with plenty of smoking, drinking and mutual 'chaffing' in the fashion of the day ('Banter reigns every where, even amongst the scientific men', runs another of Chambers's London notebook entries). Sometimes they did not go much beyond this. The Rationals Club, for example, to which Jerrold belonged in the late 1830s, along with Mayhew, Cruikshank, Lemon, Keeley, Stanfield and others of his circle, seems to have been mainly a drinking club. It met on Saturday afternoons at the Garrick's Head in Bow Street, migrating later in the day to the Wrekin in Broad Court, and financed its flow of liquor by a preposterously elaborate system of fines for various kinds of rule-breaking, such as for dropping one's h's, swearing, or 'starting a discussion on the immortality of the soul before two o'clock in the morning'. This often led to scenes of rowdy merriment and horseplay such as the one described by Athol Mayhew in his *Jorum of 'Punch'* that resulted from Jerrold's fierce refusal to pay the fines he had incurred.[16] The Museum Club was more dignified and aimed at higher things. It was a good place for networking, as young David Masson discovered when he got reviewing work for the *Athenaeum* through meeting its editor there. Its premises in Henrietta Street, Covent Garden, were open all day for breakfast or dinner. But it was at its liveliest in the evenings when 'a considerable number used to meet ... for talk and smoke in an upper room', with Jerrold as 'a kind of chief'.[17] Looking back over his long life, the publisher George Smith thought these were the most entertaining parties he had ever experienced:

> The wit was brilliant, the jokes abundant, the laughter uproarious. ... often I came away ... with sides that were literally sore with laughter ... . The best talkers of the club were Douglas Jerrold, Father Prout and G.H. Lewes. ... Lewes had a wonderful gift for dramatic representation ... Jerrold's flow of wit was unfailing, his repartee was of lightning-like swiftness. Father Prout's humour was more subtle and refined.[18]

No doubt, says Smith later on, the wit at these Museum soirées would be counted 'too personal for these days' (he is writing in the 1890s) because 'repartee of the old bludgeon, or broad-sword, type has, fortunately, disappeared'. 'But,' he continues somewhat wistfully (and oblivious, apparently, of Oscar Wilde), 'there are no talkers to-day, I fancy, to equal the men of the by-gone generation, and few raconteurs.'

At the heart of social and literary London for Jerrold was *Punch*, which with its highly convivial weekly dinners, functioned very like a club such as the Museum. In both places Jerrold would have been on the receiving end of jokes as well as dishing them out. Years after both he and à Beckett were dead, for example, the latter was remembered at the *Punch* table as 'a quiet pleasant talker – answering Douglas Jerrold's fulminations with a pithy pregnant joke'.[19]

The Museum had eventually to close through lack of funds. To it succeeded the Hooks and Eyes Club, which met weekly at the Albion in Covent Garden, and this eventually gave place to the rather grander 'Our Club' which met every Saturday evening from November to May on an upper floor of Clunn's Hotel in Covent Garden and which was, like the *Punch* table, a favourite resort of Thackeray's who became its acknowledged chief after Jerrold's death. Its special characteristics, writes Masson, 'were a perpetual brilliant chaff and repartee; a wit, a banter, a certain habit of mutual fooling ... all difficult to describe, impossible to reproduce now, but very pleasant to remember'.[20]

The great majority of admirers of Jerrold's wit would not, of course, have experienced it at first hand but rather through seeing his plays or through reading his work, especially his writings in *Punch*. Here, divorced from the experience of its delivery, they would seem to have needed constant reassurance that his wit was *not* an expression of bitterness, misanthropy, cynicism, or even atheism, but was rather the product of strong, 'healthy' feelings, a passionate concern for social justice, hatred of the abuse of power, cruelty, militarism, and so forth. There certainly were plenty who accused Jerrold of misanthropic sourness and bitter class hatred, like the anonymous campaigner for a National Theatre in 1847 who wanted his plays excluded from it 'until he ceases to exercise his great talent at the expense of a class; for how can taunts and bitter jests unite or ameliorate society?'[21] Jerrold writhed under the constant accusations of 'bitterness' and complained in the preface to the first volume of his *Collected Writings* (1851), 'were my ink redolent of myrrh and frankincense, I well know the sort of ready-made criticism that would cry, with a denouncing shiver, "aloes; aloes"' (one has to presume that he had never actually smelled myrrh). Nathaniel Hawthorne, introduced to him by Mackay, editor of the *Illustrated London News*, at the Reform Club early in 1856, put his foot in it by using the word 'acrid' in connection with his impression of Jerrold's writings. Jerrold's reaction was dramatic (Hawthorne thought afterwards that this may have had something to do with the fact that they were now on to their second bottle of Burgundy):

> ... he was indeed greatly hurt by that little word 'acrid'; he knew, he said, that the world considered him a sour, bitter, ill-natured man; but that such a man as I should have the same opinion, was almost more than he could bear. As he spoke, he threw out his arms, sank back in his seat, and I was really a little apprehensive of his actual dissolution into tears.[22]

Part of the problem for Jerrold was that wit for the mid-Victorians was, quite apart from any class-warfare implications, a deeply suspect commodity as tending towards 'heartlessness', amorality – even blasphemy. They looked back with fascinated horror to the reign of Charles II[23] when, as Horne wrote in 1844, 'the laugh was raised indiscriminately at vice and virtue, honesty or knavery, wisdom or folly' and 'licentious poison ... spurted glistening from the pens of Wycherly, Farquhar, Congreve, and Vanbrugh, who had no noble aim or object'. The muse of Restoration Comedy was, said Thackeray, 'a disreputable, daring, laughing, painted French baggage' who 'came over from the Continent with Charles ... at the Restoration', and it was with relief that reviewers of *Time Works Wonders* felt they could detect Jerrold's emergence from Congrevian influence.[24] For the *Illustrated London News* (3 May 1845) the new play's dialogue was 'just as brilliant' as that of its predecessors but was now 'natural and kindly', the hearts of the characters being 'all well placed'. *The Times* (28 April 1845) believed that, even when he was imitating Congreve, Jerrold's 'natural kindliness ... spoke deep-toned from beneath the glitter in a manner unknown to the old wit' and rejoices that now he has 'followed the Congrevian wit less and nature more – has looked deeper into humanity for the genuine sources of humour – and has come out with a truth and freshness formerly unknown'.

The key word here is 'humour'. Humour, famously defined by Carlyle as 'inverse sublimity', was generally felt to be a truly English, Shakespearian, sort of thing that was found in glorious abundance in the writings of Dickens. It appealed to the human heart, not just to the intellect, ranged over all humanity, and had no programme or purpose beyond the promotion of sympathy, 'warm, tender fellow-feeling with all humanity', to quote

Carlyle again. Once the 'broad genial glorious humour of England' becomes 'forked with sarcasm, and takes to ... tearing the roof off men's houses and shaking down steeples, then it is not true English humour', declared the philanthropist Frances Power Cobbe.[25] It was not the humorist's business to focus on the dark side of life (the idea of 'black humour', which fits exactly so much of what Jerrold wrote, e.g. *A Man Made of Money*, would have been simply a contradiction in terms to the Victorians). Jerrold, his critics argued seemed often to focus too exclusively on the dark side of life:

> His wit is too cynical, it is the 'wit blanket' which he has elsewhere so pleasantly described. The reader laughs at his command, and pities at his bidding, but rarely loves at his suggestion. The miser, the usurer, the hardened prodigal son are his favourite figures; he seems to delight in representing all the accidents, sufferings and disappointments of life ....[26]

Jerrold's defenders argued for him as a true reforming satirist in the tradition of Swift and his 'savage indignation'. His 'bitter vein of satire' arose

> not from innate gall in his own disposition, but from a desire to correct, by exposure, the many hideous defects which ... so shrewd an observer as himself cannot fail to recognise. Severity towards oppression is humanity towards the oppressed ... .[27]

They would point also to certain of his writings, notably *The Story of a Feather* ('full of humour and tenderness'[28]) and 'The Chronicles of Clovernook', as revelatory of the warm tenderheartedness and kindness that was so familiar to everyone who actually knew Jerrold personally. If he had the sting of a bee, said Leigh Hunt, he 'also had its honey'.[29] His 'large light blue eye beamed nothing but benevolence, and to this expression the feeling of his heart fully responded', wrote the *Examiner* obituarist (presumably Forster) on 13 June 1857, and he went on to assert, as did many others, that there was never any malice in Jerrold's jests: 'like all wits, he loved his joke, and if an opportunity for uttering a repartee presented itself he was not the man to let the forelock escape his grasp.'

One notable sufferer from Jerrold's wit who did not take such a benign view was the flamboyant manager of Covent Garden and Drury Lane Theatres, Alfred Bunn. Tormented beyond endurance by *Punch*'s persistent mockery of him as 'the Poet Bunn', 'Hot Cross Bunn', 'Alfred the Little', and so forth, Bunn published, with help from Albert Smith and G.A. Sala, a devastating rejoinder in November 1847 called *A Word With Punch* in which he particularly attacked Lemon ('Thickhead'), à Beckett ('Sleekhead') and Jerrold ('Wronghead'). Depicted by Sala, Bunn's artist, as both a wasp and a serpent, Jerrold is called 'a man of undoubted genius' (as distinct from the other two) to whom *Punch* is principally indebted for its success, but he is deplorably twisted mentally, being 'one of the most ill-conditioned, spiteful, vindictive and venomous writers in existence ...

Wronghead . . . Mr. DOUGLAS JERROLD.

whatever honey *was* in his composition, has long since turned to gall'. (Surprisingly, the Punchites never responded to Bunn's onslaught and by ceasing to ridicule him tacitly admitted defeat.)

If Jerrold's wit, whether applauded or condemned, was the prime cause for his celebrity, there were also other contributing factors. Notably, there was his remarkable life-story, that of a true Samuel Smiles hero. 'In the teeth of many setbacks and bitter disappointments, such as enduring poverty,' while, as *Eliza Cook's Journal* put it, 'the town resounded with the fame of his dramas',[30] he had risen from near the very bottom of the social heap to become a recognised gentleman and established middle-class paterfamilias as well as one of the most famous and influential writers of his day and the familiar friend of many leading figures in the world of literature and the arts. We have noted above Hannay's obituary tribute, 'No man of our age had so thoroughly fought his way', but this was not something that people had to wait until his death to learn about, as was the case with Dickens. Jerrold himself proclaimed it in the preface to the first volume of his *Collected Writings*:

> Self-helped and self-guided, I began the world at an age when, as a general rule, boys have not laid down their primers ... the cock-pit of a man-of-war was at thirteen exchanged for the struggle of London.

Before this, George Holyoake knew all about it when praising 'The Chronicles of Clovernook' in 1847 and Jerrold's 'giant's advocacy of humanity': 'None struggle for humanity as he does who have not struggled against the world. No other education would have given him his pre-eminence.' Again, in his *Men of the Time* (1856) Charles Knight quotes an unidentified writer as warning 'sonnet-writing young men' that Jerrold had not achieved his distinction with ease: 'no one leap into the seat of honour was his; but a painful, heart-breaking, toiling up that hill, which always reminds us of the labour of Sisyphus.' 'Dread was his fight,' adds Knight, 'but his heart held out and he triumphed.' And so, writing out of the known harshness of his own experience, Jerrold made himself into the powerful 'people's advocate' that Lewes called him. Caroline Chisholm probably does not much exaggerate Jerrold's reputation as a hero when she has one of her characters say in *Little Joe*, her story of emigrant life that was published in the Australian paper *The Empire* (1859-60):

> Douglas Jerrold was indeed a man … . We hear of testimonials and monuments erected which cost thousands; but fame – fame; what is fame, but the cottager's breath? Thousands upon thousands have felt the generous heroism of Douglas Jerrold's spirit, and if they cannot raise a monument of granite to his memory, they will leave one of feeling, by leaving his name a cherished one in the hearts of their children.[31]

Since he was no revolutionary, not even a Chartist, but rather what one might call a liberal-radical, or perhaps radical-liberal, Jerrold did not alarm or alienate the mass of the lower or even the tradesman classes, any more than did Dickens. Hero-worship of them could flourish untainted by anxiety. A *Punch* office-boy called Francis Eason had toothache and was sent by Lemon, with half a crown to pay the fee, to a Mr Canton in St Martin's Lane, and told to say he 'came from Mr Jerrold'. Thereupon, after endeavouring to satisfy Canton's curiosity about what the great man was like, he got his tooth drawn for nothing because, Canton said, 'they didn't charge Punch anything'.[32] We have here a little anecdote which gives us a telling glimpse of the kind of popularity Jerrold enjoyed, also the way in which he was regarded as the very incarnation of *Punch*.

Another factor in his popularity was his perceived 'thorough Englishness'. This was partly a matter of his notorious refusal to have anything to do with adapting French dramas to the English stage (cf. *The Times* review of *Retired from Business* quoted below, p. 246), and partly a feeling that he was reviving genuine English literature, 'the old genius of the land', at this time often identified with our Saxon heritage:

> … he writes with the Saxon pith of yore, and with Saxon simplicity; in an age when many a writer does not even read the old authors, he emulates them; he steps in the footprints of their muses. He has got the true trick of the old craft … .[33]

It is difficult to guess just which 'old authors' Sinnett has in mind here but perhaps such 17th-century classics as Bunyan or Walton. This 'Englishness' of Jerrold's, however, went beyond his literary style, and was closely linked with his championship of the poor. 'He is himself thoroughly English', said the writer in *Eliza Cook's Journal* already cited:

227

– in his feelings, his tastes, and his genius. And what, above all other things, we love him for, is his strong sympathy for the suffering, the poor, and the down-trodden classes of our community. Indeed, among all the able and earnest vindicators of the claims of the wretched to forbearance and sympathy, we can call to mind no name more honoured and distinguished than his.

As we have seen, Jerrold's 'summit' year of 1845 was a summit one also in respect of organised public homage. On 7 May he presided at the Annual Conversazione of the Birmingham Polytechnic Institution where he was greeted with enormous enthusiasm and received a congratulatory address, as well as the commemorative ring from 'the Operative Committee of the Fancy Trades of Birmingham'. After a nervous start to his speech, which is quoted by Walter Jerrold, he delighted his audience with the joking, if still sexist, reference to the impossibility of the existence of such a person as Mrs Caudle that I have already quoted (above, p. 165). He remained dissatisfied with the speech, however, telling Forster 'I was ill and nervous'.[34] On 23 October, he was the main speaker at the Anniversary of the Manchester Athenaeum. Knight records that when Jerrold

> rose in the Free Trade Hall to address an assembly of three thousand people, the shouts were so continuous that the coolest platform orator might have lost for a moment his presence of mind. I looked upon the slight figure bending again and again, as each gust of applause seemed to overpower him and make him shrink into himself.

He rallied sufficiently, however, to provide some of the 'witty' oratory his audience would have been hoping for:

> The lady knowledge, too long pent up in her tower, guarded not only by giants, but more provoking still, by dwarfs! (laughter) ... is no longer a prisoner. We have killed the giants – we have slain her dwarfs; and how have we killed them! Why, as Luther rebuked the devil – by throwing inkstands at them. (Loud laughter and cheers.). Her music is no longer made the idle luxury of the few, but is acknowledged as the daily want of the many ... .[35]

A third such occasion in 1845 would have been a gathering with himself as guest of honour at the Sheffield Mechanics' Institute on 30 October but he had to cry off at the last minute owing to the effects of 'a severe attack of influenza'.[36]

Jerrold's appearance was very well known to the public – more, perhaps, in caricature through *Punch* than in 'straight' prints like the one in *Reynolds' Miscellany* in 1847 and formal depictions like the Baily bust. The *Reynolds'* picture is taken from a photograph by Richard Beard, the leading daguerreotypist of the day, which was engraved by T. Prior and advertised for sale in the *Athenaeum* on 24 April 1847 under the banner headline 'A Portrait of Douglas Jerrold'[37]. Opportunities for his admirers to compare such images of him with his actual physical presence at some public event were rare, however. The two occasions in 1845 were exceptional because, in marked contrast to Dickens, Jerrold was reluctant and uncomfortable when it came to public speaking and greatly preferred the print medium. It was probably with some relief that he found himself in February 1852 'disabled by an accident' from attending a meeting of the association for repeal of the so-called 'taxes on knowledge' (newspaper taxes) so that he could instead send a letter, very like one of his *Punch* articles, to be read out at the meeting.[38] A few months later, there were apparently some moves to get him to stand for Parliament as liberal member for Finsbury but this was not an option for him, not only because of his distaste for making speeches but also because he was, as he told his son Blanchard, 'not rich enough': 'to be anything beyond a cypher a man must work hard in the House – and I must work at home'.[39]

Given his dislike of public speaking, it is surprising that in the autumn of 1852 Jerrold seems to have been seriously considering the giving of a series of lectures. He tells Dr Hudson, the Secretary of the Athenaeum, that this is partly the result of an invitation from the Philosophical Institution of Edinburgh but the great success of Thackeray's London lectures on 'English Humourists of the Eighteenth Century' (May/June 1851) may have had rather more to do with the matter. His subject, wrote Jerrold, was 'some way out of the beaten track' and needed 'much consideration' but we have no indication as to just what it was. By May 1853, however, he had put the project on hold. '*You* can easily understand,' he wrote to Cowden Clarke, 'that to write a series, merely for Edinburgh, would not suffice to the outlay of time: and – for a while – I see no chance of my being able to *make a mark*, [through the lectures, presumably] as I intend, life lasting, to do.'[40] We do not know if he received any lecture-tour invitations from America but Thackeray, who was on such a trip in 1855, wrote to Bradbury and Evans about the number of times he was asked if Jerrold would be coming over: 'When he wants 1500 or 2000£ this is the place for him.'[41]

Jerrold was a prominent supporter of liberal causes abroad as well as at home but, rather than going about making speeches, his activism took the form of writing leading articles and satirical pieces in *Punch*, and of lending his name to certain organisations. Along with such associates as Goodwyn Barmby, Thomas Cooper and William Shaen, he is listed as a member of the Council of the People's International League, for example. This was the liberal alternative to the more radical, Chartist-related Fraternal Democrats (promoted by George Julian Harney, editor of the *Northern Star*) which welcomed Marx as a speaker to one of its meetings on 29 November 1847. The League was inaugurated by Mazzini and others in 1847, following Austria's suppression of the Republic of Cracow with the connivance of Russia and Prussia, and it had for one of its main objects 'to embody and manifest an efficient Public Opinion in favour of the right of every People to Self-government and the maintenance of their own Nationality'. It also advocated world-wide free trade. Mazzini welcomed an attack on the League by *The Times* in May because it 'means we are a more important body than is admitted in the article'. He added, 'Still, somebody, Douglas Jerrold, for instance, in his paper ought to mention the article, just as a good omen for the League.'[42] We do not know how active Jerrold was in attending meetings of the League, the only relevant document that has come to light so far being a letter in which he apologises for being 'unavoidably prevented' from attending on 15 November.[43] The letter from Mazzini to Jerrold from which Blanchard Jerrold quotes certainly makes it sound as though it was primarily the latter's support in print for which Mazzini was thanking him. 'Whenever you do sympathise,' Mazzini told him, 'you are ready to act, to embody your feelings in good, visible, tangible symbol; and this is not the general rule.' Privately, however, Mazzini had reservations about Jerrold's style. After hearing of his death, he wrote to Emilie Hawkes (née Ashurst),

> Yes, dear, I am sorry for Douglas Jerrold, because you like him, because I met him at Muswell Hill, and because there was some genuineness in him. Individually, I was not sympathising much with him. He was writing very good things but clothing them in a rather gross, vulgar, materialistic shape, which was not to my taste.[44]

The French Socialist leader Louis Blanc, exiled in London from 1848, was another European political figure whom Jerrold supported in his journalism. Blanc wrote to thank him in October 1855 and to ask for a review of his latest book in Jerrold's 'patriotic and valuable paper'.[45] But it was on behalf of the great Hungarian patriot Lajos Kossuth that Jerrold led a characteristically romantic-literary campaign that went beyond leader-writing. Kossuth arrived as an exile in England in 1849, after Austria had crushed the shortlived Hungarian Republic over which he had presided. He was given a triumphal reception by the British public and greeted as a great democratic hero by *Punch*. Jerrold's imagination was fired, too, by the report that Kossuth had learned English from reading Shakespeare in an Austrian prison. 'An Englishman's blood kindles,' he wrote, 'with the thought that, from the quiver of the immortal Saxon, Kossuth has furnished himself with those arrowy words that kindle as they fly ...' Jerrold launched a newspaper campaign aimed at the working men of Britain for a penny subscription to raise a fund to present Kossuth with a sumptuously-bound set of Shakespeare's works. The pennies poured in and at Jerrold's suggestion a case to hold the books was made modelled on Shakespeare's birthplace in Stratford. On 8 May 1853 a grand presentation ceremony was held at the London Tavern and Jerrold had once more to nerve himself, amidst scenes of tumultuous enthusiasm, to deliver a long oration.[46]

For a celebrated author in Victorian England another aspect of public life, in addition to helping to promote good causes, was 'moving in Society' but Jerrold seems to have done very little of this, greatly preferring to centre his social life around his clubs or his own home. There does exist a

WELCOME TO KOSSUTH!

note to him from Caroline Norton conveying a last-minute dinner invitation from Lord Melbourne but we do not know whether he went. The only member of the upper classes with whom Jerrold associated at all closely was 'the frank and hearty Lord Nugent', as Forster calls him, an author and, according to the *DNB*, 'extreme whig or whig-radical' in politics, also an opponent of capital punishment. Jerrold enjoyed visiting Lillies, Nugent's country house (where a stone engraved with his name that the host set up to commemorate his visits may still be seen) and Nugent himself was a frequent visitor to Jerrold at Putney, attracted thither, wrote Blanchard, by Jerrold's 'simple habits and country fare'.[47]

Those privileged like Nugent to see him in his own home saw a somewhat different Jerrold from the celebrated 'bantering' wit of the clubs and the *Punch* table. His warm hospitality was especially extended to younger men seeking to make their way in the world,[48] exiled foreign liberals , or working-class aspirants to literary fame like William Thom. His lively table-talk and infectious delight in his Putney garden and its produce (fine asparagus, strawberries 'big and square as pincushions', and so on) and in the family pets like Mouse, his little black-and-tan terrier, who accompanied him on all his walks and lay on a rug in the study while he worked, all combined to make a visit to West Lodge both delightful and memorable. Sunday was his day for keeping open house when anyone might drop in and partake of 'cottage fare'. In summer visitors ate and drank wine in a tent pitched in the garden under Jerrold's beloved mulberry tree, at other times they might gather in his snug study: the image of him there 'with a cigar, a flask of Rhine wine on the table, a cedar log on the fire, and half-a-dozen literary youngsters round the board listening to his bright wit and his wisdom' was, wrote Hepworth Dixon in his *Athenaeum* review of Blanchard's biography of his father, the image that would live 'most brightly and permanently in the minds of those who knew him'.

Leech might snobbishly seek to amuse the *Punch* table after Jerrold's death by imitating his former colleague at home in 'Rose Cottage' (presumably his Haverstock Hill home – see above, p. 114) 'throwing hair back and sprinkling salt with gusto over gooseberry tart!' but it was the hearty simplicity of their host's manner, his complete unaffectedness, that so charmed his many visitors. 'He was', J.H. Stirling recorded of his first visit to Jerrold at home, as 'natural, simple, open as a boy'.[49] Nor was Jerrold himself the only boyish one on domestic-social occasions. His guests, too, seem to have revelled in the informal ambience he created, especially at the tent dinners, and, if Blanchard Jerrold is to be believed (and there is no reason to doubt him just because of his effusive style) scenes took place the like of which would be a somewhat startling aftermath to any literary dinner-party nowadays:

> Basting the bear was, one evening, the rule, on which occasion grave editors and contributors 'basted' one another with knotted pocket-handkerchiefs, to their hearts' content. The crowning effort of this memorable evening was a general attempt to go heels over head upon haycocks in the orchard – a feat which vanquished the skill of the laughing host, and left a very stout and very responsible editor, I remember, upon his head, without power to retrieve his natural position. Again; after a dinner-party under canvas, the hearty host, with his guests, including Mr Charles Dickens, Mr Maclise, Mr Macready, and Mr John Forster, indulged in a most active game of leap-frog ... .[50]

(No word of all this larking about, we notice, gets into Macready's account of the dinner quoted above, p. 210.)

Less boisterous was the small dinner-party at West Lodge attended by Sydney Cooper and Hepworth Dixon and which Cooper records as 'the merriest repast I ever was at, for Jerrold kept us in one continued course of laughter the whole time'. Jerrold's being in such good form astonished Cooper since it was less than twenty-four hours since he had seen him, helplessly drunk after a *Punch* dinner, being put into a cab by his companions 'with a label tied round his neck, on which was written: "Douglas Jerrold, Esq., Lower Heath, Putney"'. When Cooper remonstrated with Jerrold's fellow-Punchites about this, they answered, 'What can we do with him? He will be delivered quite safe – it is not new to him.'[51] The alternative, presumably, would have been to leave him staggering about the streets to be rescued, if he was lucky, by a passing acquaintance, as happened once when George Smith came to his aid:

> One night I met Jerrold, who appeared to have taken too much wine, in Regent Street, in charge of a policeman. It was the only time I ever saw him the worse for liquor. I said to the policemen, 'I know the gentleman; I will call a cab and see him home.' The policeman said, 'Well, I don't want to take him in charge; but he will meet with an accident if I leave him.' I made myself responsible for Jerrold's safety, and the policeman, as he moved off, said 'I am much obliged to you; he seems to be a gentleman.' Jerrold heard the remark, and stammered out in reply, 'You are right, policeman. I was well bred, but I have been very badly brought up!'[52]

We notice that Smith says he saw Jerrold drunk only this once whereas his *Punch* colleagues tell a different story, as does the publisher Richard Bentley in his unpublished diary, where he notes (7 May 1859) that Jerrold

> was fond of the Garrick Club, or of any boozing place. There he remained till the small hours, and his brougham with half sleepy coachman then drove him to Putney well soaked to bed ... .

Bentley hated Jerrold, calling him 'a little waspish cur' and 'venom itself, crystallized vinegar', so he is perhaps not the most reliable of witnesses (possibly, the two men had quarrelled over Jerrold's non-fulfilment of the contract to write Bentley a novel about Nell Gwynne – see above, p. 112). Jerrold was not a member of the Garrick and never owned a brougham, as far as we know, and an anecdote of Sala's that Bentley records, about finding Jerrold crying drunk in Covent Garden at 2 a.m., 'declaring he was a good man – not the cruel harsh man he was said to be', was probably spiced up by Sala to curry favour with Bentley.[53] Nevertheless, there does seem to be enough surviving evidence to suggest that Jerrold was, at least occasionally, rather the worse for drink at the end of one of his festive evenings. A story Tennyson liked to tell about himself and Jerrold leaving a Society of Authors dinner presided over by Talfourd is perhaps another case in point – at the very least, Jerrold would seem to have become rather over-excited. Tennyson remembered:

> I happened to say to my neighbour 'I wonder which of us will be alive 500 years hence'. On which Talfourd burst forth into a speech about me, saying 'I was the one likely to live!' ... I drove away afterwards with old Douglas Jerrold who fell on his knees, seized me by the hand and kissed it and kissed it and said 'I haven't the smallest doubt that *you* are the one who will live five hundred years'.[54]

One would give a good deal to know how Jerrold was received at Putney if he really was sometimes delivered home with a label tied round his neck (the Punchites may have been pulling Cooper's leg, of course, when they said he was well used to it). His helplessness about dress and belongings, mentioned by his son,[55] would have been even more extreme at such times, and Mary Ann's patience must have been sorely tried. It becomes tempting to believe what Jerrold allegedly told Kalisch about the Caudle Lectures being closely based on his own marital existence (above, p. 160). Mr Caudle, returning home very late from his club 'The Skylarks', is severely lectured:

> it's no use, Mr Caudle, your calling me a good creature: I'm not such a fool as to be coaxed in that way. No; if you want to go to sleep, you should come home in Christian time, not at half-past twelve. There was a time when you were as regular at your fireside as the kettle. That was when you were a decent man, and didn't go amongst Heaven knows who, drinking and smoking, and making what you think your jokes. I never heard any good come to a man who cared about jokes. No respectable tradesman does ... .

On another occasion, Caudle is clearly drunk when he comes back from a Masonic dinner, wearing someone else's hat and repeatedly asking where his watch is:

> *You must find your watch? And you'll get up for it?* Nonsense – don't be foolish – lie still. Your watch is on the mantelpiece. Ha! Isn't it a good thing for you, you've somebody to take care of it?
> What do you say? *I'm a dear creature?* Very dear, indeed, you think me, I dare say. But the fact is, you don't know what you're talking about tonight. I'm a fool to open my lips to you – but I can't help it.
> *Where's your watch?* Haven't I told you – on the mantelpiece ....

These harangues may or may not reflect real-life scoldings by Mary Ann Jerrold. As in the case of Rose Trollope, the 'great unknown' in Anthony's life,[56] we have so little testimony to go on, and are so completely in the dark about the Jerrolds' marital relationship, that we can only speculate. Like Rose Trollope, Mary Ann seems to have participated hardly at all in her husband's social life outside the home. When Dickens's Amateur Players travelled to Liverpool in 1847, for example, many of their wives went along also, including Catherine Dickens, Helen Lemon, Agnes Lewes and Mrs Dudley Costello: but not Mary Ann. Nor did she accompany him when he was being honoured in Birmingham and Manchester – though, as we have seen, she *was* present at the gala opening of the Whittington Club. Whether she stayed home on other occasions because of delicate health (there are frequent references to her illnesses in Jerrold's letters) or because she was of a retiring disposition and may not have felt comfortable among all the literary folk we do not know. A postman's daughter with presumably very little in the way of education in lady-like 'accomplishments', she perhaps felt uneasy off her home ground, in the literary and artistic society frequented by her husband. Dickens seems to be trying to reassure her through Jerrold when inviting him to join the Dickens household in Genoa: 'If you were disposed to give Mrs Jerrold a Christmas holiday, I will warrant my Wife to be as gentle a little woman, and as free from affectation or formality of any kind, as ever breathed.'[57] Mary Ann did go on the foursome holiday trip to Switzerland with the Hepworth Dixons in 1854, but the Dixons were intimate friends of the family by that time. It is perhaps worth noting that the only literary anecdote about Jerrold in which his wife features is one that has a domestic setting. He was recovering from an illness and had been left by her one morning to go shopping:

> ... a parcel of books from London arrived. Among them was Browning's 'Sordello' which he commenced to read. Line after line, and page after page was devoured by the convalescent wit, but not a consecutive idea could he get ... . The thought then struck him that he had lost his reason during his illness, and that he was so imbecile that he did not know it ... . When his wife returned, he thrust the mysterious volume into her hands, crying out, 'Read this, my dear!' After several attempts to make any sense of the first page or so, she returned it, saying, 'Bother the gibberish! I don't understand a word of it!' 'Thank Heaven' cried the delighted wit; 'then I am not an idiot!'[58]

The lack of participation in her husband's public life may possibly have had something to do, also, with the fact that he seems to have been unable to resist making her as much the object of his 'chaff' as anyone else when a chance offered itself and she may have found this easier to deal with in private than in public. Once, for example, when she was with him at a ball and someone asked him who she was dancing with, he replied, 'Oh, someone from the Humane Society, I believe.' Those who saw them at home and recorded Jerrold's husbandly chaff felt the need to state that Mary Ann quite entered into the spirit of the thing. According to Sydney Cooper, for example,

> Mrs Jerrold perfectly understood her husband, and they were very cordial in their relations with each other, though he often made her the butt for his jokes. He once told her that he thought a man might be allowed to treat his wife like a bank-note after she had turned forty, and change her into two twenties![59]

Speculation about Jerrold's attitude towards his wife, and hers to him, inevitably merges into some consideration of all his markedly sexist comicalities, which, like Thackeray's comic treatment of the Irish, seems to be decidedly in excess of the norm for mid-Victorian merriment on the topic. One of Jerrold's chief female admirers, Mary Cowden Clarke (he was one of her 'supremest' idols'[60]), adopts the standard 'true satirist' defence of Jerrold that we have encountered before:

> He would pour forth his keen flights of pointed arrows chiefly with the view of rousing to improvement his butt, whom he knew capable of better things ... . This was the origin of many of the sharp things he said against woman ... . He reserved to himself the right to snub the Mrs Jerichos and the Mrs Caudles among the sex, to rebuke their shrewish use of tongue, their henpeckings, their unworthy wheedling and meannesses; but he had faith in

the innate worth of womanhood, and its superiority to such baseness ... . Of woman's generous unselfishness and quiet heroism Jerrold had full perception, as we had many opportunities of noticing ...[61]

It was true that Jerrold fully bought into the contemporary 'Angel-in-the-House'-type idealisation of women, as did Mary Cowden Clarke herself. This is most clearly demonstrated in his 'Fireside Saints' series for *Punch*'s 1857 Almanack. How far this affected his domestic behaviour we cannot tell but the fact that he should get so excited about giving his wife a workbox as a special present is suggestive.[62] On the other hand, it seems pretty clear, as noted above, that he found Sarah Stickney Ellis's prescriptions for perfect wifely behaviour a fair target for mockery, hence the creation of Mrs Caudle. He seems crassly sexist when he writes to his older sister, 'It isn't your fault that you're a woman, and consequently, can with difficulty be made to understand that a journal, to be powerful and respected, must have a reputation' (she had asked him to review a friend's book which turns out to be 'arrant trash').[63] On the other hand, there is all his encouragement of young women writers and his championship of female membership of the Whittington. 'He had,' wrote Camilla Crosland, 'considerable faith in woman's capacity for intellectual pursuits, while fully recognising the difficulties under which they laboured when struggling in the battle of life.'[64] It certainly seems too simplistic to write Jerrold off as a standard mid-Victorian male chauvinist but one cannot, on the other hand, frequent his writings – especially his various series for *Punch* – without getting more than a whiff of misogyny.

Whatever Jerrold was like as a husband, he seems to have been a loving and caring father. He was deeply concerned for his elder daughter married to such an irresponsible husband as Henry Mayhew. If it is true, as Spielmann says,[65] that he refused to allow Mary to marry Henry's brother Horace on the grounds that one Mayhew in the family was quite enough, that seems entirely understandable (or he may have discouraged the relationship because of what Sutherland Edwards calls Horace Mayhew's 'peculiarity', a 'consistent tendency towards marriage, from which at the critical moment he abruptly turned away'[66]). Surviving letters from Jerrold to his younger daughter are warmly humorous and affectionate, and she was proud enough of his memory after his death to wish to create some form of memorial to him. As for the boys, Camilla Toulmin wrote that they were 'most affectionately trained, the father avowing that there were only two faults for which he should corporeally punish a boy – namely, telling a falsehood and cruelty to animals'.[67] Blanchard Jerrold's filial piety in all his writings about his father is a bit glutinous but a clear picture does emerge of a happy childhood for himself and his siblings, as does another showing Jerrold's great fondness for his grandchildren. Only Edmund, the middle son, seems to have baffled his father's efforts to settle him in life. He perhaps took after his uncle Henry, Jerrold's younger brother and the black sheep of the family.[68]

It seems right that the last word in this attempted sketch of Jerrold the private man should concern his well-attested generosity, his readiness to help friends and acquaintances by lending money, or putting his name to a bill, or commissioning work for one of his journals. 'I am myself squeezed pretty dry for a little time,' he writes to G.H. Lewes, answering to a request for a loan, 'but if my name be of any use to you for £20 for two months (you can write it off by then) 'tis humbly at your service.' In other words, Lewes can use Jerrold's credit to raise a £20 loan for two months and can work it off before that time through contributions to (probably) the *Shilling Mazagine*. Not infrequently, this signing of one's name to a friend's bill could lead to much anxiety, as readers of Victorian novels like Trollope's *Framley Parsonage* will know. A surviving letter of Jerrold's to T.K. Hervey, editor of the *Athenaeum*, about a bond that he and others had entered into three years earlier to save a brother of Hervey's from 'imminent ruin', and that is now costing him dear, probably represents many such entanglements resulting from his readiness to help those in financial straits. Blanchard Jerrold writes about the exploitation of his father's good nature by designing friends and others comment on how he injured his own journals by accepting inferior work for publication out of kindness (the help he gave R.H. Horne in this respect is a notable example). 'He was always kind to young men,' said Lemon defending him against Leech's accusation of meanness, and it was this aspect of Jerrold, his unfailing kindness and generosity, that was hidden from those persistent and vociferous critics who saw only an embittered and sneering cynic in a writer seen by so many more as the deeply caring champion of, and spokesman for, the poor and the oppressed.[69]

Chapter Fourteen

Last Plays and *Lloyd's Weekly Newspaper*

1850-1857

The year 1850 opened with Jerrold's journalistic outlets for lambasting all oppressors and neglecters of the poor confined mainly to *Punch*. He was, however, happy to find that the son-in-law who had caused him so much grief, Henry Mayhew, that 'blasted philosopher not worth a straw', was now showing himself to be a remarkable exposer of the hardships and desperate survival-strategies of the poor in the series of articles he had been writing for the *Morning Chronicle* since the previous October under the by-line of 'Our Metropolitan Correspondent'. Here was another stick, and a good stout one, with which to beat the bishops. Jerrold wrote to Mary Cowden Clarke:

> Do you read the Morning Chronicle? Do you devour those marvellous revela-
> tions of the *inferno* of misery ... smouldering under our feet? We live in a
> mockery of Xtianity that ... makes one sick. We know nothing of this terrible
> life that is about us – us, in our smug respectability. To read of the sufferings
> of the one class, and of the avarice, the tyranny, the pocket cannibalism of
> the other, – makes one almost wonder that the world should go on – that the
> misery and wickedness of the earth are not, by one almighty fiat, ended. And
> when we see the spires of pleasant Churches pointing to heaven, and are told
> – paying thousands to bishops for the glad intelligence – that we are Xtians!
> The cant of this country is enough to poison the atmosphere.[1]

He is, he says, 'very proud' that these articles, unprecedented in their 'comprehensiveness of purpose and minuteness of detail', should be being written by the man 'who married my girl'. Mayhew would, he believed, 'cut his name deep'. He mentioned the articles also to Lord Nugent, urging him to read about the 'sorrows of the doll-makers' in that day's issue of the *Chronicle*.[2] Within a few months, however, Jerrold had to recognise that, for all the energy and organisation that Mayhew was putting into his formidable detailed survey of the London poor, he had not really changed his spots. Relations between the *Chronicle*'s 'Metropolitan Correspondent' and his employers became strained, and his finances were once again in a mess. Jerrold, from the Eastbourne summer retreat where he was working on two plays for two different managers, wrote to Forster that he had to come up to London '*in re* Mayhew, whom God make wiser' and, a few days later, lamented, also to Forster, that '*Weekly News*, sons and son-in-law have finished me'.[3] (As will be seen, difficulties concerning his second and third sons, Edmund and Tom, were to be a recurrent problem during the last years of his life.) On 13 July he wrote to his eldest son that he would be in town 'on Friday and Sat/y, called there (as usual) by the folly and neglect and recklessness of Harry', adding bitterly, 'More loss of time – of money – of quiet.'[4]

Nothing much seems to be known of Jerrold's subsequent relations with Mayhew, or indeed with Jane. She herself seems never to have deserted her somewhat Micawberesque mate (would Mayhew have finally made good in Port Middlebay, one wonders?); she bore him two children, acted as his secretary and amanuensis, and for many years shared his wandering existence in Germany 'living on £300 a year'.[5] (When she died in 1880, however, she chose to be buried with her father at Norwood.) From Blanchard Jerrold we learn that by the time Jerrold was on his deathbed he and Mayhew had become completely estranged. Horace Mayhew (who had continued as a *Punch* staffer after his brother's early departure from the journal) gently asked the dying man if he was now friends with his son-in-law and received the answer, 'Yes, yes. God bless him!'

As to the cutting deep of names, Jerrold doubtless later felt he had reason to revise the optimistic view of Mayhew's potential fame he had formed reading the *Chronicle* letters, and he would have been surprised by the degree to which his original prophecy has been proved true during the last half-century. As regards his own hopes for leaving behind him a deeply-cut name, he unfortunately continued to base them on two kinds of writing that were so essentially the products of the contemporary cultural climate that they were doomed to obsolescence. They were his fanciful, 'philosophical' narrative satires, 'Clovernook' and *The Man Made of Money*, and his satirical, sub-Sheridanian 'high' comedies. He evidently set great store by the new play in this format on which he had so long been working for Webster. 'For both our sakes this must not be a failure,' he wrote at one point to the Haymarket actor-manager, adding, 'I think I am, from past experience justified in expecting from the play large success; that is, if not scrambled up.'[6] By dedicating the new comedy, entitled *The Catspaw*, to Bulwer, he was presumably seeking to align it with *Money*, the one contemporary 'high comedy' to have enjoyed both critical and commercial success. Jerrold, however, was a good deal less skilful in the matter of comic characterisation than Bulwer (himself but a pale follower of Jonson's in the Comedy of Humours tradition). And, as always, he was deficient in plot and dramatic structure, even though the very title of this new play clearly promises its audience the pleasures of a comedy of intrigue. The *Era* reviewer found some difficulty, indeed, in piecing together the story 'out of the separate characters loosely tacked together by the author', the characters themselves being 'mouthpieces that amuse, but work to no great end' (12 May 1850).

What *The Catspaw*, which opened on 9 May, did have going for it was its brilliantly talented cast, and Jerrold's by now legendary 'wit'. He had gone to work on the play in the customary way for contemporary drama-tists, that is, with his eye on the particular talents of particular actors. There was a soubrette part for Mrs Keeley, a bustling role for Wallack as a quack physician called Dr Petgoose, a virtuoso double role for Buckstone (as Appleface, a comic soldier sometimes disguising himself as Boggle, a comic lawyer) and an even more virtuoso tripartite one for Webster (as Coolcard, a confidence trickster who disguises himself first as a pedantic scholar and then as a foreign Chevalier). The *Theatrical Journal* reviewer, like other critics, found the whole production 'admirably well cast and acted' and had special praise for Webster's kaleidoscopic performance – tellingly described, however, as being 'almost entirely independent of the piece'. As to the wit, here is the verdict of the *Times* reviewer on 10 May 1850:

> The language uttered by the various characters is more than usually epi-grammatic, even for Mr Jerrold, who always writes comedy on the theory that a series of pointed repartees is absolutely essential. The 'hits' fell thick and fast, and the laughter excited by strange and unexpected similes and combinations was loud and frequent.

The *Illustrated London News* enjoyed the play as 'a comedy of conversa-tion, rather than as one of intrigue and human interest': 'We laugh at the jokes, but care little for the persons.' And 'C.M.', introducing the New York printing of the play, compares it to 'a battery, with a rapid discharge of bullet-moulded speeches upon the audiences', some of the 'hits' being local to London but with plenty of 'girding' at 'the infirmities and eccentricities of human nature generally'.[7]

As one-liners such as 'Self-defence is the clearest of all laws; and for this reason – the lawyers didn't make it', or 'Not to blush for poverty is to want a proper respect for wealth', rained down upon them, the packed first-night audience at the Haymarket on 9 May gave the play an almost unanimously rapturous reception. They would also have relished Jerrold's elaborate mockery of such 'bubbles of the day' as the contemporary fashion for medievalising ('the moon that shone on Coeur-de-lion's battle-axe – ha! that was a moon. Now our moon at the brightest, what is it? ... a pewter shilling'). There was, *The Times* noted, some 'slight opposition at the end' but 'the curtain rose, in answer to repeated acclamations' and 'after Mr Webster had announced the piece for repetition amidst loud applause, he led forward Mr Jerrold'. This tumultuous enthusiasm undoubtedly owed something to the presence in the audience of a large number of Jerrold's friends and well-wishers, but there was also a strong mustering of review-ers and of all the Dangles of the day. As the *Era* commented (with a loftiness of tone somewhat strange in a journal so devoted to the theatre):

> Mr Douglas Jerrold is known to be a clever man, and his name, which he fearlessly attaches to the announcement of the piece [why 'fearlessly', one wonders? Might the author of a literary *succès d'éstime* like *A Man Made of*

Money have been considered as going downmarket by returning to playwriting?], was a promise calculated to excite the curiosity of playgoing people, particularly the illustrissimi who make up the world of superficial literature [i.e. journalism, one presumes] to which Mr Jerrold belongs. Newspaper critics, if we may dignify them by such a title, and all the patterers who boldly write or freely talk, *pro* and *con*, of matters theatrical, mustered strong upon this occasion, manifesting to its importance.

The comedy ran for a month at the Haymarket (until 8 June) so could be accounted a moderate success.

After its opening Jerrold and Charles Knight took off on another journey in search of the picturesque. This time they went to the Lake District and visited Harriet Martineau, who accompanied them on a four-day tour of the region based on her own *Complete Guide* to the Lakes. We learn from Walter Jerrold that Jerrold's 'remarkable appearance' put her in mind of Coleridge, and that she was struck by his 'gentle and thoughtful kindness' as he tactfully ensured that she did not miss any of his *bon mots* by taking care to drop them into her far-famed ear-trumpet. And yet, she reflected, this was the man who, as the embodiment of *Punch*, had such a fearsome reputation for biting wit and withering sarcasm! To Martineau his wit always appeared 'as gentle as it was honest' and she saw no reason 'why any but knaves and fools should fear him'. One wonders, though, how much she relished his much-quoted quip about the anti-theological views she expressed the following year in a book written jointly with the mesmerist H.G. Atkinson and called *Letters on the Laws of Man's Social Nature and Development*. The book's message, said Jerrold, was: 'There is no God – and Harriet Martineau is his prophet.'

Home again in Putney, Jerrold began thinking in earnest towards two more plays he had committed himself to write, another Haymarket comedy for Webster (in three acts rather than the hallowed but cumbersome five, however) and yet another comedy, also in three acts, called *A Heart of Gold* for – surprisingly – the new manager of the Princess's Theatre in Oxford Street, Charles Kean, whom he had so long ridiculed in *Punch*. Ever since 1838 when he had aroused Macready's jealousy as a result of his success in *Hamlet* at Alfred Bunn's Drury Lane, Kean, son of the legendary Edmund, had been the object of a sustained campaign of belittlement and ridicule by Macready's friends and admirers such as Forster, Dickens and Jerrold himself.[8] For many years this kept Kean in the provinces where he built up a tremendous reputation but could still be loftily dismissed by Macready as 'that young man who goes about the country'.[9] When, however, Victoria and Albert decided in 1848 to try and give British drama a boost it was the gentlemanly, Eton-educated Kean who was chosen to organise an annual series of theatrical performances at Windsor Castle, a function he was to carry out for the next nine years. His appointment and organisation of these performances inevitably caused a good deal of jealousy and heartburning in the profession.[10] Given the history of Jerrold's merciless baiting of Kean in *Punch*, it says much for the latter's generosity of spirit that, even allowing for the bankability of Jerrold's name as a dramatist, he should have commissioned a new play from him at the going rate of £300 for three acts. Walter Jerrold notes that £100 was paid in advance as requested by Jerrold on 24 September. Later, Kean accepted on the same terms a second three-act comedy, *St Cupid*, proposed to him by Jerrold.

Jerrold found himself distracted from work on the new plays by a number of things. There was, in the first place, his regular commitment to *Punch*, and it was about this time that he contributed to that journal the first version of a phrase that quickly passed into the language as the name by which Paxton's building housing the Great Exhibition came for all time to be known. During 1850 Jerrold wrote a series for *Punch* using yet another of his comic female personae. This one was called Mrs Amelia Mouser (of 'The Honeysuckles'), a sort of joke proto-feminist, who takes 'a proper pride' in being a woman and scorns the 'hundreds of unmanly vulgar errors that the other sex invent against us'. Into her mouth Jerrold puts a series of rambling monologues, under the series title 'A Bit Of My Mind', in which she discursively comments on various events and issues of the day. In 'Bit the Eleventh' (13 July 1850) she deplores the fact that the forthcoming Great Exhibition is being planned entirely by men: 'Unless the mind of woman sets her mark upon the show, it will be nothing more than a big, selfish bachelor's party of all the world.' She describes a dream she has had of the Exhibition housed in 'a palace of very crystal, the sky looking in through every bit of the roof' (the anti-militarist Jerrold's satirical ventriloquism becomes a bit more complex when Mrs Mouser advocates holding in it 'a great Petticoat Meeting of all the World' which 'would send gunpowder out of fashion; and pluck all the armies of the earth of their feathers like geese at Michaelmas'). This 'Bit' appeared just a week after Paxton's engraving of what became the Crystal Palace was published in the *Illustrated London News* and well before his proposal had been officially accepted. As Dr Nick Fisher has suggested to me, it may well be seen as part of Mr Punch's campaign to support his good friend. Jerrold's phrase was soon picked up by others and in the early autumn the seductive name, 'the Crystal Palace', had become so current in the papers that it no longer needed to be enclosed in quotation marks.

Punch work apart, Jerrold had other matters to preoccupy him at this time including anxieties about his wife's health, moving the family to a cottage in Eastbourne for the summer and an attempted burglary at the cottage carried out by 'the Lewes gang' ('only think of the name!' he wrote to Knight). He was also struggling to get his son Edmund settled in life. Edmund, who had just come of age, seems already to have disappointed Jerrold by rejecting some proffered career help from Paxton.[11] He was, Jerrold wrote to Forster, 'healthy, strong and active' and 'rather of the stuff for the bush than for the clerk's desk'. After what seems to have been a fair amount of wire-pulling, and some anxious following-up of enquiries by his father, the young man was at last nominated by the Prime Minister, Lord

John Russell, to a post in the Commissariat Department in Canada, and departed to take up the appointment in 1852.[12]

Jerrold was evidently anxious as he returned, after a five-year gap, to the world of the theatre in which he had, over so many years, suffered so much injustice and disappointment. A great deal of both his self-esteem and his financial hopes had been riding on the new comedy, which had been so long in preparation. It is not surprising, therefore, that he reacted so strongly to a certain passage in Leigh Hunt's *Autobiography* which appeared soon after the opening of *The Catspaw*. Hunt claimed to have been told by a theatre manager that managers were afraid to reject plays written by influential journalists in case they should subsequently be ruined by press attacks on them. 'It is to be doubted,' Hunt wrote, 'whether even Douglas Jerrold, with all his popularity, and all his wit to boot, would have found the doors of a theatre opened to him with so much facility had he not been a journalist and one of the leaders in *Punch*.'[13] In the *Athenaeum* for 5 July, Jerrold angrily ridiculed the implication that Webster had staged his last two comedies out of 'timid deference' to himself as 'a leader in *Punch*' and bitterly pointed out:

> I have served full three apprenticeships to the English drama, and though even its best rewards haply fall very short of the profits of a master cotton-spinner, they have never, in my case, I can assure Mr Hunt, been levied on the fears of a manager, with a threat of 'Your stage or *my* journal'.

(Blanchard Jerrold says that his father was so disgusted that he threw away all his copies of Hunt's books as 'he could no longer believe in them'. If Jerrold did, in fact, do this, he could hardly have made a very clean sweep since some Hunt titles were still present in the sale-catalogue of his library – see above, p. 37).

Hunt, though he touched Jerrold on a raw nerve, was glancing at something that was a real problem with regard to dramatic reviewing in the Victorian age and this was the 'great anomaly', as a writer signing himself 'Audax' wrote in an open letter to Jerrold in the *Theatrical Journal* (7 March 1855) that 'the dramatic critics of the leading Journals of this island are more or less dramatic authors' so that the public might 'sigh in vain for truth, impartiality and justice'.[14] 'Audax' was remonstrating with Jerrold about his evidently personally-motivated attacks in the press on Kean both as actor and as manager (by this date Jerrold had, as we shall see, renewed and intensified his hostility to Kean).

Meanwhile, Jerrold had to look to other journalistic outlets besides *Punch* to augment his income. He wrote an allegorical fairy-tale, 'The Sick Giant and the Doctor Dwarf', for the 1850 Christmas Number of the *Illustrated London News*, where it appeared illustrated by William Harvey. Its sentimental-Liberal message was clear. Bakkuk, the ignorant and inarticulate giant whose sufferings drive him to destructive frenzy, is succoured and educated by the wise dwarf Zim when all his fellow-dwarves want only to crush the dangerous monster. Zim holds that 'it is nobler to reform than to destroy' and, through compassionate kindness and instruction, reforms the 'brute mass of power' that is Bakkuk (i.e. the British proletariat) and sets him to constructive work:

> And thus the labours of the Giant filled the island with blessings; and the Giant was blessed in the reward of his labours – in the wages of respect and love he enjoyed of his masters. They had taught him the true dignity of life; and while he ministered to their higher delights, they repaid him with gentleness and affection.

The first Jerrold play to be seen on the London stage the following year, the Great Exhibition year of 1851, came, in fact, not from the pen of Douglas but from that of Blanchard, who scored a hit at Madame Vestris's Lyceum with a one-act farce entitled *Cool As A Cucumber*. This was written as a vehicle for Vestris's partner Charles Mathews the Younger, who specialised in airy light-comedy roles like that of Dazzle, the role he created in Boucicault's *London Assurance. Cool As A Cucumber* opened to good notices on 24 March and played continuously till at least 5 April, and was still in the theatre's repertory at the end of May.[15] Blanchard was one son whose future career Jerrold did not have to worry about, even though his finances did give occasional cause for concern. He was already an established journalist, having been a staffer on the *Daily News*, and was now writing regularly for the *Weekly News*. During 1847-48, moreover, he had, as already noted, published a novel, *The Disgrace to the Family: a Story of Social Distinctions* (in six monthly parts, with illustrations by 'Phiz') which, according to J.C. Jeaffreson writing in 1858, had 'attracted much attention'.[16] He had wanted to follow this up with a three-volume 'political satire against Ultra-Radicalism' to be called *The Man Of The People* but the publisher Frederic Shoberl, to whom he offered it in November 1849, must have turned it down. He was surely on to a much better thing now in 1851 when Bradbury and Evans accepted for publication his guide-book *How To See The Exhibition*.[17]

Jerrold's new comedy for Webster, *Retired from Business*, opened at the Haymarket on 3 May 1851. Like Blanchard's novel, it satirised what Blanchard had called in the preface to his novel 'the emptiness of certain widely condemned and widely practiced distinctions, alike petty and provocative of social discord'. Jerrold sets his play in the agreeable village of Pumpkinfield, full of retired London merchants and tradesmen, and satirises the petty snobbery that causes the 'billocracy' (the merchants and their families) to snub and shun the 'tillocracy' (the tradesmen and their families). Such plot as there is involves the negotiation of these social barriers by two pairs of young lovers and the efforts of the wife of a former London greengrocer, Mrs Pennyweight, to pass herself and her family off as part of the 'billocracy' (she recruits a footman and alters the family name to Fitzpennyweight). Once again, there were meaty, broad-comedy character-parts for Webster, Buckstone and Wallack. Also in the cast was the vivacious comedienne Mrs Fitzwilliam, sister of Jerrold's brother-in-law, the Liverpool manager William Copeland. Like Madame Vestris though not on the same scale, Mrs Fitzwilliam was celebrated both for her personal attractions and for her skills as a comic actress, and, like Vestris, she had often played breeches roles. She did so here again, taking the part of the more important of the two male lovers. Since she was by this time 50 years old it is perhaps not surprising that the *Era*, reviewing the production on 4 May 1851, should ungallantly have found her performance as 'an enamoured youth' unsatisfactory 'because of physical developments, which, by this time, should in our humble opinion, keep her out of breeches'.

Apart from a fierce attack in the *Leader* (10 May 1851) by G.H. Lewes, addressed directly to Jerrold and telling him that that this was '*not* a comedy worthy of your powers' ('Don't talk to me about Friendship; if one can't speak the truth to one's friends, to whom can it be spoken?'), the critical reception of *Retired from Business* was very like that of its predecessor and along lines that must by now have been tediously familiar to Jerrold. Unstinted praise for his 'brilliant' witty dialogue was accompanied by regrets that he could neither construct a neat plot nor create 'truthful' characters (the idea that these might be conflicting desiderata never seems to have occurred to the reviewers): 'a hundred pointed, and even witty remarks, do not compensate for the absence of interest, which nothing but truth, as we really find it in human nature, can give.' Some reviewers, however, took comfort in the inclusion among the dramatis personae of the charmingly innocent young lovers and in the morally uplifting (not to say sanctimonious) tailpiece to this play,[18] quite unlike the satirical ending of *The Catspaw*. This reassured them that Jerrold the allegedly 'bitter' satirist and ironist was in actual fact 'much more a writer of kindliness than of satire' and a man who sympathised with 'all that is wise and good in humanity'.[19]

The *Times* reviewer was one of those thus comforted and it is worth quoting his notice more fully since it sets out the reasons (patriotic as much as literary, it almost seems) why Jerrold was held in such high esteem as a playwright in the 1840s and 1850s.

Mr Jerrold is the most thoroughly English writer now working for the stage, and while he has all the luxuriant fancy and vigour of language which belongs to our old prose dramatists, he has also in common with them that looseness of construction which the French have ever avoided. But balance the account fairly, and where shall we find his equal among the playwriters of the day? If he is ever occasionally led from the path of probability, it is by the sport of an unequalled fancy; if his personages, like those of Congreve, utter more good things than is consistent with their position, let us bear in mind that they are 'good things' notwithstanding; and if he has not the quality of neatness in point of construction, he has other qualities, which though they do less towards forming the finished dramatist, are truer exponents of the poetical nature [i.e., demonstrate more accurately Jerrold's gifts as a literary artist].

Bulwer also came out with a new comedy this year, a full-blown five-act 'high' one, set in the coffee-house London of the late 17th century and called *Not So Bad As We Seem*, but it was not intended for the commercial theatre. Bulwer wrote it for Dickens's Amateur Players, who had already been re-assembled the previous November at Knebworth, Jerrold among them, to perform *Every Man In His Humour* again. This new burst of activity on the Amateurs' part was to support a new scheme, grandly named 'The Guild of Literature and Art', which Bulwer and Dickens were trying to set up for the sake of helping impoverished writers and artists. Bulwer's play, with its picturesque setting, star part for Dickens (obviously) and tailor-made ones for other leading amateurs such as Forster and Jerrold ('Mr Shadowly Softhead'), was intended to be a great fundraiser. It had its first performance on 16 May, at Devonshire House in Piccadilly before the Queen, Court and a highly fashionable audience, with the actors being shown upstairs by liveried footmen with epaulettes of silver bullion. 'All acted well,' wrote the Queen, 'Dickens (the celebrated author) admirably, and Dr Jerrold, a funny little man who writes in "Punch" extremely well ... The dresses and scenery were beautiful.'[20] (Sadly, Jerrold never knew about the honorary doctorate thus conferred on him by Royalty.) At the ball and supper given afterwards by the Duke of Devonshire to the players and members of the audience, Jerrold seems to have become somewhat over-excited by mingling with so many high-class beauties and, if Horne as reported by Walter Jerrold is to be believed, was not contented with mere silent indulgence in what we would today call 'the male gaze': he

> moved hastily about, his large eyes gleaming as if in a walking vision; and when he suddenly came upon any of the 'Guild' he uttered glowing and racy ejaculations, at which some laughed, while others felt disposed to share his raptures.

Horne does not, alas, give us any specimens of Jerrold's 'racy ejaculations'.

Other performances of the play followed during 1851 both in London and in the country. Jerrold is supposed to have remarked of this production, '"Not so bad as we seem" but a great deal worse than we ought to be', but this surely was a joke about the Amateur Players' acting rather than one directed at the play itself. Bulwer's 'high' comedy would hardly have struck him, any more than it would have done Dickens, as being the preposterous farrago of high-flown nonsense that we might well deem it today.

Meanwhile, his by now established position as one of England's foremost literary figures was confirmed by the announcement that Bradbury and Evans were to begin issuing a collected *Writings of Douglas Jerrold* in three-halfpenny weekly and sevenpenny monthly numbers from January 1851, a project eventually completed in eight volumes, price four shillings each, in June 1854. Pride of place was given to *St Giles and St James* which inaugurated the edition and the two final volumes consisted of selected plays (nothing earlier than *The Rent Day* was included apart from *Black Eyed Susan*; the 'illegitimate' productions of the 'sorry Shakespeare' were buried in oblivion).

That Jerrold's income was by no means proportionate to his fame was also a fact, however. Apart from his *Punch* salary and the notoriously meagre earnings that still were all that even a successful dramatist could expect, he had no regular income and still needed freelance commissions, like the *Illustrated London News* Christmas story, to keep his pot boiling. He seems, on the evidence of a letter to Eliza Cook dated only 'June 6' but most probably belonging to this period, to have written for *Eliza Cook's Journal* which began in 1849 ('Dear Miss Cook, / You have, I fear, paid me liberal wages very far in advance – I can hardly hope to live to earn half their value'[21]). And he was generally on the look-out for other openings. There is a definite undercurrent of seriousness in the following jocose letter to the comic artist Alfred Henry Forrester, alias 'Crowquill', which presumably related to some joint project proposed by the artist:

> West Lodge Putney Lower Common
> Feb: 2: 1852
>
> My dear Crowquill,
> What will you have? If I could think of something very brilliant – the most brilliant – it should be at your service; as I cannot, you must take that which is the most dull, and that is
> Yours (nevertheless truly)
> Douglas Jerrold

Accompanying the letter is the following slip:

> Douglas Jerrold salutes the shoe-tie of Alfred Crowquill!!
> The 'whereabout' of DJ is as above; and he takes this opportunity of 'assuring his best friend the public and its publishers' that he 'continues to do' all sorts of literary jobs 'with dispatch, punctuality and on very liberal terms.'[22]

It is interesting to contrast the jokiness of this, with its undercurrent of bitterness, with the serene loftiness of his self-description in the 1851 Census. There he wrote against the 'Rank/Profession/Occupation' slot: 'Literature, Drama, Novels, Essays'.

The winter of 1851/52 was a trying one for Jerrold in his personal life. He was laid low by a bad bout of 'flu in November, apologising to Forster on the 29th for not having seen him that week: 'I passed the first 3 days in bed, and am now so exhausted, I feel *nowhere*. I never knew influenza in its might before.' Then Mary Ann fell ill and Jerrold wrote on 12 December to Hepworth Dixon (with whom he had developed a close friendship by this time) to cancel a Christmas invitation: 'My wife remains so ill – she *has* been *very* ill – that I have no expectation of the probability of her being able to play hostess on the 25th.' Shortly afterwards, he was summoned to his brother-in-law's home in Liverpool to see his seventy-six-year-old mother whom he found, he told Dickens, 'in a condition all but hopeless'. He came back to act in *Not So Bad As We Seem* at Reading on 23 December and on New Year's Day received the news that Mary Jerrold had died – 'a somewhat sudden visitation', he wrote to Forster, 'tho she had long been ailing'.[23] These references to his mother in the last days of her life seem, like Dickens's a few years later, to be remarkably unemotional, and when he writes to thank Wilkie Collins on 6 January for his 'charming little book' (*Rambles Beyond Railways*, 1851), he does not even specify that it is his mother who has died, saying merely, 'I have had a sudden loss which must explain the postponement of our too-long-deferred meeting at the Club.'[24] It is, of course, always dangerous to build up too much biographical speculation on the basis of a few scanty bits of evidence and the absence of other bits (in this case any evidence at all that Mary Jerrold participated in the domestic or public life of her celebrated son) but it would certainly seem clear that she played no significant role in his adult life.[25]

In the spring of 1852 a very big 'literary job' came along, one that was to last Jerrold for the remaining five years of his life, and which, although he was never to be completely free of financial anxieties (for one thing, the debt that he had contracted as a result of the collapse of *Douglas Jerrold's Weekly Newspaper* still remained unpaid), certainly placed him in far easier circumstances than he had ever been in before. He was invited to become the editor of *Lloyd's Weekly Newspaper* by that paper's energetic and enterprising proprietor Edward Lloyd.

Lloyd had first struck it rich in the later 1830s by publishing cheap part-issue imitations of Dickens like *The Penny Pickwick* or *Oliver Twiss*, as well as sensational pulp fiction with titles like *The Maniac Father* and *Ada the Betrayed*. Sala, one of Dickens's 'young men' (journalistic protégés), quotes a comment that Lloyd supposedly scribbled on an illustration Sala had submitted for one of these novelettes: 'The eyes must be larger, and there must be more blood – much more blood!'[26] Lloyd moved into newspaper publishing in 1842 with *Lloyd's Illustrated London Newspaper* priced at the astonishingly low figure of two pence (*The Times* cost seven pence), thus putting 'regular, hard news within range of the lower classes again'.[27] By 1851 the price had increased to threepence and the name of the journal had been changed to *Lloyd's Weekly Newspaper*. *Mitchell's Newspaper Press Directory* for 1851 described it as 'Democratic and Anti-Poor-Law' and as appealing to the million 'on the two great principles of cheapness and quality'. 'Peculiarly the poor man's paper', it gives prominence to police reports and 'similar matters of *popular* interest' but presents 'an immense mass of matter for the money ... so that even if its readers saw no other paper, they would not be much behind the rest of the world as to news'. Its great rival, *Reynolds' Weekly Newspaper*, established in 1850 by an extraordinary gentleman-Chartist and republican,

G.W.M. Reynolds, whose sensational and melodramatic *feuilletons* like *The Mysteries of London* far outsold any of Lloyd's titles, was published at the same price. But the violent politics of Reynolds, that 'ruffian' as Jerrold called him, that 'Pandar to the basest passions of the lowest natures' as Dickens (whom he also much outsold) called him,[28] would have repelled the 'respectable' working-class or lower-middle-class readers that Lloyd was seeking to cultivate. *Lloyd's Weekly Newspaper*, writes Virginia Berridge in her *Popular Journalism and Working-class Attitudes 1854-1886*,[29] was

> the preserve of the shopkeeping, small property-owning classes ... householders and small landlords ... [some] skilled working men ... a large number of female readers, carried over perhaps, despite Edward Lloyd's attempts to alter the paper's image, from his earlier serial publications. Female clothing workers took the paper in its first years ... later on ... their place was taken by girl servants.

Its circulation had been steadily rising since 1843 and in 1850 stood at 49,000.[30]

Lloyd's decision to ask so prominent a member of the liberal wing of the literary establishment as Jerrold to become the editor of his paper can only, as Hoggart puts it, 'be seen as a determined bid for respectability on Lloyd's part'.[31] It is also, of course, a clear sign of the extent of Jerrold's popularity among lower-middle and lower-class readers. Jerrold demurred at first, pleading his prior commitment to *Punch*, but came to terms when Lloyd proposed a salary of £1,000 a year; his only stipulation was that it should be paid to him at the rate of £20 per week. (We might recall here, for purposes of comparison, that the salary Dickens demanded, and got, in 1845 for editing a daily paper was £2,000; this clearly shows what a very high value Lloyd put on Jerrold's services.) In the 11 April 1852 issue of *Lloyd's* appeared the announcement that 'the Proprietor has availed himself of the very valuable services of DOUGLAS JERROLD ESQ as from next Sunday' and thereafter the legend 'EDITED BY DOUGLAS JERROLD' appears in large type on the front page of each issue which had previously featured no editorial name. Lloyd was an amazingly energetic and resourceful advertiser of his wares and made sure that Jerrold's name was very prominent in all the many advertisements for his paper. It is interesting to note, also, that Mitchell's description of the paper in his 1854 *Directory* is word for word the same as it had been in 1851 except that the sentence 'It is peculiarly the poor man's paper' is replaced by 'It is under the editorship of Mr Jerrold'.

As we have seen, Blanchard joined his father on the paper and so, later on, did Jerrold's problem son Edmund, who seems to have soon abandoned his Canadian appointment and gone in for a journalistic career.[32] Horace Mayhew also wrote for the paper as did Hepworth Dixon, who was commissioned to write the kind of fancifully-titled column of miscellaneous news items and brief comments that Jerrold seemed to have regarded as a *sine qua non* for any journal, like 'The Button-holder' in the *Illuminated* and *Douglas Jerrold's Weekly Newspaper*. Here it is called 'Cock-crow'. Jerrold himself wrote, according to one of his editorial successors, Thomas Catling, 'about three columns of leaders each week, and also the literary reviews'.[33] Vizetelly comments that the increase in the sales of the paper under Jerrold's editorship 'was something remarkable'.[34] According to Catling, however, there was no increase during the first six months, and it was the reporting of the death and funeral of the Duke of Wellington in the autumn that sent the circulation soaring to 150,000 a week after which it still continued to rise.[35] Thackeray wrote to Percival Leigh on 12 April 1854:

> F.P. [the comic journalist and former 'Fraserian' Francis Mahony whose pen name was 'Father Prout'] was telling me of the immense rise of Lloyds Newspaper, under the Douglas, by Jupiter I am very glad to hear it: and am quite pleased at myself at finding myself pleased at men getting on in the world. Please the Gods D J will lay by a little money. What's the business of us fathers of families but that? ... [36]

It may have been true that Lloyd was, as Vizetelly says, something of a vulgarian, 'glad to get the few literary men connected with his paper to tuck their legs under his dinner-table at his country house in Essex', and to regale them with his 'fiery wines' and 'abominable port'. No doubt he was delighted to hear it said that his very downmarket newspaper had been 'annexed to literature' by Jerrold.[37] It seems clear, however, that he inspired in his new editor a real personal affection. According to Blanchard, his father 'spoke of Mr Lloyd, on his deathbed, with the utmost tenderness, and begged to be most heartily remembered to him'.[38] Blanchard comments also that Jerrold 'found unmixed pleasure' in this last journalistic undertaking of his literary life – which is hardly surprising in that he had overall editorial control of the paper but did not need to worry himself about any of the business aspects of the enterprise.

Indicative of Jerrold's changed financial circumstances was an announcement in the *Builder* of 26 June 1852 of a tender for 'A Mansion for Mr Douglas Jerrold at Barnes, Mr T. Allom, architect' (Jerrold had been, according to Allom's obituary in the *Builder* [1872] among the architect's 'early companions and valued friends', along with Orrin Smith, Kenny Meadows and Mark Lemon).[39] Tenders received for the work ranged from £1,332 to £1,710 but it was not proceeded with, perhaps because Jerrold, who was spending the summer in temporary accommodation in Hastings, decided that he needed a new home more quickly – also, probably, one within easier reach of central London than Barnes. In October he moved his household into one of the pretty semi-detached villas in Circus Road, St John's Wood. In *The London Encyclopaedia* (1983) Weinreb and Hibbert describe St John's Wood at this time as having an 'idyllic' character:

> The calm, the variety and charm of the comparatively inexpensive houses ... and the convenience of its proximity to London, combined with the purity of

the air, made this an area chosen and inhabited by artists, authors, philoso-
phers and scientists as well as by more prosaic members of the middle
classes.

The Jerrolds were well established in their new home by 3 January 1853
when the head of the family hosted a party to celebrate his fiftieth
birthday. Hodder records him as having been 'in remarkably good health
and spirits' and the evening as having been 'one of the merriest' he had
ever passed in Jerrold's company; according to Walter Jerrold, it was so
much enjoyed by one of the guests, the sculptor Edward Hodges Baily, that
he determined to make a marble bust of Jerrold. Now in the National
Portrait Gallery, this bust is an idealised portrayal presenting its subject
as a sort of cross between a Roman consul and a handsome young hero of
the French Revolution with flowing, swept-back hair, a high 'intellectual'
forehead, large eyes, and a firm-set mouth.

The image of Jerrold that at least his more middle-class readers in
Lloyd's are more likely to have had in their minds would also have
incorporated the mane of hair, but it but would have been of the tiny, bent
figure with leonine head and dangling eyeglass familiar from cartoons in
Punch. And there was, as James Fitzjames Stephen sourly noted in a
survey of the Sunday newspapers in the *Saturday Review*, a continuity
between Jerrold's *Lloyd's* editorials and his longer articles in *Punch*. All
Jerrold's leaders, wrote Stephen on 19 April 1856,

> have a strong family likeness to those dreary serious articles which are
> familiar to readers of *Punch* – articles which read like sermons which were
> originally unctuous, but which have had gall substituted for the unction,
> without however, entirely, removing all traces of the original condiment.
> They are a constant series of growls ... . One characteristic sentence will
> illustrate the sort of writing to which we allude – we all know where endless
> columns of the same material may be had: – 'Austria's coat is for the present
> white, white as her liver – who knows how soon it may be red, red as her
> crimes?'

Stephen, who was later in the year (1 November) to lambast the Caudle
Lectures in the same journal, was deeply antipathetic towards Jerrold
politically and detested his style which, he asserted, was of a sort that
made sense only when affected by upper-class writers, being 'deeply
imbued with the bitter contemptuous cynicism which nothing can excuse,
but which the satiety arising from high social position might enable us to
understand'. In the passage just quoted he picks out, perhaps deliberately,
a particularly mechanical example of Jerroldian 'wit' but his main point
about the continuity of the *Lloyd's* leaders with Jerrold's *Punch* writings
is a valid one, however unsympathetically put. And, as appears from the
paper's circulation history, this rhetoric was as much relished by the
lower-class readers of *Lloyd's* as it had long been by the middle-class
readers of *Punch* (Stephen imagines the typical reader of a Sunday news-

paper as 'a man who has passed six days of the week in carting parcels from one railway station to another, in unloading ships, in watching the wheels of a machine, or in any other mechanical occupation').

Jerrold's *Punch* readers would certainly have felt very much at home with the first issue of *Lloyd's* published under his editorship. A front-page leader headed 'The Inapproachable Bishops' attacked the Bishop of Bath for endorsing the Marchioness of Bath's presentation of a notoriously Puseyite (High Church) priest to the living of Frome in Somerset. A second leader inside the paper ridiculed Sir Fitzroy Kelly, the Conservative Solicitor-General, as 'the Cabinet Conjurer' for making a somewhat contorted speech opposing Free Trade: 'the state fool is a thing of the past; but the Cabinet Conjurer – Fire-Eater – tumbler – Sleight-of-Hand Man flourishes among us!' And the 'Answers to Correspondents'[40] column includes a long and scathing denunciation of the perfunctory funerals accorded to those who died in workhouses and the 'disgraceful system of harrying paupers to their graves like dogs' (the situation would seem to have changed little since Dickens had satirised it a quarter-century before, in chapter five of *Oliver Twist*). The pre-Jerroldian, more sensationalist, *Lloyd's* is also still very much present in this issue, however. Three and a half columns of detailed description are devoted to a particularly gruesome case of matricide in Kennington, and there are numerous other accounts of 'horrible murders/suicides'. By 1856, however, this kind of reporting had been very considerably toned down in *Lloyd's* as in all the Sunday papers, and James Stephen noted with satisfaction in his review-article there was very little indeed in any of them 'which a man would feel inclined to skip if he were reading aloud to his wife or daughter' (his survey did not, incidentally, include *Reynolds' Weekly Newspaper* – no doubt he considered it to be simply beyond the pale).

One can get a good sense of Jerrold's editorial writings in *Lloyd's* from a collection of them for the first two years of his editorship made by Blanchard Jerrold in 1868.[41] Hailed by the *Illustrated London News* as 'a text-book for advanced Liberals',[42] this compilation contains frequent attacks on the aristocratic monopoly of political power and the fruits of office ('Lord Whig and Lord Tory have had a long, long sitting at the loaves and fishes. Suppose, if only for a trial, a penny loaf or so, with a few of the smallest sprats were given to the Men of the People'). There is much support for Richard Cobden, and for such measures as Gladstone's budget of 1853, acclaimed as 'the poor man's budget' in that it removed or reduced taxes on many such basic goods as fruit, cheese, soap, tea and so on. What Jerrold saw as the down side of the budget was the continuation and extension of the intrusive and inequitable Income Tax, that 'mean, tyrannical impost ... contemptuously [denying] to see any difference between a clerk on 300*l.* a year and ... Mr Gladstone's "bloated fundholder" with 10,000*l.* hoarded and fructifying in the Bank of England'.[43] The Protectionist Tory leader Lord Derby, an 'emblazoned Earl', is contrasted with Peel, 'the Spinner's son who has given us the blessings of cheap and plenteous food'. The campaign for a secret ballot is strongly supported since under the present system 'a general election does more to corrupt and degrade tens of thousands of Englishmen, than any political operation soever'. The Government's plan to demolish the Crystal Palace ('emphatically the People's Palace') is denounced as a purely class measure (stemming partly from aristocratic families whose mansions are adjacent to Hyde Park: 'Lady Stonehenge will not have the rabble continually swarming, with their wives and brats, before her windows'). Another aspect of Jerrold's populism, his anti-Sabbatarianism, is not much represented in this collection but it was prominent enough in his *Lloyd's* editorialising to provoke someone calling himself 'a Biblical Economist' to publish a remonstrance, addressed to Jerrold as 'one of the Pillars of our literary temple'.[44]

Many editorials were devoted to foreign affairs. Jerrold continued to champion such European liberal and nationalist heroes as Kossuth and Mazzini. He abated nothing of his hostility towards Austrian tyranny (exemplified by the expulsion of the Swiss from the Ticino) and towards Louis Napoleon, first as President of the Second Republic and then as Napoleon III ('the very type of human treason ... possessed as with an evil spirit, with the belief that to him is appointed the destiny of avenging the defeat of France'). Jerrold's intense patriotism flames out in his celebration of Wellington, whom he sees as having become 'the embodied assurance to all men of the might, the forethought, and the serene grandeur of Britain', and it is constantly linked with his passion for the Navy, 'that girdle of floating wood and iron round England', which 'has achieved its victorious greatness in spite of the venality, the absurdity, and the ignorance of the men who, for generations, have controlled it'. When Mazzini, after the failure of the Italian uprising, was rescued by a British warship, Jerrold's rhetoric soared to fit the occasion – and may echo uncomfortably in our ears today for more reasons than one:

> Yes; thank God, a British man-of-war *is* an Ark of Refuge! Thank God, the British oak *is* sacred wheresoever it may float. Still a part of England; still it carried with it the blessings of the English soil that developed the forest-giant from an acorn – in its slow growth and vastness, and unbending strength, a glorious type of English freedom. ... a part and parcel of this glorious land, whose greatest glory is her protection of the hapless fugitive ... .

(The modulation from the grandly imperial 'British' to the sturdily ancient 'English' is also worth noting.)

His long-standing anti-militarism notwithstanding, Jerrold welcomed the Crimean War. If ever there was a Just War this was it. 'Never since men resorted to the terrible arbitration of the sword – never was the weapon grasped by a purer or juster hand than the weapon now drawn by England.' Czar Nicholas I was 'an evil principle, warring against the true dignity of the human race ... an incarnate plague that would visit with moral death and desolation the liberty of the whole world' (2 April 1854). *Lloyd's* was contemptuous of Bright's Peace campaign, supportive of Lord Raglan, and not very responsive to W.H. Russell's sensational *Times* reports of the catastrophic mismanagement of the War by the British High Command during the winter of 1854/55 (a relatively mild leader of 21 January advocated 'more corporals and less coronets'). Jerrold was severely critical of the Peace Treaty Armistice signed on 1 April 1856. His loathing of Napoleon III was almost as great as his loathing of Russian despotism and he argued that France was gaining a great deal as a result of the War and paying very little for it whereas Britain was gaining nothing and yet paying an enormous bill:

> Some tens of thousands of brave men will have been laid in their early graves; some thousands of widows made desolate, some thousands of orphans left fatherless – and for what? Why, for the further security of France: for the stronger consolidation of Louis Napoleon's power, and for the final alliance of France with Russia; ... John Bull in the [peace] conference is the same John Bull he was at Eton; and as a matter of course and custom, pays for the rod that birches him. (30 March 1856)

There is nothing in *Lloyd's* akin to Dickens's scathing satire in *Household Words* on the whitewashing of Lords Lucan and Cardigan at the Chelsea Board of Enquiry, only some mockery of municipal fêting of Cardigan as a hero of the Crimea and the jeer that 'peers and the sons of peers have escaped by the prescribed privilege that allows aristocrats to plunder and blunder' (10 August 1856).

Jerrold's combination of aggressive nationalism in foreign affairs involving strong support for European liberal nationalists and his constant championship of the rights and virtues of the English masses against the domination of Church and Aristocracy went down well with the ever-increasing readership of *Lloyd's*. But he needed always to keep a good expanse of clear blue water (a modern political cliché he would surely have delighted in) between himself and the Radical politics of G.W.M. Reynolds's rival organ. A surviving letter written to Forster from Boulogne in September 1856 enables us to catch him in the act:

> I have directed that an early Friday's copy of my paper should be sent to you. If you've time to look at it, and liking it, will quote somewhat of what I've written on Frost, you will much oblige me. I wish very much to obliterate a still lingering notion that I fear may exist as to the ultra-democratic tendencies of the paper; and a quotation from the aforesaid in the *Ex* [*The Examiner*] would do much I am sure to effect this. ...[45]

John Frost (1784-1877) was a Welsh Chartist leader who had been sentenced first to death, then to transportation for life, for high treason as a result of leading an armed band into Newport during the disturbances there in 1839. Pardoned in 1854 but not allowed to return to Britain, he toured America lecturing and publishing on the evil effects of aristocratic rule on the government of Britain. In 1856 he received a full pardon and returned home. The middle-class Chartist leader and poet Ernest Jones arranged a triumphal reception for him in London on 15 September and Jerrold pours vicious scorn on both Frost himself (a 'graceless, incorrigible brawler [spitting] in the face of mercy'), Jones, and the whole event in a two-column front-page leader in *Lloyd's* on 21 September. It is clearly Frost's association with revolutionary political activity that rouses Jerrold's rhetorical fury (pumped up, evidently, by the anxiety to distance his paper from any such association) and he notes with horror the presence in the procession honouring Frost of 'French ruffians and desperadoes' carrying 'a *crimson* banner with on one side the inscription, "Liberty, Equality, and Fraternity" and on the other "République, Democratique et Sociale"'. Why not, asks Jerrold, carry a working model of the guillotine and have done with it?

He excuses the length of his diatribe on the grounds that 'it is especially at the hands of such men [as Frost] that true liberty suffers':

> They only defile what they affect to worship. By vain brawling, they lead away certain of the industrious classes whose political rights, in their fullest operation, are to be obtained by self-culture and self-respect.

Certainly, all this should have fully reassured any nervous readers of *Lloyd's* that they need not be apprehensive about any 'ultra-democratic tendencies' arising in the paper.

Jerrold's devotion to *Lloyd's* is emphasised by Blanchard Jerrold. He reports that only severe bouts of illness such as his father suffered in early 1854 when he was all but blind, 'hardly [able to] distinguish the wall from the window', stopped him writing for the paper. Later that year Jerrold took a brief sabbatical in order to go with his wife and the Hepworth Dixons on a trip to France and Switzerland (the Austrian Consul in London refused him a visa for Italy, which prompted the caustic comment, 'That shows your weakness, not my strength'). At such times Blanchard would assume the editorship and it must have been an enormous relief and comfort to Jerrold to have had such a reliable and handy coadjutor in his own eldest son.

The youngest son Tom seems, on the other hand, to have resembled Edmund in being a cause of some worry to his father. He failed to pay his tailor's bill, even though he had been sent the money to do so, and Jerrold found himself the recipient of what he considered a 'grossly impertinent' solicitor's letter that brought out all his prickly sense of achieved social status ('even an attorney', he responded, 'might possibly write as a gentleman'[46]). Tom went later to Liverpool to stay with his aunt and uncle, Elizabeth and William Copeland. Mrs Copeland arranged for him to go as a farming pupil to a Mr Longton, on terms that seemed to Jerrold somewhat exorbitant. He wanted Tom to go there as quickly as possible, however. In a letter to his sister quoted by Walter Jerrold he writes that Tom, 'has wasted time enough; and I can only hope that he will not add another year to the years he has already dawdled away':

> It is necessary that Tom should know ... that the year being out he must depend upon his own exertions. I have his mother and sister to provide for (and my health is none of the strongest) in the event of what may come at any moment.

But Tom was still on his father's hands a year later, in 1856, and Jerrold wrote to Paxton for help in getting him a job somewhere in the country:

> he can't bear London; nor is it prudent that an unoccupied young man should be open to its temptations ... for his sake, even more than for mine, it is necessary that at his age he should be self-supporting.[47]

'My health is none of the strongest.' Jerrold's well-founded anxieties about his own physical condition, and about the future financial security of his wife and unmarried daughter, perhaps made him even touchier than usual, so helping to ignite or to fuel the public row with Charles Kean that led to his disgusted definitive withdrawal from all participation in the contemporary theatre industry. This row, it has to be said, reflects little credit on Jerrold; indeed, it shows him at his vindictive worst (we should bear in mind also that long history of Kean-baiting in *Punch* that has already been mentioned). It would be merely tedious to rehearse this long-forgotten quarrel in any detail so what follows is an attempt to summarise the matter.

Of the two three-act plays that Jerrold wrote for Kean (and for which he had been paid the going rate) it was the second, *St Cupid; or Dorothy's Fortune*, that was produced first, having been chosen (it is not clear by whom) for presentation before the Queen at Windsor on 21 January 1853. Victoria was very much amused. The play, a slight romantic comedy relating to the Jacobite plot of 1715, was, she wrote in her Journal, 'very pretty' and it was 'admirably given'. She praised especially Ellen Kean, Harley and, above all, Edward Wright, whose impersonation of 'Queen Bee', an old Gipsy woman, 'kept us in fits of laughter'.[48] Her only regret was that the play was 'almost too short'. Jerrold was not present. On his dignity as a literary man, he was offended at not being invited to attend and brusquely refused Kean's offer to 'take him under his wing' and arrange for him to watch the performance from the wings.[49] Kean subsequently produced the play at the Princess's Theatre in repertory with *Macbeth* and Boucicault's melodrama *The Corsican Brothers* (*St Cupid* was given thirty-one times up to the end of April) but it attracted only poor houses and Kean failed to recoup his expenses. Jerrold's play was, wrote F.C. Wemyss in his prefatory 'Remarks' to the New York printing of the text, rather old-fashioned, wanting in 'everything that a comedy of the present day should have, but brilliancy of dialogue'.[50]

In April Kean asked Jerrold about 'the Nautical Drama' for which he had advanced him £100 a year earlier. Jerrold flatly denied that the play had been intended to be nautical ('I have had enough of nautical pieces by which fortunes have been made by others, and comparatively twopence-halfpenny by your humble servant'), and promptly paid back Kean's advance, plus interest. He also complained that the first play he had written for Kean, *A Heart of Gold*, still remained unproduced. An increasingly acrimonious correspondence followed in which justice and accuracy of remembrance (as well as reason and moderation in language) seem to have been mostly, not to say wholly, on Kean's side.[51] When he finally staged the play a year later (9 October 1854) Kean did not play the major role Jerrold had written for him but gave it to another well-known actor, John Ryder. Jerrold had violently objected to this change – with some inconsistency, we might think, given his constant mockery of Kean's acting – and accused Kean of breaking faith with him. The play, once again set in the inevitable 18th century, this time in rural Essex, features characters with names like Nutbrown, Michaelmas and Yewberry and turns on a flimsy love-plot. E.L. Blanchard, who attended the first night, commented that it was 'not one of Jerrold's best – House very full but not very enthusiastic'.[52]

Jerrold, who until the late summer of 1853 had been praising in *Lloyd's* both Kean's acting and his productions at the Princess's (though continuing to lampoon him anonymously in *Punch*) now switched to regularly attacking him and all his works. For this, and for similar attacks on E.T. Smith, the manager of Drury Lane,[53] Jerrold was himself fiercely criticised by 'B.W.W.' and 'Audax' in the *Theatrical Journal* ('The Scurrility of Jerrold', 8 February 1854; 'More Jerroldian Quacking!!', 15 March 1854; 'Mr Charles Kean and Mr Douglas Jerrold. In the Form of an Epistle to the latter Gentleman', 7 March 1855).[54] Jerrold's onslaughts on Kean included accusations that the latter was, in his double capacity of star actor and manager, both monopolising and profiteering from the Windsor theatricals ('Jerrold worked himself into a white heat over the matter, which gave the Queen the deepest annoyance and pain', recalled William Bodham Donne, Examiner of Plays from 1857[55]).

On 14 October 1854 in a *Lloyd's* article entitled '"A Heart of Gold" at the Princess's' Jerrold suddenly announced his 'farewell to all dramatic doings'. He indignantly related the history of his quarrel with Kean, explaining why he finally felt himself obliged to communicate with him only through solicitors.[56] Of Kean's production of *A Heart of Gold* he wrote (creating, deliberately or inadvertently, confusion as to whether or not he himself had actually attended a performance):[57]

> Yet it is under such wilful injuries [as changing the originally-planned cast] committed by management that a drama is, nevertheless, to be buoyant! It is through such a fog of player's brain that the intention of the author is to shine clearly forth. With a certain graceful exception, there never was so

much bad acting as in 'A Heart of Gold.' Nevertheless – according to the various printed reports – the piece asserted its vitality, though drugged and stabbed, and hit about the head, as only some players *can* hit a play – hard and remorselessly.

On the same day Forster backed him up in the *Examiner* calling the play an 'excellent' one that was 'inadequately, we might almost say contemptuously presented' with actors playing parts not written for them and which they were 'quite unequal' to performing properly.[58] And in the *Athenaeum* Hepworth Dixon after quoting Jerrold's column from *Lloyd's* besought him, on patriotic grounds, not to desert the theatre, being as he was

> a writer who, beyond all his contemporaries, has upheld the glorious traditions of the English drama, in an age when public indifference and managerial bad taste have combined to subject this part of *our literary empire* to the *domination of foreign influence* and the *degradation* of foreign models. Now, less than ever, can the national drama afford to lose Mr Jerrold. (21 October 1854, my italics.)[59]

The national drama might have lost Jerrold as playwright but it certainly did not lose him as jaundiced commentator. He might in sour-grapes fashion, write to Blanchard, 'With regard to Theatres they have become almost of no consequence'[60] so that it was hardly worth bothering to publish dramatic reviews of them ('I have myself done a sprinkling,' he adds off-handedly), but as the *Theatrical Journal* protests show, he just could not leave Kean alone. Kean's memoirist Cole lists no less than seventeen further attacks on the Queen's favourite actor-manager in the columns of *Lloyd's* between 12 November 1854 and 15 March 1857.[61] With his hugely popular Shakespearian spectaculars (Jerrold dismissed one such production as 'the usual thing, all scenery and Keanery'), his Royal patronage, his starriness as an actor and his prosperity as a manager Kean seems to have become for Jerrold in the middle 1850s the focus of all his long-nurtured feelings of resentment at having been being exploited in the theatre for the material benefit of others, and at having had his strenuous efforts to 'revive the drama' frustrated by the meanness of money-grubbing managers and the vanity and greed of self-important star actors. The situation was perhaps intensified by the fact that the Eton-educated Kean was, like Thackeray, a Victorian gentleman, so that Jerrold's highly ambivalent class attitudes also came into play; as, no doubt, did his view of Kean as the unworthy son of the great Edmund, whom he had so worshipped as a supreme interpreter of Shakespeare when he was a theatre-going boy in London.[62] Sniping anonymously at Kean in the pages of *Punch* had been all very well. But now that he had complete editorial control over a mass-circulating weekly Jerrold behaved like many an editor or newspaper proprietor before and since; he could not resist using his power to pursue a personal vendetta.

Despite his commitment to writing so much in *Lloyd's* every week

Jerrold continued to be a prolific contributor to *Punch* with a falling off only in 1854, the year of his severe illness and of the trip to Switzerland.[63] His last *Punch* serial, 'Our Honeymoon', ran from 1 January to 3 September 1853 and seems not to have made much mark. It is written in the form of a journal kept by Charlotte, a young bride on her honeymoon. She is the last of the comic female narrators Jerrold created for *Punch*, a Mrs Caudle in the making, much given to pettishness and complaints about the insufficiently romantic behaviour of her (as she acknowledges in her better moments) infinitely kind, generous and good-humoured husband.

Most of Jerrold's *Punch* contributions during the last three years or so of his life were either facetious pieces about the petty problems of social and domestic life, like 'Our Honeymoon', or they were reversions to his old 'Q' vein like 'Christmas Day in the Workhouse' (3 January 1857). The latter group, it is worth noting, included at least one piece supporting some proposed legislation to give married women the right to keep their own earnings ('The Cry of the Women', 12 April 1856). They do not, however, have quite the urgency and the sustained elaborate ferocity of the original Q Papers. These qualities are rather to be found in the numerous other contributions by Jerrold that relate to foreign affairs and that are very much in alignment with his leaders in *Lloyd's*. Among the chief Jerrold targets in both papers are the brutal autocracy of Tsar Nicholas I, Austrian tyranny, the shabby imperial masquerade (as he saw it) of Louis Napoleon ('the late special constable of St James's Street'), the squalid regime of 'King Bomba' (Ferdinand of Naples), and the scarcely less disreputable government of the Papal States. In addition to all this, Jerrold wrote most of the prefaces to the six-monthly volumes during this period and contributed to *Punch*'s Almanacks for 1856 and 1857. His writing for the second of these took the form of a series of saccharine, sub-Ruskinian thumbnail sketches of 'Fireside Saints', illustrative of those domestic virtues that were so deeply ingrained in the Victorian male imagination as being, supposedly, the quintessence of 'womanliness' and that most of his female monologists in *Punch* had been shown as subverting.

By the mid-1850s Jerrold was reasonably prosperous but still had to think of the pennies. He wrote to Mackay some three months after the Reform Club dinner with Hawthorne that he was soon going to Boulogne for the summer and would like 'to cover expenses' by writing a longish tale for the Christmas Supplement of the *Illustrated London News* ('I've a good subject but would cover some five columns'[64]). No such tale seems to have been written, perhaps because Jerrold became distracted by his wife's ill-health. She had a bad attack of rheumatism in the ankle when the couple were on a brief visit to the French resort in early July and apparently became, after their return to London, 'very, very ill', perhaps from other causes.[65] This determined Jerrold to move his household to Boulogne-sur-Mer earlier than he had planned and he returned there on 25 July, with Mary Ann and their daughter Mary ('Polly') – also, no doubt, little Mouse – to settle in lodgings in the Rue Boston. Blanchard Jerrold and his wife and their young son Evelyn had been established in Boulogne since 18 June so it was quite a family gathering.[66]

Gilbert à Beckett also brought his family to Boulogne in the summer of 1857 and his son Arthur records a genial meeting between him and Jerrold on the sands in front of the Etablissement des Bains:

> I remember the little gentleman with the leonine head and the bright blue eyes talking and laughing with my father ... I was duly presented to the author of *Black Eyed Susan*, who graciously pinched my cheek and, to the delight of my mother, approved of my Sunday go-to-meeting hat and feathers [the weather in Boulogne was at this time stiflingly hot!]. Later on I heard my father say that he was very glad to have met Douglas 'away from the table' as they were not always quite as friendly as he would wish to be in Bouverie Street.[67]

Shortly afterwards, however, there was a virulent outbreak of a disease known as 'Boulogne sore throat' in the town. This disease, caused, according to Arthur à Beckett, by Boulogne's 'wretched drains', was later classified as diphtheria; it proved fatal both to à Beckett's nine-year-old son Walter and, a few days later, may have helped kill à Beckett himself (30 August). The latter's sudden death was a terrible shock for Jerrold, reinforcing his anxieties about the possibility of a similar demise for himself, that event which might 'come at any moment' and leave his family in financial distress.[68] Dickens, who was also in Boulogne for the summer, and who promptly sent his children away with his sister-in-law Georgina (referred to by Jerrold as 'Georgy'), later recalled Jerrold coming up to see him every day to report on à Beckett's condition and walking about the garden with him 'talking about these sudden strikings-down of men we loved, in the midst of us'.[69] At the time Jerrold wrote to Forster that he did not believe the cause of à Beckett's death was local but rather 'the murderous heat of Paris [to which à Beckett had made an excursion], with the anxiety for his boy'.[70] He went on (letter dated 2 September):

> Never was a family so united, so suddenly and so wholly made desolate. Competence, position, mutual affection, 'all that makes the happier man', and all now between four boards! We leave next week (there is a charnel taint upon this place, and I never tarry here again), abridging our intended stay by a fortnight. My wife, though made nervous and much agitated by this horror, is, on the whole, much better.

Jerrold would seem to have changed his plans, however, since he made only a flying visit to London by himself the following week and did not leave Boulogne for good, accompanied by his wife and presumably his daughter also, until 26 September. Since his daughter-in-law and her child left only the day before, Jerrold's conviction that à Beckett's death, at least, was not the place's fault would seem to have prevailed in the family. Perhaps the real reason that he vowed never to return to Boulogne was that it was where his own worst nightmare about sudden death and dependents left exposed to misery and want was actually realised by the fate of a close colleague very similarly situated to himself.

Just before this shock Jerrold had had to endure yet one more slight on those attempts to 'revive' the English drama to which he had devoted so much of his life. A leading article in *The Times* of 9 August deplored the fact that

> English dramatists of the present day — we except the farce-writers, who are rich and racy of the soil and ply their craft in an unexceptionable manner — are nothing better than sycophantic copyists of French Filth.

'Isn't this,' Jerrold asked Forster when sending him the cutting (signing it "Racy" of Burlington Arcade!') 'a little *too* sweeping?' The *Times* leader-writer had ignored Jerrold's Haymarket comedies when he warmed to his work of denouncing English followers of 'the Satanic drama of Paris':

> Our petty hod-carriers in the drama business have not even the merit of originality, but are content to take this filth at second-hand. Surely something better might be accomplished on the supposition that men of ordinary ability would turn their attention to this subject, as they might to the making of shoes. Sir EDWARD LYTTON and Mr SHERIDAN KNOWLES, in our own day, have contrived to obtain a reasonable amount of success without converting themselves into nightmen for the Parisian cesspools ... . Are our English dramatic writers so entirely destitute of invention that they cannot concoct a plot and imagine a series of characters without plagiarism of the most contemptible kind?

It is difficult to imagine anything that would have rubbed salt into Jerrold's wounds as a dramatic author more viciously than this. Ever since the days when he had proudly announced that he would come into Drury Lane as 'an original dramatist, or not at all',[71] he had striven for just the kind of originality the *Times* leader-writer calls for but had had to endure constant galling criticism about his evident deficiencies both as regards plot-structure and as regards characterisation. And insult was added to injury by the fact that Oxenford, the *Times*'s principal dramatic critic, was himself a noted translator of plays from French and German, and had also, so Jerrold asserted, debased himself as a critic in that 'for years [he] praised every obscenity to the skies; especially if reeking from the Princess's [Kean's theatre, of course]'.[72] In his vigorous response to *The Times* in *Lloyd*'s (17 August 1856) Jerrold ironically applauds the paper's promise to chastise purveyors of 'cesspool drama' from across the Channel: 'Mr Charles Kean, the greatest and finest offender of all the culprits (for his upholstery has been unexceptional) has fair warning' and the *Times* critic, 'himself unfortunately a translator, although endowed with talents and scholarship that should have stirred him to better doings', may next season 'fit his fingers with a new, clean, unpartial pen'.

Back in London, Jerrold determined on another house-move after only three and a half years at Circus Road. He may have been anxious about his family's future in the event of his sudden death but his financial self-confidence in the present was reflected in his decision to move, in the late autumn of 1856, from Circus Road to a grander abode, No. 11 Greville Place, Kilburn Priory.[73] This was still in the borough of St Marlylebone but further north than St John's Wood. Several of the handsome villas built in Greville Place from c.1820 onwards still survive (not including No. 11, however). They are built in varying styles but blend well together, and, as the Camden History Group observe in their *Streets of West Hampstead* (1992), Greville Place and its immediately surrounding neighbourhood still retain 'an air of peace and spaciousness'.

Another sign of Jerrold's financial confidence at this time was his 'resolute determination', confided to the Cowden Clarkes, 'to spend some weeks at Nice next autumn with my wife and daughter' (he will, he tells the Clarkes, give them due notice of the family's going to Nice so 'that we may avail ourselves of your experience as to *location*, as those savages the Americans yell in their native war whoop tongue'[74]). His buoyant spirits showed themselves also at a New Year's Eve gathering for family and friends in the new house. Jerrold was, his eldest son remembered, 'the merriest of the party, and even tried to dance', and altogether he seems to have finished the year in very good heart.

263

Chapter Fifteen

Death and 'Funeral Games'

1857

One of Jerrold's earliest engagements in 1857 was to attend the last night of some private theatricals at Dickens's home in Tavistock Square on 14 January. The play was a melodrama called *The Frozen Deep*, written specially for the occasion by Wilkie Collins. It featured Dickens in spectacular histrionic form as Wardour, the villain-hero of the piece ('If that man now would go upon the stage', said Thackeray, who was also in the audience, 'he would make his £20,000 a year'). William Howitt recorded this and wrote that the audience present on this last night consisted of 'a very brilliant company of celebrated people and, as Jerrold said, 'Judges enow to hang us all'.[1] Within a few short months, death would no longer be for Jerrold a subject for joking but a stark reality, and Dickens would be busy organising, with his customary energy, public performances of this same play as part of his fund-raising efforts on behalf of Jerrold's widow and unmarried daughter.

For the present, however, no-one dreamed that Jerrold's days were numbered, despite his obvious physical frailty: 'We never thought of the brilliant and radiant Douglas in connection with the black river,' wrote Hannay a few months later; 'He would have sunk Charon's boat with a shower of epigrams, one would have fancied, if the old fellow ... had dared to ask *him* into the stern-sheets.'[2] He continued to be a very hands-on editor of *Lloyd's* and kept up his regular contributions to *Punch*. It was for the sake of his wife's health, not his own, that he went down to Brighton for a few days in April (the sea air and the beautiful warm weather soon restored her). Shortly afterwards came his Thackeray-supported election to the Reform Club, an outward and visible sign of his acceptance as a paid-up member of the Liberal establishment. But, however gratified he may have been by this election, he probably felt more at home as *primus inter pares* in the chummier atmosphere of Saturday evenings at Our Club. Hannay records last seeing him at the Club on 16 May adding, 'and on no evening do I remember him more lively and brilliant'. Two days later, Jerrold wrote to his friend the eminent photographer Dr Hugh Welch Diamond scheduling a session for the following week, and the fine portrait-photographs that Diamond took of him on that occasion show him looking alert and vigorous.

He had at this time acquired a distinguished new protégé in William Howard Russell, whose despatches to *The Times* from the Crimea during the winter of 1854/55 had first exposed the appalling administrative muddle and incompetence that had led to so much misery and suffering for British soldiers in the Crimea, and had caused Jerrold to bestow upon him the title of 'the Pen of the War'. Blanchard Jerrold quotes a letter from Russell to his father in which he says, 'You are indeed a leal and kind good friend to me, my dear Douglas Jerrold' and tells us that Jerrold 'admired him profoundly'.[3]

The opera impresario Willert Beale, who was a great friend of Jerrold's, had arranged for Russell to give three public readings from his 'Personal Narrative' of the Crimean campaign in London in late May. A trial run was held before an audience of Russell's fellow-journalists at a supper-meeting in a small London club. Russell proved to be an ineffective reader and, according to Beale, Jerrold showed him how it should be done by jumping up on the table, 'among the debris of the supper', and delivering an impassioned rendering of Russell's narrative of the Battle of the Alma:

> It would be difficult to imagine a more dramatic reading. The tone of voice, the gesture, appearance, fire and energy of the little figure under the gas-lamp certainly thrilled the audience, and seemed a revelation to Russell ... .[4]

Russell exclaimed that he could not possibly absorb in one lesson all that Jerrold could teach him about dramatic reading, whereupon Jerrold promptly offered to give him some regular coaching at Kilburn, an offer Russell was happy to accept.

The last lecture in the series was scheduled for Monday 1 June and Russell had invited Beale, Jerrold, Dickens and a number of other friends to dine with him at Greenwich the evening before. Jerrold and Dickens had arranged to meet him in the afternoon at the venue for the lectures, the Gallery of Illustration in Lower Regent Street, in order to go over the lecture with him but when Dickens arrived at the Gallery he found the place shut up and Jerrold waiting outside as he had been already for a quarter of an hour. Dickens recalled:

> I sat down by him in a niche in the staircase, and he told me that he had been very unwell for three or four days. A window in his study had been newly painted, and the smell of the paint (he thought it must be that) had filled him with nausea and turned him sick, and he felt quite weak and giddy through not having been able to retain any food. He was a little subdued at first and out of spirits; but we sat there half an hour, talking, and when we came out together he was quite himself.[5]

Seeing him in the open air, however, Dickens thought he looked really ill and wanted to send him home in a cab but Jerrold now felt so weak that he was afraid of fainting unless he could have some 'restorative'. They had by this time reached Leicester Square and Dickens hesitated about going on while Jerrold leant on the railings in the Square 'looking, for the moment, very ill indeed'. When they did walk on, however, Jerrold quickly recovered, and after Dickens and Russell (who had by this time joined them) had got him some refreshment at Covent Garden, declared that he felt 'quite a new man' and that it would do him good to go to Greenwich. Dickens's note continues:

> We strolled through the Temple on our way to a boat and I have a lively recollection of his stamping about Elm Tree Court, with his hat in one hand and the other pushing his hair back, laughing in his heartiest manner at a ridiculous remembrance we had in common, which I had presented in some exaggerated light, to divert him .... It was a bright day, and as soon as we reached Greenwich we got an open carriage and went out for a drive about Shooter's Hill. In the carriage, Mr Russell read us his lecture, and we discussed it with great interest; we planned out the ground of Inkerman, on the heath, and your father was very earnest indeed. The subject held us so, that we were graver than usual; but he broke out again in the same hilarious way as in the Temple; and he over and over again said to me with great satisfaction, how happy he was, that he had 'quite got over that paint'.

Dickens did not sit by Jerrold at the dinner but went round the table to him before leaving. Jerrold showed him that he had kept to the sherry-and-water that he and Dickens had agreed beforehand was all that he should drink and said, 'I have kept to the prescription; it has answered as well as this morning's, my dear old boy; I have quite got over the paint, and I am perfectly well.' He was, Dickens recalled, 'really elated by the relief of having recovered, and was as quietly happy as I ever saw him. We exchanged "God bless you!" and shook hands.' Beale, who sat opposite to Jerrold at the dinner, paints a somewhat different picture: 'He looked pale and wan, spoke little, and was evidently suffering.' When Beale went to sit by him after the dinner was over, Jerrold confessed that he was feeling 'very ill' and was present 'against the doctor's orders'. Beale's efforts to cheer him up at first seemed hopeless but when he mentioned the opera Jerrold rallied as quickly and suddenly as he had when walking with Dickens that afternoon:

> His eyes brightened; his mind seemed to cast aside its burden, his body its ailment; he laughed and talked with the gaiety natural to him. 'Do you know', he said, 'I believe it would cure me completely if I could hear Don Giovanni next Tuesday at Covent Garden. Shall we go together?'

Beale readily agreed but, when he escorted Jerrold to the carriage of Dr Quain, one of Jerrold's medical friends, who was to take him back to London, he found him 'so feeble as to be hardly able to walk without support'.[6] During the drive back Jerrold complained again about the paint but was generally cheerful and in good spirits.

The next day, however, he was seized with fits of vomiting and violent stomach pains and so began a week of much suffering, described in harrowing detail in his son's memoir. At first there were intervals of remission when he would try, with Blanchard's help, to carry on with his *Lloyd's* work, or would lie upon his study sofa where he could see his beloved garden, 'his white hair streaming upon the pillow, and his thin hand upon the head of little Mouse, who had followed him from his bedroom and was lying by his side'. On the Friday when Mark Lemon came to see him for the second and last time, Jerrold had, Dickens reported to Russell, 'begun to be confident of getting better' and spoke with pleasure of the recent jaunt to Blackheath.[7] By the weekend, however, he knew he was dying. He had to fight for breath and was again suffering acute stomach pains. Sitting in an arm-chair before an open window as the evening sunlight glowed in the room and gilded the trees outside, he kissed his weeping wife and family (of his children only Edmund, now seeking his fortune in America, was absent[8]), and asked Horace ('Ponny') Mayhew, who was in the room, to take a message to his *Punch* comrades: 'Tell the dear boys that if I've ever wounded any of them, I've always loved them.' As we have noted earlier, he also told Ponny that he forgave his trouble-some son-in-law. When on the Sunday another doctor, his friend Henry Wright, physician at the Samaritan Hospital, arrived and asked Jerrold how he was, he answered 'faintly', 'As one who is waiting – and waited for.' Wright (whom Shirley Brooks later blamed for fatally failing to make a correct diagnosis of Jerrold's case[9]) tried to cheer him with promise of recovery but Jerrold, who had no fear of death, rejected such facile comfort. 'Let me pass – let me pass!' he murmured as he gasped for air and waved people away from in front of the open window. He had still to endure another night, and more doctoring. In the morning Wright bled his ex-hausted patient, no doubt in an effort to relieve the agony that ischuria resulting from kidney failure was causing him.[10] 'Why torture a dying creature, doctor?' Jerrold asked him. Mercifully, the end was not delayed much longer and he died peacefully at last, lovingly held in the arms of both his eldest and youngest sons and murmuring, 'This is as it should be.'

Because of its utter unexpectedness Jerrold's death caused a great sensation. Dickens, who had dreamed that night of Jerrold showing him 'a writing (but not in his hand) which he was pressingly anxious that I should read for my own information, but I could not make out a word of it',[11] was travelling up to London from his Gad's Hill home in Kent on 8 June, when he was startled by a fellow-passenger's opening his morning paper and exclaiming, 'Douglas Jerrold is dead!' That morning paper may well have been *The Times*, which began its obituary by noting that the news would 'probably take the whole literary public of England completely by surprise':

But a few days ago Mr Douglas Jerrold was a prominent figure in London life. An assembly of 'wits' would hardly have been deemed complete without his presence, and his last *bon mot* was one of those items of news that everybody was glad to hear.

'Yorick', the editor of the *Thespian and Dramatic Record*, was, appropriately, more flowing in his lamentation:

> The sad tidings of his decease came upon us with awful suddenness; we paused in the pursuit of our own avocations, unable for the moment to comprehend the full extent of our bereavement, or to realise the fact that a great man was gone from amongst us – that the keen and searching eye of Douglas Jerrold was glazed in death, the thin white hand, once so deft in the use of the quill, now lay stiff and cold by his side. His place in English literature is vacant, and we seek in vain for one worthy to stand in the breach. (17 June 1857)

Obituarists in general were concerned to emphasise the thorough 'Englishness'[12] of Jerrold's literary achievement (his style, said 'Yorick' was 'English to the core'), his 'fearless independence and frank sincerity' (*Daily News*) and his constant advocacy of 'the great duty of human brotherhood' (*Illustrated London News*). Much insisted on also was the fact that 'by sheer ability ... he [had] forced his way from an obscure station to literary eminence and social distinction' (so wrote Forster, who had done much the same thing himself, in the *Examiner*), also his pre-eminence as a brilliant satirist, 'a desperate foeman' of 'the world's shams', who 'not only smote with vigour' but 'unmanned his adversary by the expression of scorn' (*Sunday Times*). Nearly every obituarist felt the need to assert that, even though there might be occasionally be a bitter flavour to Jerrold's satire, there was never any actual malice, and that its driving force was always his great pity and compassion for the poor and the oppressed. 'His keen arrows', commented the *National Magazine*, in a phrase Jerrold himself might have relished, 'flew from his heartstrings'.[13]

One sharply dissentient voice made itself heard amidst all the eulogy. Not surprisingly, G.W.M. Reynolds, whose weekly paper was *Lloyd's* great competitor, and who had all a real Radical's contempt for liberal 'compromisers', took a rather more jaundiced view of the man who had been hailed as 'the people's champion'. Jerrold's death, he asserted, 'had given birth to a vast amount of disgusting and pernicious falsehood respecting the character and productions of that gentleman':

> He was a man of strong animosities, and both his tongue and his pen were the slaves of those animosities. To offend his vanity, however involuntarily, was to make of him a bitter, if not an implacable enemy. His fierce and persistent attacks upon Charles Keane ... are well known ... . It is all very well for the clique of littérateurs, of whom the deceased satirist was the chief and centre, to howl over his tomb .... But they must understand that there are in the world more sacred things than the miserable vanity of frivolous jesters and second-hand wits ... .[14]

Reynolds scored a palpable hit with his reference to Jerrold's animus against Keane but his was very much a minority report. The memorial verses in *Punch* (20 June 1857) were, however lamentable they may be as poetry, far more representative of the general public's perception of the dead man. Here are the first three verses (of six):

> Low lies the lion-like grey head;
> The broad and bright-blue eye is glazed;
> Quenched is that flashing wit, which blazed,
> The words that woke it scarcely said.
>
> Those who but read the writer's word,
> Might deem him bitter: we that knew
> The man, all saw the sword he drew
> In tongue-fence, was both shield and sword.
>
> That sword, in the world's battle-throng,
> Was never drawn upon the meek:
> Its skill to guard was for the weak,
> Its strength to smite was for the strong.

Within an hour or two of hearing of Jerrold's death Dickens determined to organise an extensive and ambitious programme of public events in memory of his late friend, with the intention of raising a fund for Mary Jerrold and her unmarried daughter. Jerrold had not, in fact, 'left his family penniless' as *Reynolds' Weekly Newspaper* later asserted. His estate was valued at £3,500[15] and, although there were other debts to be met, the main one, deriving from the failure of *Douglas Jerrold's Weekly Newspaper*, was provided for by a dedicated insurance policy. Blanchard Jerrold was intending to petition Palmerston, the Prime Minister, for a civil list pension for his mother and felt himself to have been pre-empted by Dickens (although he did eventually write to Palmerston[16]). Dickens's precipitate decision to organise these 'extraordinary funeral games', as the *North British Review* disapprovingly called them ('one of the most grotesque shapes that benevolence has yet assumed, even in this practical century'[17]), stemmed in part no doubt from a genuine desire to help Mrs Jerrold and her daughter. It surely resulted also, however, from his own desperate need at this time to plunge himself into a whirl of frenetic activity – he had just completed the writing of *Little Dorrit* and his restless reaction to the sudden cessation of the enormous pressure this had placed him under for the past twenty months was no doubt compounded by his growing marital misery.

The fund-raising was not, Dickens told Forster, to be done 'beggingly' (he was perhaps mindful of the 'almost insane' horror Jerrold had once expressed to him about the idea of the hat being sent round for his dependants after his death – see above, p. 199) but to be announced only as being a 'tribute' that Jerrold's friends were paying to his memory. Dickens recruited Albert Smith's brother Arthur ('the best man of business I know') as secretary to the Fund and enlisted an impressive number of leading actors and writers either to serve on the Committee or to perform for the benefit of the Fund, or to do both. He himself gave a public reading

of the *Carol* and the septuagenarian T.P. Cooke came out of semi-retire-
ment to play *Black Eyed Susan*'s William one more time (hornpipe and all)
at a 'Jerrold Night' at the Adelphi Theatre, where *The Rent Day* was also
on the programme. Another 'Jerrold Night' was held at the Haymarket
where Phelps, Buckstone, Farren and the Keeleys were among those who
performed in *The Housekeeper* and *The Prisoner of War* and an 'occasional
address' beginning 'Welcome! In Jerrold's name' was spoken by Phelps.
Russell gave a special lecture on his Crimean experiences and Albert
Smith (generously putting aside memories of Jerrold's frequently-dis-
played animosity towards himself) participated in a St Martin's Hall
concert alongside a number of distinguished singers. In the same venue
Thackeray, in rueful mood following his electoral defeat at Oxford, gave
his 'Charity and Humour' lecture, introducing into it a special tribute to
Jerrold as we have seen (above, p. 188), while at the Gallery of Illustration
Dickens, Collins and their amateur company staged a full-scale public
performance of *The Frozen Deep*. All these events took place before
crowded and enthusiastic audiences during June and July and there was,
additionally, a Royal Command performance of Collins's play before the
Queen at the Gallery (Victoria was mightily impressed both by the drama
itself and by Dickens's electrifying performance as Richard Wardour[18]). In
late August Dickens took his Amateurs to play *The Frozen Deep* for two
nights in the great Free Trade Hall in Manchester, substituting for his
sister-in-law and daughters a family of professional actresses, Frances
Ternan and her daughters Maria and Ellen (and thereby, as they say,
hangs a tale). Again, there were overflowing, wildly enthusiastic, audiences and when the final accounts came to be rendered, Dickens was able
to announce in *The Times* on 1 September that the Fund had reached
£2,000, the target at which he had aimed, and that this sum would be used
'in the purchase (though trustees) of a Government annuity for Mrs
Jerrold and her unmarried daughter, with the remainder to the survivor'.

Poor Blanchard seems, understandably, to have been rather over-
whelmed by all this Dickens enterprise, but was concerned to make it
known, in *Lloyd's* (13 September) and elsewhere, that his family stood in
no need of a hand-out and that he would not accept anything 'that should
wear the appearance of charity'. He said also, however, that his mother
and sister would, in fact, accept the money raised by Dickens and his
committee regarding it 'as an addition to [Jerrold's] estate'. This the *Era*
called (20 September), somewhat unfairly, a mere 'jargon of words' whilst
Dickens's gruff response in a letter to W.H. Wills of 17 September was,
'Young Jerrold, just contemptible'. Earlier, on 3 August Dickens had
warned Paxton, who had been promising some financial help to his former
student, young Tom Jerrold, that he suspected Tom of believing the money
being raised 'would be placed at the disposal of the whole family – like a
sort of pecuniary skittles, to be bowled down by whomsoever may have a
fancy to Go in'. His final word on the subject appeared in a letter to *The
Times*, co-signed by Arthur Smith as the previous one had been, on 6

October. This made a scathing reference to Blanchard's statement in *Lloyd's* and, by way of justifying Dickens's own intervention, quoted the solicitor to Jerrold's estate as testifying that it was in danger of becoming 'absolutely insolvent'.[19] Dickens's letter was copied by the *Morning Post* and on 12 October Blanchard responded in that paper with a lengthy letter justifying his *Lloyd's* statement and quoting a 16 June letter of Dickens's to a Mr Wells that suggested he (Blanchard) should, 'when our little campaign is over', do just what he had done by way of setting the record straight.[20]

Happily, by the time Blanchard Jerrold came to publish his life of his father in 1859, he and Dickens had become reconciled (as he put it, 'Hands have long since been shaken heartily all round') and he was glad enough, as well he might have been, to include in his memoir Dickens's moving account of his last meeting with his father. As to the money, on Mary Jerrold's death (also 1859), her daughter Mary Ann (Polly) became the sole beneficiary of the Trust Fund that had been set up with Dickens and Hepworth Dixon as co-trustees. Polly lived on until 1910 and under her will the capital went to found the Douglas Jerrold Scholarship in English Literature at Christ Church College, Oxford. Dixon's son, the distinguished chemist, Harold Baily Dixon (1852-1930), who presumably succeeded his father as one of the trustees, had been an undergraduate at Christ Church and was responsible for making the arrangement. We do not know whether the idea for setting up the scholarship came from Dixon or from Polly herself but we can well understand how the idea would have appealed to her. Here was an opportunity to create a lasting memorial to her father's contribution to English literature while at the same time helping generations of young men to access the kind of education that young Jerrold the printer's apprentice, so thirsty for learning, had been able only to dream of. The scholarship continues to be awarded to this day, among the most notable of its past recipients being a poor young Cornish student called A.L. Rowse.[21]

Epilogue

Echoes

1857-2002

Given the fact that he had been one of the most popular and highly-regarded writers in Britain for upwards of twenty years, the rapid eclipse of Jerrold's fame following his death is remarkable, although not difficult to understand. Of all his voluminous writings only two of his lighter works, *Black Eyed Susan* and 'Mrs Caudle's Curtain Lectures', remained genuinely popular. Both still have some currency even today.[1] Some of his other works were reprinted at least once during the half-century following his death and one of his 'high' comedies was revived on the stage. Bradbury and Evans brought out a lavish edition of *The Story of a Feather* in 1867 (superlatively illustrated by George Du Maurier[2]) and in the same year this title was also included by Routledge in the 'Railway Library' series; there was a moderately successful revival of *Time Works Wonders* at the Globe Theatre in 1873.[3] *The Brownrigg Papers* was included in Chatto & Windus's 'Select Library of Fiction' in 1874, *Cakes and Ale* was included in Cassell's popular 'Red Library' series in 1888, and a collection of some of the shorter fiction under the title *Tales by Douglas Jerrold* appeared in 1891 edited by J. Logie Robertson. In his preface Robertson regretted that it was Jerrold's witty sayings ('of a severely sarcastic order') rather than his writings that kept his name alive, even though as 'a man of feeling and noble aims' he wrote much 'brilliantly, powerfully, and honestly' ('Was it merely a wit that wrote the "Story of a Feather"?'). Logie's choice of items to reprint was hardly a happy one, however – it included, for example, several of the heavily formulaic *Men of Character* sketches from *Blackwood's*.

Jerrold naturally featured prominently in M.H. Spielmann's monumental *History of 'Punch'* (1895), where his wit and fearless championship of the people were celebrated and his 'defects as a political economist' deprecated,[4] but it was the pious industry of Blanchard Jerrold and of his nephew, Tom's son Walter (1865-1929), that was mainly responsible for keeping Jerrold's name in print during this period. In 1859 Blanchard's *Life and Remains of Douglas Jerrold* was given a generally benign reception but was, predictably enough, savaged in the *Saturday Review*. The reviewer, presumably Fitzjames Stephen, had earlier lambasted both *St Giles and St James* and Mrs Caudle in the *Saturday*'s columns but in 1857 had relented so far as to call Jerrold 'a rather favourable sample' of the 'rabidly honest' Liberal journalist, 'honest enough in his detestation of all

273

existing institutions, but … also utterly uninstructed and hopelessly perverse'. Now, he declared, Blanchard's *Life* clearly revealed Jerrold as belonging to

> what would be the most contemptible, if it were not one of the most danger-ous, schools of modern politicians – the bastard Rousseaus of whom Mr Dickens and Mr Jerrold were the leaders. Their poetry is a sentimental growl about the virtues of the poor and the wickedness of the rich – their prose a 'dabbling in statistics to prove the exact sum given away in sinecures'.[5]

A more judicious assessment both of Jerrold himself and of Blanchard's memoir appeared in a long review-article in the *North British Review*. The as yet unidentified writer of this was fascinated by Jerrold as 'a man, who by force of his individuality, had come to occupy a certain place before the public' and also 'as exemplifying in his life some special conditions of literary adventure in our day', such as the way in which those who now wished to live by writing had, at least in their earlier days, to 'depend upon the periodical press', a 'bondage' from which Jerrold could never liberate himself. This constant pressure to supply to order a certain amount of writing, combined with Jerrold's 'copious flow of language' and lack of mental discipline (the result, in part, of defective education), led to shrillness, vulgarity, and an over-reliance on melodramatic effects. For all his great talent Jerrold could not be placed 'in the class of men of genius' but 'happier circumstances of moral and intellectual training' might have made him eligible for such classification.[6]

Undeterred by such judgments, Blanchard Jerrold, who was almost as prolific a writer as Jerrold himself, published, also in 1859, a compilation called *The Wit and Opinions of Douglas Jerrold* and this was followed over the next fifteen years by four further collections of Jerroldiana. After Blanchard's death in 1884 the baton passed to Walter Jerrold, very much a late Victorian/Edwardian 'bookman' and 'man of letters' as famously studied by John Gross.[7] In 1891 Walter edited yet another Jerrold anthology called *The Handbook of Swindling and Other Papers*, followed in 1893 by a bijou volume called *Bon Mots of Charles Lamb and Douglas Jerrold*, embellished with arabesques designed by no less a personage than Aubrey Beardsley. In 1901 came Walter Jerrold's edition of *Mrs Caudle*, together with various stories and essays, for the Oxford World's Classics series, and in 1903 his *Essays of Douglas Jerrold*, handsomely produced by J.M. Dent and charmingly illustrated by H.M. Brock. This little volume includes several of Jerrold's fanciful essays on Shakespeare as well as 'Elizabeth and Victoria', 'The Manager's Pig', 'Fireside Saints', 'The Folly of the Sword' and the *Handbook of Swindling*. In his introduction Walter Jerrold plausibly attributes the public's neglect of his grandfather's work to the fact that so much of it was highly topical journalism and expresses the hope that his anthology will direct attention towards Jerrold's 'general or more philosophical' writings (he makes a wistful reference to 'Clovernook', 'that little book of golden philosophy').

If Jerrold was indeed, as John Fyvie called him in *Macmillan's* in 1902, 'A Forgotten Jester',[8] the neglect he was suffering could certainly not be blamed on his descendants. Having in his Dent anthology urged the merits of Jerrold's 'philosophical' writings as showing 'the deeper side of his nature', Walter then tried to resuscitate interest in Jerrold's work for *Punch* by publishing *Douglas Jerrold and 'Punch'* in 1910. But in it he chooses to reprint in full such sub-Caudle series as 'Capsicum House' and 'Miss Robinson Crusoe'. For us today, of course, probably the most striking thing about these pieces is their sexism, remarkable even for a mid-Victorian 'jester'. For E.V. Lucas, however, reviewing the book anonymously in the *Times Literary Supplement* for 29 December 1910, they were simply tedious, 'pure mechanism', and Walter's attempt to revive interest in his grandfather's work could only have been the result of 'some freakish atavistic prompting'. 'Jerrold's personality,' wrote the urbane 'Evoe' of a very different *Punch* from the one Jerrold knew, 'not too alluring in life, died with him: there is no interest in him today, nor can one after perusing this work see why there should be.'

This was too sweeping a judgement. The assertion that there was 'no interest' in Jerrold in the early 1900s is contradicted by the fact that the fiftieth anniversary of his death was marked in at least two national papers, the *Daily Telegraph* and the progressive weekly the *Tribune*. The *Telegraph* filled one and a half columns with examples of Jerroldian witticisms while the *Tribune*, which devoted an equal amount of space to the subject (and supplied a portrait as well), drew attention not just to

276

Jerrold's wit, his 'way of packing much fruit of thought or ready wit into brief sentences, or happy phrases', but also to his anti-militarism and progressive views on such matters as the income tax, capital punishment and international arbitration, as well as his naming of the Crystal Palace. (It should perhaps be added that the *Tribune*'s piece was probably prompted, if not actually written, by Walter Jerrold whose young daughter Ianthe was a contributor to the paper's children's column.) Five years later St John Adcock wondered in his *Literary Shrines of London* whether anyone still read Mrs Caudle but said that Jerrold's 'best jokes and witticisms' were 'much too well known to leave me an excuse for repeating any of them here'. He, too, emphasised the social-crusader side of Jerrold: 'For all his bitter tongue, he was kind, generous, sensitive, afire with with a fine scorn of wrong, injustice, and every variety of social humbug and snobbery.'[9]

Walter Jerrold's full-length biography of his grandfather should have been published in 1914 but was delayed by the War. When it did appear in 1918 it was respectfully received, by the *Times Literary Supplement* as well as other papers. Even though the plays, to which Walter devotes an inordinate amount of space, were deemed unrevivable, the *TLS* reviewer, the drama critic and former actor Harold Hannyngton Child, lovingly recalled several of the comic 'humour' characters from *Time Works Wonders* and *The Catspaw*, and even disinterred *Thomas à Beckett* to commend it as 'a very respectable effort at historical drama'. But it was as a man rather than as a writer that reviewers of the biography believed Jerrold deserved to be remembered. He was a 'Humanitarian Radical', a 'perpetrator of fine and active services to humanity', a 'typical Victorian Radical' who 'helped to make men kinder', and a staunch champion of the people. As for his wit, one paper, the *Nation*, interestingly found it outdated, as much tied to its day as his topical journalism (of which it is part and parcel):

> The wit of Wilde and Whistler ... has spoiled our taste for such simple-hearted jests. We have learned a new fashion of joking. Jerrold in his wit was a great journalist, not a great artist.[10]

During the great post-Lytton Strachey slump of serious interest in all things Victorian during the 1920s and 1930s Jerrold pretty much disappeared from view, being mentioned only in the work of literary antiquarians or theatre historians.[11] There was also one other group that kept his name alive, namely the pacifists, for whom his *Illuminated Magazine* essay, 'The Folly of the Sword', retitled 'The Glory of War', became something of a sacred text. It was reprinted, for example, as an appendix to Guy Aldred's *At Grips with War* (1929) along with Tolstoy's 'Way to Peace' and Anatole France's 'Martial Glory', and reprinted again in 1940, in an abridged form, together with France's essay, by the Strickland Press in

Glasgow ('Strickland's Classics No. 4') where it was noted as having been originally written by 'the great English humorist' in 1843.

Not until 1950 was Mrs Caudle again reprinted in Britain (The Moray Press, Edinburgh, with a foreword by the *Punch* writer H.F. Ellis and illustrations by Mackay), though a selection of the lectures had appeared in a collection entitled *Whimsical Tales of Douglas Jerrold* published by the Roedale Press in Allentown, Pennsylvania in 1948. This particular collection would have pleased Jerrold himself since it included stories from 'The Chronicles of Clovernook'. In his lengthy and well-informed introduction the volume's editor, Edward J. Fluck, seeks to get away from the traditional focus on Jerrold as a caustic wit, 'a sort of male Dorothy Parker of his day', and to highlight instead 'Clovernook' as the work in which all the qualities of Jerrold's genius shine at their brightest: 'The study of benignant nature is rich and rare; the legends have "purposes" in them, a characteristic seriousness from which the author could never for long divorce himself.' This volume is splendidly illustrated with black and white pictures, admirably responsive to Jerrold's text, done in lithograph crayon by Lewis C. Daniel who testifies in the volume to the inspiration he derived from Jerrold's outstanding qualities of 'humour and clarity of statement'.

From the 1950s onwards, there began, both in Britain and America, that great efflorescence of scholarly interest in Victorian literature and culture generally that has grown into such a mighty industry today. In the course of this Jerrold, along with many another 'minor Victorian' (as the old phrase went) has been brought somewhat out of the shadows and figures often in the footnotes (as well as sometimes in the main text) of the endless stream of 'Victorian Studies' books, scholarly essays and editions that cascade annually from academic presses on both sides of the Atlantic. His dramas and other works have been the subject of several theses, the writer of one of which, Richard M. Kelly, went on to publish a handsome selected edition of Jerrold's *Punch* contributions, *The Best of Mr Punch* (1970) and an illuminating study of his whole oeuvre in the Twayne's English Authors series (1972). Meanwhile, the rediscovery of Henry Mayhew as one of the great explorers of the lower depths of mid-Victorian London involved some rediscovery of Jerrold also, both as Mayhew's colleague and as his father-in-law. Writing on Mayhew and the *Morning Chronicle* in his and Eileen Yeo's *The Unknown Mayhew* (1971), E.P. Thompson, the great historian of working-class England, characterised Jerrold as

> the continuer, in a somewhat softened and sentimentalised form, of a democratic and anti-clerical tradition which was consciously derived from the radicalism of John and Leigh Hunt of the *Examiner*. It was Jerrold who gave to *Punch* both its radical attack and its 'occasional gravities' in its first five years. ... Jerrold's wit had a rasping edge, but the edge was directed always towards the 'Right' – towards pomp and ceremony, towards capital punishment and militarism ... .

278

This is certainly a more positive view of Jerrold the man than that of the theatre historian Robertson Davies who echoed Thackeray's letter to Elwin (above, p. 188) when he wrote in 1975: 'With Jerrold, nobody who was a success could really be fully honest or admirable [how, if this were true, to account for his love and admiration for Dickens?], and this attitude gives his plays a savour not of satire, but of gall.'[12] The persistence of the two conflicting views of Jerrold so common in his own day – on the one hand the acerbic but fearless and right-feeling champion of the people and, on the other, the literary man warped by envy and bitterness – is remarkable.

With the advent, over the last quarter-century or so, of Feminism, Cultural History, New Historicism, Cultural Materialism, and such-like preoccupations of contemporary university Departments of English, Drama and the Humanities, the study of the work of popular writers such as Jerrold, previously largely ignored by those concerned only with 'canonical' English literature, has been found rewarding from several points of view. Raymond Williams found great significance in Jerrold's *Rent Day* and *Factory Girl* as 'quite open attempts to dramatise a new social consciousness' and saw the rejection of the latter play at Drury Lane as 'a significant moment in nineteenth-century culture'.[13] *The Mutiny at the Nore*, also, has been the subject of some lively discussion.[14] And Richard D. Fulton, writing on Jerrold's shorter fiction in 1996 in the monumental *Dictionary of Literary Biography*, supplies a detailed analysis of three stories but finally judges this fiction to be 'less literature than an artifact of Victorian popular culture'. One of Jerrold's neatest and most effective satirical sketches, 'Kind Cousin Tom' from *Cakes and Ale*, is certainly treated as literature by Harold Orel, however. He includes it in his Everyman anthology *Victorian Short Stories* (1987) and discusses it at some length in his introduction as an example of a very vital genre of early Victorian writing that may seem 'overdone' to modern readers and difficult to come to terms with.[15]

Outside the walls of Academe, Jerrold continues today to be saved from oblivion by four things – a handful of *bon mots*, his naming of the Crystal Palace, *Black Eyed Susan* and 'Mrs Caudle's Curtain Lectures'. As regards the *bon mots*, he scored fifteen entries in the 1953 edition of the *Oxford Dictionary of Quotations* but by the 1999 edition his total had dwindled to only four. In the *Macmillan Dictionary of Quotations* (1987) he scored only eight entries and two less than that in the *New Penguin Dictionary of Quotations* (1991). One hardy survivor in the more recent anthologies was a favourite of the Victorians and survives now mainly on account of its period flavour, I would imagine (certainly not on account of its truth!). It is the one from *A Man Made of Money* about the earth being so kind in Australia that you need only 'just tickle her with a hoe and she laughs with a harvest' (writing in 1957, R.G.G. Price considered that this had a 'Churchillian' ring to it). The handful of other Jerroldisms that survive into the late 20th century quotation-books, however, are generally crisper, freer from rhetoric, and have by no means lost their edge: 'Religion's in the heart, not in the knees'; 'Love's like the measles – all the worse when it comes late in life'; (on a practical man) 'Talk to him of Jacob's ladder and he would ask the number of steps'; (on a comic author – most probably Albert Smith!) 'That fellow would vulgarise the Day of Judgment'.

Black Eyed Susan was seldom off the stage, in one form or another, during the 19th century (not even Gilbert and Sullivan's brilliant burlesque, *H.M.S. Pinafore* [1878] could kill it). 'When it once gets to business', wrote Shaw, reviewing William Terriss's celebrated production at the Adelphi in December 1896, *Black Eyed Susan* 'is an excellent play'.[16] It ceased to be performed after the very early years of the 20th century, though the date of its first production in 1829 remained a landmark in theatre history – on 6 June 1957 the *Stage*, for example, ran a feature headed 'The Man Who Wrote Black Eyed Susan', to mark the centenary of Jerrold's death. Ten years later *Susan* was given an effective 'chamber' production at the Toynbee Theatre in London by an amateur group, the Stewart Headlam Players,[17] but, as I have shown elsewhere, it was not until the development of the concept of 'community theatre' in the 1980s and 1990s that the professional theatre found a way of dealing with this play. With a small group of actors and minimal scenery but plenty of song and dance and audience-involvement, productions like the one at the Croydon Warehouse in 1986 and the Channel Theatre's touring production in Kent in 1991 managed to breathe theatrical life back into Jerrold's most famous drama. Again, in 1993 patrons of various London pubs with gardens found themselves invited to enjoy a nautical melodrama by, as the mock-Victorian handbill called him, 'the Father of the Genre DOUGLAS JERROLD'.

As for the Caudle lectures, despite being scorned by one early feminist writer Alice Meynell (see above, p. 165) and subverted by another, the novelist Sarah Grand,[18] the little book went on being steadily reprinted for the first two decades of the 20th century. Then, as noted above, there was a long gap with only one reprint in 1950. In 1974 it was rediscovered by that omnivorous reader Anthony Burgess, who celebrated it as a great anti-feminist joke ('the skill with which … Jerrold has recorded the Eternal Sound of Woman, especially in Bed') and 'one of the funniest books in the language'.[19] The joke seems to have had a distinctly dark tinge to it for some later readers, however. Reviewing Burgess's edition Robertson Davies found that the value of Jerrold's work for us today was that

> it captures in a concise form an area of Victorian life which was often written about by serious novelists, but which the humorists discussed only by indirection: it is the region of the marriage of incompatibles, a welter of jealousy, suspicion and cruelty.[20]

This dark view of the book is still present in R.B. Henkle's fine study *Comedy and Culture in England 1820-1900* (1980) in which he comments on the 'pyschic desperation' of the Caudles as they struggle with 'the advent of our modern economy of mass production and mass consumption'. Even Frank Muir, including one of Mrs Caudle's best lectures in his *Oxford Book of Humorous Prose*, sees as much pathos as humour in it as Jerrold poignantly depicts 'the lack of confidence of a lower middle-class wife in the status-conscious, materialistic London of the 1840s'.

The most recent judgement on Mrs Caudle has been a good deal more upbeat, however, and I will end this brief survey with Peter Ackroyd's salute to Jerrold's comic achievement in his introduction to the reprinting (2000) of the Caudle Lectures in the Prion Humour Classics series:

> Mrs Caudle's Curtain Lectures might almost be described as a Victorian Arabian Nights except, alas, in this case the ending is not deferred for ever. A psychologist might argue that the talk before sleep was some kind of substitute for sex – hence the note of barely restrained hysteria – if it were not for the fact that there also seems to be an unlimited supply of children. But analysis is useless in the face of a phenomenon such as Margaret Caudle. It need only be stated that, with his creation, Douglas Jerrold has earned a place with Oscar Wilde and Mark Twain as one of the great comic geniuses of his century. He died young, at the age of fifty-four, but Mrs Caudle is ageless.

Appendix

The Jerrold Family After Jerrold

(This Appendix supplies information about some of the descendants of three of Jerrold's five surviving children, as well as the little that is known about what became of his middle son. His youngest daughter Mary Anne ['Polly'] died unmarried – see above p. 272)

William Blanchard Jerrold survived his father for 27 years. Having succeeded him as Editor of *Lloyd's Weekly Newspaper*, he retained that position until his death. The paper evidently flourished under his editorship, with a 40,000 increase in circulation between 1863 and 1884,[1] but it can hardly be said to have had his undivided attention. Between 1857 and his death he published some two dozen books, mainly relating to Paris and Parisian life such as *On the Boulevards* (1867), or on the English in Paris such as *Cockayne in Paris* (1871, wittily illustrated by Gustave Doré), or else to food, for example *The Dinner Bell* (1878), 'a gastromic manual: teaching the mistress how to rule a dainty and thrifty cuisine, and the cook how to prepare a great variety of dishes with economy'. Under the pen-name of 'Fin-Bec' he edited (1871-72) a cheap periodical entitled *Knife and Fork* dedicated to the art 'of eating healthily, with refinement and with economy'. Extraordinarily for such a devoted son of Douglas Jerrold, Blanchard became an apologist for Napoleon III, publishing (1874-82) a four-volume authorised life of the Emperor. Its preface gratefully acknowledges the help 'abundantly bestowed by the Imperial family'. The only work of Blanchard's still in print owes its survival to the artist who worked with him on it. This is *London. A Pilgrimage*, first published in thirteen parts in 1872. Through his powerful, haunting illustrations for this work Doré has probably done more than anyone else, Dickens always excepted, to form our image of Victorian London. Blanchard's somewhat vapid text is seldom cited, however.

Blanchard's collaboration with Doré (of whom he wrote a biography which was published posthumously) added considerably to his income, as Sala noted in a letter to Edmund Yates of 30 March 1874: 'Bill, I think, is prosperous. Chislehurst and Doré have made him fat.'[2] Considering this, and the fact that he had his continuing *Lloyd's* editorial salary (a good deal less than his father's had been, however), we may feel surprised that when he died intestate in 1884 his personal estate amounted to no more than £2,047. 16s. 2d. He was buried with his father at Norwood.

Blanchard's son Evelyn (1851-85), based in Paris, and his daughter Alice (1850-92) both became journalists. Alice 'reviews the mags in *Lloyds*', Sala told Yates. She married, much against her father's wishes, a fellow-journalist Adolphe Smith who collaborated with the photographer John Thomson on a remarkable monthly series entitled *Street Life in London* (?1877). Evelyn and his son Laurence (1872-1918) continued the family tradition of writing about France for English readers (e.g. *The Real France*, 1911). Laurence's son Gilbert (1909-50) had a distinguished career in the French Air Corps and founded the Ecole Nationale Professionelle de l'Air at Cap Matifou in Algiers in 1943. Blanchard Jerrold's younger son Sidney (1857-?1933), a barrister and author, was a Russian scholar who published a translation of Turgenev in 1884. His son, Douglas Francis Jerrold (1893-1964), having fought in the Great War and been severely wounded at Gallipoli, became a prominent right-wing writer and publisher during the 1930s. He co-founded the firm of Eyre and Spottiswoode and was Editor of the *English Review*, the journal of intellectual Toryism. A strong Catholic (his sister became a nun[3]), he vigorously supported Franco's fight against the 'irreligious' Spanish Republicans. In 1937 he published his autobiography *Georgian Adventure*.

Jerrold's daughter Jane Mayhew was, as we have seen, for many years a loyal and supportive wife to her disorganised spouse but Anne Humpherys records that 'Mayhew's final years brought a more or less permanent if friendly separation' and he was not present at her deathbed in 1880.[4] Their grand-daughter Mary (1877-1955) became, as Mary Jerrold, a leading actress on the West End stage and in British films during the 1930s, but achieved her greatest success co-starring with Lilian Braithwaite as one of the two lethal old ladies in Joseph Kesselring's *Arsenic and Old Lace*. This enjoyed a run of three and a half years at the Strand Theatre from 1942 to 1946. Mary married the actor Hubert Harben and their daughter Joan Harben (1909-53) made her first appearance on stage as a babe in arms, like her great-great grandfather. In later life she created the role of the immortal character Mona Lott with her catch-phrase, 'It's being so cheerful as keeps me going' in Tommy Handley's radio comedy show I.T.M.A. Mary Jerrold's son Philip Harben (1905-70), also made a niche for himself in the BBC, becoming Britain's first TV chef in the 1950s when his shows attracted huge numbers of viewers.

Jerrold's restless middle son, Douglas Edmund (born 1828), always known as 'Ned', turned up in Austin, Texas, in the early 1870s, according to a letter published by Gaines Kincaid in *Notes and Queries* in January 1971. Kincaid states that Edmund arrived in Austin as a touring actor but found employment, after the company he was with folded, as a political cartoonist working for the local Republican paper. Apparently the Democrats refused to believe that he was Jerrold's son. After the Republicans were defeated Edmund returned to acting and appeared in one of his father's plays. But he was chiefly known, says Kincaid, as a painter – and a photograph of one of his paintings, depicting the 1874 gubernatorial inauguration, is still extant. Kincaid appealed for further information about Edmund but none seems to have been forthcoming.

Jerrold's youngest son, Paxton's former pupil Thomas Serle (1833-1907), married his cousin Jane Matilda Copeland in 1858. She was the daughter of Jerrold's sister Elizabeth and the theatre manager William Copeland and thus the niece of both Mrs Fitzwilliam, William's sister, and J.B. Buckstone, who was married to William's sister Bella. Despite their intensely theatrical ancestry, Tom and Jane devoted themselves to market gardening[5] and wrote, separately or jointly, a number of books on the subject, e.g. *The Garden That Paid the Rent* (1860) and *Our Kitchen Garden. The Plants We Grow And How We Cook Them* (1881). In his preface to the latter book, dated from Bromley in Kent, Tom Jerrold urges the better-off to eat more vegetables and less meat so that there might be more of the latter available for poorer customers. The poor do not eat vegetables, he claims, bread being 'more handy' and 'Among the middle classes it is idleness on the part of the servants, and supineness on the part of the mistresses, which causes an almost total disregard of the value of our cheap and health-sustaining vegetables … cook will bristle up and vow she cannot remain where "them nasty foreign messes" are eaten and "all her time taken up cleaning vegetables".'

Tom's son, Walter Copeland Jerrold (1865-1929) was a journalist who worked on the *Daily Telegraph* 1904-14, a bookman and a miscellaneous writer. As noted above, he more than maintained the family tradition of prolific publishing in that he authored or edited a stream of anthologies and biographical, historical or topographical works – *Henry VIII and His Wives*, *Highways and Byways in Kent*, *Kitchener of Khartoum*, *The Heart of London*, *Five Queer Women*, *A Book of Famous Wits*, etc. etc. Walter's numerous biographies included the two-volume life of his grandfather, *Douglas Jerrold. Dramatist and Wit* frequently cited in the present work. One of Walter's four daughters, Ianthe Bridgman Jerrold (died 1977), 'being a member of a family devoted to books and bookmen, began writing as soon as she could hold a pencil, and as early as her eleventh year had the pleasure of seeing herself in print', according to the 'Editor's Note' prefixed to her book of poems, *The Road of Life* (1915) (readers were reassured that despite her literary precocity, Ianthe's 'hobbies and pursuits are those of any other healthy schoolgirl – hockey, cricket, tennis, swimming'). Between 1923 and 1966 she published upwards of twenty novels, mainly mystery stories or stories about young girls growing up. With Ianthe's last novel *My Twin and I* (1966) the Jerrolds' remarkable tradition of literary and theatrical work seems to come to a pause but it is hard to believe, given the genetic history of this family, that this will be of long duration.

Notes

The following abbreviations have been used throughout the Notes:

Berg   Berg Collection of English and American Literature, The New York Public Library, Astor, Lenox and Tilden Foundations

BJ   Jerrold, Blanchard, *The Life And Remains of Douglas Jerrold*, 1859

BJ2   Jerrold, Blanchard, *The Life of Douglas Jerrold*, Second Edition (issued as vol. 5 of re-issue of the 4 vol. *Works of Douglas Jerrold*, n.d.).

BL   The British Library

Bodleian   Bodleian Library, University of Oxford

Brotherton   The Brotherton Collection, The University of Leeds Library

DJ   Douglas Jerrold

DNB   The Dictionary of National Biography

Fales   The Fales Library, New York University Library

Forster   The Forster Collection, National Art Library, Victoria and Albert Museum

Forster, *Dickens*   Forster, John, *The Life of Charles Dickens*, ed. J.W.T. Ley, 1928

Harvard   Houghton Library, Harvard University

Iowa   University of Iowa Libraries, Department of Special Collections

Morgan   Pierpont Morgan Library, New York (accession no. MA4500)

Pilgrim   British Academy/Pilgrim Edition of the Letters of Charles Dickens, ed. M. House, G. Storey et al., 12 vols., 1965-2002

PRO   Public Record Office

Spielmann   Spielmann, M.H., *The History of 'Punch'*, 1895

TM   Theatre Museum, London

WJ   Jerrold, Walter, *Douglas Jerrold, Dramatist and Wit*, 2 vols., [1918]

Full titles and dates of publication of secondary works are given in the Notes for books referred to only once or twice and therefore not included in the Section C of the Bibliography where full publication details are given for all more frequently-cited works. Those elements of dates that are enclosed within square brackets in references to Jerrold letters are conjectural.

Notes to Overture

1. Spielmann, p.286.

2. J.A.V. Chapple and A. Pollard, eds, *Letters of Mrs Gaskell*, 1966 (Gaskell to Anne Green, 13 May 1849); D. Masson, *British Novelists and their Styles*, p.236; A. Ainger, 'Mr Dickens's amateur theatricals: a reminiscence', *Macmillan's Magazine*, vol. 23, Jan. 1871, pp.111-15; W. Beale, *The Light of Other Days*, p.79.

3. G.H. Lewes, *Selections from the Modern British Dramatists*, Leipzig, 1867, vol. 2, p.4.

4. Leigh Hunt to Dickens, 15 Jun. [1857]. MS. Iowa; Carlyle to Monckton Milnes, 15 Jun. 1857. MS. Trinity College, Cambridge; *Illustrated London News*, 20 Jun. 1857; for DJ on Carlyle see Hannay, 'Douglas Jerrold', *Atlantic Monthly*, vol. 1, Nov. 1857, p.10.

5. E. Yates, *Edmund Yates; his Recollections and Experiences*, 1884, vol. 1, p.293.

6. D. Masson, *Memories of London in the Forties*, p.242f.

7. Blanchard's tomb, since destroyed, is pictured in the *Illustrated London News*, 3 Jan. 1857 (p.675) and the elaborate inscription is given.

8. E.S. Dallas to W. Blackwood, 22 Jun. [1857]. MS. National Library of Scotland. (MS. 4123).

9. Transcription made by Eric Smith before the tomb was destroyed, preserved in the Minet Library, Lambeth.

Notes to Chapter One

1. 'Bajazet Gag, or The Manager in Search of a Star', *New Monthly Magazine*, vol. 44, Feb. 1842, pp.188-89. In naming his manager Jerrold is alluding both to the despotic behaviour of managers (Bajazeth is the name of a Turkish emperor) and to theatrical slang (a 'gag' was some trick of the trade designed to divert or bamboozle an audience).

2. W. Hazlitt, 'The Drama, No. 3', *London Magazine*, Mar. 1820 (Howe, ed., *Collected Works*, vol. 18, pp.294-95).

3. BJ, p.13. All subsequent unattributed quotations in this chapter derive from this work.

4. Highfill et al., eds, *A Biographical Dictionary of Actors, Actresses ... and Other Stage Personnel in London 1660-1800*, Carbondale Southern Illinois University Press, vol. 7, 1982: entries for Jerrold, Samuel; Jerrold, Mrs Samuel (1); Jerrold, Mrs Samuel (2).

5. T. Dibdin, *The Reminiscences of Thomas Dibdin*, 1827, vol. 1, pp.80-81. See also R. Dyer, *Nine Years of an Actor's Life*, 1833, p.128: 'A person who is in possession of sundry scenes and dresses calls himself a manager, and fits up a theatre. He then collects his adventurers, and the probable receipts are agreed to be shared amongst them. Out of each night's receipts the expense of rent, printing, and lighting is divided in equal shares, SIX of *which* go to the liquidation of the stock debt – FOUR to the manager – and ONE each to the company ... Every thing is shared after the performance; the very candle-ends are objects of competition ...'.

6. C.B. Hogan, *The London Stage 1660-1800, Part Five, 1776-1800*, 1968, p.2109.

7. W. Oxberry, *Dramatic Biography*, vol. 1, s.v. Oxberry.

8. Hazlitt, 'The Drama, No. 3'.

9. See entry for Robert Jerrold in Highfill et al., eds, *Biographical Dictionary*; for further details re. both Robert and Charles see WJ, pp.32-36. For a hostile account of Robert as manager see J. Cowell, *Thirty Years Passed Among the Players in England and America*, p.30f. ('He was actually the *unnatural* son of old Gerald [*sic*], the manager of a little strolling company through some small towns on the coast of Kent ... ')

10. W. Oxberry, *Oxberry's Dramatic Biography*, vol. 1, p.233.

11. Quoted from *Monthly Mirror*, 17 Nov. 1803, in WJ, p.15.

12. T. Dibdin, *Reminiscences*, vol. 1, p.81.

13. W. Oxberry, *Oxberry's Dramatic Biography*, vol. 1, s.v. Harley.

14. For an illuminating re-reading of the 'legend' of Sarah Baker see J.S.

Bratton, 'Sarah Baker: the Making of a "Character"' in R. Foulkes, ed., *Scenes From Provincial Stages. Essays in Honour of Kathleen Barker*, Society for Theatre Research, 1994.

15. M.T. Odell, *More About the Old Theatre, Worthing*, 1945, pp.184-86.

16. M.T. Odell, *The Old Theatre, Worthing*, 1938, p.15.

17. S. Judge, *The Isle of Sheppey*, Rochester Press, 1983, p.93. I am indebted to Ms Judge's book for most of the details about Sheerness in the next paragraph, also to her 'The Saga of Sheppey's Water Supply', *Bygone Kent*, vols. 9 and 10, 1988-89.

18. J. Hannay, 'Sheerness Revisited', *National Magazine*, vol. 1, Jan. 1857, pp.148-52. This smell was no doubt one of the reasons the town acquired the nickname among sailors and marines of 'Sheernasty'.

19. For DJ on Sheerness see 'Minor-ies, No. 7', *Mirror of the Stage*, 16 Feb. 1824, p.20; 'ruder realities of life': see *North British Review*, vol. 30, 1859, p.339. This reviewer adds, comfortably, 'But there is, after all, a protective power in youth which makes such realities less dangerous than we usually suppose.'

20. Judge, *Isle of Sheppey*, p.93.

21. W. Jerrold, 'Douglas Jerrold's *Facts and Fancies*', *Fortnightly Review*, vol. 124, 1928, p.348. Blanchard Jerrold calls Henry the younger son and this is supported by the evidence of a Sheerness playbill which lists him as 'Master J.H. Jerrold' with DJ shown simply as 'Master Jerrold'. Walter Jerrold, however, always refers to Henry as the elder but gives no evidence for this; he reprints (WJ, pp.501-02) a begging letter written to an unidentified person by Henry in later life (in it he complains, 'my brother Douglas assuredly possesses the power to serve me, but wants the heart ...').

22. *The Roscius*, vol. 1, 9 Aug. 1825, pp.147-48.

23. BL: Playbills/231.

24. 'Recollections of Guy Fawkes' – collected in W. Jerrold, ed., *The Essays of Douglas Jerrold*, 1903.

25. *Quarterly Review*, vol. 11, p.178.

26. Reproduced in WJ, facing p.18.

27. See J.K. Melling, *Southend Playhouses from 1793*, 1969, p.45; S. Everitt, *Southend Seaside Holiday*, 1980, p.9f.

28. Melling, *Southend Playhouses*, p.46.

29. Information about licensing from Essex Record Office; playbills held at Southend Branch Office. I am grateful to the Librarian, Pat Tomlinson, for help in locating this material.

30. Elizabeth married the actor William Copeland (1799-1867) who managed several theatres in Liverpool (see R.J. Broadbent, *Annals of the Liverpool Stage*, 1908). According to Sala, she had 'a slightly too strong *penchant* for playing Ophelia and Juliet, when perhaps parts of a more matronly type would have suited her better' (*Life and Adventures of George Augustus Sala*, 1895, vol. 1, p.140). Jane married another actor-manager W.J. Hammond (?1797-1848) who was also active in the Liverpool theatre world but also in London and for a while co-managed the New Strand Theatre with DJ (see below, p.109).

Notes to Chapter Two

1. For details regarding Charles Austen see B. Southam, *Jane Austen and the Navy*, 2000, *passim*; for Jane Austen quotation see D. Le Faye, ed., *Jane Austen's Letters*, 1995, p.239; Jane reports Charles and his family as being 'now all at Southend together' in early July 1813 (p.216).

2. Order in Council quoted by B. Lavery, *Nelson's Navy*, p.88.

3. The Muster Books of the *Namur* in the PRO (ADM 37/4056) show the date of DJ's entry from shore and give his age as eleven.

4. L. Kalisch, 'Englische Schriftsteller. II Douglas Jerrold', *Kölnische Zeitung*, Nr.222, 12 Aug. 1855. I am indebted to my friend Mr J.A. Williams for much help with translating and backgrounding Kalisch.

5. Included in the unpublished 1826 volume *Facts and Fancies* – see below, p.51.

6. Southam points out (*Jane Austen and the Navy*, p.272, note) that it would not have been the complete 44 volumes of the original French edition that Austen would have had in his cabin but one of the many English condensed versions in circulation by 1813.

7. 'Masonic Reminiscences', *Freemason's Quarterly Review*, 31 Mar. 1836, p.58. Quoted from another source in WJ, p.275.

8. See *The Spectacular Career of Clarkson Stanfield 1793-1867*, Tyne and Wear County Council Museum, 1979, p.14.

9. D. Le Faye, ed., *Jane Austen's Letters*, p.241. 'Young Kendall' was presumably William Webb Kendall, shown on the *Namur* muster-roll for 22 Dec. 1813 as having entered from shore as a Volunteer Ist Class on 1 Aug.1813. His age is not given.

10. J. Hannay, 'Sheerness Revisited', *National Magazine*, vol. 1, Jan. 1857, pp.148-52.

11. The only chaplain shown on the Namur muster-rolls for 1813 was called Fearon. No chaplain appears on the muster-rolls for 1814.

12. B. Jerrold, 'Introductory memoir', *The Works of Douglas Jerrold*, vol. 1, p.viii.

13. BJ, p.40.

Notes to Chapter Three

1. *The Town*, 20 Apr. 1839, p.789.

2. Blanchard Jerrold claims his father wrote a critique of a production of Weber's *Der Freischütz* at the English Opera House which he dropped one night into Bigg's letter-box. Next day he was thrilled to find himself asked to set up his own notice in type. Walter Jerrold reports, however (WJ, p.71), that the *Monitor* files do not bear out this story. DJ may well have made contributions to the paper, nevertheless, and at some later stage he became part-proprietor of it (see below, p.101).

3. I have not come across any references to Hazlitt in DJ's letters, and his coarse satire on Hazlitt's *Liber Amoris*, 'The Metaphysician and the Maid' (*New Monthly Magazine*, vol. 56, May 1839, pp.106-20), scarcely suggests veneration. He re-printed it in *Cakes and Ale* but omitted it from his Collected Writings after a remonstrance by Horne. See M.B. Friedman, 'Hazlitt, Jerrold, and Horne: *Liber Amoris* Twenty Years After', *Review of English Studies*, vol. 22, 1971, pp.455-62.

4. DJ to Leigh Hunt, 22 Oct. [1841]. Text from L. Brewer, *My Leigh Hunt Library: the Holograph Letters*, Iowa City, 1938, p.150. Misled by DJ's plainly joking reference to his own age as being 25 later in the letter, Brewer conjectures the date of writing to be '*circa* 1828'.

5. DJ to Leigh Hunt [?Nov. 1846]. MS. Iowa. In his essay 'Mayhew and the *Morning Chronicle*' in Thompson and Yeo, eds., *The Unknown Mayhew. Selections from The Morning Chronicle 1849-1850*, 1971, Thompson notes the continuity between Leigh Hunt's Radicalism and DJ's (see below, p.278).

6. Knight was reviewing the journal in *The Printing Machine*, 15 Feb. 1834.

7. Sala to Edmund Yates, 25 Mar. 1879 (J. McKenzie, ed., *Letters of George*

Augustus Sala to Edmund Yates, Victorian Research Guides 19/20, Dept. of English, University of Queensland, 1993.

8. *Oxberry's Dramatic Biography*, vol. 1 s.v. Oxberry.

9. See 'Samuel Phelps's Early Days', *Lloyd's Weekly Newspaper*, 9 Jan. 1887.

10. Reproduced in B. Manley, *Islington Entertained*, Islington Libraries, 1990, p.112.

11. W.M. Phelps and J. Forbes-Robertson, *Life and Life-Work of Samuel Phelps*, 1886, p.34; J. Coleman, *Memoirs of Samuel Phelps,* 1886, pp.41-42.

12. For more detailed discussion see the following in Section B of the Bibliography: Booth, Davis, T., Davis, J., and Emeljanov, Ganzel, Moody, Rowell.

13. Rowell, *Victorian Theatre*, p.10.

14. Davis, *Economics of the British Stage*, p.20.

15. *The Puppet-Show*, 11 Nov. 1848.

16. Unidentified 1822 cutting in Sadler's Wells Collection, Finsbury Library.

17. Playbill in Percival Collection, BL, vol. 10, Playbills 1816-22.

18. Sadler's Wells playbill for week beginning 6 Aug. 1821 (Percival Collection, BL).

19. Sadler's Wells playbills for 30 Jul. and 27 Aug. 1821 (Percival Collection, BL).

20. Contemporary review quoted in WJ p.64.

21. See I. McCalman, *Radical Underworld*, pp. 204-05, 220-21.

22. Lytton's 'Memoir' prefixed to L. Blanchard's *Sketches from Life*, vol. 1, p.vi: Vizetelly, *Glances Back*, vol. 1, p.143. Vizetelly states that DJ and Laman Blanchard were fellow-apprentices in the printing trade but there seems to be no other evidence to support this assertion. Blanchard Jerrold says they first met 'by accident' (BJ, p.56), McCalman that they were introduced to each other by John Duncombe (McCalman, p.220).

23. BJ, p.59.

24. BJ refers grandly to his mother as 'the daughter of Thomas Swann, Esq., of Wetherby, Yorkshire, a gentleman who held an appointment in the Post Office' (p.68). Almost certainly, this is the 'Thos. Swan' who was appointed an Inland Letter Carrier with Soho Square as his district on 26 May 1800 (Establishment Book: Inland Letter Carriers, Post 59/24. PRO). In the Appointments Book for 1810-1824 (Post 58/4) it is recorded under the date of 8 Sep. 1812 that a certain Wm. Johnson was appointed to be a Carrier 'in the room of Swan deceased'. I am indebted to Ms C. Doidge Ripper for these references.

25. Printed in BJ, pp.65-8. MS. Iowa.

26. Hodder, *Memories*, p.127. To 'turn down' a pair of socks is to fold them back in such a way that they are easy to slip on.

27. The story of how one set of the sheets was rescued and bound up by F.G. Tomlins after the discovery of the publisher's stock many years later is told by Walter Jerrold in his 1928 *Fortnightly Review* article.

28. Note by DJ in the *Illuminated Magazine*, vol. 1, Sep. 1843, p.253, prefacing some verses entitled 'The Mulberry Tree' by the recently-deceased actor Edward Elton, who had been a member of the Club.

29. Lytton, 'Memoir' prefixed to L. Blanchard, *Sketches from Life*, vol. 1, p.xi.

30. Quoted from Coburg playbill dated 3 Jun. 1826 (TM)

31. Sullivan, *British Literary Magazines*, p.314.

32. G. Stamp, 'From Battle Bridge to King's Cross: Urban Fabric and Change' in M. Hunter and R. Thorne, eds., *Change at King's Cross*, 1990, p.19.

Notes to Chapter Four

1. G. Rowell, *The Old Vic Theatre*, p.22.
2. The *Theatrical Examiner* is bound in with the *Theatrical Observer* at the BL, both runs being imperfect. The *Theatrical Observer* constantly praised the Coburg and Davidge who, it claimed, was 'ready at all times to treat with authors of merit, and pay like a tradesman for novelty ... respectable authors are sure to be fairly remunerated for their labours' (15 Dec. 1826). DJ's experience of Davidge was clearly very different from this.
3. TM Playbill.
4. W. Moncrieff, Introduction to text of play in Richardson's New Minor Drama series.
5. Scarborough playbill in BL (Playbills/281); copy of 1860 playbill in my possession. Gwinnet was also played at the Britannia Theatre, Hoxton, on 20 Sep. 1865 and 27 Sep. 1871 (see J. Davis, ed., *The Britannia Diaries of Frederick Wilton*, 1992).
6. TM Playbill.
7. L. James, 'The Bottle with No Label: the Curious Case of British Temperance Drama' unpublished conference paper 1992.
8. BJ, p.87.
9. BJ, p.93.
10. Cooke had served, probably as a powder-monkey, at the Battle of Cape St Vincent, and, later, narrowly escaped with his life when his ship was wrecked. He was eventually awarded a St Vincent medal and took great pride in wearing it.
11. For an excellent, comprehensive study of the genesis of the stage sailor and detailed discussion of Jerrold's nautical melodramas see J. Davis, 'British Bravery, or Tars Triumphant: Images of the British Navy in Nautical Melodrama', *New Theatre Quarterly*, vol. 4, 1988, pp.122 -43. Valuable discussion of the topic is also to be found in ch.1 of J.S. Bratton et al, eds., *Acts of Supremacy. The British Empire and the Stage, 1790-1930*, 1991.
12. See R. Gollin, 'Justice in an Earlier Treatment of the *Billy Budd* Theme', *American Literature*, vol. 28, 1956-57, pp.513-15.
13. Quoted in Lavery, *Nelson's Navy*, p.134.
14. Keats in a letter to John Taylor, 27 Feb. 1818 (F. Page, ed., *Letters of John Keats*, OUP World's Classics, 1954, p.84).
15. See W. Knight, *A Major London 'Minor'*, pp.58-59.
16. BJ, p.86.
17. See DJ's evidence to the 1832 Select Committee on Dramatic Literature.
18. TM playbill.
19. DJ's preface to first edition of *Thomas à Becket* quoted by WJ, pp.136-37.
20. BJ, p.87. According to J.F. Molloy, (*Life of Edmund Kean*, Part 2, 1888, p.244) DJ was known among his associates at this time as 'Little Shakespeare in the Camlet Cloak' (camlet is a kind of cheap, hard-wearing, waterproof cloth).
21. Quoted by WJ, pp.149-50.
22. Queen's Bench Prison Commitment Book, PRO: PRIS 4, Piece 41. The order for Jerrold's release on 16 March may be found at PRIS 7, Piece 49. On the frequency of arrests for debt in the 1830s and the reasons for this see Cross, *Common Writer*, p.40.
23. TM playbill.
24. DJ's letters to Mrs Cooke are quoted by WJ, pp.157-61. MSS. Morgan, Fales.
25. Guildhall playbill.
26. *The Press Gang* remained therefore unpublished. My quotations come from

the MS. Copy in the Pettingell Collection in the Templeman Library, University of Kent. Pasted into this is a bill for an unidentifiable theatre dated 8 Nov. 1847, advertising as an 'entire original Nautical Domestic Drama' *Arthur Bright! The Tar of All Weathers!! Or, Archibald of the Wreck!!!* starring Henry Reeves. No mention of DJ's name. Also pasted in is an alternative ending in which Arthur's sweetheart rushes in with a Royal pardon that she has personally obtained from the King.

27. DJ to Leigh Hunt, 22 Dec. 1830. MS. Harvard (MS. Eng 883 (Ib)).

Notes to Chapter Five

1. BJ, p.128.

2. Letter to Thomas Gaspey, 11 Aug. 1836. MS. Morgan.

3. Information from Mr Hamill, Director of Communications, Freemasons Hall.

4. BJ, p.76; S.A. Pope, *The Bank of England Lodge of Ancient Free and Accepted Masons of England, No. 263, its history and the lifework of its members ... 1788-1931*, 1932.

5. He seems later, as Walter Jerrold notes (WJ, p.199) to have been able to buy back the copyright and in 1835 was paid a fee by Covent Garden when they brought the play into their repertoire (Stephens, *Profession of the Playwright*, p.43).

6. J.P. Collier, *An Old Man's Diary*, 1871, p.27 (under date 24 Feb. 1832).

7. Blurb on playbill (Guildhall Collection) for first performance of *Martha Willis*, probably written by DJ himself.

8. Farrell appeared in Hessian boots and Jerrold exclaimed, 'D – n it, sir, I expected brains, not boots!' (E. Stirling, *Old Drury Lane,* 1881, vol. 1, p.75).

9. Letter of 27 Jan. 1832 from Wilkie to Stanfield quoted in the anon. Introduction to French's ed. (French's Standard Drama, no.28, New York, n.d.) of *The Rent Day*, Harvard Theatre Collection. For the definitive discussion of the stage picturing of Wilkie's paintings in this play and the political resonances involved see M. Meisel, *Realizations*, ch. 8.

10. J. Kenney's 'Advertisement' to *Masaniello* (Drury Lane, 3 May 1830), Lacy's Acting Ed. Jerrold's reunion with Stanfield at Drury Lane features in earlier biographical studies but it seems likely that he would have come across him earlier, at the Coburg, where Stanfield first worked at scene-painting.

11. *The National Omnibus*, 31 Aug. 1832 (noticing the pirated production of the play at the Haymarket); ibid., 27 Jan. 1832.

12. See D. Duffy, 'Heroic Mothers and Militant Lovers. Representations of Lower Class Women in Melodrama of the 1830s and 1840s', *Nineteenth Century Theatre*, vol. 27, Summer 1999, pp.41-65.

13. The *National Omnibus* protested against the Haymarket appropriation of the play with no payment to Jerrold: 'With actors and managers, men of genius are considered somewhat in the light of dogs – they may be treated as unceremoniously as possible – they are persons of the smallest possible consequence ... ' (31 Aug. 1832, p.278).

14. If he did say this, Jerrold was overlooking his friend J.B. Buckstone's hugely successful *Luke the Labourer* (1826) which Louis James calls 'a good early example of the way in which the "heroic" style of Pixérécourt becomes transferred into a domestic situation' (Bradby, ed., *Performance and Politics in Popular Drama*, 1980, p.13). In his prefatory remarks to *Luke* in the Cumberland's Minor Theatre edition of the play, George Daniel says, 'It is scenes of every-day life, as approximating nearer to *our own* condition, that affect us most'; Luke's bitter agony and his savage revenge on Farmer Wakefield are called 'truly heart-rending'.

15. The Chartist Ernest Jones seems to have overlooked Jerrold's and two or

three other 'factory' plays of the 1830s when he condemned the drama in 1847 for having been the 'pander to wealth and fashion': 'We have the misfortunes of younger sons, the mishaps of injured daughters of noble houses, but when has the Bastille victim, when the lost child of labour, when has the hapless operative [the martyrs of the nineteenth century], when have these been brought before the public eye in the drama, or when will they?' (quoted in Y.V. Kovalev, ed., *An Anthology of Chartist Literature,* 1956, p.22).

16. Quoted, like the dialogue in the play, from MS. in the Lord Chamberlain's Collection (loc. cit.). Of the eight scene-settings called for by the script, only the last is designated 'Interior of Cotton Factory'.

17. A much starker and more realistic play than Jerrold's, John Walker's *The Factory Lad,* was produced at the Surrey nine days after the débâcle at Drury Lane and ran for six nights. It was also printed both by Duncombe and Dick (the latter text showing it was revived at the Surrey in 1834). Walker's factory owner is anything but benevolent (but no melodrama villain either), there is much outspoken social criticism and no happy ending. Clearly, the predominantly working-class Surrey audience had no problem with this strongly Radical play. For excellent discussion of Walker's play see R. Estill, 'The Factory Lad: Melodrama as Propaganda', *Theatre Quarterly*, vol. 1, 1971, pp.22-26. Both S. Vernon, 'Trouble Up At T'Mill: the Rise and Decline of the Factory Play in the 1830s and 1840s', *Victorian Studies*, vol. 20, 1977, pp.117-39, and K. Newey, 'Climbing Boys and Factory Girls: Popular Melodramas of Working Life', *Journal of Victorian Culture*, vol. 5, 2000, pp.28-43, discuss Jerrold's play in illuminating detail.

18. The farces were both one-acters, *Swamp Hall* (Haymarket, 11 Sep. 1833) and *The Man's An Ass* (Queen's, 26 Oct. 1833) and both failures; the 'burlettas' were *Hearts and Diamonds* (Olympic, 13 Feb. 1835) and *Birds of Paradise* (Queen's, 5 Mar. 1835), the former of which at least seems to have been moderately successful, no doubt partly because of Vestris's presence in the cast – she was managing the Olympic at this time. *Doves in a Cage* (Adelphi, 18 Dec. 1835) was billed as 'a new Burletta' – it could not be billed as 'a Comedy' at a minor theatre but was so designated by Jerrold when he printed it.

19. Charles II is so designated by George Daniel in his prefatory 'Remarks' to Cumberland's edition of *The Bride of Ludgate*. He also calls him 'a profane wit, a gentlemanly ruffian, on whom the sweet uses of adversity were lost'.

20. Preface to *The Housekeeper; or, The White Rose,* Miller's Modern Acting Drama, 1833.

21. Serjeant Talfourd, acting for Jerrold in his case against Morris, the Haymarket manager, over payment for *Beau Nash* observed that it 'was completely settled by the authority of both the *Spectator* and the *Tatler* ... that nine representations were all that was required to establish the success of a dramatic production' (*The Times*, 18 May 1835, p.3).

22. 'For several years,' Balfe wrote to DJ (6 Mar. 1856), 'I have had my mind fixed upon your "Housekeeper" she would make a delightful opera! Will you allow it? ... ' MS. Private.

23. *Figaro in London* on *Nell Gwynne* 19 Jan. 1833; the *Morning Chronicle* on *Beau Nash*, 17 Jul. 1834: *New Monthly Magazine* on *The Wedding Gown* (Drury Lane, 2 Jan. 1834), vol. 40, p.254.

24. *Morning Chronicle* on *The Wedding Gown* (3 Jan. 1834), Forster on *Beau Nash* (quoted WJ, p.237) *Figaro in London* on *The Wedding Gown* (1 Jan. 1834).

25. WJ, p.149.

26. E. Yates, ed., *Celebrities at Home*, 1877, p.293. According to DJ's obituarist in the *Gentleman's Magazine* (July 1857), however, 'At the least demur ... he would surrender his most happy allusions and his most trenchant hits.'

27. WJ, p.205. Walter Jerrold adds: 'Of the earlier and later fortunes of *Jack Dolphin* I have not been able to ascertain anything.'

28. See D. Barrett, 'The Dramatic Authors' Society (1833-1883) and the Payment of English Dramatists', *Essays in Theatre*, Dept. of Drama, University of Guelph, vol. 7, no. 1 (Nov. 1988), for a full discussion of the subject; also Stephens, *The Profession of the Playwright*, p.93.

29. WJ, p.228.

30. WJ, p.227.

31. Advertisement on back wrapper of Fitzball's *The Note-Forger* (Drury Lane, 21 Apr. 1835), Duncombe's British Theatre, No. 130 (BL copy).

32. Summary and quotation of letter in Jarndyce Books Catalogue No. 3, Autumn 1971, item 201.

33. Copy seen in Harvard Theatre Collection.

Notes to Chapter Six

1. S.S. Sprigge, *The Life and Times of Thomas Wakeley*, 1899, p.493.

2. MS. Churchill Archives Centre, Cambridge (CAC/RENDI/7). For DJ's contributions to the *Athenaeum* see R.D. Fulton, 'Douglas Jerrold', in J. Greenfield, ed., *Dictionary of Literary Biography*, vol. 159.

3. Spielmann, p.25: J. Hatton, 'The True Story of "Punch". An Historical, Biographical and Critical Gossip', *London Society*, vol. 28, 1875, pp.240-41. J. Hatton, *Journalistic London*, 1882, pp.12-26. The BL set of *Punchinello* was destroyed by bombing during the Second World War.

4. Sir Charles Wetherell, the Tory MP for Boroughbridge, was violently anti-Reform. The reference to speaking in 'the unknown tongue' relates to the preacher Edward Irving (1792-1834) and his followers; the first 'speaking in tongues' at one of his services was uttered by a Scottish farm-girl in March 1830.

5. WJ, pp.243-44.

6. DJ to J.P. Collier, 15 Jan. 1835. MS. Folger Shakespeare Library.

7. DJ to 'Dear Sir', 21 Apr., n.y. MS. Morgan.

8. M. Oliphant, *Annals of a Publishing House: William Blackwood and His Sons, Their Magazine and Friends*, 1897 vol. 2, p.241.

9. DJ to Laman Blanchard, n.d. MS. Beinecke. Dating from internal evidence, e.g., the reference to Lord Durham in Canada: 'Could you in one of your leaders [Blanchard was editing *The Courier*] insinuate to Lord Durham that there is in the neighbourhood of Hampstead, an intelligent active young man, whose suavity of manner might be of considerable use to him in his task of dulcifying the Canadians?'

10. DJ to Forster, 12 Dec. 1835, printed in WJ pp.268-70. MS. Fales.

11. A. Mayhew, *A Jorum of 'Punch'*, p.21.

12. DJ to Talfourd, 5 May [1836]. MS. Harvard. No doubt Forster was responsible for the laudatory notice of the published text of the *Painter* in the *New Monthly* (Jun. 1836, vol. 49, p.242) where it is called 'a small but delicately cut jewel' that could have been conceived only by 'a man of decided genius'.

13. C. Rice, *The London Theatre in the Eighteen-Thirties*, eds. A.C. Sprague and B. Shuttleworth, Society for Theatre Research, 1950, p.3.

14. DJ to C. Cowden Clarke, 26 Mar. and 14 Apr. [1837]. MS. Brotherton.

15. Baker, *London Stage*, vol. 2, p.128.

16. F.G. Tomlins, *The Relative Values of the Acted and Unacted Drama*, 1841, p.6.

17. Gordon N. Ray, *Letters and Private Papers of W.M. Thackeray*, vol. 1, p.303 (14 Apr. 1836). For the history of *The Constitutional* see Ray, *Thackeray: the Uses*

of Adversity, 1955, pp.190-93. The only surviving file of the paper appears to be in the Henry E. Huntington Library in California. I am grateful to Dr Alan Stewart for examining it for me.

18. BL Bentley Papers (Add. MSS. 46612 ff. 314, 316).

19. BJ, p.331. He quotes from Wigan's *A New View of Insanity. The quality of the mind proved by the structure, functions and diseases of the brain ... and shown to be essential to moral responsibility*, 1844, p.264. Wigan refers to Jerrold as 'a celebrated man of literature'.

20. WJ notes (p.284f.) that the water-colour originals in the Forster Collection at the V&A are 'delightful examples of Thackeray's pictorial humour, but the reproductions in the volumes are so woodeny that a reader might well have thought that the stories in which they were set would have been better unadorned'.

21. WJ, p.285.

22. DJ to S.L. Blanchard, 15 Feb [1838]. MS. Beinecke (Osborne Files Jerrold). A 'go' was the colloquial word for a small measure of gin or some other spirit.

23. For a description of M. Bonnefoy and his school see R.D. Altick, *The Cowden Clarkes*, 1948, ch.1.

24. DJ to Mary Russell Mitford, 17 Jul. [1838]. MS. Fales. A.G. L'Estrange, *Life of Mary Russell Mitford*, 1870, vol. 3, p.98.

25. DJ to Leigh Hunt, 16 Feb [1840]. MS. Fales; Vizetelly, *Glances Back*, vol. 1 p.140.

26. W. Toynbee, ed., *Diaries of Macready*, entries for 8 and 9 Jan. 1839.

27. DJ to Leigh Hunt, 16 Feb. [1840] congratulates him on his play *The Legend of Florence* which may lessen 'the effect of that vile sentimentalism that, under the authority of what is called a great name, has of late done great injury to the dramatic taste. Two or three more *Legends*, and farewell to *Ladies of Lyons*.' MS. Fales.

Notes to Chapter Seven

1. The Census of 1841 shows many English families resident in this suburb, especially of the rentier or professional class (information from Mme J. Watrin).

2. Hodder is so described by Sutherland Edwards (*Personal Recollections*, p.53) though another acquaintance thought him 'amazingly peppery' with a way of 'stamping his feet, shaking his fist, and exclaiming "By Gad!" which was thought to be highly amusing' (Beale, *Light of Other Days*, p.240).

3. Hodder, *Memories of my Time*, p.21.

4. According to Spielmann (p.273), Mayhew took over the editorship of *Figaro in London* from Gilbert à Beckett in Dec. 1834 'in the height of its prosperity' (its circulation reached 70,000 apparently) and ran it until its demise.

5. Spielmann, p.284. For more on the journal's origins and early years see R.D. Altick's magisterial *Punch: the Lively Youth of a British Institution 1841-1851*.

6. See B.A. White, 'Douglas Jerrold's "Q" Papers in *Punch*', *Victorian Periodicals Review*, vol. 15, 1982, pp.131-37.

7. W. Toynbee, ed., *Diaries of Macready*, vol. 2, p.183; F.G. Kenyon, ed., *Letters of Elizabeth Barrett Browning*, 1898, vol. 1, p.203 (EBB to Mrs Martin, 5 Oct. 1844); *The Independent Magazine* 22 Oct. 1988, p.63: 'The very name "Crystal Palace" suggests something fantastic and unreal. Ever since Douglas Jerrold, the editor of *Punch*, coined that nickname ... the idea of the Crystal Palace became more important than the reality.'

8. Named thus in the 1841 Census (information from Mme J. Watrin): WJ gives the name as 'Fevrillier' (p.330). The school was run by a mother and her two daughters and there were 12 'élèves pensionnaires'.

9. Text from L. Brewer, *My Leigh Hunt Library: the Holograph Letters*, Iowa City, 1938, p.150.

10. The piece is entitled 'The Bishop of the Seventy-second Highlanders', 5 Feb. 1842.

11. Dickens wrote to DJ on 14 Feb. 1847 that Boucicault was 'one of a school that I utterly detest, abominate and abjure, as you do' and goes on to protest against what he sees as the preposterous artificiality of Grace Harkaway's praise of an English country morning in Act 3 of *London Assurance*: 'as like any honest sympathy or honest English as the rosepink on a Sweep's face on May Day, is to a beautiful complexion'.

12. Frederick Reynolds no doubt had DJ in mind, among others, when he appended a footnote (p.317) to his novel *A Playwright's Adventures* (1831) in which Vivid, the hero, rashly determines to write a 'strong, original and satirical five-act comedy' entitled *The Vulgarity of Fashion*: 'none but a rich or independent author can afford to devote a whole year's labour to the composition of that *precarious* commodity, a comedy in five acts.'

13. Letter to 'Dear Madam', Chicago University Library (in extra-illustrated copy of J.T. Fields's *Yesterdays with Authors*, 1874).

14. WJ, p.336. *Bubbles* was played in repertory with appearances by Adelaide Kemble singing the title role in *Norma*, Susanna in *Figaro*, etc. It was performed for the fifteenth time on 9 Apr. and soon thereafter the theatre was devoted nightly to the German Opera.

15. Hollingshead, *My Lifetime*, 1895, vol. 2, p.20. Talking at the *Punch* table in 1860, Tom Taylor said, 'Jerrold's plays won't live because they've no human interest or skilful plot – sheer wit only won't do for the stage' and denied 'the assertion that the intellectual play-goer is the best judge of a play – apt to be lead away by the neatness of the writing, whereas the less educated better appreciate the naturalness of the characters, etc.' (Silver Diaries, entry for 30 Oct. 1860. Punch Library).

16. Coleman, *Memoirs of Samuel Phelps*, p.182. As reported by Coleman, Phelps goes on to recount a prickly exchange between himself and DJ backstage after the performance. Greeting him as 'little scorpion', Phelps called DJ 'a good playwright but a bad prophet', reminding him of his scornful dismissal of Phelps's histrionic efforts many years before whereupon DJ retorted, 'Bah! … the biggest fools have the biggest luck.' 'One thing is quite certain,' Coleman reports Phelps as saying, 'if he could ever say a smart or satirical thing at the expense of his nearest and dearest friend, the spiteful little wasp never deprived himself of the pleasure of inserting his envenomed sting.'

17. G.H. Lewes, *On Actors and the Art of Acting*, 1875, pp.85-87. He includes the play along with *The Rent Day* to represent 'Domestic Drama' in his *Selections from Modern British Drama*, Leipzig, 1867.

18. See Goodman, *The Keeleys: on Stage and At Home*, 1895, p.84.

19. Receipt in BL (Add. MS. 46650 f.204).

20. In *The Times* for 24 Jun. the Haymarket announced *Bubbles* for the third time.

21. DJ to Webster, 2 July 1842. MS. Harry Ransom Humanities Research Center, University of Austin, Texas.

22. The receipt for the money, in Jerrold's autograph, is in the Bradbury Family Letter-Book in the *Punch* Library. Interestingly, it includes a provision allowing Jerrold, in the case of *Punch* ceasing publication, to repurchase for 2 guineas each any Letters in the series remaining unpublished.

23. Quoted from unidentified reviews of *Cakes and Ale* in Moran Collection, BL.

24. DJ to Forster 15 Sep. [1842]. MS. Forster.

25. WJ, p.351.

26. WJ, p.341.

27. Letter to Bradbury and Evans 23 Nov. 1842. MS. Bodleian (MS. Eng.Lett.d.397, fols.1-15). Jerrold offers the publishers the copyright for the 'Letters', to be printed with his name (they had of course been anonymously published in *Punch*) but expresses his perfect willingness to abide by any other arrangement Bradbury and Evans might suggest or require.

28. Jerrold's signed receipt is in the Bodleian (MS. Eng.Lett.d.397, fols. 1-15).

29. *Punch*, vol. 4, p.126.

30. See Spielmann, p.49 and description of Herne Bay in 'Punch's Guide to the Watering Places', vol. 3, pp.47-48 (30 Jul. 1842).

31. Hodder, *Memories*, p.28.

32. DJ to Laman Blanchard, 1 Aug. 1843. MS. Private.

33. DJ to Mrs Talfourd, 1 Dec. [1843] apologising for not being able to accept a social invitation because of 'the illness that still holds me in four walls'. MS. Berg.

34. DJ to Lemon, 'Sunday' [Dec. 1843] MS. Morgan.

35. DJ to Bradbury and Evans, 31 Dec. [1843]. MS. Bodleian (MS. Eng.Lett.d.397 f. 15.

36. G.N. Ray, ed., *Letters and Private Papers of W.M. Thackeray*, vol. 2, p.54 (Thackeray to Mrs Carmichael-Smyth, 11-? Jun. 1842).

37. See statistical table of contributors printed in Spielmann, p.260.

38. W. Jerrold, *Douglas Jerrold and Punch*, p.18.

39. *Punch*, vol. 7, p.166; vol. 7, pp.156 and 157; vol. 7, p.100; vol. 7, p.233.

40. DJ to Forster, 20 Sep. [1844]. MS. Forster.

41. DJ to S.L. Blanchard, 6 Oct. [1844]. MS. Iowa.

42. Baylis's verses are quoted in Edwards, *Personal Recollections*, p.61.

Notes to Chapter Eight

1. Cooke and Ingram successfully marketed an aperient pill, the secret ingredients for which they claimed to have learned from a descendant of 'Old Parr' who supposedly lived to the age of 152.

2. See Hatton, *Journalistic London*, p.91f.; Vizetelly, *Glances Back*, vol. 1, p.238. The *DNB* entry for Lemon supports Hatton's account.

3. H.R. Fox Bourne, *English Newspapers*, vol. 2, p.124.

4. Vizetelly, *Glances Back*, vol. 1, p.249.

5. Jerrold contrasts current legislative concern over cruelty to animals with apparent indifference towards the maiming and brutalising of human beings: 'Nay, in the vigilance of its humanity the law walks Billingsgate, and with fingers tremulous with excess of sensibility, draws out the wooden pegs inserted in the claw-joints of live lobsters' (*Pictorial Times* leader, 25 Mar. 1843).

6. Unidentified cutting in the Moran Collection, BL. In fact, three colours – crimson, gold and blue – were used on the 'dashing, flashing cover', as it is called in another cutting which says it is 'executed in the old missal style, and is brightly tinted'.

7. Hodder blamed this 'unwieldy size' for the shortness of the magazine's life 'for it can scarcely be supposed that a monthly periodical, whose page presented almost as many superficial inches as that of the *Illustrated London News*, would be regarded as a convenient form for the ultimate operation of binding' (*Memories*, p.37).

8. Unidentified cutting, Moran Collection, BL.

9. B. Maidment, *Reading Popular Prints 1790-1870*, 1996, p.166.

10. *Illuminated Magazine*, vol.1, pp.209-11.

11. DJ to R.H. Horne, 27 Jul. [1843]. MS. Berg. There is a long eulogistic review in the *Illuminated* ('a singularly bold and original poem'; vol. 1, pp.119-21) perhaps by Jerrold himself – he definitely noticed it in the *Pictorial Times*, telling Horne so in another letter (5 Aug. 1843; MS. Berg).

12. DJ to R.H. Horne, 18 Mar. [1843]. MS. Berg.

13. DJ to Laman Blanchard, 1 Aug. [1843]. MS. Private.

14. DJ to Dickens, 7 Aug. [1843]. MS. Private.

15. DJ to Forster 8 Oct. [1842]. MS. Forster.

16. G.J. Holyoake, 'Douglas Jerrold's Chronicles of Clovernook', *The People's Press*, 1847, p.187. There is a letter dated from Putney 1 July, n.y., from Jerrold to 'Dear Sir' in the Pierpont Morgan Library (Gordon N. Ray Collection) making an appointment to meet 'at my office' and acknowledging the receipt of a copy of the *People's Press*. 'I wish I could really feel deserving of what is therein said; but I feel sure of your sincerity which I cannot but acknowledge at the expense of what others may deem your judgment.'

17. After many disputes with his laundress about his missing buttons, says the Hermit, the single man grows tired of it 'and in this, his hour of weakness, a voice – a demon voice – whispers to him, "Fond, foolish man! Why trust thy buttons to an alien? Why helplessly depend upon the needle and thread of one who loves thee not, but thy shilling? Take a wife! Have a woman of thy own, who shall care for thy buttons!"' Her enslavement by her husband's buttons is the burden of Mrs Caudle's complaint in the tenth of her curtain lectures.

18. DJ to S.L. Blanchard, 6 Oct. [1844]. MS. Iowa.

19. In 1845 Ingram and Cooke re-issued the first four volumes of the *Illuminated* with an engraving of Jerrold facing the title-page of vol. 1 and the title-page for vols. 1-3 reading 'The Illuminated Magazine / edited by Douglas Jerrold, Esq. / With contributions from the writers of "Punch" &c. / With illustrations / By Phiz and Other Artists / Four Volumes / Vol. 1 / London: Published by the Proprietors, / 111 Fleet Street / MD CCC XLV'.

Notes to Chapter Nine

1. 'The Health of the Labourers' (15 Feb. 1845; vol. 8, p.77) and 'The Reconciliation: a Prophecy by Punch' (15 Mar. 1845; vol. 8, p.122).

2. *Manchester and Salford Advertiser*, 24 May 1845, p.3, copied from *Eddowe's Journal* (I owe this reference to Dr Adrian Harvey); report in the *Examiner*, 1 Nov. 1845.

3. DJ to John Fowler, 3 Nov. 1843. MS. Morgan.

4. As he told W.B. Hodgson a few months later. See J. Meiklejohn, ed., *Life and Letters of W.B. Hodgson*, 1883, p.58.

5. BJ, p.77.

6. Jerrold borrows this joke from Farquhar's *Beaux' Stratagem* (Act 2, sc.1).

7. Altick cites 'the expressed appreciation of such readers as Elizabeth Barrett, Elizabeth Gaskell, Charlotte Brontë, and Lady Palmerston' as indicating that '*Punch* was enjoyed by almost as many women as men' (p.513) but this seems rather doubtful. Three exceptionally literary women and the wife of a politician who was one of *Punch*'s heroes are hardly representative of the female half of the Victorian reading public.

8. Hodder, *Memories*, p.9.

9. Hodder, *Memories*, p.27.

10. Kelly, *Douglas Jerrold*, p.87.

11. See H. Twycross-Martin, 'Woman supportive or woman manipulative? The "Mrs Ellis" woman' in C.C. Orr, ed., *Wollstonecraft's Daughters. Womanhood in*

England and France 1780-1920, 1996. Twycross-Martin argues that one of Jerrold's subsequent (far less successful) *Punch* series, 'Capsicum House for Young Ladies' (Jan.-Jun. 1847) satirises Ellis's Rawdon House School (footnote 19 of her article).

12. Reviewed in the *Illustrated London News* 5 Jul. 1845. The reviewer notes that 'a slight plot is tacked on to the "Curtain Lectures", relative to some Gravesend flirtations, which will not bear analysis', that Oxberry was 'immensely funny' as Mrs Caudle 'and Mr Compton, as the spouse, was equally droll ... There was loud applause at the conclusion, mingled with considerable disapprobation; this latter arose, we expect, from one or two situations which had more equivocal breadth than humour to recommend them.'

13. MS. BL (Lord Chamberlain's Plays, 42987 [6]). Included in this collection are the MSS of four other dramatisations of the Caudle Lectures, including one by Jerrold himself (42986-87).

14. DJ to Mark Lemon, 'Thursday' [1845]. MS. Morgan. The Caudle Lectures were extensively pirated much further afield than provincial Britain. See Elizabeth Webby, 'English Literature in Early Australia', *Southerly*, vol. 30, 1976, p.300f.: 'Douglas Jerrold ... had his works, especially the famous *Mrs Caudle's Curtain Lectures* ... reprinted in nearly every newspaper in Australia ...'

15. *Punch*, vol. 9, p.33.

16. See Altick, *Punch*, p.15f. for an account of the trial.

17. This First Series is undated but the Second one is dated 1 Dec. 1847. WJ notes (p.385) that a 'Caudle Duet' was sung at another London pleasure-spot, Rosherville Gardens, and a set of 'Mrs Caudle's Quadrilles' were composed and dedicated to DJ by J.H. Tully.

18. A copy of the 'Judge and Jury' Caudle handbill is in the Dickens House Library (Staples Collection). For the broadsheet see R. Collison, *The Story of Street Literature*, 1973, p.98.

19. See *Marx-Engels Collected Works*, 1975 –, vol. 38, p.533.

20. These featured on BBC TV's 'Antiques Road Show' in 1997 and were illustrated in the *Radio Times* for 11-17 Jan. of that year.

21. P. Quennell, ed., *Mayhew's London*, 1949, p.525.

22. See her 1890s' essay 'Victorian Caricature' collected in *Essays of Alice Meynell*, 1922, p.161-62. 'There is in some old "Punch" volume a drawing by Leech ... where the work of the artist has vied with the spirit of the letterpress. Douglas Jerrold treats of the woman's jealousy, Leech of her stays. They lie on a chair by the bed, beyond description gross. And page by page the woman is derided ....'

23. See Altick, *Punch*, p.16.

24. Crosland, *Landmarks of a Literary Life*, p.154.

25. Altick, *Punch*, p.187f.

26. For fuller discussion of 'The English in Little' and the other later Jerrold series for *Punch* see W. Jerrold, *Douglas Jerrold and Punch*, which reprints some of them and R. Kelly, *Douglas Jerrold*; see also A. Easson, 'Tom Thumb versus High Art: Douglas Jerrold's "The English in Little"', *Victorian Newsletter*, vol. 42, 1973, pp.25-26.

27. Vol. 9, p.135 (20 Sep. 1845). On pp.130-31 are two large cuts by Leech entitled 'An Historical Parallel; or, Court Pastimes. Elizabeth – 1580 Victoria – 1845' showing Elizabeth watching a bear-baiting and Victoria watching Albert massacre the deer. For DJ's earlier attacks on Victoria's apparent fondness for blood sports see above p.138.

28. Hodgson, *Life and Letters*, p.58f.

29. Hodder, *Memories,* p.128.

30. Hodgson, *Life and Letters*, pp.50, 59.

Notes to Chapter Ten

Notes to Chapter Ten

1. 'Pendennis and Copperfield', *North British Review,* vol. 15, May 1851, p.57.

2. For a full exploration of the topic see R.B. Martin, *The Triumph of Wit. A Study of Victorian Comic Theory,* 1974.

3. Martin, *Triumph,* p.24

4. Hunt ignores – what he could hardly have been unaware of – Jerrold's vitriolic, and highly personal, attacks in *Punch* on various individuals such as Sir Peter Laurie, the 'Pigskin Solomon' (see above, p.122) and 'the Poet Bunn' (see below, p.225).

5. 'On the Combination of Grave and Gay', *Musical Times,* 15 June 1854; reprinted in L. Houtchens, *Leigh Hunt's Literary Criticism,* 1956, p.563f. Cf. Emerson's observation in 1847 that 'the wit and humour of England, as in *Punch,* so in the humorists, Jerrold, Dickens, Thackeray, Hood [had] taken the direction of humanity and freedom' (quoted by Amy Cruse in her *The Victorians and Their Reading,* 1935, p.408).

6. W. Jerrold, *Douglas Jerrold and 'Punch',* p.27.

7. 'The Spirit of Chivalry in Westminster Hall', reprinted in M. Slater, ed., *Dickens: The Amusements of the People,* pp.73-80. For DJ and the *Daily News* see below p.197.

8. See A. Lohrli, ed., *Household Words. Conducted by Charles Dickens. Table of Contents List of Contributors and Their Contributions,* 1973, p.325. For the anecdote about DJ's '*mon*onymous' quip see F. Perkins, *Charles Dickens,* New York, 1870, p.88.

9. Dickens to DJ, 23 Jan. 1844. The editor of this volume of the Pilgrim Dickens Letters, K. Tillotson, notes that Horne mentions the story in his discussion of Jerrold in *A New Spirit of the Age* (1844) as illustrating 'the deep importance of national education'.

10. DJ to Dickens, 30 Jan. [1844]. MS. Private.

11. See Forster, *Dickens,* p.342 and M. Slater, 'Carlyle and Jerrold into Dickens. A Study of the *The Chimes*' in A.Nisbet, ed., *Dickens Centennial Essays,* 1970, pp.184-204.

12. Dickens to DJ, 16 Nov. 1844 (Pilgrim, vol. 4, p.219).

13. See Pilgrim, vol. 4, 1977, p.183.

14. See M. Slater, ed., Dickens: *The Amusements of the People,* p.159.

15. Forster *Dickens,* p.342.

16. Miss Tucker, an elderly schoolmistress, is a comic figure in a recognisably Dickensian vein. Her school having been ruined by Florentine's attempted elopement, she becomes dependent on her former pupil's charity and, though treated with the greatest consideration, is always complaining about her situation under the guise of humbling herself. She ends by falling for the mercenary charms of the con-man Professor Truffles.

17. Dickens to DJ, 9 Jul. 1845 (Pilgrim, vol. 4, p.329).

18. DJ to Dickens, 6 Feb. [1847]. MS. Private.

19. DJ to CD, Putney, 20 May [n.y.]. MS. Huntington Library, HM27939.

20. Dickens to DJ, 26 May 1846 (Pilgrim, vol. 4, p.557). In the same letter Dickens thanks Jerrold for a copy of 'the Hermit' (i.e., 'The Chronicles of Clovernook'): 'He took my fancy mightily, when I first saw him in the Illuminated; and I have stowed him away in the left-hand breast pocket of my travelling coat, that we may hold pleasant converse together on the Rhine. You see what confidence I have in him!'

21. Dickens to DJ, 24 Oct. 1846 (Pilgrim, vol. 4, p.644).

22 Quoted by A. Locker in F.G. Kitton, *Dickens By Pen and Pencil,* 1890, p.173.

23. Vizetelly, *Glances Back*, vol.1, p.142.

24. E. Kintner, ed., *Letters of Robert Browning and Elizabeth Barrett Browning*, 1969, vol. 1, p.210; J. Froude, ed., *Letters and Memorials of Jane Welsh Carlyle*, vol. 1, p.340 (23 Sep. 1845).

25. DJ to Dickens [Oct. 1846]. MS. Private.

26. Forster, *Dickens*, p.462.

27. 'Mrs Bib's Baby' ran for only seven instalments between between 24 Jan. and 14 Mar. 1846 and its joke about a foolish interfering grandmother, Mrs Daffy (daffy was a cheap mixture to make babies sleep) does not allow for the variations that keep the Caudle Lectures from becoming simply tedious. 'The Life and Adventures of Miss Robinson Crusoe' terminated very much *in medias res* on 10 Oct. 1846, after fourteen instalments. A parody of Defoe's novel, it was, like 'Mrs Bib's Baby', yet another of Jerrold's anti-women jokes without the humour that (at least for some readers) redeems the Caudle Lectures. Thus, Miss Crusoe's Girl Friday escapes not from cannibals but from Amazons who make war on all married women who 'forgetful of their true dignity in the world, which was to do entirely as they like – had basely betrayed the independence of their sex by allowing themselves to "love, honour, and obey" brutes, their husbands' (*Punch*, vol. 11, p.153).

28. DJ to CD [Oct. 1846]. MS. Private. DJ quotes from Sheridan's *School for Scandal*, Act 2, sc. 2..

29. CD to DJ, 24 Oct. 1846 (Pilgrim, vol. 4, p.643).

30. In his *Glances Back* Vizetelly asserts incorrectly (vol. 1, p.292) that after the 'calamity' of the sudden termination of 'Mrs Bib's Baby', 'Jerrold's hand was missed from "Punch" for some considerable time'. The *Punch* ledgers on which W. Jerrold bases his listing of DJ's contributions in *Douglas Jerrold and 'Punch'* show that in actual fact he continued to contribute as regularly as ever. W. Jerrold's listing is complete only to the end of vol. 15 (Jul.-Dec. 1848).

31 The Hon. Mrs Norton – see W. Jerrold, *Douglas Jerrold and 'Punch'*, p.103.

32. Compare Dickens's article 'Ignorance and Crime', written anonymously for the *Examiner* 22 Apr. 1848 (Slater, ed., *Dickens: The Amusements of the People*, pp.91-95).

33. G.N. Ray, ed., *Letters and Private Papers of W.M. Thackeray*, vol. 2, p.248.

34 See John Sutherland's introduction to his edition of *The Book of Snobs* in the University of Queensland's 'Victorian Texts' series, 1978, p.12.

35. Dickens to the Editor of *The Times*, 13 Nov. 1849 (Pilgrim, vol. 5, p.644).

36. Dickens to DJ, 17 Nov. 1849 (Pilgrim, vol. 5, p.650). Ned Ward was the tavern-keeper Edward Ward (1667-1731) whose *The London Spy* contained coarsely humorous descriptions of London scenes and characters.

37. Dickens to the Editor of *The Times*, 17 Nov. 1849 (Pilgrim, vol. 5, p.654).

38. V. Gatrell is less than fair to DJ in his monumental *The Hanging Tree. Execution and the English People 1770-1868*, 1994, when he writes (p.297) that all the pro-abolitionists of the early 1840s changed their mind by the end of the decade and 'thought it was all right to hang murderers after all' provided 'the messy business' was 'hidden behind prison walls'. He does not mention DJ, instead subsuming him under '*Punch*'.

39. A five-act comedy written expressly for the Amateur Players to perform in order to raise money for the Guild of Literature and Art, a scheme Bulwer and Dickens had concocted to help indigent authors and artists.

40. After reading the script for the first time Dickens wrote to Bulwer of the Softhead role, 'As to Jerrold – there he stands, in the play!' (Pilgrim, vol. 6, p.257).

41. G. Rowell, *Queen Victoria Goes to the Theatre*, p.72f.

42. Dickens to Bulwer, 10 July 1851 and 4 Feb. 1852 (Pilgrim, vol. 6, pp.425 and 590). Cf. Dickens's letter to the Duke of Devonshire (Pilgrim, vol. 6, p.602) in which he reports Jerrold's defection: 'It is no new infirmity of his, however, never to be true to himself. I am mistaken if he do not bitterly repent this false step, long after it is too late.'

43. BJ, p.338. Another version of this incident appears in J.M. Barrie's *An Edinburgh Eleven*, 1894, p.24, with David Masson as the source. This identifies the club as the Garrick where Masson says he was Jerrold's guest. This can hardly be right, however, since Jerrold was never a member of the Garrick and it is difficult to think what club it could have been since Jerrold did not become a member of any of the gentlemen's clubs that would have had a 'Stranger's Room', until 1856 when he joined the Reform. But then Dickens was never a member of the Reform. The only solution would seem to be that Jerrold was himself a guest and had brought Masson along by arrangement with his host. Barrie perhaps somewhat mangled the story in his memory of Masson's telling it. His version has Jerrold and Dickens sitting back to back but not speaking. 'At last Jerrold could stand it no longer. Turning, he exclaimed, "Charley, my boy, how are you?" Dickens wheeled round and grasped his hand.'

44. Dickens to A.H. Layard, 3 Apr. 1855 (Pilgrim, vol. 7, p.582). As the Pilgrim editors note, a leader supporting Layard appeared in *Lloyd's* entitled 'BRAIN v. BIRTH' on 15 Apr.

45. G.N. Ray, *Thackeray. The Age of Wisdom*, p.172.

46. For Lemon's background, see A. Adrian's *Mark Lemon*, ch.1.

47. Spielmann, p.74. Thackeray was referring to the highly convivial weekly dinners attended by all the *Punch* staff at which the subject for the next 'big cut' or main full-page cartoon, was decided. According to Frith, 'discussions on a proposed theme waxed fast and furious, Thackeray and Douglas Jerrold generally taking opposite sides ... Jerrold, being the oldest as well as the noisiest, generally came off victorious' (*John Leech*, vol. 2, pp. 31, 33).

48. Thackeray to Lemon, 24 Feb. 1847 (Ray, ed., *Letters and Private Papers of W.M. Thackeray*, vol. 2, p.282). DJ, who had often satirised wealthy bishops, apparently thought Thackeray was especially reflecting on him in a passage in 'Clerical Snobs' (16 May1846) which deplored anti-clerical satire on the grounds that vast numbers of poorly-paid clergymen led exemplary lives of charity and self-denial (yet in another part of the same article Thackeray himself jeered at the wealth of Irish bishops). DJ protested and, according to Thackeray writing to John Allen on 18 Feb. 1847, 'Jerrold and I had a sort of war & I came off conqueror' (Ray, ed., *Letters and Private Papers of W.M. Thackeray*, vol. 2, p.274). There were fewer anti-bishop jokes in *Punch* after this but they did not disappear altogether.

49. Silver Diaries 26 Feb. 1862. Punch Library.

50. Thackeray to Mrs Sartoris, Oct.-3 Nov. 1850 (Ray, ed., *Letters and Private Papers*, vol. 2, p.700).

51. Silver Diaries 26 Jan. 1859. Punch Library.

52. Vizetelly, *Glances Back*, vol. 1, p.290f.

53. See B. Hardy, *The Exposure of Luxury. Radical Themes in Thackeray*, 1972, for a full and illuminating discussion of Thackeray's social critique.

54. Ray, ed., *Thackeray: Contributions to the Morning Chronicle*, pp.70-77.

55. Thackeray to Lemon, 24 Feb. 1847 (Ray, ed., *Letters and Private Papers of W.M. Thackeray*, vol. 2, p.282).

56. Thackeray to Mrs Brookfield, 13 Jul. 1850 (Ray, ed., *Letters and Private Papers of W.M. Thackeray*, vol. 2, p.681).

57. *Quarterly Review*, vol. 96, March 1855, p.82.

58. Thackeray to W. Elwin, 1 Feb. 1855: Thackeray to G. Smith, 5 Feb. 1855; Thackeray to P. Leigh, 5 Feb. 1855 (Ray, ed., *Letters and Private Papers of W.M. Thackeray*, pp.414, 417, 418).

59. 'Fashionable Movements', *Punch* , 6 Jun. 1846 (vol. 10, p.249).

60. Chesterton commented that Dickens or Jerrold or 'many others' might have come up with the idea for a Book of Snobs but only Thackeray could have added the 'great sub-title' 'By One of Themselves' (Introduction to *The Book of Snobs*, 1911).

61. Vizetelly, *Glances Back*, vol. 1, p.292.

62. *Illuminated Magazine*, vol. 1, Jun. 1843, p.118. Ref. to *Vanity Fair* mislaid.

63. Spielmann, p.74; W. Jerrold, *Douglas Jerrold and 'Punch'*, p.26.

64. WJ, pp.645-46.

65. See Silver Diaries, 3 Feb. 1864. Punch Library. Thackeray himself relished this joke and repeated it to an English convert he met in Rome: 'I daresay,' he wrote to Mrs Procter (Jan.-4 Feb 1854), 'the good fellow went home and asked his favorite saint to *convert* me – all but my nose and that is past praying for' (E. Harden, ed., *Letters and Private Papers ... A Supplement*, vol. 1, p.621).

66. Hodder, *Memories*, p.302f.

67. Hugh Diamond to J.I. Dibdin, 29 Jun. 1874 (MS. National Portrait Gallery).

68. W. Jerrold, *Douglas Jerrold and 'Punch'*, p.32.

69. Vizetelly quotes (*Glances Back*, vol. 1, p.286) an invitation to a breakfast-party he received from Thackeray in which the latter says he has invited Tom Taylor, Leech and others but not Jerrold who 'if asked, would most likely not come, but if he did, he'd take especial care that his own effulgence should obscure all lesser lights'.

70. Report in *The Times*, 23 Jul. 1857 (p.12).

71. Thackeray to W. Elwin, 26 Mar. 1855 (E. Harden, ed., *Letters and Private Papers. A Supplement*, vol. 1, p.677). Later, however, in a letter to his wife of 2 Dec. 1858, Elwin reported Thackeray as speaking far more harshly, and indeed snob-bishly, of his former colleague: 'He hated me like the plague, and I scorned him as I should a dustman' (quoted in E. Lutyens, *A Blessed Girl: Memoirs of a Victorian Childhood Chronicled in an Exchange of Letters*, 1953, p.329).

Notes to Chapter Eleven

1. DJ to Leigh Hunt, 15 Jan. [1845]. MS. Folger Shakespeare Library.

2. Mrs Newton Crosland (Camilla Toulmin) – see below p.196.

3. Hollingshead, *My Lifetime*, vol. 1, p.166. In his *Relative Values of the Acted and Unacted Drama* (1841) Tomlins had paid tribute to the 'pungency' of Jerrold's wit and the 'truthfulness of his pathetic writing'.

4. See p.4 of M. Fryckstedt's excellent, comprehensive discussion of the journal in her 'Douglas Jerrold's Shilling Magazine', *Victorian Periodicals Review*, vol. 19, 1986, pp.2-27. Fryckstedt provides a contents list for each number for the whole run indicating authorship wherever possible.

5. B. Maidment, 'Essayists and Artizans – the Making of Nineteenth Century Self-taught Poets', *Literature and History*, vol. 9 (1983), pp.74-91.

6. Hodder, *Memories*, p.109. I cannot identify 'Mr H.' – there was an article on the Sanatorium in the *Illuminated* for Aug. 1844 but that was by Reach whom DJ knew very well.

7. DJ to Leigh Hunt, 15 Jan. [1845]. MS. Folger Shakespeare Library.

8. DJ to J.H. Stirling, 19 Mar. [1845]. MS. Fales; reprinted WJ, p.391. Only two further articles by Stirling seem to have been published, 'The Novel Blowers, or, Hot-Pressed Heroes' (May 1845) and 'A Peep into a Welsh Iron Valley' signed 'Fluellen' (Oct. 1847), the latter subject suggested to him by DJ.

9. To an unknown correspondent, 26 Dec. [? 1845]. MS. Fales.

10. The bound volumes have stamped on their covers a design which is a combination of a loom and a plough.

11. For the *Ainsworth's* and *Chambers's* circulation figures see Altick, *Common Reader*, p.394.

12. Quoted by Fryckstedt, 'Douglas Jerrold's Shilling Magazine', p.5.

13. R. Colby, 'Oliver's Progeny: Some Unfortunate Foundlings', *Dickens Quarterly*, vol. 4 (1987), pp.109-21. Colby quotes Dickens's words, 'Nor did I doubt that there lay festering in St Giles's as good materials towards the truth as any flaunting in St James's.' The phrase was also used by Edward Stirling in the title of his 1841 play, *The Rubber of Life; or, St James's and St Giles's.*

14. J. Mitchel, *Jail Journal*, The University Press of Ireland (n.d.), p.72. Mitchel's journal, written between 1848 and 1853, was published in America in 1854. I am indebted to Ms D. McFeely for this reference.

15. 'Hedgehog Letters' nos. 13 (May 1846) and 23 (Oct.1846), *Shilling Magazine,* vol. i, pp.446-51 and vol. ii, pp.544-48.

16. Based on the figures supplied by Spielmann, p.260.

17. *Punch*, vol.10, p.250.

18. For Jerrold's help to Cooper see *The Life of Thomas Cooper.Written By Himself* (1872) ch. 25; for Goodwyn Barmby see Bellamy and Saville, *Dictionary of Labour Biography* (1982), vol. 6; for Cooper and Thom see B. Maidment, ed., *The Poorhouse Fugitives. Self-taught Poets and Poetry in Victorian Britain*, 1987. Jerrold's *Punch* allusions to Thom occur in his report of the 1844 Burns Festival (vol. 7, p.129).

19. Mrs Alexander Ireland, ed., *Selections from the Letters of Geraldine Endsor Jewsbury to Jane Welsh Carlyle,* 1892, p.202f. Jewsbury's brief article entitled 'To-Day' dealt in Carlylean terms with contemporary loss of faith and the dearth of widely-accepted spiritual guides or 'overseers'.

20. For a full listing and discussion of Jewsbury's work for Jerrold see M. Fryckstedt, 'Geraldine Jewsbury and *Douglas Jerrold's Shilling Magazine*', *English Studies,* vol. 66, 1985, pp.326-37.

21. See 'Divinity from Rags' (vol. 3, pp.541-57) and 'The Market – Old and New' (vol. 5, pp.519-28).

22. Camilla Toulmin has her Jerrold character in *Mrs Blake* say, 'I have not the least objection to dimity in the magazine, so long as it is hidden.'

23. See *Mrs Blake*, vol. 1, pp.212, 191f., 197.

24. DJ was also assigned two 'literary shares' in the new paper – see K. Tillotson, 'New Light on the *Daily News*', *The Dickensian*, vol. 79, 1982, pp. 89-92.

25. DJ to unknown correspondent, 22 Feb. [1846]. MS. Morgan.

26. D. Roberts, 'Charles Dickens and the *Daily News*: Editorials and Editorial Writers', *Victorian Periodicals Review*, vol. 22, 1989, pp.51-63.

27. DJ to Forster, 17 Apr. [1846]. MS. Forster.

28. Report in *The Times* (12 Feb. 1847) of Mayhew's examination before the Commissioner for Bankruptcy. See also Humpherys, *Travels into the Poor Man's Country*, p.9.

29. DJ to Lemon, n.d. MS. Morgan.

30. DJ to Dickens, [Oct. 1846]. MS. Private.

31. DJ to R.J. Lane, 8 Jun. [1846]. MS. Morgan.

32. DJ to Mark Lemon [1846]. MS. Morgan.

33. See his letter to H.F. Chorley quoted in WJ, p.454f.

34. Leigh Hunt to DJ, 29 Dec. [1847]. MS. Private.

35. G.T. Harney, *The Harney Papers*, ed. F.G. and R.M. Black, 1969, p.245. The 'Address' that DJ refused to insert was directed to 'the Working Classes of Great Britain and the United States' and argued that the interests of workers in both countries would be adversely affected if the Oregon boundary dispute were to result in war. DJ, as we have noted (above, p.197), was opposed to war on principle in this case, not for class reasons. DJ did, however, quote approvingly from the Address in his 'Hedgehog Letters' (*Shilling Magazine*, vol. 3, Apr.1846, pp.369-73). Addressing his letter to the American pacifist Elihu Burritt, Hedgehog mocks the warmongering speeches of John Quincy Adams, much to the pleasure of the *Northern Star*, which greatly commends DJ for quoting the Fraternal Democrats (*Northern Star*, 25 Apr. 1846).

36. DJ to Dickens, 'Friday' [1847]. MS. Private.

37. See A. Humpherys, 'G.W.M. Reynolds: Popular Literature and Popular Politics' in J. Wiener, ed., *Innovators and Preachers. The Role of the Editor in Victorian England*, 1985, pp.15-18, for interesting discussion of this feature of Victorian periodicals.

38. Dickens to DJ, 24 Oct. 1846 (Pilgrim, vol. 4, p.643).

39. Introduction to DJ, *The Barber's Chair and The Hedgehog Letters*, 1875.

40. Elihu Buritt (1810-79) was a self-taught shoemaker's son from Connecticut who had been apprenticed to a blacksmith. He campaigned actively for pacifism on both sides of the Atlantic and founded the League of Universal Brotherhood in 1846.

41. Lewes to George Combe, 24 Dec. 1849 (W. Baker, ed., *Letters of George Henry Lewes*, 1995).

42. DJ to W.J. Fox, 3 Nov. [1846]. MS. Iowa; DJ to Charles F. Dennet, 6 Apr. [1847]. MS. Harvard (Autograph File).

Notes to Chapter Twelve

1. 'The title, so happy from a literary point of view, so exactly descriptive of what Jerrold meant, was, in a business light, utterly bad. The name would exclude all who were not clerks; and there were thousands of young men in the city who, clerks as they were, might not wish to place themselves under the patronage of Dick Whittington.' (Edwards, *Personal Recollections*, p.30).

2. J.S. Sinnett, 'The Whittington Club', *Reynolds' Miscellany*, 14 Aug. 1847, p.222. Sinnett hailed the Whittington as 'the first truly National Club of our country' of which Jerrold fully deserved to be President.

3. *The Puppet Show*, 21 Oct. 1848, pp.69, 74. Further mockery of 'The Whittington Slap-Bang [slang term for cheap eating-house]' and 'the progress gang' who started it appears on p.104, together with ridicule of Jerrold's *Punch* series 'Mrs Bib's Baby', as well as in later issues.

4. DJ to Lord Nugent, 6 Feb [1847]. MS. Harvard (MS Eng 883 (It)).

5. See C. Kent's excellent article, 'The Whittington Club: a Bohemian Experiment in Middle Class Social Reform' (*Victorian Studies*, vol. 18, 1974-75, pp.31-55) for a full discussion of the Club's history from the beginning through to its transformation in 1873 into a proprietory club called the Temple.

6. Playbill in the present writer's collection.

7. DJ to Dickens, 'Wednesday'. MS. Private.

8. DJ to Dickens, 6 Jul. [1847]. MS. Private. All reference works give 1849 as the date of Blanchard Jerrold's marriage but the marriage certificate is very clearly dated 25 June 1847.

9. W. Toynbee, ed., *Diaries of Macready*, entry for 24 Jul. 1847.

10. He had apparently had a holiday in the Channel Islands during Aug./Sep. 1846 (WJ, p. 440).

11. DJ to Leigh Hunt, 'Thursday evening' [Jul./Aug.1847]. MS. Iowa. DJ to H.F. Chorley, n.d., quoted in H.G. Hewlett, ed., *H.F. Chorley: Autobiography, Memoir and Letters*, 1873, vol. 2, p.5f. DJ's first quotation is from Thomson's *The Castle of Indolence*; I cannot identify his second one.

12. DJ to Lord Nugent, 27 Aug. [1847]. MS. Fales.

13. London Metropolitan Archives, B/SPL/9/1. I owe this reference to Ms C. Doidge Ripper.

14. I am grateful to Ms Carole Walker for information about Chisholm's connections with Jerrold.

15. Hodder, *Memories*, pp.114-18

16. Charlotte Brontë to W.S. Williams, 28 Feb. 1848 (M. Smith, ed., *Letters of Charlotte Brontë*, vol. 2, 2000, p.35).

17. 'It left him responsible for a heavy debt, a debt which was only discharged at his death by an insurance policy, duly set aside for the purpose, which then fell due' (WJ, p.491).

18. Frith, *John Leech*, 1891, vol. 1, p.178.

19. Reviews quoted on the monthly-part covers of *The Man Made of Money*. I am grateful to Dr Michael Harris for allowing me to examine his (incomplete) set of parts of this novel.

20. *The Examiner*, 14 Apr. 1849, pp.227-29; *British Quarterly Review*, vol. 10 (1849), pp.192-208; *Atlantic Monthly*, vol. 1, pp.8-9.

21. Information from Professor J. Farrell who kindly examined for me the complete set of monthly parts of the novel in the Harry Ransom Humanities Research Center, University of Texas at Austin.

22. DJ to C. Cowden Clarke, 'Friday' [1849], WJ, p.503; DJ to H. Holl, 25 Jun. 1849. MS. John Rylands Library, University of Manchester.

23. DJ to Mark Lemon, 'Wednesday' [Jul. 1849]. MS. Morgan.

24. See R. Foster, *Paddy and Mr Punch: Connections in Irish and English History*, 1993.

25. See Knight, *Passages of a Working Life*, 1865, vol. 3, pp.95-100.

26. DJ to Mrs Knight, 5 Jul. [1849]. It begins, 'Unless your husband shall be scorched to tinder by the eyes of the Irish girls, or carried clear away by their white teeth, – he purposes being home on Tuesday.' MS. Morgan.

27. DJ to Paxton, 23 Apr. and 21 May [1849]. MSS. Chatsworth. The *Gardener's Chronicle* obituary of Paxton (17 Jun. 1865) said, 'nothing pleased him more than to lend a helping hand to those who were desirous of improving themselves' (Paxton himself had begun his career as a gardener's boy) and the *Illustrated London News* commented in 1851, 'the gardens at Chatsworth form an excellent finishing school for young men'. I owe these references to Dr N. Fisher.

28. DJ to Mark Lemon, 'Thursday' [11 Sep. 1849]. MS. Kent State University. I am grateful to Professor F.S. Schwarzbach for bringing this letter to my attention.

29. DJ to Benjamin Webster, 14 Dec. [1845]. MS. Chicago University Library (in extra-illustrated edition of J.T. Fields, *Yesterdays with Authors*).

30. F.M. Evans to DJ, 1 Nov. 1849. MS. Bodleian (Eng.Lett.d.387, ff 6-7).

31. MS Bodleian (Eng.Lett.d.397, ff 13-14). I am grateful to Dr Klaus Stierstorfer for drawing this item to my attention.

32. Silver Diaries, Punch Library.

Notes to Chapter Thirteen

1. Lewes, *Selections from the Modern British Dramatists*, 1867, vol. 2, p.3; Hannay, 'Douglas Jerrold', *Atlantic Monthly*, vol. 1, Nov. 1857, p.9; G.A. Sala, *Twice Round the Clock or the Hours of the Day and Night in London*, 1859, p.248.

2. See 'Mr Dickens's Amateur Theatricals: a reminiscence', *Macmillan's*, vol. 23, Jan. 1871, pp.206-15.

3. 'Cuthbert Bede', i.e. Edward Bradley, 'Unpublished Anecdotes of Charles Lamb, Douglas Jerrold, and Charles Dickens', *The Figaro*, 15 Apr. 1874, p.10.

4. J.B. Atkins, *The Life of Sir William Howard Russell*, 1911, vol. 1, p.109.

5. *National Magazine*, Jan. 1857, p.179.

6. T.S. Cooper, *My Life*, 1890, pp.34-5; G. Haight, ed., *Letters of George Eliot*, vol. 7, 1955, p.31.

7. MS. National Library of Scotland. Quoted by permission of Mr A.S. Chambers.

8. Re. Coyne see Spielmann, p.272; re. Forster see Sir Joseph Crowe, *Reminiscences of Thirty Five Years of my Life*, 1895, p.77, and the Silver Diaries, Punch Library, entry for 12 Mar. 1862.

9. Shirley Brooks, *The Gordian Knot*, 1860, p.50. I am grateful to Ms F. Morris for drawing my attention to this novel and its portrait of Jerrold.

10. *Theatrical Journal*, 5 Jul. 1845, 'Sketches of Public Characters. No.5'.

11. Described by Yates as '"Chaffing" Hal Baylis, one of Jerrold's closest friends, and in the practice of verbal repartee, closest rivals' in his obituary of Shirley Brooks in the *Observer*, 1 Jan. 1874. For more on Baylis and some grim examples of his 'chaff' see Hodder, *Memories*, p.69ff.

12. H. Sutherland Edwards, *Personal Recollections*, pp.52-3.

13. W. Frith, *Autobiography*, 1887, vol. 2, p.177, and *John Leech*, 1891, vol. 2, p.31.

14. DJ to Forster, 'Monday': 'I am desirous that you should withdraw my name from the Garrick. I learn from certain members ... that the black-balling power is vested in the hands of too few. I don't wish to trust myself to the *lords*.' MS. Forster. Possibly, he was smarting from having been black-balled at the Athenaeum. Elizabeth Barrett wrote to Browning on 30 Jan.1846 that she had reproached John Kenyon 'with what they had been doing at his club in blackballing Douglas Jerrold ... and he had not heard of it ... Dickens was so enraged at the repulse of his friend that he gave in his own resignation like a privy counsellor' (E. Kintner, ed.,*Letters of Robert Browning and Elizabeth Barrett Browning*, Harvard 1969). There is no record of this incident in the Athenaeum archives. See N. Cross, *The Common Writer*, p.107ff. for a good description of the 'Bohemian' type clubs to which DJ belonged.

15. DJ to Dickens 6 Feb. [1847]. MS. Private. Jerrold continues à propos of Boucicault, 'By the way, a new comedy by that ingenious forger was played last night [*The School For Scheming* at the Haymarket]. I religiously resolved *not* to see it. ... I hear that *The School for Swindling* would have been the fittest title; all the *dram:pers* as it appears being first form scholars in that social art.'

16. Mayhew, *Jorum of 'Punch'*, ch.2.

17. Masson, *Memories of London in the Forties*, p.213.

18. Quoted from Smith's MS. in the National Library of Scotland by J. Glyn in *Prince of Publishers. A Biography of George Smith*, 1986, p.40.

19. Silver Diaries, Punch Library, entry for 27 May 1863.

20. Masson, *Memories*, pp.218, 221.

21. 'Dramaticus', *The Stage As It Is*, 1847, p.22..

22. Hawthorne, *The English Notebooks*, here cited from vol. 21 of T. Woodson, ed., *The Centenary Edition of the Works of Nathaniel Hawthorne*, Ohio State University Press, 1997, p.474. Mackay later published a somewhat different account of the occasion in his *Forty Years Recollections* – see notes to the Centenary Edition.

23. After his death DJ was seen by Chambers as having been eighth in succession to Charles II in a line of 'prime jokers of London' (Chambers's *Book of Days*, 1863, p.46).

24. Horne, *A New Spirit of the Age*, 1844, vol. 1, p.279f.; Thackeray, *The English Humourists of the Eighteenth Century. Congreve and Addison*, 1853.

25. 'The Humour of Various Nations', *Victoria Magazine*, Jul. 1863, pp.193-206.

26. The *Athenaeum* review of *Cakes and Ale*, 2 Apr. 1842.

27. Unidentified cutting in the Moran Collection, BL. The *Saturday Review* would have none of this and called Jerrold 'the greatest living professor of the cynical code of morality' who 'thinks that virtue can be taught by sneers – that charity is to be recommended by gibes and sarcasms' (1 Dec. 1855).

28. *Ainsworth's Magazine*, vol. 6 (1844), p.116.

29. B. Jerrold, *The Best Of All Good Company*, p.415.

30. 'Douglas Jerrold', *Eliza Cook's Journal*, 28 Dec. 1850. About this date around half of the contents of this journal were written by Samuel Smiles, according to his *Autobiography* (pp.164-5) but this piece on DJ was clearly written by a London-based contributor. Smiles himself was still in Leeds.

31. I am grateful to Ms Carole Walker for drawing this item to my attention.

32. Francis Eason to M.H. Spielmann. MS. Punch Library (Eason File).

33. John Taylor Sinnett, 'Mr Douglas Jerrold', *Reynolds' Miscellany*, 5 Jun. 1847, p.57.

34. DJ to Forster, 16 May [1845]. MS. Forster.

35. Report in the *Examiner*, 1 Nov. 1845, p.696.

36. See correspondence with J. Fowler, Hon. Sec. of the Sheffield Mechanics' Institute, 12 Sep.-3 Nov. 1845 in Morgan and in the Forster Collection.

37. I am grateful to Dr J. Plunkett for drawing this item to my attention. Proofs before letters of this engraving cost five shillings, India proofs half that amount, and prints one shilling.

38. For the text of the letter (MS. in Berg) see WJ, pp.582-84. Jerrold expresses his optimism that the taxes will be repealed now that Disraeli, 'a successful man of letters' with 'ink in his veins' is Chancellor of the Exchequer.

39. DJ to Blanchard Jerrold, 23 Jun. [1852]. MS. Private.

40. DJ to Dr Hudson, 22 Oct. 1852. MS. Fales. DJ to C. Cowden Clarke, May [1853]. MS. Brotherton.

41. E. Harden, ed., *Letters and Private Papers of W.M. Thackeray. A Supplement*, 1994, vol. 1, p.724.

42. E.F. Richards, ed., *Mazzini's Letters to an English Family*, 1920, vol. 1, p.55f. For Mazzini and the League see D. Mack Smith, *Mazzini*, 1994, p.52f.

43. DJ to Dr John Bowring, 15 Nov. [1847]. MS. Morgan.

44. BJ, p.275; Richards, ed., *Mazzini's Letters to an English Family*, vol. 2, p.79.

45. Letter printed in WJ, p.626f. Having read Blanc's *Organisation du Travail*, Thackeray wrote to his mother that he thought Blanc's remedy for the evils of the present system were 'absurd and detestable ' (Ray, *Thackeray: the Age of Wisdom*, p.120).

46. 'An Englishman's blood glows ...': see WJ, p.595; DJ's presentation speech to Kossuth is reprinted in WJ, pp.596-600.

47. Caroline Norton to DJ, 'Monday Evening'. MS. Iowa; Forster, *Dickens*, p.529; B. Jerrold, 'Introductory memoir', vol. 1 of *Collected Works of Douglas Jerrold*, (5 vols., n.d.) p.xxxi.

48. 'At Douglas Jerrold's own villa in Putney we youngsters had a constant welcome, and there the patriarch, though witty as usual, was seldom so biting as when we met him elsewhere' (Sir J.A. Crowe, *Reminiscences of Thirty-five years of my Life*, 1895, p.77).

49. Silver Diaries, Punch Library, entry for 2 Jul. 1862; Stirling quoted by WJ, p.428.

50. BJ, p.261. The stout editor who got into difficulties was no doubt Mark Lemon.

51. T.S. Cooper, *My Life*, vol. 2, pp.39, 38.

52. G.M. Smith, *Recollections of a Long and Busy Life*, p.76. MS. National Library of Scotland.

53. I am indebted to Professor P. Leary for information about Bentley's diary and transcriptions therefrom. Quotations by permission of the University of Illinois at Urbana-Champaign. Professor Leary reports that, for all his loathing of Jerrold, Bentley was, on the evidence of his diary, a compulsive recorder of Jerroldian witticisms.

54. R.B. Martin, *Tennyson – The Unquiet Heart*, 1980, pp.303-04.

55. 'He was the most helpless among men. He never brushed his hat; never opened a drawer to find a collar; never knew where he had put his stick' (BJ, p.262).

56. N. John Hall, *Trollope*, 1991, p.87.

57. Dickens to DJ, 16 Nov. 1844 (Pilgrim, vol. 4, p.219).

58. T. Powell, *Living Authors of England* (New York), 1849, p.243. The story is also recorded by N. Crosland in his *Rambles Round My Life*, 1898, p.174.

59. T.S. Cooper, *My Life*, vol. 2, p.39.

60. R.D. Altick, *The Cowden Clarkes*, 1948, p159.

61. Mary Cowden Clarke, *My Long Life*, 1896, p109f.

62. See BJ, p.306.

63. DJ to Elizabeth Copeland, 13 Feb. [?1847]. MS. Fales.

64. Mrs Newton Crosland (Camilla Toulmin), *Landmarks of a Literary Life*, p.154.

65. Spielmann, pp.328-29.

66. Edwards, *Personal Recollections*, p.64.

67. Crosland, *Landmarks*, p.156.

68. See note 21 to ch. 1.

69. DJ to G.H. Lewes, 'Friday', MS. Brotherton; DJ to T.K. Hervey, 23 Jun.. n.y. MS. Fales; Silver Diaries, Punch Library, entry for 19 Jan. 1859.

Notes to Chapter Fourteen

1. DJ to Mrs Cowden Clarke, 22 Feb. [1850]. WJ pp.529-30; printed here from MS. in Brotherton.

2. DJ to Lord Nugent, 28 Feb. [1850]. MS. Fales. He quotes a detail of the kind that always appealed to him as a satirist: '"Here" says the progenitor of the dolly "nothing goes down but blue eyes". *Because*, that's the colour of the Queen's Eyes!'"

3. WJ, pp.547, 548. This is the only evidence we have that DJ continued to contribute to his former paper after it had become *Jerrold's Weekly News and Financial Economist* (6 Jan.-14 Jul. 1849), then *The Weekly News and Financial Economist* (21 Jul. 1849-31 May 1851) and finally *The Weekly News And Chronicle* (1851-54).

4. DJ to Blanchard Jerrold, 12 Jul. 1851. MS. Private.

5. Silver Diaries, Punch Library, 8 Jan. 1862. For the best account of Mayhew's life see Humpherys, *Travels into the Poor Man's Country*.

6. DJ to Ben Webster, 14 Dec. [?1845]. MS. University of Chicago Library (bound in extra-illustrated edition of J.T. Fields, *Yesterdays with Authors*).

7. *The Catspaw* (Modern Standard Drama no.84), New York: William Taylor & Co., n.d. Copy seen in Harvard Theatre Collection. Crabb Robinson, seeing it on 3 Jun., found it 'a low comedy, or rather farce in five acts' with 'no probable action – but merely an absurd incident'. He added, 'All that I recollect is the comic effect of these three capital actors [Buckstone and the Keeleys]'. See E. Brown, ed., *The London Theatre 1811-1866. Selections from the Diary of Henry Crabb Robinson*, Society for Theatre Research, 1966, p.191.

8. See M. Glen Wilson, 'Charles Kean and the Victorian Press', *Victorian*

Periodicals Review, vol. 8, 1975, pp.95-108; also V.R. Francisco, 'Mr Charles Kean, Actor: A Reevaluation', *Theatre History Studies*, vol. 9, 1989, pp.55-68.

9. L. Wallack, *Memories of Fifty Years*, 1889, p.97.

10. See Rowell, *Queen Victoria Goes to the Theatre*, ch.4.

11. In a letter to Paxton of 23 Apr. DJ refers to 'those advantages that you so kindly proferred to my boy Edmund, advantages that he so foolishly neglected, and for which folly he is now suffering, I believe, the truest compunction'. Devonshire MSS; Chatsworth: Paxton letters 525.1.

12. See WJ, pp.538, 552, 564, 585f. According to G. Kincaid (*Notes and Queries*, Jan. 1971, pp.36-37) '*Les Archives du Canada* fail to show that [Edmund] ever showed up to accept the post.'

13. This passage appears as a footnote added to the index of the *Autobiography*, 1850, vol. 3, p.326, which states that it had been accidentally omitted from its intended place in vol. 3, p.256 – at the end of a section attacking theatre managers for their purely commercial approach to their business. The whole passage is cancelled in the revised 1859 edition of the *Autobiography*.

14. See further M. Glen Wilson's discussion in his 'Charles Kean and the Victorian Press', *Victorian Periodicals Review*, vol. 8.

15. Information from *Times* theatre notices (no Lyceum advertisements appear 7-19 Apr.). M. Booth praises the inventiveness of the ending of *Cool As A Cucumber* in his *English Plays of the Nineteenth Century*, vol. 4, 1973, p.18. In it Blanchard plays with theatre conventions (division between stage and auditorium, etc.) in a way that anticipates Tom Stoppard's *The Real Inspector Hound*. For a detailed account see the profile of Blanchard in the *Illustrated Review*, 13 Mar. 1873, pp.268-73.

16. J.C. Jeaffreson, *Novels and Novelists. From Elizabeth to Victoria*, 1858, vol. 2, p.363.

17. Blanchard Jerrold to 'Mr Shoberl', 9 Nov. 1849. MS. Punch Library. A number of rather desperate letters asking for financial help from Blanchard Jerrold to Bradbury and Evans in the Punch Library, written at various times during 1851-1853 show that he had pressing money worries at this time.

18. The last speech is made by Captain Gunn (played by Webster) and asks who is ever truly 'retired from business': 'Life has its duties ever: none wiser, better, than a manly disregard of false distinctions, made by ignorance, maintained by weakness. Resting from the activities of life, we have yet our daily task – the interchange of simple thoughts, and gentle doings. When, following those already passed, we rest beneath the shadow of yon distant spire, then, and only then may it be said of us – "Retired from Business".' *Writings of D. J.*, vol. 7, 1853, p.303.

19. *The Times*, 5 May 1851; *Illustrated London News*, 10 May 1851.

20. Rowell, *Queen Victoria Goes to the Theatre*, p.72f.

21. DJ to Miss Cook, 6 Jun. [?1849] MS. Harvard (Lowell Autograph).

22. DJ to A.H. Forrester, 2 Feb. 1852. MS. Huntington Library (FR132).

23. DJ to John Forster, 29 Nov. [1851]. MS. Forster; DJ to W. Hepworth Dixon, 12 Dec. [1851]. MS. University of Chicago Library (MS.621); DJ to Dickens, 'Friday' [Dec. 1851]. MS. Huntington Library HM 27940; DJ to John Forster, 1 Jan. 1852. MS. Forster.

24. DJ to 'My dear Collins' (presumably Wilkie), 6 Jan. [?1852]. MS. Princeton University Library (General Manuscripts [misc.] Boxes JA-JE, Manuscripts Division, Dept. of Rare Books and Special Collections).

25. Since 1846 Mary Jerrold had been in receipt of a pension of £30 a year from the General Theatrical Fund, granted on grounds of incapacity.

26. Quote by P.R. Hoggart in his 'Edward Lloyd "The Father of the Cheap

Press"', *The Dickensian*, vol. 80, 1984, pp.33-38. See also L. James, *Fiction For the Working Man*, 1963, p.25.

27. Hoggart, 'Edward Lloyd', p.34.

28. WJ, p.547; Dickens, 'A Preliminary Word', *Household Words*, 30 Mar. 1850 (Slater, ed., Dickens: *The Amusements of the People*, p.178).

29. Ph.D. thesis, University of London, 1976.

30. Altick, *English Common Reader*, p.394.

31. Hoggart, 'Edward Lloyd', p.36.

32. DJ to BJ, 4 Oct. 1855: 'Edmund at once rejects the notion of the Paris Correspondentship .... When he entered upon Dixon's place [writing the 'Cock-crow' column – see below], he was wholly unemployed and helpless – flung off by the Leader people [G.H. Lewes and others]. When you return the Paris Letters must be dropt .... Possibly Edmund may change "Crows" for "Theatres" – but that must be purely a matter for him; *I* can't displace him.' MS. Private.

33. 'Mr Edward Lloyd and his Newspapers', Letter to the Editor, *Pall Mall Gazette*, 12 Apr. 1890.

34. Vizetelly, *Glances Back*, vol. 1, p.278.

35. This seems to have been something of an exaggeration. Altick (*Common Reader*, p.394) gives a circulation figure of 96,000 for 1854-55. Blanchard Jerrold, who succeeded his father as editor, states that the circulation at Jerrold's death was 182,000 (BJ, p.241). Six years later the figure was 350,000 (Altick, p.395).

36. G.N. Ray, ed., *Letters and Private Papers of W.M. Thackeray*, vol. 3, p.363.

37. Vizetelly, *Glances Back*, vol. 1, p. 278.

38. We should perhaps bear in mind, however, that Blanchard had succeeded his father as editor of *Lloyd's* and so was Lloyd's employee when he wrote this.

39. I am indebted to a descendant of Allom's, Mrs Diana Brooks, for bringing the *Builder* announcement to my notice and supplying information.

40. See note 37 to ch. 11, above.

41. *Other Times being Liberal Leaders contributed to Lloyd's Weekly Newspaper by Douglas Jerrold and Blanchard Jerrold. Part 1 1852-54*, Simpkin, Marshall & Co., 1868 (no further Parts published).

42. *Illustrated London News*, 18 Jan. 1868 (vol. 52, p.55).

43. For an illuminating discussion of the complexity and ambivalence of the attitude of reformist MPs like Cobden and Hume towards the question of direct taxation see M. Taylor, *The Decline of British Radicalism 1847-1860*, 1995, p.137-43.

44. *The Key to the Sabbath Question: or, A Letter to Douglas Jerrold, Esq. on Sabbath Observance. By a Biblical Economist*. Edinburgh [1854]. Copy seen at National Library of Scotland.

45. DJ to Forster, 17 Sep. [1856]. MS. Forster. Forster duly extracted seven paragraphs from DJ's *Lloyd's* leader in the *Examiner* for 20 Sep. 1856.

46. DJ to Mr James Bampton/Tailor/Edensor/Chatsworth, 9 Jun. [?1855]. MS. Fales.

47. DJ to Paxton, 18 Oct. 1856. Information from Sophie Dupré of Clive Farahar & Sophie Dupré, in letter to present writer of 22 Jan. 1996.

48. Quoted from Queen Victoria's Journal in the Royal Archives by gracious permission of Her Majesty Queen Elizabeth II.

49. See J. Westland Marston, *Our Recent Actors*, 1888, vol. 2, p.206.

50. F.C. Wemyss, 'Remarks', *St Cupid,* The Minor Drama no. 50, W. Taylor, New York. On the play's unsatisfactory run at the Princess's and its deficiencies as a drama see J.W. Cole, *Life ... of Charles Kean*, 1859, vol. 2, p.47f.

51. For the complete correspondence see Cole, *Life ... of Charles Kean,* vol. 2, ch.4.

52. *The Life and Reminiscences of E.L. Blanchard*, 1891, vol. 1, p.123f. DJ himself, thought the play had 'a strong, homely, domestic interest' (see his letter to the New York manager J.W. Wallack, 12 Aug. [1854], Harvard Theatre Collection).

53. During the severe winter of 1853/54 Smith distributed soup to 200 poor people twice a week at his theatre. DJ scorned this in *Lloyd's* as a self-promoting gimmick (22 Jan. 1853: 'Soup at Drury Lane') and was robustly answered by Smith, who dubbed him a 'queer and querulous man [notoriously] at war with human nature', in the *Theatrical Journal*, 1 Feb. 1853. See also J. Davis and V. Emeljanov, *Reflecting the Audience. London Theatre-going, 1840-1880*, 2001, p.204.

54. 'Audax' deplores DJ's 'continual and even cowardly attacks' on Kean in *Lloyd's* and other journals, 'the same monotonous sarcasm, the same vulgar vituperation, the same bad ill-natured puns, and the same bitter invective', *Theatrical Journal*, 7 Mar. 1855. I am grateful to Dr P. Schlicke for drawing my attention to the anti-Jerrold campaign in this penny weekly.

55. Quoted by T. Hughie Jones from *The Private Life of the Queen, by One of Her Majesty's Servants* in *Theatre Notebook*, vol.55, 2001, p.38. One of DJ's *Lloyd's* leaders attacking 'the great Kean monopoly' of the Windsor Theatricals is quoted by Rowell in *Queen Victoria Goes To The Theatre*, p.53.

56. Kean had published his correspondence with DJ in a pamphlet entitled *Mr Douglas Jerrold and Mr Charles Kean*. DJ declares in his *Lloyd's* article that he 'would have no written or personal communication with an individual who had violated the confidence of honourable minds by printing "for private circulation only" private letters; letters that – had the writer's consent been, as is usual in such cases, demanded – might, for him, have been posted in the market-place'.

57. According to the *Times* report (10 Oct. 1854), 'The applause at the end of the piece was loud, though not quite unmixed, and the call for the author was answered by Mr Ryder's statement that the management was not aware whether Mr Jerrold was in the house.' On the play itself the reviewer commented that its 'sole merit' consisted in 'the eloquence and sparkle of certain portions of the dialogue. Maud's description of London, as seen from the summit of St Paul's, is a choice bit of fanciful word-painting in Mr Jerrold's best style ...'.

58. *Examiner*, 14 Oct. 1854, p.650. The writer, almost certainly Forster, promises to 'take an early opportunity of speaking of [the play] as a literary work, which will perhaps be more just to the writer than to regard it, for the present at least, as an acted play' but this promise seems to have remained unfulfilled.

59. On the identification by British critics of imported French plays as one of the main reasons for the 'decline of the drama' see J. Bishop, '"They manage things better in France": French Plays and English Critics 1850-1855', *Nineteenth Century Theatre*, vol. 22, 1994, pp.5-29.

60. DJ to Blanchard Jerrold, 4 Oct. 1855. MS. Private.

61. Cole, *Life ... of Charles Kean*, 2nd ed., 1859, p.92. For choice examples of DJ's denigration of Kean and his productions see Clement Scott, *Drama of Yesterday and Today*, 1899, vol. 1, p.253ff. and Errol Sherson, *London's Lost Theatres*, 1925, p.138.

62. '... But to Edmund Kean did "young Douglas" give all his enthusiasm. He kept in his soul always a happy remembrance of the actor who, according to him, approached nearer to Shakespeare's *Hamlet* than any player he ever saw. Whenever Edmund Kean appeared, there his devoted young admirer endeavoured to be, his eager blue eyes drinking in the genius of his model.' (BJ, p.50). In his *Yesterdays with Authors*, 1872, James T. Fields quotes (p.373) Jerrold as saying that Edmund Kean's performance as Shylock was 'like a chapter out of Genesis'.

63. Information from ledgers in the Punch Library. R.G. Price is incorrect in stating (*A History of Punch*, p.79) that DJ was doing 'less and less work' for the magazine. I give the total for the year before he became editor for purposes of comparison:

1851 105 columns

1852 96.5 columns (became editor of *Lloyd's* in April)

1853 74.75 columns

1854 57.5 columns

1855 97 columns

1856 108.75 columns

1857 51.75 columns (died in June)

64. DJ to Charles Mackay, 28 Jun. 1856. MS. Harvard (FMS Eng 945).

65. DJ to 'My dear Polly' [Mary Jerrold, daughter], Terminus Hotel, Boulogne 11 Jul. 1856. MS. Fales; DJ to Forster, 142 Rue Boston, 2 Sep. [1856]. MS. Forster.

66. Dates established by reference to the *Registres des Débarquements et des Embarquements* in Boulogne municipal archives. I am indebted to Mme J. Watrin for much help in researching these records.

67. A.W. à Beckett, *The à Becketts of 'Punch'*, 1903, pp.65-66.

68. Thackeray was also horrified: 'My poor friend A Beckett's death has shocked me. He has left no money and hasn't insured his life – Down from competence and comfort goes a whole family into absolute penury. One boy 1/2 through the University ... another at a public school daughters with masters and mamma with tastes for music and millinery – What is to happen to these people? Had I dropped 3 years ago my poor wife and young ones would have been no better off.' (G.N. Ray, *Letters and Private Papers of W.M. Thackeray*, vol. 3, p.617).

69. CD to William Howard Russell, 10 Jun. 1857 (Pilgrim, vol. 8, p.346).

70. DJ to Forster, 2 Sep. [1856]. MS. Forster.

71. WJ, p.150.

72. DJ to Forster, 142 Rue Boston, 11 Aug. [1856]. MS. Forster.

73. The previous occupant was William James Robson who had issued fraudulent shares in the Crystal Palace Company. He fled the country in Sep. 1856 but was captured in Belgium, and extradited; tried at the Old Bailey in November and sentenced to twenty years' transportation.

74. DJ to Mr and Mrs Cowden Clarke, 20 Oct. [1856]. MS. Brotherton. WJ misreads 'some' as 'nine' (p.648).

Notes to Chapter Fifteen

1. Howitt to A.J. Symmington, 15 Jan.1857. MS. National Library of Scotland.

2. Hannay, 'Douglas Jerrold', *Atlantic Monthly*, Aug. 1857, p.11.

3. BJ, p.287. A check through DJ's *Lloyd's* leaders for 1854/55 does not, somewhat surprisingly, show any supporting, or indeed even alluding to, Russell and his revelations. For DJ's general attitude towards the War see above, p.254f.

4. Beale, *Light of Other Days*, p.257.

5. Dickens's reminiscences of DJ sent to Blanchard Jerrold 26 Nov. 1858; printed from the MS. in Pilgrim, vol. 8, pp.762-64.

6. Beale, *Light of Other Days*, p.259-60.

7. Dickens to Russell, 10 Jun. 1857 (Pilgrim, vol. 8, p.346).

8. See Appendix for those details that are known of Edmund's career.

9. See G.S. Layard, *A Great 'Punch' Editor*, 1907, p.157f. Layard suppresses Wright's name in his quotation from Brooks's manuscript diary entry for 14 Jan. 1869. The diary is now in the London Library and I am grateful to Professor P. Leary for information about it.

10. The obituary notice in the *Lancet*, which could well have been written by Jerrold's old comrade and admirer, Thomas Wakely, stated: "long-existing disease of the aortic valves had rendered him peculiarly susceptible to unhealthy influences; and pulmonary and renal congestion, terminating in ischuria renalis, ended his earthly career. He died in his fifty-fifth year, leaving vacant a place in literature that no one living is competent to fill, and which he had attained by his unaided exertions and the greatness of his own genius' (reprinted in the *Examiner*, 13 Jun. 1857).

11. Dickens to Russell, 10 Jun. 1857 (Pilgrim, vol. 8, p.347).

12. See quotation from *The Times* review of *Retired from Business*, above, p.246.

13. *National Magazine*, Aug. 1857.

14. 'Gossip of the Week', *Reynolds' Weekly Newspaper*, 21 Jun. 1857, p.5, col. 1.

15. See Pilgrim, vol .8, p.423, note 4.

16. Blanchard wrote angrily to his sister Polly on 7 Sep. 1857 that Dickens's letter in *The Times* announcing the final amount realised for the Fund 'destroyed all hope of a pension from government since Lord Palmerston will have seen it'; seven weeks later, however, he told her he had written twice to Palmerston, 'much against my will'. I am indebted to Mr B. Lake for supplying me with photocopies of these letters in 1991.

17. 'Literary Adventure. Life of Douglas Jerrold', *North British Review*, vol. 30, 1859, p.337.

18. Rowell, *Queen Victoria Goes to the Theatre*, p.73.

19. For the Dickens letters quoted see Pilgrim, vol. 8, pp.449, 400, 463.

20. Dickens's 16 Jun. letter, from which Blanchard Jerrold quotes at some length in the *Morning Post*, is not in Pilgrim.

21. After 1931, however, the Douglas Jerrold Scholarship ceased to be distinguished in the University Calendar from the other Christ Church scholarships in English; 'names of subsequent holders are buried in the voluminous tutors' books' (Mark Curthoys, Christ Church College Archivist, to the present writer, 23 Jan. 1992).

Notes to Epilogue

1. See M. Slater, 'The Transformations of Susan: the Stage History of Douglas Jerrold's *Black Eyed Susan* 1829-1994', *Theatre Notebook*, vol. 50, 1996, pp.146-75, and M. Slater, 'How Mrs Caudle Went On and On; or, The Afterlife of a Minor Victorian Classic' in B. Garlick and M. Harris, eds, *Victorian Journalism: Exotic and Domestic. Essays in Honour of P.D. Edwards*, Queensland University Press, 1998 pp.38-45.

2. Paul Goldman calls Du Maurier's work for this edition 'a model of outstanding comic invention and facility' (*Victorian Illustration*, 1996). The fantastic initial letters, praised by Percy Muir (*Victorian Illustrated Books*, 1971), at the beginning of each chapter (see illustrations pp.274 and 275) are, I think, particularly responsive to Jerrold's text.

3. It ran for six weeks and was, wrote the *Times* critic 'received with evident satisfaction': 'Although it is somewhat old-fashioned, and as a work of dramatic art is by no means a model which any novice should seek to imitate, it is well worth seeing as a theatrical curiosity, and as a work of one of the most brilliant wits that ever gave sparkle to the age in which he lived' (10 Mar. 1873). See also E. Dutton Cook, *Nights at the Play*, 1883, pp.264-68.

4. Later historians of *Punch* were less concerned about his inadequate political economy. Price praises Jerrold's prose in the 'Q' papers, 'still vivid with their sweep of passion and their wonderful fertility of illustration' and concludes, 'Jerrold still lives as a prose writer and ought to be better remembered as a wit' (*History of Punch*, 1957). For Altick's judgment see above, p.166.

5. For Stephen's 1857 comment on DJ see *Saturday Review*, 11 Jul. 1857, pp.34-35. For his review of BJ see *Saturday Review*, 15 Jan. 1859, pp.74-75. In his *Life of Sir James Fitzjames Stephen* (1895), Leslie Stephen remarks (p.155) that 'there was something inexpressibly repugnant to Fitzjames in the tone adapted by the school of which he took Dickens and Douglas Jerrold to be representatives'.

6. 'Literary Adventure. Life of Douglas Jerrold', *North British Review*, vol. 30, 1859, pp. 337-66.

7. See J. Gross, *The Rise And Fall of the English Man of Letters*, 1969.

8. *Macmillan's*, vol. 87, 1902/03, pp.382-89. Fyvie quotes many examples of Jerroldian wit but says, 'a writer's fame must rest upon his writings; and it cannot be contended that Jerrold was one of the great artists. But the four closely-printed volumes into which the best of his work has been compressed form a very store-house of quaint conceit and burnished epigram. Much of it is too pyrotechnical for steady and continuous reading, but all of it is good to dip into now and again, both for pleasure and profit.'

9. A. St John Adcock, *Literary Shrines of London*, 1912, p.246.

10. *Times Literary Supplement*, 19 Dec. 1918; *Spectator*, 18 Jan. 1919, pp.74-75; *Athenaeum*, Jan. 1919, p.39; *The Nation*, 4 Jan. 1919, p.418.

11. For example E. Beresford Chancellor in his *Literary Ghosts of London* (1934): '[Jerrold's] books are largely forgotten, with the exception of *The Caudle Lectures,* which have become proverbial ... . *The Story of a Feather* ... and ... *Black Eyed Susan* ... [are] also occasionally remembered.' Also E. Fagg in *The Old 'Old' Vic* (1936): 'in spite of his hack work Jerrold had some original resource, as may be seen in his "Mrs Caudle" and "The Story of a Feather"' (p.40).

12. R. Davies in *The Revels History of Drama in English*, vol. 4 (1975), p.235. Earlier (p.224), Davies praises Jerrold's dramatic dialogue as 'neat and witty, and, by melodramatic standards, compressed. It is through his dialogue that he creates tension and reveals character, and we may guess his plays acted even more pungently than they read, for the savour and relieving tartness of his lines render them eminently speakable.'

13. R. Williams, 'Social environment and theatrical environment: the case of English naturalism' in Axton and Williams, eds., *English Drama: Forms and Development*, 1977, p.212.

14. See J. Moody, 'The Silence of New Historicism: a Mutinous Echo from 1830', *Nineteenth Century Theatre*, vol. 24, 1996, pp. 61-89; and J.N. Cox, 'The Ideological Tack of Nautical Melodrama' in Hays and Nikolopoulou, eds., *Melodrama. The Cultural Emergence of a Genre*, 1996, pp.167-89.

15. 'Kind Cousin Tom' tells the story of Tom who is rising in the world, cultivating upper-class friends and wooing an heiress but who is constantly embarrassed in public by the cheerful friendly familiarity of his poor cousin Jack who has no sense of the shame of poverty and so no notion of the mortification he is causing Tom. Eventually, Tom pays Jack to take himself and his family off to a remote part of Wales and live there as his pensioner. Jack innocently sees this as a further example of genuine kindness on his cousin's part, and is full of gratitude accordingly.

16. G.B. Shaw, *Our Theatre in the Nineties*, 1932, vol. 3, p.6.

17. The Stewart Headlam Players, named after a member of the old London School Board, and later the London County Council, who promoted the study of Shakespeare in adult education, produced plays in conjunction with courses run by the Inner London Educational Authority.

18. In her novel *The Heavenly Twins* (1893) Grand has her serious-minded young heroine, Evadne, see in Mrs Caudle no comic figure but a type of oppressed womanhood ('The rule of her life is weariness and worry from morning till night, and for relaxation in the evening she must sit down and mend the children's clothes … ').

19. *Mrs Caudle's Curtain Lectures.* With a Foreword by Anthony Burgess. Harvill Press, 1974. Burgess notes that Joyce in *Finnegans Wake,* makes it clear what prototype he has in mind for Anna Livia Plurabelle – our geomater or earth-mother – when Henry Chimpden Earwicker is invited to 'list to her caudle'. Joyce also refers to 'the caudlelectures' in the Library Scene in *Ulysses.* (I owe this reference to Professor Steve Connor.)

20. *Victorian Periodicals Newsletter,* vol. 9, Sep. 1976.

Notes to Appendix

1. Altick, *English Common Reader,* p.395.

2. McKenzie, ed., *Letters of George Augustus Sala to Edmund Yates,* p.167. Chislehurst was the home of Napoleon III's widow, the Empress Eugenie.

3. Sydney E. Jerrold. She became Marie Christopher of the Order of the Assumption and in 1940 published *Parvulus. Collected Poems by Sydney E. Jerrold.*

4. Humpherys, *Travels into the Poor Man's Country,* p.23. Like Blanchard and all her other siblings, Jane Mayhew was buried in the Jerrold family grave at Norwood.

5. Tom did, however, write the lyrics (mainly an adaptation of DJ's original dialogue), for W. Meyer Lutz's operatic version of *Black Eyed Susan* called *All In The Downs*; it was produced at the Gaiety Theatre under John Hollingshead's management on 5 Nov. 1881.

Bibliography

[All items published in London unless otherwise stated]

A: PRIMARY MATERIAL

1: Letters of Douglas Jerrold

The main repositories of Jerrold letters are as follows:

Beinecke Rare Book and Manuscript Library, Yale Unversity
Henry W. and Albert A. Berg Collection of English and American Literature, New
    York Public Library, Astor, Lenox and Tilden Foundations
The Brotherton Collection, University of Leeds Library
Chicago University Library
The Fales Library, New York University Library
The Forster Collection, National Art Library, Victoria and Albert Museum
University of Iowa Libraries, Department of Special Collections
The Pierpont Morgan Library, New York (Gordon Ray Collection)

For detailed references for this material and location of other letters see Notes
pp.287-317.

2: Other Jerrold-related material, excluding
his published works

Jerrold, D.W., *Facts and Fancies*, (uncorrected proofs), British Library
*Catalogue of the Library of the late Eminent Author Douglas Jerrold Esq... which
    will be sold by Auction by Messrs. S. Leigh Sotheby & John Wilkinson on Friday
    26 August 1859*, (copies in Bodleian and London Libraries)
Prospectus for *The Capitol Goose*, Bodleian Library, Oxford (Lett.d.397.ff.13-14)
Moran, E.R., *Collections relating to Charles Dickens and Douglas Jerrold*, Manu-
    scripts Collection, British Library
The Silver Diaries, Punch Library
Contributors' payments ledgers, Punch Library
*Report from the Select Committee on Dramatic Literature, 1832, with the minutes
    of evidence*
Percival, R., *Collection relating to Sadler's Wells Theatre, formed by Mr R. Percival,
    comprising pamphlets, play bills...*, 14 vols., British Library
Sadler's Wells Collection, Finsbury Public Library
Playbills Collection, Guildhall Library
Playbills, Essex Record Office (Southend Branch)
Playbills, Theatre Museum

3: Douglas Jerrold's works: plays

For performance and publication details and location of manuscripts, see *Cambridge Bibliography of English Literature (3rd edition)*, vol. 4, 1800-1900, ed. J. Shattock, pp.2001-05. Dates below are years of first performance.

Ambrose Gwinett; or, a Sea-side Story, 1828
Bampfylde Moore Carew, 1829
Beau Nash, the King of Bath, 1834
The Bill-sticker; or, an Old House in the City, 1836 (unpublished)
Birds of Paradise, 1835 (unpublished)
Black Eyed Susan; or, All in the Downs, 1829
The Bride of Ludgate, 1831
Bubbles of the Day, 1842
The Catspaw, 1850
The Chieftain's Oath; or, the Rival Clans, 1821 (unpublished)
Descart, the French Buccaneer; or, the Rock of Annaboa, 1828
The Devil's Ducat; or, the Gift of Mammon, 1830
Dolly and the Rat; or, the Brisket family, 1823
Doves in a Cage, 1835
The Factory Girl, 1832 (unpublished)
Fifteen Years of a Drunkard's Life, 1828
The Flying Dutchman, 1829
A Gallantee Showman; or, Mr Peppercorn at home, 1837 (unpublished)
Gertrude's Cherries; or, Waterloo in 1835, 1842
Gervase Skinner; or, Penny Wise and Pound Foolish, 1830 (unpublished)
The Gipsy of Derncleugh, 1821
The Golden Calf, 1832
The Hamper of Wine, 1829 (unpublished)
The Hazard of the Die, 1835
A Heart of Gold, 1854
Hearts and Diamonds, 1835 (unpublished)
The Housekeeper; or, the White Rose, 1833
The Island; or, Christian and his comrades, 1823 (unpublished)
John Overy, the miser; or, the Southwark ferry, 1829
Law and Lions, 1829
The Living Skeleton, 1825 (unpublished)
London characters; puff! puff!! puff!!!, 1825 (unpublished)
The Lonely Man of Shiraz, 1829 (unpublished)
The Man for the Ladies, 1836
The Man's an Ass, 1835 (unpublished)
Martha Willis the Servant Maid; or, Service in London, 1831
Matthew Hopkins the Witchfinder, 1829 (unpublished)
More Frightened than Hurt, 1821
The Mother, 1838 (unpublished)
Mrs Caudle's Curtain Lectures; or, a Matrimonial Chapter, 1845 (unpublished)
The Mutiny at the Nore; or, British Sailors in 1797, 1830
Nell Gwynne; or, the Prologue, 1833
The Painter of Ghent, 1836
Paul Pry, A Comedy 1827
The Perils of Pippins; or, the Man who 'couldn't help it', 1836
Popular Felons, 1826 (unpublished)

Bibliography

The Press-gang; or, Archibald of the Wreck, 1830 (unpublished)
The Prisoner of War, 1842
The Rent Day, 1832
Retired from Business, 1851
St. Cupid; or, Dorothy's fortune, 1853
Sally in our Alley, 1830
Saul Braintree, the poacher, 1831 (unpublished)
The Schoolfellows, 1835
The Smoked Miser; or, the Benefit of Hanging, 1823
The Spendthrift, (?)1850 (unpublished)
The Statue lover; or, Music in Marble, 1828
Swamp Hall; or, the Friend of the Family, 1833 (unpublished)
Thomas à Becket, 1829
Time Works Wonders, 1845
The Tower of Lochlain; or, the Idiot Son, 1828
Two eyes between two; or, Pay me for my eye, 1828
Vidocq! The French police spy, 1829
The Wedding Gown, 1834
The White Milliner, 1841
Wives by Advertisement; or, Courting in the Newspapers, 1828

4: Douglas Jerrold's other works

The Writings of Douglas Jerrold. Collected Edition, Bradbury & Evans, 8 vols., 1851-54
The Works of Douglas Jerrold, ed. W.B. Jerrold, Bradbury, Evans & Co., 4 vols., [1863]
The Works of Douglas Jerrold, ed. W.B. Jerrold, Bradbury, Agnew & Co., 5 vols., n.d., [vol. 5 being a rev. ed. of *The Life and Remains of Douglas Jerrold* by B. Jerrold]

Cakes and Ale, 2 vols., 1842
The Chronicles of Clovernook; with some account of the Hermit of Bellyfulle [and Essays from *The Illuminated Magazine*], 1846
The Brownrigg Papers, ed. W.B. Jerrold, 1860
Tales by Douglas Jerrold, ed. J. Logie Robertson, 1891
Essays of Douglas Jerrold, ed. W. Jerrold, 1903
The Whimsical Tales of Douglas Jerrold, ed. E.J. Fluck, Allentown, Pa., 1948
The Best of Mr Punch, ed. R. Kelly, Nashville, Tenn., 1970

Men of Character, 3 vols., 1838
The Handbook of Swindling by Captain Barabbas Whitefeather, 1839
The History of St Giles and St James, 1841
Punch's Letters to his Son, 1843
The Story of a Feather, 1844
Punch's Complete Letter Writer, 1845
Mrs Caudle's Curtain Lectures, 1846
A Man made of Money, 1849

Heads of the People; or, Portraits of the English, 2 vols., [essays by Douglas Jerrold and others, illustrated by Kenny Meadows],1840-1

For details of Jerrold's periodical contributions, see R. Kelly, *Douglas Jerrold*, 1972, pp 156-7

5: Newspapers and other periodicals

Files of all periodicals listed are in the British Library unless otherwise specified. Dates are included where more than one periodical of that title is held.

Actors by Daylight
The Athenaeum
Blackwood's Magazine
Boulogne Gazette (Boulogne Public Library)
The Daily News
Douglas Jerrold's Shilling Magazine
Douglas Jerrold's Weekly Newspaper
The Drama (1821-1825)
The Dramatic Magazine (Theatre Museum)
The Era
The Examiner
The Figaro
Figaro in London
The Illuminated Magazine
The Illustrated London News
The Illustrated Review
The Kentish Gazette
Lloyd's Weekly Newspaper
The London Literary Gazette
The Man in the Moon
The Mirror of the Stage
The Monthly Magazine
The Morning Chronicle
The Morning Herald
The National Omnibus and General Advertiser
New Monthly Magazine
The Northern Star
Oxberry's Dramatic Biography
The People's Press
The Pictorial Times (1843-1848)
Punch
Punch in London
The Puppet-show
Reynolds' Miscellany
Reynolds' Weekly Newspaper
The Roscius (Harvard Theatre Collection)
The Saturday Review
The Stage; or, The Theatrical Inquisitor (1828-1829)
The Stage (1844), (Garrick Club Library)
The Sunday Monitor
The Sunday Times
The Theatrical Examiner
The Theatrical Inquisitor (1812-1820)
The Theatrical Journal
The Theatrical Observer

Bibliography

The Times
The Weekly Times

6: Other primary sources (non-Jerrold)

Blanchard, L., *Lyric Offerings*, 1828
Chambers, R., 'Memorandum Book', (manuscript), National Library of Scotland
Dickens, C., *The Amusements of the People and other papers 1834-51*, ed. M.D. Slater, (vol. 2 of the Dent Uniform Edition of Dickens's Journalism), 1996
Dickens, C., *The Letters of Charles Dickens*, (British Academy/Pilgrim edition),12 vols., Oxford, 1965-2000
Macready, W.C., *Diaries*, ed. W. Toynbee, 2 vols., 1912
Sala, G.A., *Letters of George Augustus Sala to Edmund Yates*, ed. J. McKenzie, Brisbane, 1993
Smith, G., *Recollections of a long and busy life* (typescript), National Library of Scotland
Thackeray, W.M., *Contributions to the 'Morning Chronicle'*, ed. G.N. Ray, 1966
Thackeray, W.M., *Letters and Private Papers*, ed. G.N. Ray, 4 vols., 1945
Thackeray, W.M., *Letters and Private Papers: a supplement*, ed. E F. Harden, 2 vols., 1994

B: SECONDARY MATERIAL

This list is confined to frequently cited works, and to reference and important background works. Full bibliographical details of all works cited are given in the Notes pp.287-317.

Adrian, A., *Mark Lemon First Editor of Punch*, 1966
Altick, R.D., *The English Common Reader: a Social History of the Mass Reading Public 1800-1900*, 1957
Altick, R.D., *Punch: the Lively Youth of a British Institution 1841-1851*, Columbus, Ohio, 1997
Arundell, D., *The Story of Sadler's Wells 1683-1977*, Newton Abbot, 1978
Baker, H.B., *The London Stage*, 2 vols., 1889
Beale, W., *The Light of Other Days seen through the Wrong End of an Opera Glass*, 1890
Bernard, J., *Retrospections of the Stage*, 1830
Booth, M., *Theatre in the Victorian Age*, Cambridge, 1991
Bourne, H.R. Fox, *English Newspapers: chapters in the history of journalism*, 2 vols., 1887
Coleman, J., *Memoirs of Samuel Phelps*, 1886
Collier, J.P., *An Old Man's Diary*, 2 vols., 1871
Cooper, T.S., *My Life*, 1890
Cowell, J., *Thirty Years passed among the Players in England and America*, New York, 1845
Crosland, Mrs Newton, *Landmarks of a Literary Life 1820-1892*, 1893
Cross, N., *The Common Writer*, Cambridge, 1985
Davis, J., 'British Bravery, or Tars Triumphant: Images of the British Navy in Nautical Melodrama', *New Theatre Quarterly*, vol. 4, 1988, pp.122-143
Davis, T.C., *The Economics of the British Stage 1800-1914*, Cambridge, 2000
Dibdin, T., *The Reminiscences of Thomas Dibdin*, 2 vols., 1827
Dyer, R., *Nine Years of an Actor's Life*, 1833
Edwards, H.S., *Personal Recollections*, 1900

323

Bibliography

Egan, P., *The Life of an Actor*, 1825

Emeljanow, V., *Victorian Popular Dramatists*, Boston, Mass., 1987

Fitzball, E., *Thirty-five Years of a Dramatic Author's Life*, 2 vols, 1859

Forster, J., *Life of Dickens*, ed. J.W.T. Ley, 1928

Fryckstedt, M., 'Douglas Jerrold's Shilling Magazine', *Victorian Periodicals Review*, vol. 19, 1986, pp.2-27

Fulton, R.D., 'Douglas Jerrold', in *Dictionary of Literary Biography*, vol. 159, *British Short Fiction Writers 1800-1880*, ed. J.R. Greenfield, 1996

Ganzel, D., 'Patent Wrongs and Patent Theatres: Drama and the Law in the Early Nineteenth Century', *PMLA*, vol. 76, 1961, pp.384-396

Hannay, J., 'Douglas Jerrold, personal reminiscences', *Atlantic Monthly*, vol. 1, 1857, pp.1-12

Hazlitt, W., *Complete Works*, ed. P.P. Howe, 21 vols., 1930-34

Highfill, P.H. et al., *Biographical Dictionary of Actors, Actresses ... and other stage personnel in London 1660-1800*, 16 vols., Carbondale, 1973-93

Hodder, G., *Memories of my Time*, 1870

Hodgson, W.B., *Life and letters of W.B. Hodgson*, ed. J. Meiklejohn, 1883

Hook, T., *Gervase Skinner or the Sin of Economy*, new edition, n.d. [1870]

Humpherys, A., *Travels into the Poor Man's Country: the work of Henry Mayhew*, Athens, Georgia, 1977

Jerrold, B., *The Best of All Good Company*, 1871-73

Jerrold, B., *The Life and Remains of Douglas Jerrold*, 1859

Jerrold, W., *Douglas Jerrold, Dramatist and Wit*, 1918

Jerrold, W., *Douglas Jerrold and 'Punch'*, 1910

Jerrold, W., 'Douglas Jerrold's Facts and Fancies', *Fortnightly Review*, vol. 124, 1928, pp.343-54

Judge, S., *The Isle of Sheppey*, Rochester, 1983

Kalisch, L., 'Englische Schriftsteller, II, Douglas Jerrold', *Kölnische Zeitung*, 12 Aug. 1855

Kelly, R., *Douglas Jerrold*, New York, 1972

Knight, C., *English Cyclopaedia*, 1856

Knight, W.G., *A Major London 'Minor': the Surrey Theatre 1805-1865*, 1997

Lavery, B., *Nelson's Navy*, 1989

Lytton, E. Bulwer (ed.), *Sketches from life by the late Laman Blanchard with a memoir of the author*, 3 vols., 1846

McCalman, I., *Radical Underworld: Prophets, Revolutionaries and Pornographers in London 1795-1840*, Cambridge, 1988

Mackay, C., *Forty years recollections of life, literature and public affairs*, 2 vols., 1877

Masson, D., *British Novelists and their styles*, 1859

Masson, D., *Memories of London in the Forties*, 1908

Mayhew, A., *A Jorum of 'Punch' with those who helped to brew it*, 1895

Meisel, M., *Realizations. Narrative, Theatrical, and Pictorial Arts in Nineteenth Century England*, Princeton, 1983

Moody, J., *Illegitimate Theatre in London 1770-1840*, Cambridge, 2000

Murray, C., *Robert William Elliston, a theatrical biography*, 1975

Nicoll, A., *A History of English Drama 1660-1900*, rev. ed., vols. 3-5, Cambridge, 1952-59

Phelps, W.M. & Forbes-Robertson, J., *Life and Life Work of Samuel Phelps*, 1886

Price, R.G.G., *A History of Punch*, 1957

Ray, G.N., *Thackeray: the uses of adversity*, 1955

Ray, G.N., *Thackeray: the age of wisdom*, 1958

Rede, L., *The Road to the Stage*, 1827

Bibliography

Rowell, G., *The Old Vic Theatre: a history*, Cambridge, 1993
Rowell, G., *Queen Victoria goes to the Theatre*, 1978
Rowell, G., *The Victorian Theatre*, Oxford, 1956
Sala, G.A., *Life and Adventures of George Augustus Sala*, 2 vols., 1895
Southam, B., *Jane Austen and the Navy*, 2000
Spielmann, M.H., *The History of 'Punch'*, 1895
Stephens, J.R., *The Censorship of English Drama 1824-1901*, Cambridge, 1980
Stephens, J.R., *The Profession of the Playwright: British Theatre 1800-1900*, Cambridge, 1992
Sullivan, A. (ed.), *British Literary Magazines: the Romantic Age 1787-1836*, 1983
Taylor, D.J., *Thackeray*, 1999
Tomlins, F.G., *Brief View of English Drama from the Earliest Period to the Present Time*, 1840
Vizetelly, H., *Glances Back through Seventy Years*, 2 vols., 1893
Wemyss, F., *Theatrical Biography or the life of an actor and manager*, Glasgow, 1848
Winston, J., *The Theatric Tourist*, 1805
Yates, E., *Edmund Yates, his recollections and experiences*, 2 vols., 1884

Index

Index

Index

Index

Joyce, James: *Finnegans Wake*, 317; *Ulysses*, 317
'Judge and Jury Society', 163

Kalisch, Ludwig, 24, 31, 160, 234
Kean, Charles, 242-3, 244, 257, 258, 259, 262, 269, 313
Kean, Edmund, 8, 12, 14, 17, 65, 66, 72, 84, 109, 128, 132, 259, 313
Kean, Ellen, 257
Keats, John, 36, 37, 47, 50, 69, 149
Keeley, Mrs, 127, 128, 218, 241, 271, 310
Keeley, Robert, 43, 96, 127, 128, 162, 218, 222, 271, 310
Keene, Charles, 163
Kelly, Richard M., 160; *The Best of Mr Punch*, 278
Kelly, Sir Fitzroy, 253
Kemble, Adelaide, *see* Sartoris, Mrs
Kemble, Charles, 33, 34, 53, 72, 111, 126
Kemble, Fanny, 33, 72
Kendall, William Webb, 290
Kent, 13, 14, 147, 150, 280
Kentish Gazette, 15, 18
Kentish Town, 114, 121
Kenyon, John, 308
Kilburn, 263, 266
Killarney, Lakes of, 214-16
Kincaid, Gaines, 284
Kingsley, Charles, 172, 194
Knight, Charles, 2-3, 33, 37, 207, 208, 214-15, 228, 242, 243; *Men of the Time*, 226-7; *Penny Cyclopedia*, 3
Knowles, Sheridan, 262
Kossuth, Lajos, 230, 254
Kotzebue: *Die Spanier in Peru*, 8; *The Stranger*, 19

La Bruyère, Jean de, 55
Lake District, 242
Lamartine, Alphonse Marie Louis de, 211
Lamb, Charles, 10, 50, 56, 63, 276; 'Ellistoniana', 64
Lambeth, 40, 85
Lancet, 101, 315
Landells, Ebenezer, 119, 120, 128, 135, 141, 144, 152, 166
Landseer, Edwin, 219
Lane, R.J.: *Life at a Water Cure*, 198
Last, Joseph, 119
Laurie, Sir Peter, 122-3, 124, 138, 156, 301
Layard, Austen, 182
Leader, 246
League of Universal Brotherhood, 306
Leech, John, 3, 124, 134, 136, 141, 147, 164, 184, 188, 189, 212, 213, 215, 232, 237, 300, 304; *Pictures of Life and Character*, 185
Leigh, Percival, 185, 195, 251
Lemon, Helen, 234
Lemon, Mark, 2, 119, 120, 121, 136, 137, 138, 141, 142, 144, 160, 162, 167, 177,

183, 184, 195, 199, 214, 215, 216, 222, 225, 227, 237, 251, 268; 'The Boys of London', 146; *Prose and Verse*, 221
Lever, Charles: *St Patrick's Eve*, 184
Lewes, Agnes, 234
Lewes, George Henry, 2, 127, 199, 204, 210, 219, 220, 223, 237, 246, 312; *On Actors and the Art of Acting*, 96; *Selections from Modern British Dramatists*, 88
Lewis, 'Monk', 33; *Adelgitha; or the Fruits of a Single Error*, 22; *The Castle Spectre*, 38, 39, 67; *Rolla*, 8, 12
Lewis, C.S., 128
Lillo, George: *George Barnwell*, 12, 18, 30, 38
Linton, Eliza Lynn, 196
Linton, W.J., 153
Liverpool, 110, 177, 182, 210, 289; Mechanics' Institute, 168
Liverpool Standard, 192
Lloyd, Edward, 249, 250, 251
Llloyd's Illustrated London Newspaper, 249
Lloyd's Weekly Newspaper, 1, 182, 203, 249-56, 258, 259, 260, 262, 265, 268, 269, 271, 272, 283, 312, 313
Lohrli, Anne, 174
London Journal, 202
London Literary Gazette, 70
London theatres, 39-40, 41; licensing, 40; audiences, 63, 74, 75, 85-6, 87, 92, 100; Adelphi, 40, 54, 66, 70, 80, 87, 100, 108, 162, 271, 280; Aldwych, 109; Catherine Street, 38, 39; Coburg, 40, 45-6, 52, 53, 54, 57, 60-62, 63, 64, 66, 70, 78, 79, 85, 98, 101, 292; Covent Garden, 15, 31, 33, 34, 39, 40, 41, 42, 53, 54, 57, 65, 72, 81, 93, 94, 100, 106, 111, 116-17, 125, 126, 168, 169, 171; Drury Lane, 8, 17, 18, 25, 40, 42, 53, 54, 57, 63, 65, 74, 82, 84, 85, 87, 90, 91, 92, 93, 94, 97, 100, 106, 111, 113, 117, 125, 127, 130, 218, 242, 258, 262, 279, 294; English Opera House, 34, 39, 40; Gaiety, 317; Globe, 172, 273; Haymarket, 40, 41, 52, 90, 93, 94, 97, 98, 117, 126, 131, 155, 162, 167, 169, 218, 240, 241, 242, 245, 262, 271, 293, 294, 308; Lyceum, 34, 40, 43, 45, 162, 245; Marylebone, 175; Old Vic, 40; Olympic, 40, 44, 46, 53, 85, 109, 294; Pavilion, 77-8, 85-6, 87; Princess's, 162, 242, 257, 262; Queen's, 99, 294; Royal Pavilion, 84; Rawstorne Street, 39, 44; Royal Circus, 63; Sadler's Wells, 39, 40, 41-2, 44, 46, 53, 69, 72; Strand, 84, 93, 96, 109-10, 113, 209, 289; Surrey, 40, 41, 63, 64, 65, 69, 70, 71, 72, 74, 75, 76, 77, 78, 79, 80, 81, 101, 111, 294; Tottenham Street, 78, 100; Toynbee, 280; Victoria, 61
London, 5, 11, 31, 33, 44, 133, 136, 151, 283; demonstrations in, 35-6; 'mysteries

335